THE EMC
Write-In
READER

Reading Strategies and Test Practice

CEDAR LEVEL

EMCParadigm Publishing Company

Staff Credits

Editorial

Laurie Skiba
Managing Editor

Brenda Owens
Editor

Becky Palmer
Reading Specialist

Nichola Torbett
Associate Editor

Jennifer Joline Anderson
Associate Editor

Diana Moen
Associate Editor

Mary Curfman
Editorial Consultant

Paul Spencer
Art and Photo Researcher

Design and Production

Shelley Clubb
Production Manager

Matthias Frasch
*Cover Designer and
Production Specialist*

Jennifer Wreisner
Text Designer

Erica Tava
Production Specialist

Lisa Beller
Production Specialist

Sharon O'Donnell
Proofreader

ISBN 0-8219-2910-0
© 2005 EMC Corporation

Published by EMC/Paradigm Publishing
875 Montreal Way
St. Paul, Minnesota 55102
www.emcp.com
E-mail: educate@emcp.com

Printed in the United States of America
10 9 8 7 6 5 4 3 2 1 XXX 10 09 08 07 06 05 04

Consultants and Contributors

Maria Callis
Reading Specialist/Department Chair
Trafalgar Middle School
Cape Coral, Florida

Shari Carlson
English/Reading Instructor
Fridley Middle School
Fridley, Minnesota

T. Carolyn Coleman
Language Arts/Reading Instructor
Gwinnett County Schools
Lawrenceville, Georgia

Dr. Edmund J. Farrell
Emeritus Professor of English Education
University of Texas at Austin
Austin, Texas

Sharon Kremer
Language Arts Instructor
Denton High School
Denton, Texas

Lisa Larnerd
English Department Chairperson
Basic High School
Henderson, Nevada

Beth Lee
Language Arts Instructor
Heritage Middle School
Longmont, Colorado

Cecilia Lewis
Language Arts Instructor
Mariner High School
Cape Coral, Florida

John Oricchio
Educational Consultant
Port Washington, New York

John Owens
Literacy Specialist
Heritage Middle School
Longmont, Colorado

Mary Spychalla
English/Reading Instructor
Valley Middle School
Apple Valley, Minnesota

Contents

Overview of Skills   viii
Overview of Features   xi
How to Use This Book   xii

UNIT 1 INTRODUCTION TO READING

PURPOSES OF READING   1
Reading for Experience   1
Reading to Learn   1
Reading for Information   2
THE READING PROCESS   2
Before Reading   2
During Reading   3
After Reading   3
USING ACTIVE READING STRATEGIES   4
    1 Read with a Purpose   4
    2 Connect to Prior Knowledge   6
    3 Write Things Down   7
    4 Make Predictions   10
    5 Visualize   11
    6 Use Text Organization   12
    7 Tackle Difficult Vocabulary   13
    8 Monitor Your Reading Progress   14
UNIT 1 READING REVIEW   16

UNIT 2 ESSENTIAL READING SKILLS

READING SKILLS   17
Identify the Author's Purpose   18
Find the Main Idea   19
Make Inferences   20
Use Context Clues   20
Analyze Text Organization   22
Identify Sequence of Events   23
Compare and Contrast   24
Evaluate Cause and Effect   25
Classify and Reorganize Information   26
Distinguish Fact from Opinion   26
Interpret Visual Aids   28
Understand Literary Elements   30
Draw Conclusions   32
UNIT 2 READING REVIEW   33

UNIT 3 READING FICTION

FICTION   35
Forms of Fiction   35
Elements of Fiction   36
USING READING STRATEGIES WITH FICTION   39
Rona Maynard   "The Fan Club"   Connect to Prior Knowledge   42
Edgar Allan Poe   "The Tell-Tale Heart"   Write Things Down   54
William Saroyan   "The Hummingbird That Lived through Winter"   Write Things Down   65
Luci Tapahonso   "The Ground Is Always Damp"   Visualize   73
Morley Callaghan   "Luke Baldwin's Vow"   Make Predictions   80
UNIT 3 READING REVIEW   98

UNIT 4 READING POETRY

POETRY			101
Forms of Poetry			101
Techniques of Poetry: Imagery			102
Techniques of Poetry: Shape			102
Techniques of Poetry: Rhythm			103
Techniques of Poetry: Sound			104
USING READING STRATEGIES WITH POETRY			104
Phil George	"Name Giveaway"	Connect to Prior Knowledge	108
Carl Lindner	"First Love"	Read with a Purpose	113
Arnold Adoff	"Point Guard"		
Maxine Kumin	"400-Meter Freestyle"	Use Text Organization	119
Lillian Morrison	"The Women's 400 Meters"		
Galway Kinnell	"Blackberry Eating"	Visualize	126
Naomi Shihab Nye	"The Lost Parrot"	Write Things Down	131
Alfred, Lord Tennyson	"The Charge of the Light Brigade"	Write Things Down	137
UNIT 4 READING REVIEW			143

UNIT 5 READING FOLK LITERATURE

FOLK LITERATURE			147
Types of Folk Literature			147
USING READING STRATEGIES WITH FOLK LITERATURE			148
Frances Densmore	"Song of the Thunders" and "Songs of the Crows"	Visualize	152
Retold by Christina Kolb	"The Epic of Gilgamesh"	Write Things Down	158
Retold by Geraldine Harris	"The Secret Name of Ra"	Make Predictions	169
Retold by Fitzgerald Iyamabo	"Why the Sky Is Far Away from the Earth"	Use Text Organization	177
Retold by Carolyn Swift	"Amaterasu"	Read with a Purpose	184
UNIT 5 READING REVIEW			192

UNIT 6 READING DRAMA

DRAMA			195
Elements of Drama			195
USING READING STRATEGIES WITH DRAMA			196
Claire Boiko	*Persephone*	Read with a Purpose	201
UNIT 6 READING REVIEW			218

UNIT 7 READING NONFICTION

NONFICTION			221
Forms of Nonfiction			221
Purposes and Methods of Writing in Nonfiction			222
Types of Nonfiction Writing			223
USING READING STRATEGIES WITH NONFICTION			224
Roald Dahl	"The Green Mamba"	Visualize	228
Jerry Izenberg	"Roberto Clemente: A Bittersweet Memoir" and Roberto Clemente's Career Statistics with the Pittsburgh Pirates	Use Text Organization	241
Peggy Noonan	"The *Challenger* Disaster"	Connect to Prior Knowledge	258
Mark Mathabane	"Appearances Are Destructive"	Tackle Difficult Vocabulary	264
Cassandra M. Vanhooser	"The Price of Freedom"	Read with a Purpose	271
UNIT 7 READING REVIEW			278

UNIT 8 READING INFORMATIONAL AND VISUAL MEDIA

INFORMATIONAL AND VISUAL MEDIA

Informational Media			281
Elements of Informational Media			282
Electronic Media			282
Elements of Electronic Media			282
Visual Media			283
Elements of Visual Media			283
USING READING STRATEGIES WITH INFORMATIONAL AND VISUAL MEDIA			284
from *Literature and the Language Arts: Experiencing Literature*	"What Is Your Personality Type?"	Connect to Prior Knowledge	288
Task Force on Blood Pressure Control in Children	Variations in Vital Signs by Age	Write Things Down	294
Arthur Rothstein	Historical Photographs	Read with a Purpose	299
Ken Haedrich	"How to Chop an Onion in Four Easy Steps"	Read with a Purpose	305
Interview with Dave Schaller and Susan Nagel	"Getting into Web Development"	Use Text Organization	311
UNIT 8 READING REVIEW			317

UNIT 9 DEVELOPING VOCABULARY SKILLS

TACKLING DIFFICULT VOCABULARY AS YOU READ	321
Using Definitions, Footnotes, Endnotes, and Glossaries	321
Using Context Clues	322
Using Your Prior Knowledge	323
Breaking Words into Base Words, Word Roots, Prefixes, and Suffixes	323
Common Prefixes Chart	324
Common Suffixes Chart	325
Common Root Words Chart	326
Recognizing Combining Forms	329
Combining Forms Chart	330
Exploring Word Origins and Word Families	331
Using a Dictionary	332
Understanding Multiple Meanings	333
Understanding Denotation and Connotation	333
IMPROVING YOUR ACTIVE VOCABULARY	334
Keeping a Word Study Notebook	334
Using Mnemonic Devices	335
Categorizing and Classifying Words	335
Learning Synonyms, Antonyms, and Homonyms	336
UNIT 9 VOCABULARY REVIEW	338

UNIT 10 TEST-TAKING STRATEGIES

PREPARING FOR TESTS IN YOUR CLASSES	341
Answering Objective Questions	342
Answering Essay Questions	343
TAKING STANDARDIZED TESTS	345
Answering Multiple-Choice Questions	345
Answering Reading Comprehension Questions	346
Answering Analogy Questions	347
Answering Synonym and Antonym Questions	348
Answering Sentence Completion Questions	349
Answering Constructed-Response Questions	349
UNIT 10 TEST-TAKING REVIEW	351

APPENDICES

APPENDIX A: BUILD READING FLUENCY A-1
WORD RECOGNITION SKILLS A-2
Increase Your Automaticity A-2
Crossword Puzzle A-3
Word Race A-4
Word Matrix A-5
SILENT READING SKILLS A-6
Increase the Amount You Read A-6
How Much Can You Learn in 10 Minutes? A-6
Free Reading Log A-7
Pages-per-Minute Graph A-8
Minutes-per-Section Graph A-8
ORAL READING SKILLS A-9
Perform Rereading Activities A-9
Repeated Reading Exercise A-11
Repeated Reading Record A-12
Passages for Fluency Practice A-13

APPENDIX B: GRAPHIC ORGANIZERS FOR READING STRATEGIES B-1
READING STRATEGIES CHECKLIST B-2
READ WITH A PURPOSE B-3
Author's Purpose Chart B-3
Reader's Purpose Chart B-4
CONNECT TO PRIOR KNOWLEDGE B-5
K-W-L Chart B-5
Reactions Chart B-5
WRITE THINGS DOWN B-6
Note Taking Chart B-6
Pro and Con Chart B-6
Venn Diagram B-7
Cluster Chart B-7
Writing Ideas Log B-8
MAKE PREDICTIONS B-9
Prediction Chart B-9
Character Chart B-9
VISUALIZE B-10
Sensory Details Chart B-10
Figurative Language Chart B-10
USE TEXT ORGANIZATION B-11
Story Strip B-11
Time Line B-11
Plot Diagram B-12
Cause-and-Effect Chart B-13
Summary Chart B-13
Drawing Conclusions Log B-14
Main Idea Map B-14
TACKLE DIFFICULT VOCABULARY B-15
Word Sort B-15
Word Study Notebook B-15
Word Study Log B-16
Word Map B-17
MONITOR YOUR READING PROGRESS B-18
Fix-Up Ideas Log B-18
Your Own Graphic Organizer B-18
Reading Strategies Evaluation Chart B-19
Books I Want to Read B-20

ACKNOWLEDGMENTS
Literary Acknowledgments C-1
Art Acknowledgments C-2

Overview of Skills

READING STRATEGIES

Read with a Purpose 4, 39, 104, 113, 148, 184, 197, 201, 224, 271, 284, 299, 305

Connect to Prior Knowledge 6, 39, 42, 105, 108, 149, 197, 224, 258, 284, 288

Write Things Down 7, 39, 54, 65, 105, 131, 137, 149, 158, 197, 224, 284, 294

Make Predictions 10, 39, 80, 105, 149, 169, 197, 225, 284

Visualize 11, 40, 73, 105, 126, 149, 152, 198, 225, 228, 284

Use Text Organization 12, 40, 106, 119, 150, 177, 198, 225, 241, 285, 311

Tackle Difficult Vocabulary 13, 40, 106, 150, 198, 225, 264, 285

Monitor Your Reading Progress 14, 40, 106, 150, 198, 225, 285

READING SKILLS AND TEST-TAKING PRACTICE

Recognize Cause and Effect 51, 181

Analyze the Narrator 62

Understand Literary Elements 70

Compare and Contrast Setting 77

Identify Relevant Details 95

Identify an Author's Point of View 110

Identify Tone 116

Identify Organizational Patterns 123

Identify Main Ideas 128, 140, 174, 314

Analyze Character 134, 189, 255

Compare and Contrast 155

Put Events in Sequence 166, 308

Evaluate Cause and Effect 215

Draw Conclusions 238, 291

Recognize Author's Purpose 261, 275

Use Context Clues 268

Interpret Information 296

Interpret Visual Media 302

Answering Objective Questions 342

Answering Essay Questions 343

Answering Multiple-Choice Questions 345

Answering Reading Comprehension Questions 346

Answering Analogy Questions 347

Answering Synonym and Antonym Questions 348

Answering Sentence Completion Questions 349

Answering Constructed-Response Questions 349

VOCABULARY SKILLS

Prefixes 52

Creating a Word Study Notebook 64, 334

PAVE 71

Word Play 79

Synonyms 97, 112, 193, 319, 336

Semantic Map 99, 293

Jargon 118

Visualize 125

Using Figurative Language 130

Homonyms 136, 336

Antonyms 142, 319, 336

Create Context Clues 145, 322

Homophones 157

Classifying Vocabulary Words 168

Writing about Vocabulary Words 176, 219

Word Origins 183, 257

Using Words as Different Parts of Speech 191

Semantic Family: Tones of Voice 216

Vocabulary in Context 240, 270

Irregular Verbs—Past and Present 263

Descriptive Compounds 277

Create a Crossword Puzzle 279

Word Origins: Science Terms 298

Word Parts 304

Understanding Cooking Terms 310

Electronic Media Word Sort 315

Using Definitions, Footnotes, Endnotes, and Glossaries 321

Using Your Prior Knowledge 323

Using a Dictionary 332

Understanding Multiple Meanings 333

Understanding Denotation and Connotation 333

Using Mnemonic Devices 335

Categorizing and Classifying Words 335

LITERARY TOOLS

Act 196
Alliteration 104, 127, 129
Anecdote 243, 256
Article 221
Aside 205, 217
Assonance 104
Autobiography 221
Biography 221
Central Conflict 83, 96, 162, 167
Character 31, 36, 65
Characterization 31, 36, 190
Chorus 204
Chronological Order 158
Climax 31, 38
Concrete or Shape Poem 103
Conflict 37
Consonance 104
Dénouement 31, 38
Description 223
Dialogue 135, 196, 223
Diction 260, 262
Documentary Writing 221
Drama or Play 195
Dramatic Poem 101
Essay 221
Exposition 31, 38, 223
External Conflict 37
Fable 148
Fairy Tale 147
Falling Action 31, 38
Fiction 35
Figure of Speech 102, 121, 122, 124
Flashback 158
Folk Literature 147
Folk Song 148
Folk Tale 147
Feet 103
Historical Fiction 35
History 222
How-To Writing 222
Image 102
Imagery 102
Inciting Incident 31, 38
Internal Conflict 37
Legend 148
Lyric Poem 101

Memoir 222, 242
Metaphor 102, 121, 122, 124, 250
Meter 103
Monologue 196
Mood or Atmosphere 30, 37, 75, 78
Motif 182
Motive 171, 175
Myth 147, 201
Narration 223
Narrative Poem 101
Narrator 56, 63
Nonfiction 221
Novel 35
Novella 35
Onomatopoeia 104, 130
Opinion 266, 269
Parable 148
Parody 212
Personification 102, 121, 124, 156
Persuasive Essay 264
Playwright 195
Plot 31, 37, 83, 65, 96
Plot Diagram 38
Point of View 30, 37
Purpose or Aim 222
Repetition 139, 141
Resolution 31, 38
Rhyme 104
Rhyme Scheme 104
Rhythm 103
Rising Action 31, 38
Romance 35
Scene 196
Science Fiction 35
Script 195
Setting 36, 65, 66, 71
Short Story 35
Simile 102, 122, 124
Speaker 111
Spectacle 196
Speech 222
Stage Directions 195, 210
Suspense 232, 239
Tall Tale 147
Theme 49, 53
Tone 30, 37, 113, 117
Unity 276

INFORMATIONAL AND VISUAL MEDIA TOOLS

Aim 299, 393
Bulletin Board System 283
Chart 294
Chronological Order 309
Commentary 282
Computer News Services 282
Digital Photography 284
Editorial 282
Electronic Mail or E-Mail 282
Electronic Media 282
Essay 282
E-Zines or Webzines 282, 283
Fine Art 283
Graphic Aids 283
How-To Instructional Guide 281
Illustrations 283
Information Services or News Services 283
Instruction Manual 281

Internet 282
Interview 282, 311, 315
Media 281
Multimedia 282
News Articles 282
Newsgroups 283
Newspapers 281
Periodicals 281
Photographs 283
Photojournalism 284
Procedural Memo 281
Quiz 292
Review or Critique 282
Table 297
Technical Writing 281
Visual Arts 283, 284
Web Page 283
Web-Based Newspapers 282
Webzines or E-Zines 282, 283

Overview of Features

The EMC Write-In Reader helps you to interact with reading selections as never before! This portable anthology guides you in using reading strategies—reading tools that help you get more meaning from what you read. Questions and tips in the margins prompt you to record your thoughts and notes as you read. Using selections from the *Literature and the Language Arts* textbook, *The EMC Write-In Reader* gives you an opportunity to complete rich reading tasks, expand your reading skills, and increase your test-taking abilities.

The EMC Write-In Reader shows you how to use reading strategies before, during, and after reading and includes activities that develop your comprehension, fluency, and vocabulary skills.

The EMC Write-In Reader helps you learn how reading strategies work, how to combine them, and how to apply them to any reading task. These eight active reading strategies help you interact with a text to create meaning.

❶ Read with a Purpose
❷ Connect to Prior Knowledge
❸ Write Things Down
❹ Make Predictions
❺ Visualize
❻ Use Text Organization
❼ Tackle Difficult Vocabulary
❽ Monitor Your Reading Progress

Detailed instruction on one reading strategy is carried through the before, during, and after stages of the reading process for each selection.

The EMC Write-In Reader offers a unique text organization, including

- an **introduction to reading** unit that defines and explains the reading process, eight active reading strategies, and fix-up ideas to use when you have trouble
- a unit focusing on **essential reading skills** and tasks evaluated on standardized tests
- a unit for each **genre,** or kind of text, with an introduction on how to apply reading strategies to that genre
- a unit on **vocabulary development** to help you unlock word meaning
- a unit on **standardized test practice** to help you prepare for state and national tests
- an appendix of **fluency activities** to build word recognition skills, silent reading fluency, and oral reading fluency
- an appendix containing a multitude of **reading strategy graphic organizers**

Become a successful, active reader with *The EMC Write-In Reader!*

BEFORE READING

1 **Reader's Resource** provides background information to help you **set a purpose** for reading.

2 The **Active Reading Strategy** gives you step-by-step instruction on how to use the reading strategy **before reading**.

3 A **Graphic Organizer** for each selection helps you to **visualize** and **understand text organization** as you read.

CONNECT

1 **Reader's resource**

"The Fan Club" by Rona Maynard is a story about a high school girl's difficulty fitting in with the "popular crowd." The story depicts a typical school day, the hardships of being accepted, and what students will do to fit in.

Social groups often cause feelings of peer pressure among individuals seeking or wanting acceptance in the group. Sometimes social groups or individuals are intolerant toward others. *Intolerance*, *prejudice*, and *discrimination* are words that describe hostile feelings and actions toward a person or group based on unjustified opinions. As you read the story, look for examples of intolerance, prejudice, and discrimination between the social groups at Laura's school.

4 **Word watch**

PREVIEW VOCABULARY

billow   jostle
cynical   malicious
gaudy   submerge
gesture   throng
irrational

5 **Reader's journal**

What is more important—belonging to a group or standing by your beliefs?

"The Fan Club"

by Rona Maynard

2 *Active* READING STRATEGY

CONNECT TO PRIOR KNOWLEDGE

Before Reading   THINK ABOUT WHAT YOU KNOW

❑ Read the Reader's Resource carefully.
❑ With a partner, talk about the social groups in your school. Then answer the Reader's Journal question.
❑ Prepare to compare situations in the story to situations in your school by completing the Comparison Chart as you read.

Graphic Organizer: Comparison Chart **3**

Behavior of Students in Story	Similar Situation at My School

4 **WordWatch** gives you the opportunity to **preview** the vocabulary Words for Everyday Use for the selection.

5 **Reader's Journal** helps you to **connect** with what you know and to your own life.

The
FAN
Club

Rona Maynard

It was Monday again. It was Monday and the day was damp and cold. Rain splattered the cover of *Algebra I* as Laura heaved her books higher on her arm and sighed. School was such a bore.

School. It loomed before her now, massive and dark against the sky. In a few minutes, she would have to face them again—Diane Goddard with her sleek blond hair and Terri Pierce in her candy-pink sweater. And Carol and Steve and Bill and Nancy. . . . There were so many of them,
10 so exclusive as they stood in their tight little groups laughing and joking.

Why were they so cold and unkind? Was it because her long stringy hair hung in her eyes instead of dipping in graceful curls? Was it because she wrote poetry in algebra class and got A's in Latin without really trying? Shivering, Laura remembered how they would sit at the back of English class, passing notes and whispering. She thought of their identical brown loafers, their plastic purses, their hostile stares as they passed her in the corridors. She didn't
20 care. They were clods, the whole lot of them.

She shoved her way through the door and there they

During Reading **6**

USE WHAT YOU KNOW

❑ Listen as your teacher reads the first page of the story aloud. How does Laura feel about Diane Goddard? How do you think Diane feels about Laura? Fill in information about the students in the story in the left side of the Comparison Chart.

❑ Do you think you would fit in better with Laura or with Diane Goddard and her group? Write about a similar situation from your school in the right side of the graphic organizer.

❑ Read the rest of the story on your own. Keep making notes in your chart about how the students behave. Each time you make a note, write a note about a related experience of your own.

7

THINK AND REFLECT

Whom does Laura think this group of students is whispering about and staring at? (Infer)

_____

_____

6 During Reading instruction in the margin tells you how to apply the reading strategy as you read.

7 Think and Reflect questions deepen your understanding of what you are reading.

How to use this book

DURING READING

8 Note the **Facts** questions give you the space to **make notes** about factual information as you read (see example).

9 Use the **Strategy** reminds you to use the strategy to read actively.

10 Read Aloud activities in the margins help you to **build fluency** by giving you the chance to speak and listen to ideas you are trying to understand.

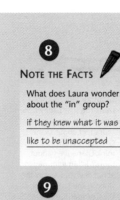

8

NOTE THE FACTS

What does Laura wonder about the "in" group?

if they knew what it was

like to be unaccepted

9

Use THE STRATEGY

CONNECT TO PRIOR KNOWLEDGE. How do you feel when you have to make a speech at school? How do you act when other students are giving speeches? How do others in the class act? Make a note in your Comparison Chart about what happens during Laura's speech and about your own experience.

10

READ ALOUD

As you read lines 190–200, read the highlighted lines aloud. Focus on the tone of voice Miss Merrill would use. What attitude does Miss Merrill have toward Rachel?

_____

_____

None of them knew what it was like to be unwanted, 170 unaccepted. Did Steve know? Did Diane?

"Most of us are proud to say that we live in a free country. But is this really true? Can we call the United States a free country when millions of people face prejudice and discrimination? As long as one person is forbidden to share the basic rights we take for granted, as long as we are still the victims of <u>irrational</u> hatreds, there can be no freedom. Only when every American learns to respect the dignity of every other American can we truly call our country free."

180 The class was silent. "Very nice, Laura." Things remained quiet as other students droned through their speeches. Then Miss Merrill looked briskly around the room. "Now, Rachel, I believe you're next."

There was a ripple of dry, humorless laughter—almost, Laura thought, like the sound of a rattlesnake. Rachel stood before the class now, her face red, her heavy arms piled with boxes.

Diane Goddard tossed back her head and winked at Steve.

190 "Well, well, don't we have lots of things to show," said Miss Merrill. "But aren't you going to put those boxes down, Rachel? No, no, not there!"

"Man, that kid's dumb," Steve muttered, and his voice could be clearly heard all through the room.

With a brisk rattle, Miss Merrill's pen tapped the desk for silence.

Rachel's slow smile twitched at the corners. She looked frightened. There was a crash and a clatter as the tower of boxes slid to the floor. Now everyone was giggling.

200 "Hurry and pick them up," said Miss Merrill sharply.

Rachel crouched on her knees and began very clumsily to gather her scattered treasures. Papers and boxes lay all about, and some of the boxes had broken open, spilling their contents in wild confusion. No one went to help. At

11

words for everyday use

ir • ra • tion • al (ir rash´ə nəl) *adj.,* lacking reason; absurd. *Because Emma had never tried squash, her dislike of the vegetable was <u>irrational</u>.*

48   THE EMC WRITE-IN READER

11 Words for Everyday Use includes the definition and pronunciation for new vocabulary. A sample sentence demonstrates the use of the word in context.

last she scrambled to her feet and began fumbling with her notes.

"My—my speech is on shells."

A cold and stony silence had settled upon the room.

210 "Lots of people collect shells, because they're kind of pretty—sort of, and you just find them on the beach."

"Well, whaddaya know!" It was Steve's voice, softer this time, but all mock amazement. Laura jabbed her notebook with her pencil. Why were they so cruel, so thoughtless? Why did they have to laugh?

"This one," Rachel was saying as she opened one of the boxes, "it's one of the best." Off came the layers of paper and there, at last, smooth and pearly and shimmering, was the shell. Rachel turned it over lovingly in her hands. White, fluted sides, like the closecurled petals of a flower; a

220 scrolled coral back. Laura held her breath. It was beautiful. At the back of the room snickers had begun again.

"Bet she got it at Woolworth's," somebody whispered.

"Or in a trash dump." That was Diane.

Rachel pretended not to hear, but her face was getting very red and Laura could see she was flustered.

"Here's another that's kind of pretty. I found it last summer at Ogunquit.[3]" In her outstretched hand there was a small, drab, brownish object. A common snail shell. "It's called a . . . It's called. . . ."

230 Rachel rustled through her notes. "I—I can't find it. But it was here. It was in here somewhere. I know it was." Her broad face had turned bright pink again. "Just can't find it. . . ." Miss Merrill stood up and strode toward her.

"Rachel," she said sharply, "we are supposed to be prepared when we make a speech. Now, I'm sure you remember those rules on page twenty-one. I expect you to know these things. Next time you must have your material organized."

The bell sounded, ending the period. Miss Merrill collected her books.

240 Then, suddenly, chairs were shoved aside at the back of the room and there was the sound of many voices whispering. They were standing now, whole rows of them, their faces grinning with delight. Choked giggles, shuffling

3. **Ogunquit.** Resort town in southern Maine

MARK THE TEXT

Underline or higlight what Laura thinks about the reaction of the other students to Rachel's speech?

13

Literary TOOLS

THEME. The **theme** is the central idea in a literary work. The theme of Laura's speech is that we all should treat others fairly and with dignity. Based on her speech, how do you expect Laura to treat Rachel?

_____

_____

_____

14

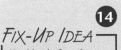

Use Margin Questions
If you are having difficulty following the story, make sure you answer all the questions in the margins. If you can't answer a question, reread the page to see if you can find the answer. The questions will help you find some of the main ideas in the story.

---

12 Mark the Text activities ask you to **underline or highlight** information in the text to help you read actively and organize your thoughts (see example).

13 Literary Tools explain **literary techniques and concepts** and help you recognize these elements as you read.

14 Fix-Up Ideas help you get back on track if you encounter problems or lose focus.

15 Footnotes explain references, unusual usage, and uncommon terms or words.

AFTER READING

16 After Reading activities follow up on the reading strategy and help you to summarize, synthesize, and reflect on the material you have read.

17 Reading Skills and Test Practice develops essential reading skills assessed on standardized tests.

18 Think-Aloud Notes help you organize your discussion ideas in writing.

16 *Reflect* ON YOUR READING

After Reading REFLECT ON YOUR CONNECTIONS

❏ Look at what you wrote down in your Comparison Chart. Do you think the situation described in the story could happen at your school? Why, or why not?

_____

_____

_____

_____

❏ With your partner from the Before Reading activity, talk about how connecting the characters to students you know helped to read the story.

Reading Skills and Test Practice **17**

RECOGNIZE CAUSE AND EFFECT

Discuss with your partner how best to answer these questions about cause and effect in the story. Use the Think-Aloud Notes to write down your reasons for eliminating incorrect answers.

____1. What causes Laura to agree to visit after school?
   a. Terri and Diane have criticized Laura's poem.
   b. Rachel praises Laura's poem.
   c. Laura feels cast out by the popular crowd.
   d. Rachel and Laura are interested in animals.

____2. What event convinces Laura to pin on a fan club card?
   a. Everyone else is wearing one.
   b. Rachel has embarrassed Laura.
   c. Everyone applauds Laura.
   d. Diane speaks directly to Laura.

How did using the reading strategy help you to answer the questions?

_____

_____

_____

_____

THINK-ALOUD NOTES
18

_____

_____

_____

_____

_____

_____

_____

_____

_____

_____

_____

_____

UNIT 3 / READING FICTION   **51**

Investigate, Inquire, and Imagine

RECALL: GATHER FACTS
1a. What does Laura do in algebra class? What does she do in Latin class?

INTERPRET: FIND MEANING
1b. Why might this behavior cause other students to act coldly toward her?

ANALYZE: TAKE THINGS APART
2a. By examining Laura's thoughts, words, and actions, identify her feelings toward the people around her. How does she feel about Rachel? What are her feelings toward the group of popular students? How does she feel about society?

SYNTHESIZE: BRING THINGS TOGETHER
2b. How do Laura's attitudes toward others reflect her personal character?

EVALUATE: MAKE JUDGMENTS
3a. How effectively does "The Fan Club" deliver important ideas about human nature?

EXTEND: CONNECT IDEAS
3b. Give an example from your own experience that you think reveals something important about human nature.

WordWorkshop

PREFIXES. Prefixes are *morphemes* (word parts) that appear at the beginning of a word. They are *bound morphemes* because they can never stand alone. In "The Fan Club," *irrational,* a Word for Everyday Use, has the prefix *ir–. Submerging* has the prefix *sub–.*

When you add a prefix to a word or word root, you do not leave out any letters. For example, look again at *irrational.* When adding *ir–* to *rational,* you do not drop an *r.* Prefixes can help you understand the meaning of words. For example, if you know that the prefix *ir–* means "not" and that *rational* means "reasonable," you can tell that *irrational* means "not reasonable."

Look through "The Fan Club" and find ten words that contain prefixes. Write the words and their meanings on the lines below.

1. _____
2. _____
3. _____
4. _____
5. _____
6. _____
7. _____
8. _____
9. _____
10. _____

19 Investigate, Inquire, and Imagine critical thinking questions further your understanding of the reading, from basic recall and interpret questions to those that ask you to analyze, synthesize, evaluate, and extend your ideas. Some questions also ask you to look at a specific point of view or a different perspective.

20 WordWorkshop activities apply vocabulary development concepts to the words from the selection.

AFTER READING

21 Literary Tools follows up on the literary techniques and concepts introduced during reading and asks you to apply your understanding.

Literary Tools 21

THEME. A **theme** is a central idea in a literary work. What theme or themes are central to "The Fan Club"? Which parts of the story convey the theme or themes most strongly?

_____

_____

_____

_____

_____

22 Read-Write Connection gives you the opportunity to write about your responses to the selection.

Read-Write Connection 22

If you were Rachel, how would you have reacted to the students in the last scene of the story?

_____

_____

_____

_____

23 Beyond the Reading activities extend the ideas, topics, and themes from the selection.

Beyond the Reading 23

ANALYZING THE MEDIA. How do the media portrait conformity and individuality? With a group of your classmates, gather several examples of television, radio, magazine, or billboard ads; movies; or other media that deal with being yourself or with following the group. Analyze each example and draw some conclusions about the media's portrayal of individuality versus conformity. How persuasive do you find each example? Why?

GO ONLINE. To find links and additional activities for this selection, visit the EMC Internet Resource Center at **emcp.com/languagearts** and click on Write-In Reader.

Unit ONE

Introduction to READING

PURPOSES OF READING

As a reader, you read for different purposes. You might **read for experience**—for insights into ideas, other people, and the world around you. You can also **read to learn**. This is the kind of reading done most often in school. When you read to learn, you may read textbooks, newspapers and newsmagazines, and visual "texts" such as art and photographs. The purpose of this type of reading is to gain knowledge. Third, you can **read for information**. When you read in this way, you are looking for specific data in sources such as reference materials, tables, databases, and diagrams.

Reading for Experience

READING LITERATURE

The most important reason to read literature is to educate your imagination. Reading literary works, which include fiction, nonfiction, poetry, and drama, will train you to think and feel in new ways. In the process of reading literary works and thinking about your own and others' responses to them, you will exercise your imagination as you encounter characters and situations that you would otherwise never know.

Reading to Learn

READING TEXTBOOKS AND NONFICTION

When you are reading to learn, you have two main goals: to expand your knowledge on a particular topic and to remember the information later. When you read to learn, you will often work with textbooks; reference books; periodicals such as newspapers, journals, and newsmagazines; and related art and photographs.

Textbooks provide a broad overview of a course of study in an objective, factual way. Other types of nonfiction works provide information about people, places, things, events, and ideas. Types of

MARK THE TEXT

Highlight or underline three purposes for reading.

NOTE THE FACTS

What goals might you have when you are reading to learn?

_____

_____

_____

nonfiction include histories, biographies, autobiographies, and memoirs. Periodicals such as newspapers, journals, and newsmagazines contain an enormous amount of information about current events around the world. While few people have time to read everything that appears in news periodicals, it is important to stay aware of what is going on in the world around you.

Reading for Information

READING INTERNET, REFERENCE, AND VISUAL MATERIALS

When you are reading for information, you are looking for information that answers a specific, immediate question; that helps you learn how to do something; or that helps you make a decision or draw a conclusion about something. One of the most important things for you to learn in school is how to find, process, and think about the vast amount of information available to you in online and printed reference works, graphic aids, and other visual materials.

THE READING PROCESS

The reading process begins before you actually start to read. Before reading, you begin to develop your own purpose and expectations for what you are about to read. These are related to what you already know and what you have experienced. During reading, you use your natural habits and responses to help you understand what you are reading, perhaps by adjusting your initial purpose and expectations. After reading, you think and reflect on what you have read. All readers use a reading process, even if they don't think about it. By becoming aware of this process, you can become a more effective reader. The reading process can be broken down into three stages: before reading, during reading, and after reading.

Before Reading

Have a plan for reading actively. Before you begin to read, establish a plan for reading actively by setting a purpose, previewing the material, and connecting with what you already know.

- ❑ **Set a purpose** for reading. Know why you are reading and what information you seek. Are you reading for experience or enjoyment, reading to learn, or reading for specific information?
- ❑ **Preview** the organization of the material. Glance at any visuals and think about how they add to the meaning of the text. Skim headings and introductory paragraphs.
- ❑ **Connect** with what you know. Think about how what you are reading connects to your own life and to your prior experience.

Before Reading

ASK YOURSELF

- ■ What's my purpose for reading this?
- ■ What is this going to be about?
- ■ How is this information organized?
- ■ What do I already know about the topic?
- ■ How can I apply this information to my life?

During Reading

Use reading strategies to read actively. Reading strategies are actions you can take on paper, in your head, or aloud that help you understand what you are reading. During reading, you will use reading strategies to read actively. Keep in mind that you will often use a combination of these strategies to read a single text.

❑ **Read aloud** to build reading fluency and give oral emphasis to ideas you are trying to understand. Hearing words aloud may help you untangle difficult ideas. Listen to your teacher read passages aloud, or read aloud by yourself or with a partner.

❑ **Write things down** to note your responses to what you are reading. Methods such as highlighting and marking a text, taking or making notes, and creating graphic organizers help you read actively and organize your thoughts. Underline or copy to your notebook the main points. Note unusual or interesting ideas or things you don't understand. Jot down words you need to define. Write your reactions to what you read.

❑ **Think and reflect** by asking questions to further your understanding of what you are reading. Asking questions helps you to pinpoint parts of the text that are confusing. You can ask questions in your head, or you may write them down.

Check your reading and use fix-up ideas. Monitor your reading comprehension by paying attention to how well you understand what you are reading. If you find yourself reading the words but not actually understanding what you are reading, get back on track by using a **fix-up idea** such as rereading, reading in shorter chunks, changing your reading rate, or trying a new reading strategy. A fix-up idea will be presented with each reading strategy accompanying the selections in this text. (For more information on fix-up ideas, see pages 14–15.)

After Reading

Reflect on your reading. After you finish reading, summarize, synthesize, and reflect on the material you have read.

■ **Summarize** what you have read to help identify, understand, and remember the main and supporting ideas in the text.

■ **Synthesize** different ideas in the material by pulling the ideas together and drawing conclusions about them. Reread any sections you don't remember clearly. Answer any questions you had.

■ **Extend** your reading by examining how your knowledge has grown and identifying questions you still have about the material.

During Reading

ASK YOURSELF

■ What is the best way to accomplish my purpose for reading?
■ What do I want or need to find out while I'm reading?
■ What is the essential information presented here?
■ What is the importance of what I am reading?

CHECK YOUR READING

■ Do I understand what I just read? Can I summarize it?
■ What can I do to make the meaning more clear?

After Reading

ASK YOURSELF

■ What did I learn from what I have read?
■ What is still confusing?
■ What do I need to remember from my reading?
■ What effect did this text have on my thinking?
■ What else do I want to know about this topic?

USING ACTIVE READING STRATEGIES

Reading actively means thinking about what you are reading as you read. A reading strategy, or plan, helps you read actively and search for meaning in what you are reading. As a reader, you are in charge of unlocking the meaning of each text you read. This book will introduce you to eight excellent strategies that develop active reading. The following strategies can be applied at each stage of the reading process: before, during, and after reading.

> **Active Reading Strategies**
>
> 1 Read with a Purpose
> 2 Connect to Prior Knowledge
> 3 Write Things Down
> 4 Make Predictions
> 5 Visualize
> 6 Use Text Organization
> 7 Tackle Difficult Vocabulary
> 8 Monitor Your Reading Progress

As you become experienced with each of the reading strategies, you will be able to use two or three strategies at a time, instead of just one. By using multiple strategies, you will become a thoughtful, active, and successful reader—not only in your English language arts classes but also in other content areas, during testing situations, and beyond the classroom. You will learn which strategies work best for you and use these strategies in every reading task you encounter.

1 Read with a Purpose

Before you begin reading, think about your reason for reading the material. You might be reading from a textbook to complete a homework assignment, skimming a magazine for information about one of your hobbies, or reading a novel for your own personal enjoyment. Know why you are reading and what information you seek. Decide on your purpose for reading as clearly as you can. Be aware that your purpose may change as you read.

> **Read with a Purpose**
>
> | Before Reading | Establish a purpose for reading |
> | During Reading | Read with this purpose in mind |
> | After Reading | Reflect on how the purpose affected the reading experience |

THE READING PROCESS

BEFORE READING
Have a plan for reading
❑ Set a purpose
❑ Preview
❑ Connect

DURING READING
Use reading strategies
❑ Read aloud
❑ Write things down
❑ Think and reflect
❑ Check your reading and use fix-up ideas

AFTER READING
Reflect on your reading
❑ Summarize
❑ Synthesize
❑ Extend

After you determine your purpose for reading, you can choose a method of reading that fits that purpose. Scanning, skimming, and close reading are three different ways of reading.

SCANNING. When you **scan,** you look through written material quickly to locate particular information. Scanning is useful when, for example, you want to find an entry in an index or a definition in a textbook chapter. To scan, simply run your eye down the page, looking for a key word or words. When you find the key words, slow down and read carefully.

SKIMMING. When you **skim,** you glance through material quickly to get a general idea of what it is about. Skimming is an excellent way to get a quick overview of material. It is useful for previewing a chapter in a textbook, for surveying material to see if it contains information that will be useful to you, and for reviewing material for a test or essay. When skimming, look at titles, headings, and words that appear in boldface or colored type. Also read topic sentences of paragraphs, first and last paragraphs of sections, and any summaries or conclusions. In addition, glance at illustrations, photographs, charts, maps, or other graphics.

READING CLOSELY. When you **read closely,** you read slowly and carefully, looking at each sentence and taking the time to absorb its meaning before going on. Close reading is appropriate, for example, when you are reading some poems for pleasure or studying a textbook chapter for the first time. If you encounter words that you do not understand, try to figure them out from context or look them up in a dictionary. You may want to record such words in a word study notebook. The act of writing a word will help you to remember it later. When reading for school, take notes using a rough outline form or other note-taking format. Outlining the material will help you to learn it.

Setting a purpose gives you something to focus on as you read. For example, you might read the user's manual for your new phone to find out how to program speed-dial numbers. Or, you might read a mystery novel to find out which character committed the crime.

A few purposes you might have for reading "First Love," a poem by Carl Lindner in Unit 4, page 114, might be to learn what the title means, to look for figures of speech, or to determine the speaker's feelings about basketball. Read the following background information from the Reader's Resource for "First Love." When you finish reading, complete the Think and Reflect activity in the margin.

NOTE THE FACTS

List three different ways to read printed material.

_____

_____

_____

NOTE THE FACTS

When should you **read closely?**

_____

_____

_____

MARK THE TEXT

Go back over the pages in this unit and highlight or underline a colored head. Then underline the boldface headings beneath the colored heading. Marking the text in this way helps you keep track of key ideas.

In 1891, James Naismith, a physical education teacher in Springfield, Massachusetts, wanted to develop an indoor game that would be fun, easy to learn, and lively. An early version of his game had players throwing balls through large peach baskets. Naismith's game caught on. His new game became known as basketball. As basketball developed, changes to the rules streamlined the game. Metal hoops took the place of baskets. Only five players per team were allowed on the floor at a time. Today, most teams have players who specialize in particular positions on the floor. A guard may be either a point guard, who runs the team's offense, or a shooting guard, who takes outside shots. The center usually stays near the basket, taking close shots and rebounding. Forwards play near the key, the painted free-throw area in front of each basket.

THINK AND REFLECT

Write a purpose for reading "First Love." (Connect)

_____

_____

_____

2 Connect to Prior Knowledge

Prior knowledge is what you already know or have already experienced before reading something. Before and during reading, think about what you already know about the topic or subject matter. By connecting to your prior knowledge, you can increase your interest in and understanding of what you read. The Reader's Journal activities that come before each selection in this book provide an opportunity to connect to experiences in your own life. Information in the Reader's Resource expands your knowledge of what you are about to read.

Connect to Prior Knowledge	
Before Reading	Think about what you already know about the topic
During Reading	Use what you already know about the topic to make inferences and predictions
After Reading	Describe how the reading experience expanded your knowledge of the topic

Read the following information from the Reader's Resource for "The Fan Club" by Rona Maynard in Unit 3, page 42. As you read, highlight or underline things you already know about social groups.

"The Fan Club," by Rona Maynard, is a story about a high school girl's difficulty fitting in with the "popular crowd." The story depicts a typical school day, the hardships of being accepted, and what students will do to fit in.

Social groups often cause feelings of peer pressure among individuals seeking or wanting acceptance in the group. Sometimes social groups or individuals are intolerant toward others. *Intolerance*, *prejudice*, and *discrimination* are words that describe hostile feelings and actions toward a person or group based on unjustified opinions. As you read the story, look for examples of intolerance, prejudice, and discrimination between the social groups at Laura's school.

THINK AND REFLECT

Based on what you know about peer pressure, how could someone face up to a group's acts of intolerance? **(Connect)**

_____

_____

_____

③ Write Things Down

Writing things down helps you pay attention to the words on a page. It is an excellent way to remember important ideas. Methods such as highlighting and marking or coding a text, taking or making notes, and creating graphic organizers help you read actively and organize your thoughts.

Write Things Down	
Before Reading	Have a plan for writing things down: sticky notes, handwritten notes, highlighters, or charts to fill in
During Reading	Use a method for writing things down; ask questions; respond
After Reading	Summarize things written down

NOTE THE FACTS

What methods of writing things down help you pay attention to words on a page?

_____

_____

_____

Highlighting and marking a text helps you locate key ideas. Mark important ideas, things you would like to come back to, things that are confusing, things you like or dislike, and things with which you agree or disagree. In this Write-In Reader or a book you own, you may highlight the text itself. With other books you may need to use sticky notes and bookmarks to keep track of your thoughts.

As you read, find a way to connect to what you are reading by **coding** your reactions. Use the following system to keep track of your reactions in the margins or on sticky notes. Create additional notations for reactions you have that are not listed.

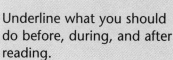

MARK THE TEXT

Underline what you should do before, during, and after reading.

Additional ways to take notes:
- outline
- make lists
- create a chart or diagram
- write down main ideas and your responses
- use a tape recorder

YES	I agree with this
NO	I disagree with this
?	I do not understand this
W	I wonder . . .
+	I like this part
–	I do not like this part
!	This is like something else I know
√	This seems important
∞	I need to come back and look at this
___	_____
___	_____

If you do not have sticky notes, keep track of your reactions in a chart like the one below.

Reading TIP

As you read the selections in this book, write down important ideas and your thoughts about them. The more things you write down in the margins, the more you will understand and remember.

Reactions Chart

Page, Column, or Line Number	Short Note about My Reactions
page 55	Even though the narrator keeps insisting he is not crazy, he sounds crazy.

After reading, summarize your reactions and compare them to those of your classmates.

Here is a summary of my reactions: I liked the story. It was scary, gory, and had a great ending.

Here is how my reactions were the same as those of my classmates: My classmates thought the story was scary and had a great ending.

Here is how my reactions were different from those of my classmates: Some of my classmates thought the story was too gory; others thought it was too old-fashioned.

Taking or making notes helps you select ideas you consider important. *Paraphrase*, or write in your own words, what you have read and put it into notes you can read later. Taking or making notes is also a quick way for you to retell what you have just read. Since you cannot write in, mark up, or highlight information in a textbook or library book, make a response bookmark like the following and use it to record your thoughts and reactions. As you read, ask yourself questions, make predictions, react to ideas, identify key points, and/or write down unfamiliar words.

Response Bookmark

Page #	Questions, Predictions, Reactions, Key Points, and Unfamiliar Words
55	Rereading the first paragraph helped me understand it.
58	The narrator sounds crazy.
59	Gory!

Graphic organizers help you organize ideas as you read. For instance, if you are reading an essay that compares two authors, you might use a Venn diagram or a cluster chart to collect information about each author. If you are reading about an author's life, you may construct a time line. As you read a selection, create your own method for gathering and organizing information. You might use your own version of a common graphic organizer or invent a new way to show what the selection describes. Signal words in the text can help you construct an organizer. (See Appendix B for examples of these and other graphic organizers.)

Signal Words	Common Graphic Organizer
descriptive words: *also, for instance, for example, in the beginning, in addition, the main reason, one point*	Character Chart, page B-8 Sensory Details Chart, page B-9 Summary Chart, page B-12
sequence words: *after, as before, next, now, on, first, second, finally*	Time Line, page B-10 Story Strip, page B-10 Plot Diagram, page B-11

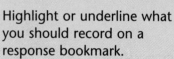

MARK THE TEXT

Highlight or underline what you should record on a response bookmark.

NOTE THE FACTS

List three examples of descriptive words.

_____

_____

_____

comparison-and-contrast words: *as well as, but, either/or, likewise, on the other hand, similarly, not only/but*	Pro and Con Chart, page B-6 Cluster Chart, page B-7 Venn Diagram, page B-7
cause-and-effect words: *as a result, because, if/then, since, therefore, this led to*	Note Taking Chart, page B-6 Cause-and-Effect Chart, page B-12 Drawing Conclusions Log, page B-13

After reading the following excerpt from "The Ground Is Always Damp" by Luci Tapahonso, Unit 3, page 73, write down the answer to the question in the margin. Highlight or underline signal words in the excerpt that direct you to the answer.

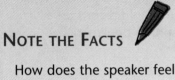

NOTE THE FACTS

How does the speaker feel about her new home?

_____

_____

_____

_____

_____

> In contrast, when Leona looks to the east most mornings, the sky is gray, the air thick with frost, and the wind blows cold dampness.
>
> "My mother, there are no mountains here, and I can't see very far because the air is thick and heavy with a scent I can't recognize. The rain seems all the same here, except in degree, and it is constant. Sometimes it lasts for two days and nights. It pours steadily until brown streams form and drain into the overflowing creek behind the house."

4 Make Predictions

When you **make predictions** during reading, you are making guesses about what the reading is going to be about or what might happen next. Before reading, make predictions based on clues from the page and from what you already know about the topic. Continue making predictions as you read. Remember, your predictions do not have to be correct. Pause during reading to gather information that helps you make more predictions and check predictions you have already made.

Make Predictions

Before Reading	Gather information and make preliminary predictions
During Reading	Continue making predictions
After Reading	Analyze and verify predictions

Read an excerpt from the short story "Luke Baldwin's Vow" by Morley Callaghan, Unit 3, page 80. Look for clues that suggest what might happen next.

> That summer when twelve-year-old Luke Baldwin came to live with his Uncle Henry in the house on the stream by the sawmill, he did not forget that he had promised his dying father he would try to learn things from his uncle; so he used to watch him very carefully.
>
> Uncle Henry, who was the manager of the sawmill, was a big, burly man weighing more than two hundred and thirty pounds, and he had a rough-skinned, brick-colored face. He looked like a powerful man, but his health was not good. He had aches and pains in his back and shoulders which puzzled the doctor.

Prediction Chart

Predictions	Clues	What Really Happens
Uncle Henry will die.	"his health was not good"	

5 Visualize

Reading is more than simply sounding out words. It is an active process that requires you to use your imagination. When you **visualize,** you form a picture or an image in your mind of what the text describes. Each reader's images will be different based on his or her prior knowledge and experience. Keep in mind that there are no "right" or "wrong" visualizations.

Reading TIP

By learning to make predictions while you read, you become more engaged in what you're reading and you remember more information.

THINK AND REFLECT

Based on the clues in the excerpt, make a **prediction** about what might happen later in the story. Record your prediction in the first column of the chart. In the second column, tell what clues led you to make this prediction. After you read the rest of the story, you would be able to record what really happened in the story and to compare that to your original predictions. **(Predict)**

Before Reading	Begin to picture what may happen
During Reading	Create mind pictures as you read
After Reading	Draw or summarize what you saw in your mind pictures

Read the following excerpt from "The Green Mamba" by Roald Dahl, Unit 7, page 228. As you read, imagine what the room and the poisonous snake look like.

THINK AND REFLECT

Make notes or draw pictures to show the images you pictured in your mind while reading this passage. (**Visualize**)

A moment later I caught sight of the snake. It was lying full-length along the skirting of the right-hand wall, but hidden from the snake-man's view by the back of the sofa. It lay there like a long, beautiful, deadly shaft of green glass, quite motionless, perhaps asleep. It was facing away from us who were at the window, with its small triangular head resting on the matting near the foot of the stairs.

❻ Use Text Organization

Text organization refers to the different ways a text may be presented or organized. If you are aware of the ways different texts are organized, you will find it easier to understand what you read. For example, knowing about typical plot elements—the exposition, rising action, climax, falling action, and resolution—is important for understanding the events in a short story or novel. Focusing on signal words and text patterns is important for understanding nonfiction and informational text. For instance, transition words, such as *first, second, next, then,* and *finally,* might indicate that an essay is written in chronological, or time, order.

Use Text Organization

Before Reading	Preview organizational features (look over headings, pictures, format)
During Reading	Be aware of organizational features as you read
After Reading	Discuss how the text organization affected your reading experience

In this excerpt from "Roberto Clemente: A Bittersweet Memoir" by Jerry Izenberg, Unit 7, page 241, look for organizational features that help you understand the excerpt.

> The record book will tell you that Roberto Clemente collected 3,000 hits during his major-league career. It will say that he came to bat 9,454 times, that he drove in 1,305 runs, and played 2,433 games over an eighteen-year span. . . . [But] those cold numbers won't begin to delineate the man Roberto Clemente was. To even begin to understand what this magnificent athlete was all about, you have to work backward. The search begins at the site of its ending.
>
> The car moves easily through the predawn streets of San Juan. A heavy all-night rain has now begun to drive, and there is that post-rain sweetness in the air that holds the promise of a new, fresh, clear dawn. This is a journey to the site of one of Puerto Rico's deepest tragedies.

7 Tackle Difficult Vocabulary

How do you deal with new or unfamiliar words as you read? Learning how to tackle difficult vocabulary on your own leads to improved reading comprehension. In some cases, you may want to identify and define new vocabulary before reading. Use context clues to guess meanings, find definitions in the dictionary, and decode words by recognizing common word parts.

Tackle Difficult Vocabulary	
Before Reading	Have a plan for tackling difficult words
During Reading	Use context, word structure, footnotes, or a dictionary; ask for help
After Reading	Describe how vocabulary affected your reading experience

THINK AND REFLECT

How does author Izenberg help readers understand this section of the text? What organizational elements do you recognize? **(Analyze)**

_____

_____

_____

_____

Reading TIP

If you take the time to learn new words, you increase your ability to understand what you read in class and on standardized tests. One of the best ways to learn new words is to associate an image with the meaning of a new word. For instance, the word *meretricious* means "falsely attractive, pretentious, superficially significant." So you could associate *meretricious* with an image of fake $100 bills. What image could you associate with the word *curtail*, meaning "to make less"? Draw that image here.

Read the following excerpt from "Appearances Are Destructive" by Mark Mathabane, Unit 7, page 264. As you read, record unfamiliar words in your notebook. After you finish, go back to each word you recorded. Using both context clues (words nearby that provide hints about the meaning) and word parts, unlock the meaning of each unfamiliar word. Consult a dictionary if context clues or word parts do not help.

THINK AND REFLECT

Based on context clues, what might *diminution* mean? (Analyze)

_____

_____

> The argument by civil libertarians that dress codes infringe on freedom of expression is misleading. We observe dress codes in nearly every aspect of our lives without any diminution of our freedoms—as demonstrated by flight attendants, bus drivers, postal employees, high school bands, military personnel, sports teams, Girl and Boy Scouts, employees of fast-food chains, restaurants, and hotels.

⓫ Monitor Your Reading Progress

All readers occasionally have difficulty as they read. The key to reading success is being aware of these difficulties. As you read, **monitor**, or pay attention to, your progress, stopping frequently to check how well you are understanding what you are reading. If you encounter problems or lose focus, use a **fix-up idea** to regain understanding. Readers who know how to apply fix-up ideas are well on the way to reading independence. They know when they are having a problem and are able to adjust and get back on track.

USING FIX-UP IDEAS

The following **fix-up ideas** can help you "fix up" any confusion or lack of attention you experience as you read. You probably use many of these already.

- **Reread.** If you don't understand a sentence, paragraph, or section the first time through, go back and reread it. Each time you reread a text, you understand and remember more.

- **Read in shorter chunks.** Break a long text into shorter chunks. Read through each "chunk." Then go back and make sure you understand that section before moving on.

- **Read aloud.** If you are having trouble keeping your focus, try reading aloud to yourself. Go somewhere private and read aloud, putting emphasis and expression in your voice. Reading aloud may help you to untangle difficult text by talking your way through it.

- **Ask questions.** As you read, stop and ask yourself questions about the text. These questions help you pinpoint things that are confusing or things you want to come back to later. You can ask questions in your head, or jot them down in the margins or on a piece of paper.

- **Change your reading rate.** Your reading rate is how fast or slow you read. Good readers adjust their rate to fit the situation. Read quickly, when you just need an overview, or if the reading task is easy. Slow down and read carefully when a text is difficult or contains a lot of description.

- **Create a mnemonic device.** A mnemonic (ni mä′ nik) device is a memory trick that helps you memorize specific information in a text. One memory trick is to make up an acronym, or abbreviation, to help you remember items in a list. For example, the acronym *HOMES* can help you remember the names of the five great lakes, **H**uron, **O**ntario, **M**ichigan, **E**rie, and **S**uperior. Another memory trick is to create a short sentence or rhyme. For instance, if you need to remember that in the eardrum, the anvil comes before the stirrup, remember "the letter *a* comes before the letter *s*."

Monitor Your Reading Progress

Before Reading	Be aware of fix-up ideas that ease reading problems
During Reading	Use fix-up ideas
After Reading	Evaluate the fix-up ideas used

READ ALOUD

Reading fluency is your ability to read something quickly and easily. Increase your reading fluency by rereading a 100–150-word passage aloud several times. Reread the passage until you are able to read through it in less than a minute without making any mistakes. Read the passage to a partner and have your partner track your errors, or read the passage into a tape recorder, play back your recording, and keep track of your own errors. For additional fluency practice, see Appendix A.

Reading TIP

As you read, use your classmates as resources to help you uncover the meaning in a selection. Working with a partner or a small group can increase your understanding of what you read.

THINK ALOUD. When you **think aloud**, you communicate your thoughts aloud to your classmates about what you are reading. Thinking aloud helps you share ideas about the text and ways in which to read it.

SHARE FIX-UP IDEAS. When you **share fix-up ideas**, you and your classmates can figure out ways to deal with difficult sections of a text.

Unit 1 READING Review

Choose and Use Reading Strategies

Before reading the excerpt below, review with a partner how to use each of these reading strategies (see pages 4–15).

1. Read with a Purpose
2. Connect to Prior Knowledge
3. Write Things Down
4. Make Predictions
5. Visualize
6. Use Text Organization
7. Tackle Difficult Vocabulary
8. Monitor Your Reading Progress

Now apply at least two reading strategies to an excerpt from a short story by Cherylene Lee, "Hollywood and the Pits." Use the margins and mark up the text to demonstrate how you use reading strategies to read actively. When you finish, summarize the excerpt in two to three sentences.

> "Thank you very much, dear. We'll be letting you know."
>
> I knew what that meant. It meant I would never hear from them again. I didn't get the job. I heard that phrase a lot that year.
>
> I walked out of the plush office, leaving behind the casting director, producer, director, writer, and whoever else came to listen to my reading for a semiregular role on a family sitcom. The carpet made no sound when I opened and shut the door.
>
> I passed the other girls waiting in the reception room, each poring over her script. The mothers were waiting in a separate room, chattering about their daughters' latest commercials, interviews, callbacks, jobs. It sounded like every Oriental kid in Hollywood was working except me.

On Your Own

Apply the reading strategies you have learned in this unit to your own reading. Select a 100–150-word passage from your favorite book, magazine, or newspaper, and try one of the following activities.

FLUENTLY SPEAKING. Reread the passage aloud several times. Reread the passage until you are able to read through it in less than a minute without making any mistakes. Read the passage to a partner and have your partner track your errors, or read the passage into a tape recorder, play back your recording, and keep track of your own errors.

PICTURE THIS. As you read, create a drawing, painting, sculpture, or other visual representation of the images that come into your mind.

PUT IT IN WRITING. Write an informal essay about the reading passage you have selected. Explain why you like to read this type of material. Discuss what you like about it and why you find it interesting. How does this passage relate to your own life?

Unit TWO

ESSENTIAL READING SKILLS

READING SKILLS

Each of the reading strategies we've discussed in Unit 1 helps you learn to think, question, and respond while you read. By using the eight active reading strategies, you will be able to demonstrate your mastery of the following reading skills:

- **Identify the Author's Purpose**
- **Find the Main Idea**
- **Make Inferences**
- **Use Context Clues**
- **Analyze Text Organization**
- **Identify Sequence of Events**
- **Compare and Contrast**
- **Evaluate Cause and Effect**
- **Classify and Reorganize Information**
- **Distinguish Fact from Opinion**
- **Interpret Visual Aids**
- **Understand Literary Elements**
- **Draw Conclusions**

Using these skills as you read helps you to become an independent, thoughtful, and active reader who can accomplish tasks evaluated on tests, particularly standardized tests. Standardized test practice connected to these skills follows each selection in this book.

Reading TIP

For more practice on test-taking skills, see Unit 10, Test-Taking Strategies, pages 341–354.

Identify the Author's Purpose

A writer's **purpose** is his or her aim or goal. Being able to figure out an author's purpose, or purposes, is an important reading skill. An author may write with one or more of the purposes listed in the following chart. A writer's purpose corresponds to a specific mode, or type, of writing. A writer can choose from a variety of forms while working within a mode.

Reading TIP

To **identify the author's purpose**, ask yourself

- Why did the author create this piece of writing?
- Is the author simply sharing information or trying to convince me of something?
- Is he or she writing to entertain or trying to make a point?

Purposes of Writing

Purpose	Mode	Writing Forms
to reflect	personal/ expressive writing	diary entry, personal letter, autobiography, personal essay
to entertain, to describe, to enrich, and to enlighten	imaginative/ descriptive writing	poem, character sketch, play
to tell a story, to narrate a series of events	narrative writing	short story, biography, legend, myth, history
to inform, to explain	informative/ expository writing	news article, research report, expository essay, book review
to persuade	persuasive/ argumentative writing	editorial, petition, political speech, persuasive essay

Once you identify what the author is trying to do, you can evaluate, or judge, how well the author achieved that purpose. For example, you may judge that the author of a persuasive essay made a good and convincing argument. Or, you may decide that the novel you are reading has a boring plot. In other words, the author has done a bad job of entertaining you!

Read the following lines from "The Price of Freedom" by Cassandra M. Vanhooser, Unit 7, page 271. Think about Vanhooser's purpose for writing about American prisoners of war. Is she trying to entertain, persuade, inform, or express her feelings?

From the Revolution to the Gulf War, more than 800,000 men, women, and children have been held captive by enemy forces. Other military museums touch on the subject, but this is the first memorial dedicated solely to the plight of American prisoners of war. Its location—on the very site of the Andersonville Prison Camp where 45,000 Union soldiers were incarcerated [put in prison]—seems fitting.

Find the Main Idea

The **main idea** is a brief statement of what you think the author wants you to know, think, or feel after reading the text. In some cases, the main idea will actually be stated. Check the first and last paragraphs for a sentence that sums up the entire passage. Usually, the author will not tell you what the main idea is, and you will have to infer it.

In general, nonfiction texts have main ideas; literary texts (poems, short stories, novels, plays, and personal essays) have themes. Sometimes, however, the term *main idea* is used to refer to the theme of a literary work, especially an essay or poem. Both deal with the central idea in a written work.

A good way to find the main or overall idea of a whole selection (or part of a selection) is to gather important details into a Main Idea Map like the one below. Use the details to determine the main or overall thought or message. This will help you to draw conclusions about the main idea when you finish reading.

Main Idea Map

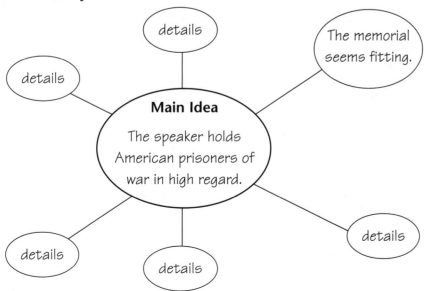

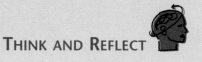

Which words or phrases in the paragraph help you determine Vanhooser's purpose? **(Infer)**

_____

_____

_____

_____

Reading TIP

To **infer the main idea,** ask yourself

- Who or what is this passage about?
- What does the author want me to know, think, feel, or do about this "who" or "what"?
- If I had to tell someone in one sentence what this passage is about, what would I say?

Make Inferences

By paying close attention to what you read, you will be able to make inferences about what the writer is trying to communicate. **Making an inference** means putting together the clues given in the text with your own prior knowledge.

Inference Chart

Text	What I Infer
The basketball player "could read / every crack and ripple / in that patch of asphalt."	The basketball player is playing outside.

Use Context Clues

You can often figure out the meaning of an unfamiliar word by using context clues. **Context clues** are words and phrases near a difficult word that provide hints about its meaning. The context in which a word is used may help you guess what it means without having to look it up in the dictionary.

The following table explains different kinds of context clues and includes words that signal each type of clue. Look for these words in the sentences around an unfamiliar word to see if they signal a context clue.

Reading **TIP**

Sometimes you can determine the meaning of a word by using the context as a clue. For example, the word choice or mood of a passage in general may help you determine the meaning of a particular word.

Context Clues

comparison clue	shows a comparison, or how the unfamiliar word is like something that might be familiar to you
signal words	*and, like, as, just as, as if, as though*

EXAMPLE

"It hardly took the mill hand a minute to reach the bank and go slinking *furtively* around the bend as if he felt that the boy was following him."—from "Luke Baldwin's Vow" by Morley Callaghan. (Since the mill hand feels as if someone is following him, when he goes slinking *furtively* around the bend, he must slink "sneakily" to avoid being followed.)

contrast clue	shows that something contrasts, or differs in meaning, from something else
signal words	*but, nevertheless, on the other hand, however, although, though, in spite of*

EXAMPLE

"But, for many minutes, the heart beat on with a muffled sound. This, however, did not *vex* me; it would not be heard through the wall."—from "The Tell-Tale Heart" by Edgar Allan Poe. (Though the heart is still beating, that the speaker is *not vexed* must mean that the speaker is "not worried or not bothered" because the sound of the beating heart cannot be heard through the wall.)

restatement clue	uses different words to express the same idea
signal words	*that is, in other words, or, namely*

EXAMPLE

"After trying all sorts of things in vain, they finally managed to invent a mirror, or *looking-glass*."—from "Amaterasu" by Carolyn Swift. (The restatement confirms that a *looking-glass* is another name for "a mirror.")

examples clue	gives examples of other items to illustrate the meaning of something
signal words	*including, such as, for example, for instance, especially, particularly*

EXAMPLE

"She mastered four *modern languages*—French, Italian, Spanish, and Flemish—as well as classic Greek and Italian."—from "Elizabeth I" by Milton Meltzer. (Since French, Italian, Spanish, and Flemish are languages that are widely spoken today, *modern languages* must mean languages that are still in use in modern times.)

cause-and-effect clue	tells you that something happened as a result of something else
signal words	*if/then, when/then, thus, therefore, because, so, as a result of, consequently, since*

EXAMPLE

"Teachers have shared their frustrations with me at being unable to teach those students willing to learn *because* classes are frequently disrupted by other students ogling themselves in mirrors, painting their fingernails, combing their hair, shining their gigantic shoes or comparing designer labels on jackets, caps and jewelry."—from "Appearances Are Destructive" by Mark Mathabane. (The word *because* signals why teachers are frustrated and follows with a list of things that frustrate teachers.)

MARK THE TEXT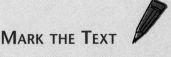

Underline or highlight what a restatement clue does.

NOTE THE FACTS

What words signal a cause-and-effect relationship?

_____

_____

_____

Analyze Text Organization

Writing can be organized in different ways. To be an effective reader you need to know how to analyze how the text is organized. When you analyze something, you break it down into parts and then think about how the parts are related to each other and to the whole.

Chronological or Time Order

Events are given in the order in which they happen or should be done. Events are connected by transition words such as *first, second, next, then, furthermore,* and *finally.* Chronological order is often used to relate a narrative, as in a short story; to write a how-to article on a topic like building a bird feeder; or to describe a process, such as what happens when a volcano erupts.

Spatial or Location Order

Parts are described in order of their location in space, for example, from back to front, left to right, or top to bottom. Descriptions are connected by transition words or phrases such as *next to, beside, above, below, beyond,* and *around.* Spatial order could be used for an article that discusses a project's physical aspects, such as describing the remodeling of a kitchen, or for a descriptive passage in literature, as in establishing the setting of a science fiction story set in a space station.

Order of Importance

Details are listed from least important to most important or from most important to least important; transition phrases are used such as *more important, less important, most important,* and *least important.* For example, a speech telling voters why they should elect you class president could build from the least important reason to the most important reason.

Comparison-and-Contrast Order

Details of two subjects are presented in one of two ways. In the first method, the characteristics of one subject are presented, followed by the characteristics of the second subject. This method could be used to organize an essay that compares and contrasts two fast-food chains, and to tell why one is superior to the other.

Reading TIP

Transition words connect ideas. They indicate how a text is organized. Look for words that
- describe main points (descriptive words)
- show sequence (sequence words)
- show comparison and contrast (comparison-and-contrast words)
- show cause and effect (cause-and-effect words)

In the second method, both subjects are compared and contrasted with regard to one quality, then with regard to a second quality, and so on. An essay organized according to this method could compare the platforms of two political parties issue by issue: the environment, the economy, and so forth. Ideas are connected by transition words and phrases that indicate similarities or differences, such as *likewise, similarly, in contrast, a different kind, on the other hand,* and *another difference.*

Cause-and-Effect Order

One or more causes are followed by one or more effects, or one or more effects are followed by one or more causes. Transition words and phrases that indicate cause and effect include *one cause, another effect, as a result, consequently,* and *therefore.* Cause-and-effect organization might be used for a public health announcement warning about the dangers of playing with fire or an essay discussing the outbreak of World War I and the events that led up to it.

Classification or Sorting Order

Items are classified, or grouped, in categories to show how one group is similar to or different from another. Items in the same category should share one or more characteristics. For example, Edgar Allan Poe, Agatha Christie, and Stephen King can be classified together as mystery writers. Transition words that indicate classification order are the same words that indicate comparison-and-contrast order, words such as *likewise, similarly, in contrast, a different kind,* and *another difference.*

Identify Sequence of Events

Sequence refers to the order in which things happen. When you read certain types of writing, such as a short story, a novel, a biography of a person's life, or a history book, keep track of the sequence of events. You might do this by making a time line or a sequence map.

Time Line

To make a time line, draw a line and divide it into equal parts like the one on the next page. Label each part with a date or a time. Then add key events at the right places along the time line.

METHODS OF TEXT ORGANIZATION

- Chronological order
- Spatial order
- Order of importance
- Comparison-and-contrast order
- Cause-and-effect order
- Classification order

NOTE THE FACTS

Underline or highlight how you can keep track of the sequence of events in a history textbook.

_____

_____

_____

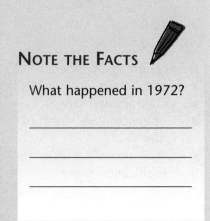
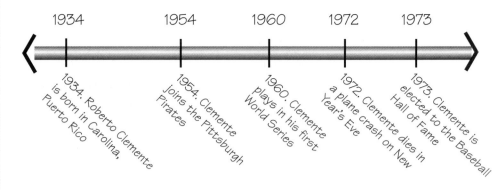

1934   1954   1960   1972   1973

1934. Roberto Clemente is born in Carolina, Puerto Rico

1954. Clemente joins the Pittsburgh Pirates

1960. Clemente plays in his first World Series

1972. Clemente dies in a plane crash on New Year's Eve

1973. Clemente is elected to the Baseball Hall of Fame

Sequence Map

In each box, draw pictures that represent key events in a selection. Then write a caption under each box that explains each event. Draw the events in the order in which they occur.

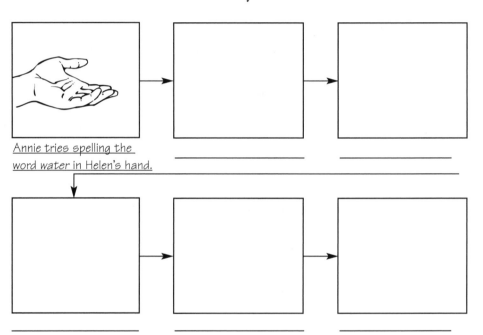

Annie tries spelling the word water in Helen's hand.

_____

_____

_____

_____

_____

Compare and Contrast

Comparing and contrasting are closely related processes. When you **compare** one thing to another, you describe similarities between the two things; when you **contrast** two things, you describe their differences. To compare and contrast, begin by listing the features of each subject. Then go down both lists and check whether each feature is shared or not. You can also show similarities and differences in a Venn diagram. A Venn diagram uses two slightly overlapping circles. The outer part of each circle shows what aspects of two things are different from each other. The inner, or shared, part of each circle shows what aspects the two things share.

Venn Diagram

Write down ideas about Topic 1 in the first circle and ideas about Topic 2 in the second circle. The area in which the circles overlap should contain ideas common to both topics.

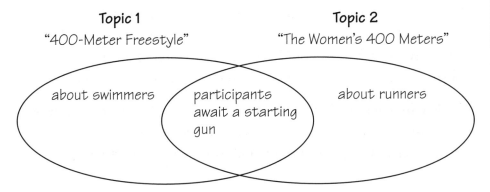

Topic 1
"400-Meter Freestyle"

about swimmers

participants await a starting gun

Topic 2
"The Women's 400 Meters"

about runners

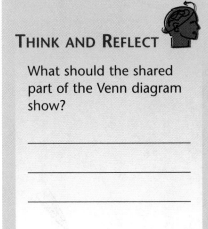

THINK AND REFLECT

What should the shared part of the Venn diagram show?

_____

_____

_____

Evaluate Cause and Effect

When you evaluate **cause and effect**, you are looking for a logical relationship between a cause or causes and one or more effects. A writer may present one or more causes followed by one or more effects, or one or more effects followed by one or more causes. Transitional, or signal, words and phrases that indicate cause and effect include *one cause*, *another effect*, *as a result*, *because*, *since*, *consequently*, and *therefore*. As a reader, you determine whether the causes and effects in a text are reasonable. A graphic organizer like the one below will help you to recognize relationships between causes and effects.

MARK THE TEXT

Highlight or underline what you do when you evaluate cause and effect.

Cause-and-Effect Chart

Keep track of what happens in a story and why in a chart like the one below. Use cause-and-effect signal words to help you identify causes and their effects.

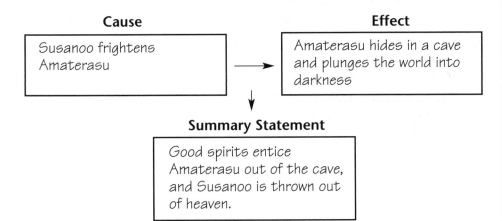

Cause

Susanoo frightens Amaterasu

Effect

Amaterasu hides in a cave and plunges the world into darkness

Summary Statement

Good spirits entice Amaterasu out of the cave, and Susanoo is thrown out of heaven.

Classify and Reorganize Information

To **classify** is to put into classes or categories. Items in the same category should share one or more characteristics. A writer may group, or categorize, things to show similarities and name the categories to clarify how one group is similar or different from another. For example, whales can be classified by their method of eating as *baleen* or *toothed*, or by their types such as *orca* or *blue*. Classifying or reorganizing the information into categories as you read increases your understanding.

The key step in classifying is choosing categories that fit your purpose. Take classification notes in a chart like the one below to help you organize separate types or groups and sort their characteristics.

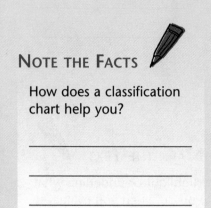

NOTE THE FACTS

How does a classification chart help you?

_____

_____

_____

Classification Chart

Category 1	Category 2	Category 3
Rear-Fanged Venomous Snakes	Fixed Front-Fang Venomous Snakes	Movable Front-Fang Venomous Snakes
Items in Category	**Items in Category**	**Items in Category**
twig snake mangrove	mambas cobras	rattlesnakes vipers
Details and Characteristics	**Details and Characteristics**	**Details and Characteristics**
large rear teeth release venom into prey as prey is swallowed	small nonmovable front teeth bite prey to insert venom	foldable fangs only come out when needed and stab at prey

Distinguish Fact from Opinion

A **fact** is a statement that could be proven by direct observation or a reliable reference guide. Every statement of fact is either true or false. The following statement is an example of fact:

> Poet Naomi Shihab Nye's heritage is Palestinian and American. (This statement is a fact that can be proven by reading birth records.)

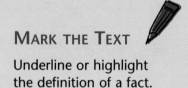

MARK THE TEXT

Underline or highlight the definition of a fact.

An **opinion** is a statement that expresses an attitude or desire, not a fact about the world. One common type of opinion statement is a *value statement*. A value statement expresses an attitude toward something.

> Naomi Shihab Nye is one of America's best modern-day poets. (This statement expresses an opinion that can be supported but not proved.)

Value statements often include judgment words such as the following:

attractive	honest	ugly
awesome	junk	unattractive
beautiful	kind	valuable
cheap	mean	wonderful
dishonest	nice	worthless
excellent	petty	
good	treasure	

THINK AND REFLECT

What are three judgment words you could add to the chart on the left? **(Apply)**

_____

_____

_____

_____

A **policy statement** is an opinion that tells not what is but what someone believes should be. Such statements usually include words like *should, should not, ought, ought not, must,* or *must not.*

> You **should** wear a seat belt when riding in a car.
> You **must not** ignore the signs urging you to buckle up.

A **prediction** makes a statement about the future. Because the future is unpredictable, most predictions can be considered opinions.

> New research will show that seat belts should be mandatory. Automobile computers may soon be able to prevent a car from operating if the driver is not wearing a seat belt.

When evaluating a fact, ask yourself whether it can be proven through direct observation or by checking a reliable source such as a reference book or an unbiased expert. An opinion is only as good as the facts that support it. When reading or listening, be critical about the statements that you encounter. It may be helpful to make a chart like the one on page 28 to help distinguish fact from opinion as you read.

Reading TIP

Facts can be proven by direct observation or by checking a reliable source. **Opinions** are supported by facts, but there is no actual proof. Use a Fact or Opinion Chart to determine whether you have proof or support.

Fact or Opinion Chart

Fact: During the 1930s, Arthur Rothstein took pictures of people living in the Dust Bowl.	**Opinion:** People in the 1930s had a tougher life in America than at any other time in America's history.
Proof: Many of Rothstein's photographs, taken while he worked for the Farm Security Administration, can be found at the Library of Congress.	**Support:** Although many people had a difficult life in the 1930s, some may argue that other times in America's history were more difficult.
Fact: **Proof:**	**Opinion:** **Support:**

NOTE THE FACTS

What are two things you can do with graphics at the During Reading stage?

_____

_____

_____

_____

Interpret Visual Aids

Visual aids are charts, graphs, pictures, illustrations, photos, maps, diagrams, spreadsheets, and other materials that present information. Many writers use visual aids to present data in understandable ways. Information visually presented in tables, charts, and graphs can help you find information, see trends, discover facts, and uncover patterns.

Reading Graphics

Before Reading	■ Determine the subject of the graphic by reading the title, headings, and other textual clues. ■ Determine how the data are organized, classified, or divided by reading the labels along rows or columns.
During Reading	■ Survey the data and look for trends by comparing columns and rows, noting changes among information fields, looking for patterns, or studying map sections. ■ Use legends, keys, and other helpful sections in the graphic.
After Reading	■ Check footnotes or references for additional information about the data and their sources. ■ List conclusions or summarize the data.

Pie Chart

A **pie chart** is a circle that stands for a whole group or set. The circle is divided into parts to show the divisions of the whole. When you look at a pie chart, you can see the relationships of the parts to one another and to the whole.

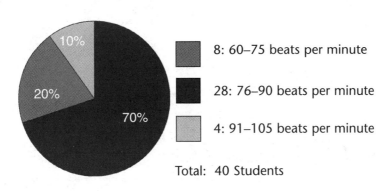

- 8: 60–75 beats per minute
- 28: 76–90 beats per minute
- 4: 91–105 beats per minute

Total: 40 Students

AVERAGE RESTING PULSE RATES IN ONE CLASSROOM

NOTE THE FACTS

What percentage of students have average resting pulse rates between 60 and 75?

_____

_____

_____

Bar Graph

A bar graph compares amounts of something by representing the amounts as bars of different lengths. In the bar graph below, each bar represents the height of the tallest peak in that state. To read the graph, simply imagine a line drawn from the edge of the bar to the bottom of the graph. Then read the number. For example, the bar graph below shows that Boundary Peak in Nevada is approximately 13,000 feet high.

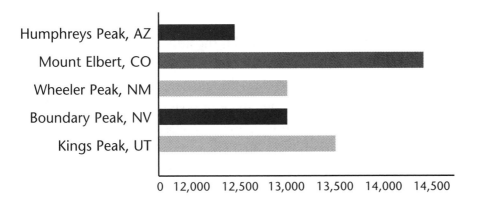

HIGHEST PEAKS IN FIVE WESTERN STATES

NOTE THE FACTS

Of the five western states in the chart, which state has the highest peak? Approximately how tall is its highest peak?

_____

_____

Map

A **map** is a representation, usually on a surface such as paper or a sheet of plastic, of a geographic area showing various significant features of that area.

NOTE THE FACTS

In which state is Grand Canyon National Park located?

_____

_____

_____

GEOLOGICAL MAP OF FIVE WESTERN STATES

Understand Literary Elements

Literary elements are the terms and techniques that are used in literature. When you read literature, you need to be familiar with the literary terms and reading skills listed below. These literary elements are explained in more detail in Unit 3, Reading Fiction, pages 36–38. Other literary elements are described in Units 4–7. Here are descriptions of the reading skills needed for some of the most common literary elements.

Reading **TIP**

An author's **writing style** can affect tone and mood. For example, sentence length, sentence variety, vocabulary difficulty (the number of mono–, bi–, and polysyllabic words), and the connotation (the association a word has in addition to its literal meaning) of words help determine the tone and mood.

- **RECOGNIZE MOOD AND TONE. Mood** is the atmosphere or emotion conveyed by a literary work. A writer creates mood by using concrete details to describe the setting, characters, or events. The writer can evoke in the reader an emotional response—such as fear, discomfort, longing, or anticipation—by working carefully with descriptive language and sensory details. The mood of a work might be dark, mysterious, gloomy, cheerful, inspiring, or peaceful. **Tone** is the writer's attitude toward the subject or toward the reader of a work. Examples of different tones that a work may have include familiar, ironic, playful, sarcastic, serious, and sincere.

- **UNDERSTAND POINT OF VIEW. Point of view** is the vantage point, or perspective, from which a story or narrative is told. Stories are typically written from the following points of view:

first-person point of view	narrator uses words such as *I* and *we*
second-person point of view	narrator uses *you*
third-person point of view	narrator uses words such as *he, she, it,* and *they*

■ ANALYZE CHARACTER AND CHARACTERIZATION. A **character** is a person (or sometimes an animal) who takes part in the action of a story. **Characterization** is the literary techniques writers use to create characters and make them come alive. Writers use the following techniques to create characters:

direct description	describing the physical features, dress, and personality of the character
behavior	showing what characters say, do, or think
interaction with others	showing what other characters say or think about them
internal state	revealing the character's private thoughts and emotions

■ EXAMINE PLOT DEVELOPMENT. The plot is basically what happens in a story. A **plot** is a series of events related to a *central conflict*, or struggle. A typical plot involves the introduction of a conflict, its development, and its eventual resolution. The elements of plot include the following:

exposition	sets the tone or mood, introduces the characters and setting, and provides necessary background information
inciting incident	introduces a central conflict with or within one or more characters
rising action	develops a central conflict with or within one or more characters and develops toward a high point of intensity
climax	marks the highest point of interest or suspense in the plot at which something decisive happens
falling action	details the events that follow the climax
resolution	marks the point at which the central conflict is ended or resolved
dénouement	includes any material that follows the resolution and that ties up loose ends

Reading **TIP**

A **character chart** can be used as a graphic organizer to keep track of character development as you read. See the example in Appendix B, page B-8.

Reading **TIP**

A graphic organizer called a **plot diagram** can be used to chart the plot of a literature selection. Refer to the example in Appendix B, page B-11.

Draw Conclusions

When you **draw conclusions,** you are gathering pieces of information and then deciding what that information means.

This passage from the short story "The Fan Club" by Rona Maynard describes a girl about to deliver a speech to her classmates.

> Then Miss Merrill looked briskly around the room. "Now, Rachel, I believe you're next."
>
> There was a ripple of dry, humorless laughter—almost, Laura thought, like the sound of a rattlesnake. Rachel stood before the class now, her face red, her heavy arms piled with boxes.
>
> Diane Goddard tossed back her head and winked at Steve.
>
> "Well, well, don't we have lots of things to show," said Miss Merrill. "But aren't you going to put those boxes down, Rachel? No, no, not there!"
>
> "Man, that kid's dumb," Steve muttered, and his voice could be clearly heard all through the room.
>
> With a brisk rattle, Miss Merrill's pen tapped the desk for silence.
>
> Rachel's slow smile twitched at the corners. She looked frightened. There was a crash and a clatter as the tower of boxes slid to the floor. Now everyone was giggling.

Use a log like the one below to keep track of key ideas and supporting points and to draw overall conclusions.

Drawing Conclusions Log

Key Idea Rachel is the target of the laughs and whispers of her classmates.	Key Idea	Key Idea
Supporting Points "a ripple of dry, humorless laughter" "Man, that kid's dumb" "everyone was giggling"	**Supporting Points**	**Supporting Points**
Overall Conclusion Rachel's classmates are thoughtless and unkind.	**Overall Conclusion**	**Overall Conclusion**

Unit 2 READING Review

Choose and Use Reading Skills

Before reading the excerpt below, review with a partner how to use each of these essential reading skills.

- Identify the Author's Purpose
- Find the Main Idea
- Make Inferences
- Use Context Clues
- Analyze Text Organization
- Identify Sequence of Events
- Compare and Contrast
- Evaluate Cause and Effect
- Classify and Reorganize Information
- Distinguish Fact from Opinion
- Interpret Visual Aids
- Understand Literary Elements
- Draw Conclusions

Read this excerpt from "Flying," a personal essay by Reeve Lindbergh. She describes what it was like to take flying lessons from her father, Charles Lindbergh. In 1927, her father was the first to fly solo across the Atlantic Ocean. As you read the excerpt, note how you can use some of the reading skills discussed in this unit. After you finish reading, summarize the excerpt in two or three sentences. Then answer the questions that follow.

There was no room in my father's lessons with me, his youngest and least experienced child, for soaring like the birds—no wind in the hair, no swooping and circling. We just droned along, my father and me.

And then, one Saturday afternoon, we didn't. I don't remember now exactly what made me understand there was something wrong with the airplane. I think there may have been a jerking sensation that repeated itself over and over. And I think too that there was a huge stillness in the air, a silence so enormous that it took me a moment to realize that it was actually the opposite of noise and not noise itself. The silence was there because the engine had stalled. Perhaps the most profound moment of silence occurred when my father realized that it was not going to start again—no matter what he did. We were in the middle of the sky, on a sunny Saturday afternoon over Connecticut, in a plane without an engine.

I don't think there was any drop in altitude, not at first. What I noticed was my father's sudden alertness, as if he had opened a million eyes and ears in every direction. I heard him say something sharp on the airplane's two-way radio to Stanley down below, and I could hear the crackle of Stanley's voice coming back. I knew enough not to say very much myself, although my father told friends later that I asked him once, in a conversational way, "Are we going to crash?" And when he told this part of the story, the part where I asked that question, he would laugh.

1. How does Lindbergh's father react when the engine stalls?

   _____

   _____

2. What does this tell you about Charles Lindbergh?

   _____

   _____

3. What context clues help you guess the meaning of *droned?* Of *profound?*

   _____

   _____

4. What might happen next? What clues in the excerpt make you think this might happen?

   _____

   _____

On Your Own

FLUENTLY SPEAKING. Select a 100–150-word passage from a book, magazine, or newspaper that you are currently reading. Working with a partner, take turns reading the passage aloud several times. Break it down into shorter sections and alternate reading paragraphs or sentences. Use the Oral Reading Skills: Repeated Reading Record in Appendix A, page A-12, to chart your progress.

PICTURE THIS. Find an article that contains data of some sort. Think about how this data can be presented using a visual aid, such as a table, chart, or graph. Do you notice any trends or patterns in the information? Draw a visual aid, such as a pie chart or bar graph, to present the information in a more understandable way.

PUT IT IN WRITING. Read a short article from a magazine or newspaper. Now go back and reread the first and last paragraphs. Write a summary of the main idea. What is it that the author wants you to know, think, feel, or do after reading this text? Is the main idea stated, or did you have to infer it?

Unit THREE

READING Fiction

FICTION

Fiction is prose writing that tells an invented or imaginary story. *Prose* is writing that uses straightforward language and differs from poetry in that it doesn't have a rhythmic pattern. Some fiction, such as the historical novel, is based on fact. Other forms of fiction, such as the fantasy tale, are highly unrealistic. Fictional works also vary in structure and length.

Forms of Fiction

The oldest form of fiction is the stories told in the oral, or folk, tradition, which include myths, legends, and fables. The most common forms of fiction are short stories, novels, and novellas.

THE SHORT STORY. A **short story** is a brief work of fiction that tells a story. It usually focuses on a single episode or scene and involves a limited number of characters. Although a short story contains all the main elements of fiction—character, setting, plot, and theme—it may not fully develop each element. The selections in this unit are examples of short stories.

THE NOVEL AND NOVELLA. A **novel** is a long work of fiction that usually has more complex elements than a short story. Its longer format allows the elements of fiction to be more fully developed. A **novella** is a work of fiction that is longer than a typical short story but shorter than a typical novel.

Other types of fiction include romances, historical fiction, and science fiction. **Romances** are tales that feature the adventures of legendary figures such as Alexander the Great and King Arthur. **Historical fiction** is partly based on actual historical events and is partly made up. **Science fiction** is imaginative literature based on scientific principles, discoveries, or laws; it often deals with the future, the distant past, or worlds other than our own.

MARK THE TEXT

Highlight or underline the definition of *fiction*.

NOTE THE FACTS

What is the main difference between a short story and a novel?

_____

_____

_____

Elements of Fiction

CHARACTER. A **character** is a person (or sometimes an animal or thing) who takes part in the action of a story. The following are some useful terms for describing characters.

protagonist (main character)	central figure in a story
antagonist	character who struggles against the protagonist
major character	character with a significant role in the action of the story
minor character	character who plays a lesser role
one-dimensional character (flat character)	character who exhibits a single dominant quality (character trait)
three-dimensional character (full or rounded character)	character who exhibits the complexity of traits of a human being
static character	character who does not change during the course of the story
dynamic character	character who does change during the course of the story
stock character	character found again and again in different literary works

CHARACTERIZATION. **Characterization** is the use of literary techniques to create characters and make them come alive. Writers use the following techniques to create characters:

direct description	describing the physical features, dress, and personality of the character
behavior	showing what the character says or does
interaction with others	showing what other characters say or think about the character
internal state	revealing the character's private thoughts and emotions

SETTING. The **setting** of a work of fiction is the time and place in which the events take place. In fiction, setting is most often revealed by description of landscape, scenery, buildings, weather, and season. Setting reveals important information about the time period, geographical location, cultural environment, and physical conditions in which the characters live.

THINK AND REFLECT

Give an example of a stock character. **(Extend)**

_____

_____

_____

Reading TIP

Motivation is the force that moves a character to think, feel, or behave a certain way. For example, a character may be motivated by greed, love, or friendship.

MOOD AND TONE. Mood is the atmosphere or emotion created by a literary work. A writer creates mood by using concrete details to describe the setting, characters, or events. The mood of a work might be dark, mysterious, gloomy, cheerful, inspiring, or peaceful.

Tone is the writer's attitude toward the subject or toward the reader of a work. The tone of a work may be familiar, ironic, playful, sarcastic, serious, or sincere.

POINT OF VIEW. Point of view is the vantage point from which a story is told. You need to consider point of view to understand the perspective from which the events in the story are being told. Stories are typically written from the following points of view:

first-person point of view	narrator uses words such as *I* and *we*
second-person point of view	narrator uses *you*
third-person point of view	narrator uses words such as *he, she, it,* and *they*

Most of the literature you read will be told from either the first-person or third-person point of view. In stories written from a first-person point of view, the narrator may be a participant or a witness of the action. In stories told from a third-person point of view, the narrator generally stands outside the action. In some stories, the narrator's point of view is *limited.* In this case, the narrator can reveal only his or her private, internal thoughts or those of a single character. In other stories, the narrator's point of view is *omniscient.* In such stories the narrator can reveal the private, internal thoughts of any character.

CONFLICT. A conflict is a struggle between two forces in a literary work. A plot involves the introduction, development, and eventual resolution of a conflict. A struggle that takes place between a character and some outside force is called an **external conflict.** A struggle that takes place within a character is called an **internal conflict.**

PLOT. When you read short stories or novels, it helps to know the parts of a plot. The plot is basically what happens in a story. A **plot** is a series of events related to a central conflict, or struggle. A typical plot involves the introduction of a conflict, its development, and its eventual resolution. The elements of plot include the following:

Reading **TIP**

The writer can cause in the reader an emotional response—such as fear, discomfort, or longing—by working carefully with descriptive language and sensory details. Sensory details appeal to any of the five senses—sight, hearing, smell, taste, and touch.

MARK THE TEXT

Highlight or underline the explanation of what omniscient point of view means.

Reading **TIP**

In fiction, the main character usually takes one side of the central conflict. That character may struggle against another character, against the forces of nature, against society, against fate, or against some elements within himself or herself.

exposition	sets the tone or mood, introduces the characters and setting, and provides necessary background information
inciting incident	event that introduces a central conflict
rising action	develops a central conflict and rises toward a high point of intensity
climax	the high point of interest or suspense in the plot where something decisive happens
falling action	the events that follow the climax
resolution	the point at which the central conflict is ended or resolved
dénouement	any material that follows the resolution and that ties up loose ends

Use a **plot diagram** like the one that follows to chart the plot of a literature selection.

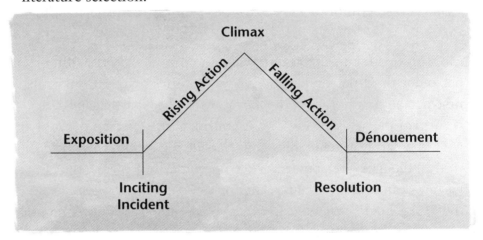

Become an Active Reader

Active reading strategy instruction in this unit gives you an in-depth look at how to use one active reading strategy for each story. Margin notes guide your use of this strategy and show you how to combine it with other strategies. Using just one reading strategy increases your chances of reading success. Learning how to use several strategies in combination increases your chances of success even more. Use the questions and tips in the margins to keep your attention focused on reading actively. Use the white space in the margins to jot down responses to your reading. For further information about the active reading strategies, see Unit 1, pages 4–15.

THINK AND REFLECT

Which point of the plot could be called the "turning point"? **(Infer)**

_____

_____

Reading TIP

Plots rarely contain all these elements in this exact order. Elements of exposition may be introduced at any time in the course of a work. Plots can have many variations. If you understand the purpose of each element, you will be able to identify them whenever they appear.

USING READING STRATEGIES WITH FICTION

Active Reading Strategy Checklists

When reading fiction, you need to be aware of the plot (or what happens), the characters, and the setting. The following checklists offer things to consider as you read fiction.

1 READ WITH A PURPOSE. Before reading about imagined events and characters, give yourself a purpose, or something to look for, as you read. Say to yourself
- ❏ I want to look for . . .
- ❏ I need to learn what happens to . . .
- ❏ I want to experience what it is like in . . .
- ❏ I want to understand . . .

2 CONNECT TO PRIOR KNOWLEDGE. Being aware of what you already know and thinking about it as you read can help you keep track of what's happening and will increase your knowledge. As you read, say to yourself
- ❏ I already know this about the story . . .
- ❏ This part of the story reminds me of . . .
- ❏ I think this part of the story is like . . .
- ❏ My experience tells me that . . .
- ❏ I like this description because . . .

3 WRITE THINGS DOWN. As you read short stories or novels, writing things down is very important. Possible ways to write things down include
- ❏ Underline characters' names.
- ❏ Write messages on sticky notes.
- ❏ Highlight the setting.
- ❏ Create a graphic organizer to keep track of plot elements.
- ❏ Use a code in the margin that shows how you respond to the characters, setting, or events. For instance, you can mark a description you like with a "+."

4 MAKE PREDICTIONS. Make predictions about characters, settings, and events in a story. Your predictions will help you think about what lies ahead. Make predictions like the following:
- ❏ I predict that this character will . . .
- ❏ The setting of this story makes me think that . . .
- ❏ I bet there will be a conflict between . . .
- ❏ This event in the story makes me guess that . . .

Reading **TIP**

Sometimes your teacher will set a purpose for reading: "Compare the narrator's experience to your own life." Other times you can set your own purpose. To set a purpose, preview the title, the opening paragraphs, and instructional information for the story. Think about what you want to get out of the reading.

Reading **TIP**

Instead of writing down a short response, use a symbol or a short word to indicate your response. Use codes like the ones listed below.

+	I like this.
–	I don't like this.
√	This is important.
Yes	I agree with this.
No	I disagree with this.
?	I don't understand this.
!	This is like something I know.
∽	I need to come back to this later.

Other tips for visualizing:

- Say to yourself, "If this were a movie, I'd see and hear . . ."

- Make quick sketches of what you imagine.

- Fill in gaps with details based on your experience or personal knowledge.

- Think about how things would sound, smell, and feel like if you were in the scene.

Keep a vocabulary notebook as you read. Jot down new words and their meanings. After you finish reading, practice using the words in sentences, word sorts, and daily conversation.

Fix-Up Ideas

- Reread
- Ask a question
- Read in shorter chunks
- Read aloud
- Retell
- Work with a partner
- Unlock difficult words
- Vary your reading rate
- Choose a new reading strategy
- Create a mnemonic device

5 VISUALIZE. Visualizing, or allowing the words on the page to create images in your mind, is one of the most important things to do while reading fiction. Become part of the action. "See" what the author describes. Make statements like

❑ I imagine the setting to look like . . .

❑ This description of the main character makes me . . .

❑ I picture that this is what happens in this section . . .

❑ I envision myself in the action by . . .

6 USE TEXT ORGANIZATION. Fiction writing has a plot that you can follow. Use the plot, or the series of events, to keep track of what is happening. Say to yourself

❑ The exposition, or introduction, tells me . . .

❑ The central conflict centers on . . .

❑ The climax, or high point of interest, occurs when . . .

❑ The resolution, or the outcome, of this story lets me know . . .

❑ Signal words like *first*, *then*, and *finally* explain . . .

7 TACKLE DIFFICULT VOCABULARY. Difficult words in a story can get in the way of your ability to follow the events in a work of fiction. Use aids that a text provides, consult a dictionary, or ask someone about words you do not understand. When you come across a word you do not know, say to yourself

❑ The context tells me that this word means . . .

❑ A dictionary definition provided in the story shows that the word means . . .

❑ My work with the word before class helps me know that the word means . . .

❑ A classmate said that the word means . . .

❑ I can skip knowing the exact meaning of this word because . . .

8 MONITOR YOUR READING PROGRESS. All readers encounter difficulty when they read, especially if they don't choose the reading material themselves. When you have to read something, take note of problems you are having and fix them. The key to reading success is knowing when you are having difficulty. To fix problems, say to yourself

❑ Because I do not understand this part, I will . . .

❑ Because I am having trouble staying interested in the story, I will . . .

❑ Because the words are too hard, I will . . .

❑ Because the story is very long, I will . . .

❑ Because I cannot remember what I have just read, I will . . .

How to Use Reading Strategies with Fiction

Read the following excerpts to discover how you might use reading strategies as you read fiction.

Excerpt 1. Note how a reader uses active reading strategies while reading this excerpt from "Zebra" by Chaim Potok.

WRITE THINGS DOWN

I'll make a plot chart for this story. One thing I know from this passage is that the main character likes to run.

His name was Adam Martin Zebrin, but everyone in his neighborhood knew him as Zebra.

He couldn't remember when he began to be called by that name. Perhaps they started to call him Zebra when he first began running. Or maybe he began running when they started to call him Zebra.

He loved the name and he loved to run.

READ WITH A PURPOSE

I want to find out why he is called Zebra.

VISUALIZE

I imagine a boy, about my age, running down the streets of his neighborhood.

MAKE PREDICTIONS

It sounds like running is very important to Zebra. I predict that he does something with his running, like win a race or save somebody's life by running.

Excerpt 2. Note how a reader uses active reading strategies while reading this excerpt from "The Fan Club" by Rona Maynard.

CONNECT TO PRIOR KNOWLEDGE

I know how Laura feels. There are some people in my school who laugh at me just because I'm not part of their group and I don't wear the "right" things.

USE TEXT ORGANIZATION

Laura's feelings toward the "in-crowd" seem to be a conflict in this story.

School. It loomed before her now, massive and dark against the sky. In a few minutes, she would have to face them again—Diane Goddard with her sleek blond hair and Terri Pierce in her candy-pink sweater. And Carol and Steve and Bill and Nancy. . . . There were so many of them, so exclusive as they stood in their tight little groups laughing and joking.

Why were they so cold and unkind? Was it because her long stringy hair hung in her eyes instead of dipping in graceful curls? Was it because she wrote poetry in algebra class and got A's in Latin without really trying? Shivering, Laura remembered how they would sit at the back of English class, passing notes and whispering. She thought of their identical brown loafers, their plastic purses, their hostile stares as they passed her in the corridors. She didn't care. They were clods, the whole lot of them.

MONITOR YOUR READING PROGRESS

I keep getting distracted by how I feel when people laugh at me. I'm going to refocus by trying to predict what Diane Goddard and her group are up to.

TACKLE DIFFICULT VOCABULARY

From context, I can guess that *exclusive* means only certain people can belong.

Reader's resource

"The Fan Club" by Rona Maynard is a story about a high school girl's difficulty fitting in with the "popular crowd." The story depicts a typical school day, the hardships of being accepted, and what students will do to fit in.

Social groups often cause feelings of peer pressure among individuals seeking or wanting acceptance in the group. Sometimes social groups or individuals are intolerant toward others. *Intolerance*, *prejudice*, and *discrimination* are words that describe hostile feelings and actions toward a person or group based on unjustified opinions. As you read the story, look for examples of intolerance, prejudice, and discrimination between the social groups at Laura's school.

Word watch

PREVIEW VOCABULARY

billow	jostle
cynical	malicious
gaudy	submerge
gesture	throng
irrational	

Reader's journal

What is more important—belonging to a group or standing by your beliefs?

"The Fan Club"
by Rona Maynard

Active READING STRATEGY

CONNECT TO PRIOR KNOWLEDGE

Before Reading ➤ THINK ABOUT WHAT YOU KNOW

❑ Read the Reader's Resource carefully.
❑ With a partner, talk about the social groups in your school. Then answer the Reader's Journal question.
❑ Prepare to compare situations in the story to situations in your school by completing the Comparison Chart as you read.

Graphic Organizer: Comparison Chart

Behavior of Students in Story	Similar Situation at My School

The FAN Club

Rona Maynard

During Reading

USE WHAT YOU KNOW

❏ Listen as your teacher reads the first page of the story aloud. How does Laura feel about Diane Goddard? How do you think Diane feels about Laura? Fill in information about the students in the story in the left side of the Comparison Chart.

❏ Do you think you would fit in better with Laura or with Diane Goddard and her group? Write about a similar situation from your school in the right side of the graphic organizer.

❏ Read the rest of the story on your own. Keep making notes in your chart about how the students behave. Each time you make a note, write a note about a related experience of your own.

It was Monday again. It was Monday and the day was damp and cold. Rain splattered the cover of *Algebra I* as Laura heaved her books higher on her arm and sighed. School was such a bore.

School. It loomed before her now, massive and dark against the sky. In a few minutes, she would have to face them again—Diane Goddard with her sleek blond hair and Terri Pierce in her candy-pink sweater. And Carol and Steve and Bill and Nancy. . . . There were so many of them,

10   so exclusive as they stood in their tight little groups laughing and joking.

Why were they so cold and unkind? Was it because her long stringy hair hung in her eyes instead of dipping in graceful curls? Was it because she wrote poetry in algebra class and got A's in Latin without really trying? Shivering, Laura remembered how they would sit at the back of English class, passing notes and whispering. She thought of their identical brown loafers, their plastic purses, their hostile stares as they passed her in the corridors. She didn't

20   care. They were clods, the whole lot of them.

She shoved her way through the door and there they

THINK AND REFLECT

Whom does Laura think this group of students is whispering about and staring at? **(Infer)**

_____

_____

THINK AND REFLECT

How do you think Laura feels? Have you ever felt this way? **(Empathize)**

_____

_____

were. They <u>thronged</u> the hall, streamed in and out of doors, clustered under red and yellow posters advertising the latest dance. Mohair sweaters, madras shirts, pea-green raincoats. They were all alike, all the same. And in the center of the group, as usual, Diane Goddard was saying, "It'll be a riot! I just can't wait to see her face when she finds out."

Laura flushed painfully. Were they talking about her?

30 "What a scream! Can't wait to hear what she says!"

Silently she hurried past and <u>submerged</u> herself in the stream of students heading for the lockers. It was then that she saw Rachel Horton—alone as always, her too-long skirt <u>billowing</u> over the white, heavy columns of her legs, her freckled face ringed with shapeless black curls. She called herself Horton, but everyone knew her father was Jacob Hortensky, the tailor. He ran that greasy little shop where you could always smell the cooked cabbage from the back rooms where the family lived.

40 "Oh, Laura!" Rachel was calling her. Laura turned, startled.

"Hi, Rachel."

"Laura, did you watch *World of Nature* last night? On Channel 11?"

"No—no, I didn't." Laura hesitated. "I almost never watch that kind of program."

"Well, gee, you missed something—last night, I mean. It was a real good show. Laura, it showed this fly being born!" Rachel was smiling now; she waved her hands as she talked.

50 "First the feelers and then the wings. And they're sort of wet at first, the wings are. Gosh, it was a good show."

"I bet it was." Laura tried to sound interested. She turned to go, but Rachel still stood there, her mouth half open, her pale, moon-like face strangely urgent. It was as if an invisible hand tugged at Laura's sleeve.

"And Laura," Rachel continued, "that was an awful good poem you read yesterday in English."

words for everyday use	**throng** (thrôn') *v.*, crowd; press upon in large numbers. *Fans <u>throng</u> the stadium on game days.* **sub • merge** (sub mərj') *v.*, put or go into or under, as in water. *Ian took a deep breath and <u>submerged</u> to the sandy lake bottom.* **bil • low** (bil´ō) *v.*, surge; swell. *The drying sheets <u>billow</u> in the wind.* **billowing,** *adj.*

Laura remembered how Terri and Diane had laughed and whispered. "You really think so? Well, thanks, Rachel. I mean, not too many people care about poetry."

"Yours was real nice though. I wish I could write like you. I always like those things you write."

Laura blushed. "I'm glad you do."

"Laura, can you come over sometime after school? Tomorrow maybe? It's not very far and you can stay for dinner. I told my parents all about you!"

Laura thought of the narrow, dirty street and the tattered awning in front of the tailor shop. An awful district, the kids said. But she couldn't let that matter. "Okay," she said. And then, faking enthusiasm, "I'd be glad to come."

She turned into the algebra room, sniffing at the smell of chalk and dusty erasers. In the back row, she saw the "in" group, laughing and joking and whispering.

"What a panic!"

"Here, you make the first one."

Diane and Terri had their heads together over a lot of little cards. You could see they were cooking up something.

Fumbling through the pages of her book, she tried to memorize the theorems[1] she hadn't looked at the night before. The laughter at the back of the room rang in her ears. Also those smiles—those heartless smiles. . . .

A bell buzzed in the corridors; students scrambled to their places. "We will now have the national anthem," said the voice on the loudspeaker. Laura shifted her weight from one foot to the other. It was so false, so pointless. How could they sing of the land of the free, when there was still discrimination. Smothered laughter behind her. Were they all looking at her?

And then it was over. Slumping in her seat, she shuffled through last week's half-finished homework papers and scribbled flowers in the margins.

"Now this one is just a direct application of the equation." The voice was hollow, distant, an echo beyond the sound of rustling papers and hushed whispers. Laura sketched a guitar on the cover of her notebook. Someday she would live in the Village[2] and there would be no more algebra classes and people would accept her.

---

1. **theorems.** Mathematical formulas
2. **Village.** Greenwich Village, a section of New York City

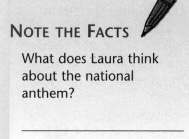

NOTE THE FACTS

How does Laura respond to Rachel's invitation?

_____

_____

NOTE THE FACTS

What does Laura think about the national anthem?

_____

_____

She turned towards the back row. Diane was passing around one of her cards. Terri leaned over, smiling. "Hey, can I do the next one?"

100 ". . . by using the distributive law." Would the class never end? Math was so dull, so painfully dull. They made you multiply and cancel and factor, multiply, cancel, and factor. Just like a machine. The steel sound of the bell shattered the silence. Scraping chairs, cries of "Hey, wait!" The crowd moved into the hallway now, a thronging, <u>jostling</u> mass.

Alone in the tide of faces, Laura felt someone nudge her. It was Ellen. "Hey, how's that for a smart outfit?" She pointed to the other side of the hall.

The <u>gaudy</u> flowers of Rachel Horton's blouse stood out
110 among the fluffy sweaters and pleated skirts. What a lumpish, awkward creature Rachel was. Did she have to dress like that? Her socks had fallen untidily around her heavy ankles, and her slip showed a raggedy edge of lace. As she moved into the English room, shoelaces trailing, her books tumbled to the floor.

"Isn't that something?" Terri said. Little waves of mocking laughter swept through the crowd.

The bell rang; the laughter died away. As they hurried to their seats, Diane and Terri exchanged last-minute
120 whispers. "Make one for Steve. He wants one too!"

Then Miss Merrill pushed aside the book she was holding, folded her hands, and beamed. "All right, people, that will be enough. Now, today we have our speeches. Laura, would you begin please?"

So it was her turn. Her throat tightened as she thought of Diane and Carol and Steve grinning and waiting for her to stumble. Perhaps if she was careful they'd never know she hadn't thought out everything beforehand. Careful, careful, she thought. Look confident.

130 "Let's try to be prompt." Miss Merrill tapped the cover of her book with her fountain pen.

Laura pushed her way to the front of the class. Before

How do the other students treat Rachel?

_____

_____

FIX-UP IDEA

Use Margin Questions
If you are having difficulty following the story, make sure you answer all the questions in the margins. If you can't answer a question, reread the page to see if you can find the answer. The questions will help you find some of the main ideas in the story.

words for everyday use
jos • tle (jäs´l) v., push roughly. *The students <u>jostle</u> one another as they board the bus.* **jostling,** *adj.*
gau • dy (gôd´ē) *adj.,* bright and showy, but lacking in good taste. *Everyone noticed Aunt Edna's <u>gaudy</u> hat pin.*

her, the room was large and still. Twenty-five round, blurred faces stared blankly. Was that Diane's laughter? She folded her hands and looked at the wall, strangely distant now, its brown paint cracked and peeling. A dusty portrait of Robert Frost, a card with the seven rules for better paragraphs, last year's calendar, and the steady, hollow ticking of the clock.

140   Laura cleared her throat. "Well," she began, "my speech is on civil rights." A chorus of snickers rose from the back of the room.

"Most people," Laura continued, "most people don't care enough about others. Here in New England, they think they're pretty far removed from discrimination and violence. Lots of people sit back and fold their hands and wait for somebody else to do the work. But I think we're all responsible for people that haven't had some of the advantages. . . ."

150   Diane was giggling and <u>gesturing</u> at Steve Becker. All she ever thought about was parties and dates—and such dates! Always the president of the student council or the captain of the football team.

"A lot of people think that race prejudice is limited to the South. But most of us are prejudiced—whether we know it or not. It's not just that we don't give other people a chance; we don't give ourselves a chance either. We form narrow opinions and then we don't see the truth. We keep right on believing that we're open-minded liberals when all
160   we're doing is deceiving ourselves."

How many of them cared about truth? Laura looked past the rows of blank, empty faces, past the bored stares and <u>cynical</u> grins.

"But I think we should try to forget our prejudices. We must realize now that we've done too little for too long. We must accept the fact that one person's misfortune is everyone's responsibility. We must defend the natural dignity of people—a dignity that thousands are denied."

words for everyday use	**ges • ture** (jes´chər) v., express or emphasize ideas and emotions with physical movement. *The politician <u>gestures</u> wildly with his arms to make a point.* **cy • ni • cal** (sin´i kəl) *adj.,* sarcastic; sneering. *The mean boy wore a <u>cynical</u> smirk.*

USE __THE STRATEGY__

CONNECT TO PRIOR KNOWLEDGE. How do you feel when you have to make a speech at school? How do you act when other students are giving speeches? How do others in the class act? Make a note in your Comparison Chart about what happens during Laura's speech and about your own experience.

MARK THE TEXT

Highlight or underline what Laura says people do about discrimination and violence.

NOTE THE FACTS

What does Laura say about responsibility and dignity?

_____

_____

THINK AND REFLECT

Do you agree with the ideas in Laura's speech? Why? **(Apply)**

_____

_____

Do you think Laura will be true to her beliefs? Why? **(Predict)**

_____

_____

READ ALOUD

As you read lines 190–200, read the high-lighted lines aloud. Focus on the tone of voice Miss Merrill would use. What attitude does Miss Merrill have toward Rachel?

_____

_____

170 None of them knew what it was like to be unwanted, unaccepted. Did Steve know? Did Diane?

"Most of us are proud to say that we live in a free country. But is this really true? Can we call the United States a free country when millions of people face prejudice and discrimination? As long as one person is forbidden to share the basic rights we take for granted, as long as we are still the victims of <u>irrational</u> hatreds, there can be no freedom. Only when every American learns to respect the dignity of every other American can we truly call our country free."

180 The class was silent. "Very nice, Laura." Things remained quiet as other students droned through their speeches. Then Miss Merrill looked briskly around the room. "Now, Rachel, I believe you're next."

There was a ripple of dry, humorless laughter—almost, Laura thought, like the sound of a rattlesnake. Rachel stood before the class now, her face red, her heavy arms piled with boxes.

Diane Goddard tossed back her head and winked at Steve.

190 "Well, well, don't we have lots of things to show," said Miss Merrill. "But aren't you going to put those boxes down, Rachel? No, no, not there!"

"Man, that kid's dumb," Steve muttered, and his voice could be clearly heard all through the room.

With a brisk rattle, Miss Merrill's pen tapped the desk for silence.

Rachel's slow smile twitched at the corners. She looked frightened. There was a crash and a clatter as the tower of boxes slid to the floor. Now everyone was giggling.

200 "Hurry and pick them up," said Miss Merrill sharply.

Rachel crouched on her knees and began very clumsily to gather her scattered treasures. Papers and boxes lay all about, and some of the boxes had broken open, spilling their contents in wild confusion. No one went to help. At

words for everyday use	**ir • ra • tion • al** (ir rash´ə nəl) adj., lacking reason; absurd. _Because Emma had never tried squash, her dislike of the vegetable was <u>irrational</u>._

last she scrambled to her feet and began fumbling with her notes.

"My—my speech is on shells."

A cold and stony silence had settled upon the room.

210 "Lots of people collect shells, because they're kind of pretty—sort of, and you just find them on the beach."

"Well, whaddaya know!" It was Steve's voice, softer this time, but all mock amazement. Laura jabbed her notebook with her pencil. Why were they so cruel, so thoughtless? Why did they have to laugh?

"This one," Rachel was saying as she opened one of the boxes, "it's one of the best." Off came the layers of paper and there, at last, smooth and pearly and shimmering, was the shell. Rachel turned it over lovingly in her hands. White, fluted sides, like the closecurled petals of a flower; a

220 scrolled coral back. Laura held her breath. It was beautiful. At the back of the room snickers had begun again.

"Bet she got it at Woolworth's," somebody whispered.

"Or in a trash dump." That was Diane.

Rachel pretended not to hear, but her face was getting very red and Laura could see she was flustered.

"Here's another that's kind of pretty. I found it last summer at Ogunquit."[3] In her outstretched hand there was a small, drab, brownish object. A common snail shell. "It's called a . . . It's called. . . ."

230 Rachel rustled through her notes. "I—I can't find it. But it was here. It was in here somewhere. I know it was." Her broad face had turned bright pink again. "Just can't find it. . . ." Miss Merrill stood up and strode toward her. "Rachel," she said sharply, "we are supposed to be prepared when we make a speech. Now, I'm sure you remember those rules on page twenty-one. I expect you to know these things. Next time you must have your material organized."

The bell sounded, ending the period. Miss Merrill collected her books.

240 Then, suddenly, chairs were shoved aside at the back of the room and there was the sound of many voices whispering. They were standing now, whole rows of them, their faces grinning with delight. Choked giggles, shuffling

---

3. **Ogunquit.** Resort town in southern Maine

NOTE THE FACTS

What does Laura think about the reaction of the other students to Rachel's speech?

_____

_____

Literary TOOLS

THEME. The **theme** is the central idea in a literary work. The theme of Laura's speech is that we all should treat others fairly and with dignity. Based on her speech, how do you expect Laura to treat Rachel?

_____

_____

_____

NOTE THE FACTS

What does Laura realize when she sees the writing on the white cards?

_____

_____

feet—and then applause—wild, sarcastic, <u>malicious</u> applause. That was when Laura saw that they were all wearing little white cards with a fat, frizzy-haired figure drawn on the front. What did it mean? She looked more closely. "HORTENSKY FAN CLUB," said the bright-red letters.

250   So that was what the whispering had been about all morning. She'd been wrong. They weren't out to get her after all. It was only Rachel.

Diane was nudging her and holding out a card. "Hey, Laura, here's one for you to wear."

For a moment Laura stared at the card. She looked from Rachel's red, frightened face to Diane's mocking smile, and she heard the pulsing, frenzied rhythm of the claps and the stamping, faster and faster. Her hands trembled as she picked up the card and pinned it to her sweater. And as she

260   turned, she saw Rachel's stricken look.

"She's a creep, isn't she?" Diane's voice was soft and intimate.

And Laura began to clap.   ■

words
for
everyday
use

ma • li • cious (mə liʹ shəs) *adj.,* marked by a desire to cause pain or distress. *The bombing was a <u>malicious</u> attack.*

Reflect ON YOUR READING

After Reading → **REFLECT ON YOUR CONNECTIONS**

❑ Look at what you wrote down in your Comparison Chart. Do you think the situation described in the story could happen at your school? Why, or why not?

_____

_____

_____

_____

❑ With your partner from the Before Reading activity, talk about how connecting the characters to students you know helped to read the story.

Reading Skills and Test Practice

RECOGNIZE CAUSE AND EFFECT

Discuss with your partner how best to answer these questions about cause and effect in the story. Use the Think-Aloud Notes to write down your reasons for eliminating the incorrect answers.

_____1. What causes Laura to agree to visit after school?
   a. Terri and Diane have criticized Laura's poem.
   b. Rachel praises Laura's poem.
   c. Laura feels cast out by the popular crowd.
   d. Rachel and Laura are interested in animals.

_____2. What event convinces Laura to pin on a fan club card?
   a. Everyone else is wearing one.
   b. Rachel has embarrassed Laura.
   c. Everyone applauds Laura.
   d. Diane speaks directly to Laura.

How did using the reading strategy help you to answer the questions?

_____

_____

_____

_____

THINK-ALOUD NOTES

_____

_____

_____

_____

_____

_____

_____

_____

_____

_____

_____

Investigate, Inquire, and Imagine

RECALL: GATHER FACTS
1a. What does Laura do in algebra class? What does she do in Latin class?

→ INTERPRET: FIND MEANING
1b. Why might this behavior cause other students to act coldly toward her?

ANALYZE: TAKE THINGS APART
2a. By examining Laura's thoughts, words, and actions, identify her feelings toward the people around her. How does she feel about Rachel? What are her feelings toward the group of popular students? How does she feel about society?

→ SYNTHESIZE: BRING THINGS TOGETHER
2b. How do Laura's attitudes toward others reflect her personal character?

EVALUATE: MAKE JUDGMENTS
3a. How effectively does "The Fan Club" deliver important ideas about human nature?

→ EXTEND: CONNECT IDEAS
3b. Give an example from your own experience that you think reveals something important about human nature.

WordWorkshop

PREFIXES. **Prefixes** are *morphemes* (word parts) that appear at the beginning of a word. They are *bound morphemes* because they can never stand alone. In "The Fan Club," *irrational,* a Word for Everyday Use, has the prefix *ir–. Submerging* has the prefix *sub–.*

When you add a prefix to a word or word root, you do not leave out any letters. For example, look again at *irrational.* When adding *ir–* to *rational,* you do not drop an *r.* Prefixes can help you understand the meaning of words. For example, if you know that the prefix *ir–* means "not" and that *rational* means "reasonable," you can tell that *irrational* means "not reasonable."

Look through "The Fan Club" and find ten words that contain prefixes. Write the words and their meanings on the lines below.

1. _____
2. _____
3. _____
4. _____
5. _____
6. _____
7. _____
8. _____
9. _____
10. _____

Literary Tools

THEME. A **theme** is a central idea in a literary work. What theme or themes are central to "The Fan Club"? Which parts of the story convey the theme or themes most strongly?

_____

_____

_____

_____

_____

Read-Write Connection

If you were Rachel, how would you have reacted to the students in the last scene of the story?

_____

_____

_____

_____

Beyond the Reading

ANALYZING THE MEDIA. How do the media portrait conformity and individuality? With a group of your classmates, gather several examples of television, radio, magazine, or billboard ads; movies; or other media that deal with being yourself or with following the group. Analyze each example and draw some conclusions about the media's portrayal of individuality versus conformity. How persuasive do you find each example? Why?

GO ONLINE. To find links and additional activities for this selection, visit the EMC Internet Resource Center at **emcp.com/languagearts** and click on Write-In Reader.

Reader's resource

Edgar Allan Poe is known for developing the psychological horror story with tales such as **"The Tell-Tale Heart,"** first published in 1843. Poe's story is about a murder that occurs as the result of the narrator's irrational fear or *phobia*. The narrators in Poe's stories are often unreliable; they do not always tell what really happened. At the beginning of "The Tell-Tale Heart," the narrator claims to be mad, or insane. While severe mental illness sometimes leads to violent behavior, it is rarely the cause of crime. Mental illnesses include schizophrenia, bipolar disorder (manic depression), and severe depression. As you read, think about whether the narrator in "The Tell-Tale Heart" is mad or sane.

Word watch

PREVIEW VOCABULARY

audacity	stealthy
concealment	stifle
conceive	suave
cunning	supposition
derision	vehement
dissimulate	vex
sagacity	

Reader's journal

Which thing or things in the world around you most frighten or horrify you?

"The Tell-Tale Heart"
by Edgar Allan Poe

Active READING STRATEGY

WRITE THINGS DOWN

Before Reading ➤ **PREVIEW SELECTION AND GRAPHIC ORGANIZER**

❑ Read the Reader's Resource and begin to think about the narrator. What questions do you have about him? What might you assume about him from the Reader's Resource?

❑ Look at the examples in the graphic organizer. As you read, you will pay attention to these and other details about the narrator.

Graphic Organizer: Character Traits Chart

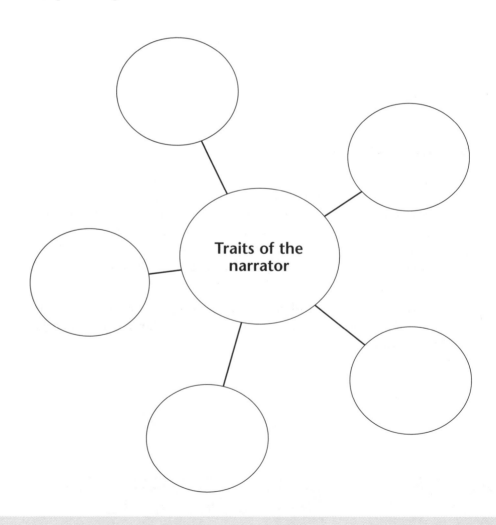

Traits of the narrator

The Tell-Tale HEART

Edgar Allan Poe

During Reading

COMPLETE THE CHARACTER TRAITS CHART AS YOU READ

- ❑ Listen as your teacher reads the first page of the selection aloud. What do you learn about the narrator? Make notes in your chart. You may also want to jot down questions you have about the narrator.
- ❑ Continue reading on your own. Keep adding notes about the narrator to your chart. If you find answers to your questions, write those down, too.

True!—nervous—very, very dreadfully nervous I had been and am; but why *will* you say that I am mad? The disease had sharpened my senses—not destroyed—not dulled them. Above all was the sense of hearing acute. I heard all things in the heaven and in the earth. I heard many things in hell. How, then, am I mad? Hearken![1] and observe how healthily—how calmly I can tell you the whole story.

It is impossible to say how first the idea entered my brain; but once <u>conceived</u>, it haunted me day and night. Object there was none. Passion there was none. I loved the old man. He had never wronged me. He had never given me insult. For his gold I had no desire. I think it was his eye! Yes, it was this! He had the eye of a vulture—a pale blue eye, with a film over it. Whenever it fell upon me, my blood ran cold; and so

10

NOTE THE FACTS

What does the narrator dislike about the old man?

_____

_____

---

1. **Hearken.** Listen carefully

words for everyday use

con • ceive (kən sēv′) v., form or develop in the mind. *She <u>conceived</u> the idea for the fund-raiser just before she fell asleep.*

Literary TOOLS

NARRATOR. The **narrator** is a person or character who tells a story. What do you think of the narrator so far?

_____

_____

NOTE THE FACTS

How does the narrator behave toward the old man during the day?

_____

_____

by degrees—very gradually—I made up my mind to take the life of the old man, and thus rid myself of the eye forever.

20 Now this is the point. You fancy me mad. Madmen know nothing. But you should have seen *me*. You should have seen how wisely I proceeded—with what caution—with what foresight—with what <u>dissimulation</u> I went to work! I was never kinder to the old man than during the whole week before I killed him. And every night, about midnight, I turned the latch of his door and opened it—oh, so gently! And then, when I had made an opening sufficient for my head, I put in a dark lantern, all closed, closed, so that no light shone out, and then I thrust in my head. Oh, you would have laughed to see how <u>cunningly</u> I thrust it in! I moved it slowly—very, very slowly, so that I might not disturb the old man's sleep. It took me an hour to place my whole head within the opening so far

30 that I could see him as he lay upon his bed. Ha!—would a madman have been so wise as this? And then, when my head was well in the room, I undid the lantern cautiously—oh, so cautiously—cautiously (for the hinges creaked)—I undid it just so much that a single, thin ray fell upon the vulture eye. And this I did for seven long nights—every night just at midnight—but I found the eye always closed; and so it was impossible to do the work; for it was not the old man who vexed me, but his Evil Eye. And every morning, when the day broke, I went boldly into the chamber, and spoke

40 courageously to him, calling him by name in a hearty tone, and inquiring how he had passed the night. So you see he would have been a very profound old man, indeed, to suspect that every night, just at twelve, I looked in upon him while he slept.

Upon the eighth night I was more than usually cautious in opening the door. A watch's minute hand moves more quickly than did mine. Never, before that night, had I *felt* the extent of my own powers—of my <u>sagacity</u>. I could scarcely contain my feelings of triumph. To think that there I was, opening

50 the door, little by little, and he not even to dream of my

words for everyday use	**dis • sim • u • late** (di sim′ yü lāt′) v., act of hiding; pretending. _Susan wore a disguise to dissimulate her identity._ **dissimulation**, n.
	cun • ning (kun′ iŋ) adj., skillful or clever. _The cunning quarterback confused the defense with a well-executed pass play._ **cunningly**, adv.
	sag • ac • i • ty (sə gas′ ə tē) n., wisdom; intelligence. _The youngsters marveled at the sagacity of the old man who had traveled the world._

secret deeds or thoughts. I fairly chuckled at the idea; and perhaps he heard me; for he moved on the bed suddenly, as if startled. Now you may think that I drew back—but no. His room was as black as pitch with the thick darkness (for the shutters were close fastened, through fear of robbers), and so I knew that he could not see the opening of the door, and I kept pushing it on steadily, steadily.

I had my head in, and was about to open the lantern, when my thumb slipped upon the tin fastening, and the old man sprang up in bed, crying out—"Who's there?"

I kept quite still and said nothing. For a whole hour I did not move a muscle, and in the meantime I did not hear him lie down. He was still sitting up in the bed listening; just as I have done, night after night, hearkening to the deathwatches[2] in the wall.

Presently I heard a slight groan, and I knew it was the groan of mortal terror. It was not a groan of pain or grief— oh, no!—it was the low, <u>stifled</u> sound that arises from the bottom of the soul when overcharged with awe. I knew the sound well. Many a night, just at midnight, when all the world slept, it has welled up from my own bosom, deepening, with its dreadful echo, the terrors that distracted me. I say I knew it well. I knew what the old man felt, and pitied him, although I chuckled at heart. I knew that he had been lying awake ever since the first slight noise, when he had turned in the bed. His fears had been ever since growing upon him. He had been trying to fancy them causeless, but could not. He had been saying to himself—"It is nothing but the wind in the chimney—it is only a mouse crossing the floor," or "it is merely a cricket which has made a single chirp." Yes, he has been trying to comfort himself with these <u>suppositions</u>: but he had found all in vain. *All in vain;* because Death, in approaching him, had stalked with his black shadow before him, and enveloped the victim. And it was the mournful

---

2. **deathwatches.** Wood-boring beetles that make a tapping noise in the wood they invade. They are thought to predict death.

| words for everyday use | sti • fle (stī' fəld) v., hold back; stop, smother. *Val buried her face in her pillow to stifle the sound of her crying.* **stifled,** adj. |
| | sup • po • si • tion (sup ə zish' ən) n., something supposed; assumption. *The supposition is that those students with the best records of attendance will do best on the test.* |

Use **THE STRATEGY**

WRITE THINGS DOWN. Remember to add notes about the narrator to your Character Traits Chart. What do you learn about the narrator on this page? Add one or more notes to your chart.

NOTE THE FACTS

How does the narrator feel about the old man's terror?

_____

_____

Reading **STRATEGY REVIEW**

CONNECT TO PRIOR KNOWLEDGE. Try connecting to what you already know (see the Active Reading Strategy for "The Fan Club" on page 42). Have you ever heard a noise at night and been frightened by it? What did you imagine it was? How did you convince yourself not to be scared?

_____

_____

FIX-UP IDEA

Read Aloud/Think Aloud
If you are having trouble completing the chart, work with a partner to do a read aloud/think aloud. Read two or three paragraphs aloud. Stop and think aloud with your partner about the section you read. Then have your partner read the next two or three paragraphs. Again, stop to think aloud. Continue this way until you have completed the selection.

NOTE THE FACTS

What increases the narrator's fury?

_____

_____

NOTE THE FACTS

How does the narrator react when he hears the sound?

_____

_____

influence of the unperceived shadow that caused him to feel—although he neither saw nor heard—to *feel* the presence of my head within the room.

When I had waited a long time, very patiently, without hearing him lie down, I resolved to open a little, a very, very little crevice in the lantern. So I opened it—you cannot imagine how <u>stealthily</u>, stealthily—until at length, a single dim ray, like the thread of the spider, shot from out the crevice and fell upon the vulture eye.

It was open—wide, wide open—and I grew furious as I gazed upon it. I saw it with perfect distinctness—all a dull blue, with a hideous veil over it that chilled the very marrow in my bones; but I could see nothing else of the old man's face or person; for I had directed the ray, as if by instinct, precisely upon the damned spot.

And have I not told you that what you mistake for madness is but overacuteness of the senses?—now, I say, there came to my ears a low, dull, quick sound, such as a watch makes when enveloped in cotton. I knew *that* sound well, too. It was the beating of the old man's heart. It increased my fury, as the beating of a drum stimulates the soldier into courage.

But even yet I refrained and kept still. I scarcely breathed. I held the lantern motionless. I tried how steadily I could maintain the ray upon the eye. Meantime the hellish tattoo of the heart increased. It grew quicker and quicker, and louder and louder every instant. The old man's terror *must* have been extreme! It grew louder, I say, louder every moment!—do you mark me well? I have told you that I am nervous; so I am. And now at the dead hour of the night, amid the dreadful silence of that old house, so strange a noise as this excited me to uncontrollable terror. Yet, for some minutes longer I refrained and stood still. But the beating grew louder, louder! I thought the heart must burst. And now a new anxiety seized me—the sound would be heard by a neighbor! The old man's hour had come! With a loud yell, I threw open the lantern

90

100

110

words for everyday use	stealth • y (stel' thē) *adj.,* secret; sneaky. *Quietly, the <u>stealthy</u> dog inched toward the scraps in the garbage.* **stealthily,** *adv.*

120 and leaped into the room. He shrieked once—once only. In an instant I dragged him to the floor, and pulled the heavy bed over him. I then smiled gaily, to find the deed so far done. But, for many minutes, the heart beat on with a muffled sound. This, however, did not <u>vex</u> me; it would not be heard through the wall. At length it ceased. The old man was dead. I removed the bed and examined the corpse. Yes, he was stone, stone dead. I placed my hand upon the heart and held it there many minutes. There was no pulsation. He was stone dead. His eye would trouble me no more.

130 If still you think me mad, you will think so no longer when I describe the wise precautions I took for the <u>concealment</u> of the body. The night waned, and I worked hastily, but in silence. First of all I dismembered the corpse. I cut off the head and the arms and the legs.

I then took up three planks from the flooring of the chamber, and deposited all between the scantlings.[3] I then replaced the boards so cleverly, so cunningly, that no human eye—not even *his*—could have detected anything wrong. There was nothing to wash out—no stain of any kind—no

140 blood spot whatever. I had been too wary for that. A tub had caught all—ha! ha!

When I had made an end of these labors, it was four o'clock—still dark as midnight. As the bell sounded the hour, there came a knocking at the street door. I went down to open it with a light heart,—for what had I *now* to fear? There entered three men, who introduced themselves, with perfect <u>suavity</u>, as officers of the police. A shriek had been heard by a neighbor during the night; suspicion of foul play had been aroused; information had been lodged at the police office, and

150 they (the officers) had been deputed to search the premises.

I smiled,—for *what* had I to fear? I bade the gentlemen welcome. The shriek, I said, was my own in a dream. The old man, I mentioned, was absent in the country. I took my visitors all over the house. I bade them search—search *well*. I

USE THE STRATEGY

WRITE THINGS DOWN. What does the narrator's reaction to the old man's death tell you about the narrator?

_____

_____

How does the narrator try to convince the reader that he is not mad?

_____

_____

THINK AND REFLECT

How do you think the narrator will react to the visit by the police? **(Predict)**

_____

_____

---

3. **scantlings.** Small beams or timbers.

words for everyday use	**vex** (veks') *v.*, bother; trouble. *She tried not to let the psychic's predictions of doom <u>vex</u> her.* **con · ceal · ment** (kən sēl' mənt) *n.*, hiding. *<u>Concealment</u> of the broken lamp was unlikely, as the pieces were scattered across the floor.* **suave** (swäv') *adj.*, smooth, graceful; polite. *The <u>suave</u> politician made lots of promises to the community.* **suavity**, *n.*

MARK THE TEXT

Highlight or underline what convinces the officers of the narrator's innocence.

THINK AND REFLECT

What does the narrator think he hears? **(Infer)**

_____

_____

THINK AND REFLECT

What does the narrator think the police see and hear? What do you think the police see and hear? **(Infer)**

_____

_____

led them, at length, to *his* chamber. I showed them his treasures, secure, undisturbed. In the enthusiasm of my confidence, I brought chairs into the room, and desired them *here* to rest from their fatigues, while I myself, in the wild <u>audacity</u> of my perfect triumph, placed my own seat upon the

160   very spot beneath which reposed the corpse of my victim.

    The officers were satisfied. My *manner* had convinced them. I was singularly at ease. They sat, and while I answered cheerily, they chatted of familiar things. But, ere long, I felt myself getting pale and wished them gone. My head ached, and I fancied a ringing in my ears: but still they sat and still chatted. The ringing became more distinct;—it continued and became more distinct: I talked more freely to get rid of the feeling; but it continued and gained definitiveness—until, at length, I found that the noise was not within my ears.

170   No doubt I now grew *very* pale—but I talked more fluently, and with a heightened voice. Yet the sound increased—and what could I do? It was *a low, dull, quick sound—much such a sound as a watch makes when enveloped in cotton.* I gasped for breath—and yet the officers heard it not. I talked more quickly—more <u>vehemently</u>; but the noise steadily increased. I arose and argued about trifles, in a high key and with violent gesticulations;[4] but the noise steadily increased. Why *would* they not be gone? I paced the floor to and fro with heavy strides, as if excited to fury by the observations of the men—

180   but the noise steadily increased. Oh God; what *could* I do? I foamed—I raved—I swore! I swung the chair upon which I had been sitting, and grated it upon the boards, but the noise arose over all, and continually increased. It grew louder—louder—*louder!* And still the men chatted pleasantly, and smiled. Was it possible they heard not? Almighty God!—no, no! They heard!—they suspected!—they *knew!*—they were making a mockery of my horror!—this I thought, and this I think. But anything was better than this agony! Anything was more tolerable than this <u>derision</u>! I could bear those

---

4. **gesticulations.** Energetic gestures or movements

words for everyday use

au • dac • i • ty (ô das′ ə tē) *n.,* bold courage; daring. *The young woman was praised for having the <u>audacity</u> to share her shocking story for the benefit of others.*
ve • he • ment (vē′ ə mənt lē) *adj.,* violent; eager; forceful. *The <u>vehement</u> storm caused flooding and crop damage.* **vehemently,** *adv.*
de • ri • sion (di rizh′ ən) *n.,* contempt or ridicule. *The narrow-minded community treated the newcomer with <u>derision</u>.*

190   hypocritical smiles no longer! I felt that I must scream or die! and now—again!—hark! louder! louder! louder! *louder!*

    "Villains!" I shrieked. "Dissemble no more! I admit the deed!—tear up the planks! here, here!—it is the beating of his hideous heart!" ■

THINK AND REFLECT

What do you think will happen to the narrator now? **(Extend)**

_____

_____

Reflect ON YOUR READING

After Reading ➤ ## SUMMARIZE YOUR NOTES

❑ Compare your notes about the narrator with a partner.
❑ Write a brief character sketch of the narrator based on what you wrote.

_____

_____

_____

_____

_____

_____

Reading Skills and Test Practice

ANALYZE THE NARRATOR
READ, THINK, AND EXPLAIN. Explain why the narrator of "The Tell-Tale Heart" is unreliable. What effect does this have on the story?

_____

_____

_____

_____

_____

_____

REFLECT ON YOUR RESPONSE. Compare your response to that of your partner. Talk about how the information you wrote down while reading helped form your response.

THINK-ALOUD NOTES

_____

_____

_____

_____

_____

_____

_____

_____

_____

_____

_____

Investigate, Inquire, and Imagine

RECALL: GATHER FACTS
1a. What about the old man bothers the narrator? Why?

INTERPRET: FIND MEANING
1b. Why might this feature be so troublesome for the narrator?

ANALYZE: TAKE THINGS APART
2a. What characteristics of the narrator make him seem sane? What characteristics of the narrator make him seem insane?

SYNTHESIZE: BRING THINGS TOGETHER
2b. Do you think the narrator's mental state changes over the course of the story? Explain why or why not?

PERSPECTIVE: LOOK AT OTHER VIEWS
3a. Do you think the old man knew who was watching him? Why do you think he reacted the way he did?

EMPATHY: SEE FROM INSIDE
3b. What would the old man have thought if he knew how the narrator felt about his eye? How would he have reacted, knowing also that the narrator "loved the old man"?

Literary Tools

NARRATOR. A **narrator** is a person or character who tells a story. Review the Character Traits Chart you completed during reading. Then answer these questions:

Which important details about the narrator are not revealed in the story?

_____

_____

_____

_____

Why do you think the author chose not to include those details?

_____

_____

_____

_____

WordWorkshop

CREATING A WORD STUDY NOTEBOOK. A word study notebook can help you learn new words and understand how to use them. Choose four words from "The Tell-Tale Heart" below. Make entries for your word study notebook by including its definition, pronunciation, and origins, along with an example sentence or drawing to help you remember it. To see an example of a page from a word study notebook, see Unit 9, page 334.

audacity	dissimulate	supposition
concealment	sagacity	vehement
conceive	stealthy	vex
cunning	stifle	
derision	suave	

1. Word: _____
   Pronunciation:_____
   Origins:_____
   Definition: _____
   Sentence: _____
   Drawing:

2. Word: _____
   Pronunciation:_____
   Origins:_____
   Definition: _____
   Sentence: _____
   Drawing:

3. Word: _____
   Pronunciation:_____
   Origins: _____
   Definition: _____
   Sentence:_____
   Drawing:

4. Word: _____
   Pronunciation:_____
   Origins: _____
   Definition: _____
   Sentence:_____
   Drawing:

Read-Write Connection

Do you think the old man knew anything about the narrator's thoughts and plans? Why, or why not?

Beyond the Reading

LEARNING ABOUT CRIMINOLOGY. Research different careers related to the justice system and criminology, such as police officer, lawyer, judge, social worker, criminologist. Use library and Internet resources to learn more about these careers. You might also visit a career center or conduct an interview with a person who works in this field.

GO ONLINE. To find links and additional activities for this selection, visit the EMC Internet Resource Center at **emcp.com/languagearts** and click on Write-In Reader.

"The Hummingbird That Lived through Winter"
by William Saroyan

Active READING STRATEGY

WRITE THINGS DOWN

Before Reading ▶ **PREPARE TO WRITE DOWN THE ELEMENTS**

❑ Review the terms *character, setting,* and *plot.* A **character** is a person or other being who takes part in the action of a literary work. The **setting** is the time and place in which a literary work happens. A **plot** is a series of events related to a central conflict or struggle. (See pages 36–38 in the introduction to this unit for more information.)

❑ Think about the title and what you read in the Reader's Resource. What do you already know about the characters, setting, and plot of the story? Make notes in the Literary Elements Chart below.

❑ As you read, you will continue to make notes about these three elements.

Graphic Organizer: Literary Elements Chart

Character	Setting	Plot

CONNECT

Reader's resource

"The Hummingbird That Lived through Winter" by William Saroyan tells about an old man and a humming-bird in the middle of winter in California. Normally, hummingbirds from the United States and Canada migrate to Mexico, Central America, or South America to spend the winter. Humming-birds are the smallest birds on earth. They are named for the sound of their wings in motion. They are the only birds able to fly up, down, forward, back-ward, and sideways. Humming-birds are known for their bold nature.

Word watch

PREVIEW VOCABULARY

distinguish
guardian
transformation
vapor

Reader's journal

What would you do if you found a sick or injured animal?

_____

_____

_____

_____

During Reading

GATHER INFORMATION

❑ Listen as your teacher reads the first two paragraphs aloud. What do you learn about the setting? What do you learn about the characters? What do you learn about the plot? Make notes in your Literary Elements Chart.

❑ Read the rest of the story on your own. Continue to write down what you learn about each element as you read. For instance, when you meet a new character, make a few notes about what you learn under the Character column. When you learn something about when and where the story takes place, make notes in the Setting column. As events happen in the story, make notes in the Plot column about what happens.

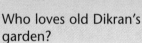

NOTE THE FACTS

Who loves old Dikran's garden?

_____

_____

Literary TOOLS

SETTING. The **setting** of the story is the time and place in which it happens. What do you learn about the setting on this page?

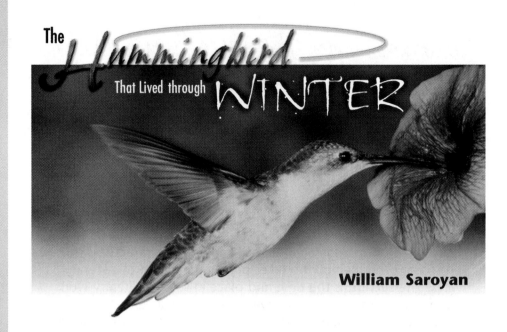

The Hummingbird That Lived through WINTER

William Saroyan

There was a hummingbird once which in the wintertime did not leave our neighborhood in Fresno, California. I'll tell you about it.

Across the street lived old Dikran, who was almost blind. He was past eighty and his wife was only a few years younger. They had a little house that was as neat inside as it was ordinary outside—except for old Dikran's garden, which was the best thing of its kind in the world. Plants, bushes, trees—all strong, in sweet black moist earth whose 10 guardian was old Dikran. All things from the sky loved this spot in our poor neighborhood, and old Dikran loved *them*.

One freezing Sunday, in the dead of winter, as I came home from Sunday School I saw old Dikran standing in the middle of the street trying to distinguish what was in his hand. Instead of going into our house to the fire, as I had wanted to do, I stood on the steps of the front porch and watched the old man. He would turn around and look upward at his trees and then back to the palm of his hand. He stood in the street at least two minutes and then at last

words for everyday use	**guard • ian** (gär' dē ən) *n.*, one that guards. *Our puppy is a loyal guardian to our baby sister, barking loudly when anyone new goes near her.* **dis • tin • guish** (di stin' gwish) *v.*, discern; detect with the eyes or with other senses. *Because the brothers looked so much alike, from a distance it was difficult to distinguish one from the other.*

20   he came to me. He held his hand out, and in Armenian[1] he said, "What is this in my hand?"

I looked.

"It is a hummingbird," I said half in English and half in Armenian. Hummingbird I said in English because I didn't know its name in Armenian.

"What is that?" old Dikran asked.

"The little bird," I said. "You know. The one that comes in the summer and stands in the air and then shoots away. The one with the wings that beat so fast you can't see them.

30   It's in your hand. It's dying."

"Come with me," the old man said. "I can't see, and the wife's at church. I can feel its heart beating. Is it in a bad way? Look again once."

I looked again. It was a sad thing to behold. This wonderful little creature of summertime in the big rough hand of the old peasant. Here and pathetic, not suspended in a shaft of summer light, not the most alive thing in the world, but the most helpless and heart-breaking.

"It's dying," I said.

40   The old man lifted his hand to his mouth and blew warm breath on the little thing in his hand which he could not even see. "Stay now," he said in Armenian. "It is not long till summer. Stay, swift and lovely."

We went into the kitchen of his little house, and while he blew warm breath on the bird he told me what to do.

"Put a tablespoon of honey over the gas fire and pour it into my hand, but be sure it is not too hot."

This was done.

After a moment the hummingbird began to show signs of

50   fresh life. The warmth of the room, the <u>vapor</u> of the warm honey—and, well, the will and love of the old man. Soon the old man could feel the change in his hand, and after a

---

1. **Armenian.** Language spoken by the people dwelling chiefly in Armenia and in neighboring regions of Turkey and Azerbaijan

words for everyday use

va • por (va′ pər) *n.*, scattered matter suspended in the air and clouding it (such as smoke or fog). *Even without hearing the teapot whistle, I knew it was ready by the <u>vapor</u> pouring out of the spout.*

MARK THE TEXT

Underline or highlight what is in old Dikran's hand.

Use **THE STRATEGY**

WRITE THINGS DOWN. Reread this page. What do you learn about old Dikran? Make notes in the Character column of your chart.

NOTE THE FACTS

What makes the hummingbird feel better?

_____

_____

Refocus

If you have trouble tracking all the elements in your chart, focus on one of the elements. For example, just take notes about the plot. Write down what happens in the story and your reaction to events in the story. You might want to use a Plot Diagram like the one in Appendix B on page B-12.

NOTE THE FACTS

Why does old Dikran tell the narrator to let the hummingbird go?

_____

_____

_____

THINK AND REFLECT

Why do you think it matters to Dikran and the narrator whether the bird lived? **(Infer)**

_____

_____

moment or two the hummingbird began to take little dabs of the honey.

"It will live," the old man announced. "Stay and watch."

The <u>transformation</u> was incredible. The old man kept his hand generously open, and I expected the helpless bird to shoot upward out of his hand, suspend itself in space, and scare the life out of me—which is exactly what happened.

60 The new life of the little bird was magnificent. It spun about in the little kitchen, going to the window, coming back to the heat, suspending, circling as if it were summertime and it had never felt better in its whole life.

The old man sat on the plain chair, blind but attentive. He listened carefully and tried to see, but of course he couldn't. He kept asking about the bird, how it seemed to be, whether it showed signs of weakening again, what its spirit was, and whether or not it appeared to be restless; and I kept describing the bird to him.

70 When the bird was restless and wanted to go, the old man said, "Open the window and let it go."

"Will it live?" I asked.

"It is alive now and wants to go," he said. "Open the window."

I opened the window, the hummingbird stirred about here and there, feeling the cold from the outside, suspended itself in the area of the open window, stirring this way and that, and then it was gone.

"Close the window," the old man said.

80 We talked a minute or two and then I went home.

The old man claimed the hummingbird lived through that winter, but I never knew for sure. I saw hummingbirds again when summer came, but I couldn't tell one from the other.

One day in the summer I asked the old man.

"Did it live?"

"The little bird?" he said.

"Yes," I said. "That we gave the honey to. You remember.

words for everyday use

trans • for • ma • tion (trans fər mā′ shən) n., change in composition, structure, or outward form and appearance. *After the addition of the new paint, furniture, carpet, and curtains, the <u>transformation</u> of the room was complete.*

The little bird that was dying in the winter. Did it live?"

90   "Look about you," the old man said. "Do you see the bird?"

    "I see humming*birds*," I said.

    "Each of them is our bird," the old man said. "Each of them, each of them," he said swiftly and gently. ■

THINK AND REFLECT

What do you think Dikran means when he says, "Each of them is our bird"? **(Interpret)**

_____

_____

Reflect ON YOUR READING

❑ With a partner, complete your Literary Elements Chart.
❑ Discuss your reaction to the story. What is your opinion of the narrator and Dikran? Did anything in the story surprise you? Why is the setting of the story important?
❑ Write a brief summary that answers the questions above.

_____

_____

_____

_____

THINK-ALOUD NOTES

_____

_____

_____

_____

_____

_____

_____

_____

_____

_____

_____

Reading Skills and Test Practice

UNDERSTAND LITERARY ELEMENTS

Discuss with your partner how to answer the following questions about the selection. Use the Think-Aloud Notes to write down your reasons for eliminating the incorrect answers.

_____1. How does the narrator feel about the hummingbird's revival?
    a. excited
    b. cautious
    c. not surprised
    d. quietly pleased

_____2. How does old Dikran feel about nature and its creatures?
    a. He fears nature because he can't see.
    b. He thinks nature is more powerful than man.
    c. He thinks nature is cruel and thoughtless.
    d. He values and cherishes it.

How did using the reading strategy help you to answer the questions?

_____

_____

_____

_____

Investigate, Inquire, and Imagine

RECALL: GATHER FACTS
1a. What do Dikran and the narrator do with the hummingbird? Who gives the instructions and who carries them out?

ANALYZE: TAKE THINGS APART
2a. What evidence do you find that old Dikran values nature and its creatures?

EVALUATE: MAKE JUDGMENTS
3a. Why do you think Saroyan made Dikran blind? How does that detail affect the story?

INTERPRET: FIND MEANING
1b. How does the narrator feel as the hummingbird begins to show signs of energy?

SYNTHESIZE: BRING THINGS TOGETHER
2b. How does old Dikran think the hummingbird he helped relates to the hummingbirds he sees the following spring? What does this say about Dikran's attitude toward life?

EXTEND: CONNECT IDEAS
3b. Who in real life do you know who takes care of the things the way old Dikran does?

Literary Tools

SETTING. The **setting** of a story is the time and place in which it happens. Review the setting column of your graphic organizer. Why is the setting, especially the season, so important in this story? What details of the setting remain the same throughout the story?

_____

_____

WordWorkshop

PAVE. A good way to help yourself remember the meaning of an unfamiliar word you encounter while reading is by using PAVE. PAVE stands for *predict, associate, verify,* and *evaluate.*

When you encounter an unfamiliar word, first try to **predict** the word's meaning based on the context and on your prior knowledge of the word or its parts. Then **associate** by writing a new sentence using the word. Next, **verify** the word's meaning using a dictionary or glossary. Select and write down the most appropriate definition. Finally, **evaluate** the sentence you wrote using the word. If necessary, rewrite the sentence to reflect the meaning you found. If you wish, draw an image that will help you remember the meaning of the word. You can include your work with PAVE in your word study notebook.

Try PAVE for the vocabulary word "distinguish" from "The Hummingbird That Lived through Winter." In your word study notebook, use PAVE to unlock the meaning of other difficult words from the selection.

EXAMPLE
transformation

Predict   an ability to change forms

Associate   Captain Heroic could undergo an amazing transformation where he would change from a wimp to a strong superhero.

Verify   the process of changing in composition, form, or structure

Evaluate   The transformation of Captain Heroic from wimp to superhero was so amazing that not only his body but his mind was radically changed.

distinguish

Predict _____

Associate _____

Verify _____

Evaluate _____

Read-Write Connection

Do you think the hummingbird lived? Why, or why not? Write your response on a separate piece of paper.

Beyond the Reading

RESEARCHING HUMMINGBIRD LEGENDS. Hummingbirds are fascinating creatures. They have been included in myths and legends of many Native American groups, including the Hopi, the Cherokee, and the Aztec. Work in small groups to research hummingbird legends. Use the library or Internet to find a myth or legend that depicts a hummingbird. With your group members, decide on a way to share the myth or legend with the class. You may want to rewrite the story in your own words, illustrate the story in a mural or story strip, or act out the myth or legend.

GO ONLINE. To find links and additional activities for this selection, visit the EMC Internet Resource Center at **emcp.com/languagearts** and click on Write-In Reader.

"The Ground Is Always Damp"

by Luci Tapahonso

Active READING STRATEGY

VISUALIZE

Before Reading ➤ **BEGIN TO PICTURE THE SETTING**

❑ Read the Reader's Resource and think about the title of the story.
❑ Look at the picture on page 74. What would you see, hear, smell, and feel if you were in the place in the picture?
❑ Begin to picture the setting of the story.

Graphic Organizer: Visualization Sketches

As you read, pause occasionally to sketch your visualizations or jot down descriptions of what you visualized.

Setting in New Mexico	Setting Where Leona Lives Now

CONNECT

Reader's resource

Luci Tapahonso, a member of the Navajo Nation, grew up in Shiprock, New Mexico. New Mexico, Utah, and Arizona are home to the Navajo Nation. Northwestern New Mexico features a dramatic landscape of river valleys, mountain ranges, desert, and mesas. **"The Ground Is Always Damp"** compares two settings: one in New Mexico, where the character Leona used to live, and one where Leona lives now. As you read, look for details about New Mexico and Leona's new home.

Reader's journal

Think of one of your favorite places to be. In what ways does being there affect your mood? What do you do when you are there?

_____

_____

_____

_____

CONTINUE TO MAKE MIND PICTURES

❑ Listen as your teacher reads the first paragraph of the story aloud. Create a mind picture of this scene. What do you see? hear? smell?

❑ As you read the rest of the story, keep picturing the scene, including all the things you would see, hear, and smell. Picture Leona and what she is doing, as well.

❑ Make sketches or write brief descriptions of what you picture in the graphic organizer on page 73.

MARK THE TEXT

Highlight or underline what Leona dreamed about one night.

NOTE THE FACTS

What does Leona imagine?

_____

_____

The Ground Is Always Damp

Luci Tapahonso

One night Leona dreamt that she was sitting outside her parents' home in the bright sunlight. The many trees, the small dusty chickens scratching nearby, and a single cloud above cast sharp dark shadows on the smooth yard. The sudden familiarity of the detailed shadows and clean air startled and awakened her, and later she spoke aloud, addressing her mother who was hundreds of miles away.

"Shimá, my mother, it's cloudy here most of the time. The ground is always damp, and Mom, I don't care to kneel down and sift dirt through my fingers. One day last week, the sun came out for a few hours, and the shadows were soft and furry on the brown grass. That's the way it is here, my mother."

Even though Leona hadn't seen her parents in months, she talked to them silently every day. She imagined that they listened, then responded by explaining things or asking long, detailed questions. Leona did this thoughtfully and felt that they did the same in their daily conversations about her and her children. They wondered what the weather was like and what kind of house Leona and her family lived in. She was certain about this. The difference was that they spoke aloud to each other, or to the various brothers and sisters who lived nearby.

In her dreams, she was always there in New Mexico, driving the winding roads to Taos, watching the harvest dances at

10

20

Laguna, or maybe selling hay and watermelons with her
brothers. In her dreams, she laughed, talking and joking easily
in Navajo and English. She woke herself up sometimes
30   because she had laughed aloud, or said, "Aye-e-e"—that old
familiar teasing expression.

The New Mexico sky is clear and empty. It is a deep blue,
almost turquoise, and Leona's family lives surrounded by the
Carriso Mountains in the west, the Sleeping Ute Mountains
in the north, the La Plata in the east and the Chuska
Mountain range[1] to the southwest. They rely on the distance,
the thin, clean air, and the mountains to alert them to rain,
thunderstorms, dust storms, and intense heat. At various
times, her brothers stand looking across the horizon to see
40   what is in store. They can see fifty miles or more in each
direction.

In contrast, when Leona looks to the east most mornings,
the sky is gray, the air thick with frost, and the wind blows
cold dampness.

"My mother, there are no mountains here, and I can't see
very far because the air is thick and heavy with a scent I can't
recognize. I haven't been able to smell the arrival of snow
here, or to distinguish between the different kinds of rain
scent. The rain seems all the same here, except in degree, and
50   it is constant. Sometimes it lasts for two days and nights. It
pours steadily until brown streams form and drain into the
overflowing creek behind the house.

"Shimá, some nights I just want to walk down the street and
smell piñon[2] wood smoke, or stew or beans boiling when I
pass a house." In the fall, we talk about the seasonal rituals at
home. "Remember," we say, "fresh green chile roasting
outside at Farmer's Market or outside of Smith's or
Albertson's? When Grandma Acoma baked bread in the
outside oven at McCarty's? We all helped. Daddy chopped
60   wood and piled it near the oven. We helped put the oven
door back in place and ran out of the house with potholders
and the long poles to bring out the bread. We would help
Grandma carry the bread, and she would say, 'Chase the dogs
off! They just get in the way!'"

---

1. **Carriso . . . Sleeping Ute . . . La Plata . . . Chuska Mountain range.** Mountain
ranges in northwestern New Mexico, southwestern Colorado, northeastern Arizona
2. **piñon.** Any of various low-growing pines or the edible seed of a pine

UNIT 3 / READING FICTION   75

Use THE STRATEGY

VISUALIZE. Read the two
highlighted paragraphs.
They describe two very
different places. Imagine
yourself in both places.
What would you see, hear,
and feel in each place?

_____

_____

_____

Literary TOOLS

MOOD. Mood is the
feeling or emotion that the
writer creates in a literary
work. The writer can evoke
emotions, such as fear,
longing, or anticipation,
by working carefully with
descriptive language. Read
lines 45–52. What mood
does this paragraph
create?

_____

_____

Reading STRATEGY REVIEW

WRITE THINGS DOWN. Writing
things down (see the Active
Reading Strategy for "The
Hummingbird That Lived
through Winter" on page 65)
can help you keep track of
things as you read. For
example, as you read, you
use a chart to keep track of
the differences between
where Leona used to live
and where she lives now.

Once Leona's elder daughter said, "Then we didn't know that those times would be memories for us. We didn't know we would leave there. It seemed like it would last and last. The bright afternoons, Grandma's soft strong hands, the smell of bread in the clear blue sky."

70   "Our laughter was different then," she said softly. ■

Reflect ON YOUR READING

After Reading **SUMMARIZE YOUR PICTURES**

❏ Share your drawings or descriptions with a partner. Tell your partner in more detail about the pictures you made in your Visualization Sketches Chart. Use various senses in your description.

❏ Talk about how visualizing helped you read this selection.

Reading Skills and Test Practice

COMPARE AND CONTRAST SETTING

READ, THINK, AND EXPLAIN. How is the author's childhood setting different from her adult setting? Use details and information from the story to support your answer.

_____

_____

_____

_____

_____

_____

_____

_____

_____

_____

REFLECT ON YOUR RESPONSE. Compare your response to that of your partner and talk about how the information you wrote down while reading helped form your response.

THINK-ALOUD NOTES

_____

_____

_____

_____

_____

_____

_____

_____

_____

_____

Investigate, Inquire, and Imagine

RECALL: GATHER FACTS ➤
1a. What does Leona tell her mother about the place where she is?

INTERPRET: FIND MEANING
1b. How do you think Leona feels about the place where she is living?

ANALYZE: TAKE THINGS APART ➤
2a. Compare and contrast Leona's family home in New Mexico and the place where Leona is living now. What do the two places have in common?

SYNTHESIZE: BRING THINGS TOGETHER
2b. What did the landscape of New Mexico offer Leona that her new landscape does not? In what ways does Leona define home?

PERSPECTIVE: LOOK AT OTHER VIEWS ➤
3a. Why might Leona speak aloud to her mother who is hundreds of miles away?

EMPATHY: SEE FROM INSIDE
3b. If you were in Leona's situation—far away from your family and the place where you feel most comfortable—how might you react? What would you do to feel more comfortable in your new home?

Literary Tools

MOOD. **Mood** is the feeling or emotion that the writer creates in a literary work. The writer can evoke emotions, such as fear, longing, or anticipation, by working carefully with descriptive language. Choose at least three of your own words that describe the mood of this story. Point out parts of the story that you think contribute to creating these moods.

_____

_____

_____

_____

_____

_____

_____

WordWorkshop

WORD PLAY. In writing "The Ground Is Always Damp," Luci Tapahanso uses powerful, simple words in just the right way to create her strong descriptions. Use the following words from her story and other precise, vivid words to write your own very short story—no longer than a paragraph—on the lines below.

dust storms   horizon   sift   turquoise

_____

_____

_____

_____

_____

_____

Read-Write Connection

The story does not tell where Leona is living. Is this important? Why, or why not? Write a brief explanation of where you think Leona is living, adding sensory details as you describe it.

_____

_____

_____

_____

Beyond the Reading

RESEARCHING PLACES IN THE STORY. Use an atlas to find the four mountain ranges mentioned in "The Ground Is Always Damp." Use the index to help you find Carriso (may also be spelled Corrizo), Ute, La Plata, and Chuska. Locate the mountains on the map. Next, identify the following areas on the map: Chaco Canyon National Monument, New Mexico; Window Rock, Arizona; Monument Valley Ruins, Arizona; and Canyon de Chelly National Park, Arizona. Use the Internet to research one of the last four places you listed on the map. Use the information you found to write a brochure for this place.

GO ONLINE. To find links and additional activities for this selection, visit the EMC Internet Resource Center at **emcp.com/languagearts** and click on Write-In Reader.

Reader's resource

"Luke Baldwin's Vow" by Morley Callaghan is a coming-of-age story. In this type of story, the main character is often faced with a challenge. The way in which the character deals with this challenge usually teaches a moral or a value, such as responsibility or honesty. Coming of age stories also allow different generations to learn from each other. Younger generations may gain wisdom from older generations, while older generations may find new ideas and renewed spirit in learning about younger generations. As you read the story, look for the challenge Luke faces and think about how he changes as a result of this challenge.

Word watch

PREVIEW VOCABULARY

aloof	methodical
apprehensive	ponderous
assess	precise
burly	proposition
competent	resourceful
divert	slow-witted
exultation	thwart
furtive	wiry
imposing	

Reader's journal

Would you describe yourself as practical, idealistic, or somewhere in between? Why?

"Luke Baldwin's Vow"

by Morley Callaghan

Active READING STRATEGY

MAKE PREDICTIONS

Before Reading ➤ **GATHER INFORMATION AND MAKE PRELIMINARY PREDICTIONS**

❏ Read the title and scan the selection. Read the Reader's Resource.
❏ Think about what the story may be about. Who will the characters be? What will be the main conflict or problem?
❏ Write down one or more predictions in the Prediction Chart below.

Graphic Organizer: Prediction Chart

Prediction #	Prediction

Luke Baldwin's VOW

Morley Callaghan

That summer when twelve-year-old Luke Baldwin came to live with his Uncle Henry in the house on the stream by the sawmill, he did not forget that he had promised his dying father he would try to learn things from his uncle; so he used to watch him very carefully.

Uncle Henry, who was the manager of the sawmill, was a big, <u>burly</u> man weighing more than two hundred and thirty pounds, and he had a rough-skinned, brick-colored face. He looked like a powerful man, but his health was not

10   good. He had aches and pains in his back and shoulders which puzzled the doctor. The first thing Luke learned about Uncle Henry was that everybody had great respect for him. The four men he employed in the sawmill were always polite and attentive when he spoke to them. His wife, Luke's Aunt Helen, a kindly, plump, straightforward woman, never argued with him. "You should try and be like your Uncle Henry," she would say to Luke. "He's so wonderfully practical. He takes care of everything in a sensible, easy way."

20   Luke used to trail around the sawmill after Uncle Henry not only because he liked the fresh clean smell of the newly cut wood and the big piles of sawdust, but because he was impressed by his uncle's <u>precise</u>, firm tone when he spoke to the men.

words for everyday use

bur • ly (bər′ lē) *adj.*, strongly and heavily built. *The <u>burly</u> waiter easily carried the tray filled with dishes.*

pre • cise (prē sis′) *adj.*, exact. *To make good dough, you must use the <u>precise</u> amount of flour.*

> **During Reading**

CONTINUE TO PREDICT

❑ Listen as your teacher reads the first two paragraphs of the story aloud. Does the information in these paragraphs match your preliminary predictions? Adjust your predictions as necessary based on the new information or make a new prediction.

❑ As you read the rest of the story on your own, keep adjusting your predictions and making new ones. Number each prediction. Then mark the number in the text where you stopped reading to make your prediction.

NOTE THE FACTS

What did Luke promise his father?

_____

_____

NOTE THE FACTS

What do other people think of Uncle Henry?

_____

_____

MARK THE TEXT

Highlight or underline what kinds of things Uncle Henry knows.

THINK AND REFLECT

Why do you think Luke chooses Dan as a companion? (Infer)

_____

_____

Sometimes Uncle Henry would stop and explain to Luke something about a piece of timber. "Always try and learn the essential facts, son," he would say. "If you've got the facts, you know what's useful and what isn't useful, and no one can fool you."

30   He showed Luke that nothing of value was ever wasted around the mill. Luke used to listen, and wonder if there was another man in the world who knew so well what was needed and what ought to be thrown away. Uncle Henry had known at once that Luke needed a bicycle to ride to his school, which was two miles away in town, and he bought him a good one. He knew that Luke needed good, serviceable clothes. He also knew exactly how much Aunt Helen needed to run the house, the price of everything, and how much a woman should be paid for doing the

40   family washing. In the evenings Luke used to sit in the living room watching his uncle making notations in a black notebook which he always carried in his vest pocket, and he knew that he was <u>assessing</u> the value of the smallest transaction that had taken place during the day.

Luke promised himself that when he grew up he, too, would be admired for his good, sound judgment. But, of course, he couldn't always be watching and learning from his Uncle Henry, for too often when he watched him he thought of his own father; then he was lonely. So he began

50   to build up another secret life for himself around the sawmill, and his companion was the eleven-year-old collie, Dan, a dog blind in one eye and with a slight limp in his left hind leg. Dan was a fat slow-moving old dog. He was very affectionate and his eye was the color of amber.[1] His fur was amber too. When Luke left for school in the morning, the old dog followed him for half a mile down the road, and when he returned in the afternoon, there was Dan waiting at the gate.

---

1. **amber.** Brownish yellow, translucent fossil resin often used for jewelry

words for everyday use   **as • sess** (ə ses') *v.*, evaluate. *We will <u>assess</u> the playground to make sure it is safe.*

Sometimes they would play around the millpond or by
the dam, or go down the stream to the lake. Luke was
never lonely when the dog was with him. There was an old
rowboat that they used as a pirate ship in the stream, and
they would be pirates together, with Luke shouting
instructions to Captain Dan and with the dog seeming to
understand and wagging his tail enthusiastically. Its amber
eye was alert, intelligent and approving. Then they would
plunge into the brush on the other side of the stream,
pretending they were hunting tigers. Of course, the old dog
was no longer much good for hunting; he was too slow and
too lazy. Uncle Henry no longer used him for hunting
rabbits or anything else.

When they came out of the brush, they would lie
together on the cool, grassy bank being affectionate with
each other, with Luke talking earnestly, while the collie, as
Luke believed, smiled with the good eye. Lying in the
grass, Luke would say things to Dan he could not say to his
uncle or his aunt. Not that what he said was important: it
was just stuff about himself that he might have told to his
own father or mother if they had been alive. Then they
would go back to the house for dinner, and after dinner
Dan would follow him down the road to Mr. Kemp's house,
where they would ask old Mr. Kemp if they could go with
him to round up his four cows. The old man was always
glad to see them. He seemed to like watching Luke and the
collie running around the cows, pretending they were
riding on a vast range in the foothills of the Rockies.

Uncle Henry no longer paid much attention to the collie,
though once when he tripped over him on the veranda,[2] he
shook his head and said thoughtfully, "Poor old fellow, he's
through. Can't use him for anything. He just eats and
sleeps and gets in the way."

One Sunday during Luke's summer holidays when they
had returned from church and had had their lunch, they
had all moved out to the veranda where the collie was
sleeping. Luke sat down on the steps, his back against the
veranda post. Uncle Henry took the rocking chair, and
Aunt Helen stretched herself out in the hammock, sighing

60

70

80

90

_____

2. **veranda.** An open porch area, usually with a roof

Literary TOOLS

PLOT AND CENTRAL CONFLICT.
A **plot** is a series of events
related to a **central conflict,**
or struggle. As you read, try
to decide what the central
conflict is. If you are having
trouble making predictions,
try writing things down
instead. Keep a list of events
in the story or make a picture
map of the story.

NOTE THE FACTS

What things does Luke say
to Dan?

_____

_____

Use THE STRATEGY

MAKE PREDICTIONS. What
does Uncle Henry think of
Dan?

_____

_____

Using what you know
about Uncle Henry, make
a prediction about what
will happen to Dan. Write
the prediction in your
chart.

VISUALIZE. Visualizing means trying to picture what you are reading about (see the Active Reading Strategy for "The Ground Is Always Damp" on page 73). Try to visualize this scene between Luke and Dan. Think about what you would see and hear. Use sounds, such as Luke tapping the step and Dan yelping.

Use THE STRATEGY

MAKE PREDICTIONS. Predict what decision Uncle Henry will make about Dan. Write the prediction in your chart.

contentedly. Then Luke, eying the collie, tapped the step with the palm of his hand, giving three little taps like a

100 signal and the old collie, lifting his head, got up stiffly with a slow wagging of the tail as an acknowledgment that the signal had been heard, and began to cross the veranda to Luke. But the dog was sleepy, his bad eye was turned to the rocking chair; in passing, his left front paw went under the rocker. With a frantic yelp, the dog went bounding down the steps and hobbled around the corner of the house, where he stopped, hearing Luke coming after him. All he needed was the touch of Luke's hand. Then he began to lick the hand <u>methodically</u>, as if apologizing.

110 "Luke," Uncle Henry called sharply, "bring that dog here."

When Luke led the collie back to the veranda, Uncle Henry nodded and said, "Thanks, Luke." Then he took out a cigar, lit it, put his big hands on his knees and began to rock in the chair while he frowned and eyed the dog steadily. Obviously he was making some kind of an important decision about the collie.

"What's the matter, Uncle Henry?" Luke asked nervously.

"That dog can't see any more," Uncle Henry said.

120 "Oh, yes, he can," Luke said quickly. "His bad eye got turned to the chair, that's all, Uncle Henry."

"And his teeth are gone, too," Uncle Henry went on, paying no attention to what Luke had said. Turning to the hammock, he called, "Helen, sit up a minute, will you?"

When she got up and stood beside him, he went on. "I was thinking about this old dog the other day, Helen. It's not only that he's just about blind, but did you notice that when we drove up after church he didn't even bark?"

"It's a fact he didn't, Henry."

130 "No, not much good even as a watchdog now."

"Poor old fellow. It's a pity, isn't it?"

"And no good for hunting either. And he eats a lot, I suppose."

words for everyday use

me • thod • i • cal (mə thä' di kəl) *adj.,* arranged in an orderly or systematic fashion. *Jan was <u>methodical</u> about tracking every penny she earned, spent, and saved.* **methodically,** *adv.*

"About as much as he ever did, Henry."

"The plain fact is the old dog isn't worth his keep any more. It's time we got rid of him."

"It's always so hard to know how to get rid of a dog, Henry."

"I was thinking about it the other day. Some people think it's best to shoot a dog. I haven't had any shells for that
140   shotgun for over a year. Poisoning is a hard death for a dog. Maybe drowning is the easiest and quickest way. Well, I'll speak to one of the mill hands and have him look after it."

Crouching on the ground, his arms around the old collie's neck, Luke cried out, "Uncle Henry, Dan's a wonderful dog! You don't know how wonderful he is!"

"He's just a very old dog, son," Uncle Henry said calmly. "The time comes when you have to get rid of any old dog. We've got to be practical about it. I'll get you a pup, son. A smart little dog that'll be worth its keep. A pup that will
150   grow up with you."

"I don't want a pup!" Luke cried, turning his face away. Circling around him, the dog began to bark, then flick his long pink tongue at the back of Luke's neck.

Aunt Helen, catching her husband's eye, put her finger on her lips, warning him not to go on talking in front of the boy. "An old dog like that often wanders off into the brush and sort of picks a place to die when the time comes. Isn't that so, Henry?"

"Oh sure," he agreed quickly. "In fact, when Dan didn't
160   show up yesterday, I was sure that was what had happened." Then he yawned and seemed to forget about the dog.

But Luke was frightened, for he knew what his uncle was like. He knew that if his uncle had decided that the dog was useless and that it was sane and sensible to get rid of it, he would be ashamed of himself if he were <u>diverted</u> by any sentimental considerations. Luke knew in his heart that he couldn't move his uncle. All he could do, he thought, was keep the dog away from his uncle, keep him out of the house, feed him when Uncle Henry wasn't around.

THINK AND REFLECT

Describe Uncle Henry's view of dogs and the purpose they should serve. Describe Luke's view of dogs. (**Compare and Contrast**)

_____

_____

_____

NOTE THE FACTS

Why is Luke frightened? What does he decide to do?

_____

_____

_____

Next day at noontime Luke saw his uncle walking from the mill toward the house with old Sam Carter, a mill hand. Sam Carter was a dull, stooped, <u>slow-witted</u> man of sixty with an iron-gray beard, who was wearing blue overalls and a blue shirt. He hardly ever spoke to anybody. Watching from the veranda, Luke noticed that his uncle suddenly gave Sam Carter a cigar, which Sam put in his pocket. Luke had never seen his uncle give Sam a cigar or pay much attention to him.

Then, after lunch, Uncle Henry said lazily that he would like Luke to take his bicycle and go into town and get him some cigars.

"I'll take Dan," Luke said.

"Better not, son," Uncle Henry said. "It'll take you all afternoon. I want those cigars. Get going, Luke."

His uncle's tone was so casual that Luke tried to believe they were not merely getting rid of him. Of course he had to do what he was told. He had never dared to refuse to obey an order from his uncle. But when he had taken his bicycle and had ridden down the path that followed the stream to the town road and had got about a quarter of a mile along the road, he found that all he could think of was his uncle handing old Sam Carter the cigar.

Slowing down, sick with worry now, he got off the bike and stood uncertainly on the sunlit road. Sam Carter was a gruff, <u>aloof</u> old man who would have no feeling for a dog. Then suddenly Luke could go no farther without getting some assurance that the collie would not be harmed while he was away. Across the fields he could see the house.

Leaving the bike in the ditch, he started to cross the field, intending to get close enough to the house so Dan could hear him if he whistled softly. He got about fifty yards away from the house and whistled and waited, but there was no sign of the dog, which might be asleep at the front of the house, he knew, or over at the saw-mill. With the saws whining, the dog couldn't hear the soft whistle. For a few

---

NOTE THE FACTS

What does Luke think his uncle is trying to do?

_____

_____

THINK AND REFLECT

Judge whether Luke is right to be worried about Dan or whether there is nothing to worry about. Explain your answer. **(Evaluate)**

_____

_____

_____

_____

---

words for everyday use

slow-wit • ted (slō wi′ təd) *adj.*, mentally slow, dull. *Lorna could be <u>slow-witted</u> about certain things, but her humor was always sharp.*

a • loof (ə lüf′) *adj.*, reserved and cool, distant. *Kara's <u>aloof</u> manner made it hard for her to find friends.*

---

minutes Luke couldn't make up his mind what to do, then he decided to go back to the road, get on his bike and go back the way he had come until he got to the place where the river path joined the road. There he could leave his

210 bike, go up the path, then into the tall grass and get close to the front of the house and the sawmill without being seen.

He had followed the river path for about a hundred yards, and when he came to the place where the river began to bend sharply toward the house his heart fluttered and his legs felt paralyzed, for he saw the old rowboat in the one place where the river was deep, and in the rowboat was Sam Carter with the collie.

The bearded man in the blue overalls was smoking the
220 cigar; the dog, with a rope around its neck, sat contentedly beside him, its tongue going out in a friendly lick at the hand holding the rope. It was all like a crazy dream picture to Luke: all wrong because it looked so lazy and friendly, even the curling smoke from Sam Carter's cigar. But as Luke cried out, "Dan, Dan! Come on, boy!" and the dog jumped at the water, he saw that Sam Carter's left hand was hanging deep in the water, holding a foot of rope with a heavy stone at the end. As Luke cried out wildly, "Don't! Please don't!" Carter dropped the stone, for the cry came
230 too late; it was blurred by the screech of the big saws at the mill. But Carter was startled, and he stared stupidly at the riverbank, then he ducked his head and began to row quickly to the bank.

But Luke was watching the collie take what looked like a long, shallow dive, except that the hind legs suddenly kicked up above the surface, then shot down, and while he watched, Luke sobbed and trembled, for it was as if the happy secret part of his life around the sawmill was being torn away from him. But even while he watched, he seemed
240 to be following a plan without knowing it, for he was already fumbling in his pocket for his jackknife, jerking the blade open, pulling off his pants, kicking his shoes off while he muttered fiercely and prayed that Sam Carter would get out of sight.

NOTE THE FACTS

What does Luke see? Why does this picture seem wrong to him?

_____

_____

_____

NOTE THE FACTS

How does Luke react to seeing Dan disappear into the river?

_____

_____

THINK AND REFLECT

Do you think Luke's actions are admirable, or do you think he should respect his uncle's wishes? (Evaluate)

_____

_____

It hardly took the mill hand a minute to reach the bank and go slinking <u>furtively</u> around the bend as if he felt that the boy was following him. But Luke hadn't taken his eyes off the exact spot in the water where Dan had disappeared. As soon

250 as the mill hand was out of sight, Luke slid down the bank and took a leap at the water, the sun glistening on his slender body, his eyes wild with eagerness as he ran out to the deep place, then arched his back and dived, swimming under water, his open eyes getting used to the greenish-gray haze of the water, the sandy bottom and the embedded rocks.

His lungs began to ache, then he saw the shadow of the collie floating at the end of the taut rope, rock-held in the sand. He slashed at the rope with his knife. He couldn't get much strength in his arm because of the resistance of the water. He grabbed the rope with his left hand, hacking with

260 his knife. The collie suddenly drifted up slowly, like a water-soaked log. Then his own head shot above the surface, and while he was sucking in the air he was drawing in the rope, pulling the collie toward him and treading water. In a few strokes he was away from the deep place and his feet touched the bottom.

Hoisting the collie out of the water, he scrambled toward the bank, lurching and stumbling in fright because the collie felt like a dead weight.

He went on up the bank and across the path to the tall

270 grass, where he fell flat, hugging the dog and trying to warm him with his own body. But the collie didn't stir, the good amber eye remained closed. Then suddenly Luke wanted to act like a <u>resourceful</u>, <u>competent</u> man. Getting up on his knees, he stretched the dog out on its belly, drew him between his knees, felt with trembling hands for the soft places on the flanks just above the hipbones, and rocked back and forth, pressing with all his weight, then relaxing the pressure as he straightened up. He hoped that he was

MARK THE TEXT

Highlight or underline the reason Luke was frightened.

---

words for everyday use

fur • tive (fər′ tiv) *adj.,* sneaky, underhanded, sly. *Joe fed his broccoli to the <u>furtive</u> dog under the table.* **furtively,** *adv.*

re • source • ful (ri sors′ fəl) *adj.,* able to deal effectively with problems and challenges. *Fayed proved himself a <u>resourceful</u> camper by acting confidently when the bear entered our camp.*

com • pe • tent (käm′ pə tənt) *adj.,* capable. *Joan can do the project—she is a <u>competent</u> manager.*

working the dog's lungs like a bellows.[3] He had read that men
who had been thought drowned had been saved in this way.

"Come on, Dan. Come on, old boy," he pleaded softly. As
a little water came from the collie's mouth, Luke's heart
jumped, and he muttered over and over, "You can't be dead,
Dan! You can't, you can't! I won't let you die, Dan!" He
rocked back and forth tirelessly, applying the pressure to
the flanks. More water dribbled from the mouth. In the
collie's body he felt a faint tremor. "Oh gee, Dan, you're
alive," he whispered. "Come on, boy. Keep it up."

With a cough the collie suddenly jerked his head back,
the amber eye opened, and there they were looking at each
other. Then the collie, thrusting his legs out stiffly, tried to
hoist himself up, staggered, tried again, then stood there in
a stupor. Then he shook himself like any other wet dog,
turned his head, eyed Luke, and the red tongue came out in
a weak flick at Luke's cheek.

"Lie down, Dan," Luke said. As the dog lay down beside
him, Luke closed his eyes, buried his head in the wet fur
and wondered why all the muscles of his arms and legs
began to jerk in a nervous reaction, now that it was all over.
"Stay there, Dan," he said softly, and he went back to the
path, got his clothes and came back beside Dan and put
them on. "I think we'd better get away from this spot,
Dan," he said. "Keep down, boy. Come on." And he
crawled on through the tall grass till they were about
seventy-five yards from the place where he had undressed.
There they lay down together.

In a little while he heard his aunt's voice calling, "Luke.
Oh, Luke! Come here, Luke!"

"Quiet, Dan," Luke whispered. A few minutes passed, and
then Uncle Henry called, "Luke, Luke!" and he began to
come down the path. They could see him standing there,
massive and <u>imposing</u>, his hands on his hips as he looked
down the path, then he turned and went back to the house.

280

290

300

310

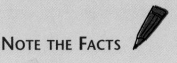

NOTE THE FACTS

What does Luke do to try
to save Dan? Why does he
think this might work?

_____

_____

Use **THE STRATEGY**

MAKE PREDICTIONS. Predict
what Uncle Henry will do
when he finds out that Luke
saved Dan's life.

---

3. **bellows.** An instrument that expands to take in air through a valve and
contracts to expel it through a tube

words for everyday use	im • pos • ing (im po' ziŋ) *adj.*, impressive in size, bearing, dignity, or grandeur. *My mother, in her evening gown, was an <u>imposing</u> figure as she came down the long staircase to join the party.*

As he watched the sunlight shine on the back of his uncle's neck, the <u>exultation</u> Luke had felt at knowing the collie was safe beside him turned to bewildered despair, for he knew that even if he should be forgiven for saving the dog when he saw it drowning, the fact was that his uncle had been <u>thwarted</u>. His mind was made up to get rid of 320 Dan, and in a few days' time, in another way, he would get rid of him, as he got rid of anything around the mill that he believed to be useless or a waste of money.

As he lay back and looked up at the hardly moving clouds, he began to grow frightened. He couldn't go back to the house, nor could he take the collie into the woods and hide him and feed him there unless he tied him up. If he didn't tie him up, Dan would wander back to the house.

"I guess there's just no place to go, Dan," he whispered sadly. "Even if we start off along the road, somebody is sure 330 to see us."

But Dan was watching a butterfly that was circling crazily above them. Raising himself a little, Luke looked through the grass at the corner of the house, then he turned and looked the other way to the wide blue lake. With a sigh he lay down again, and for hours they lay there together, until there was no sound from the saws in the mill and the sun moved low in the western sky.

"Well, we can't stay here any longer, Dan," he said at last. 340 "We'll just have to get as far away as we can. Keep down, old boy," and he began to crawl through the grass, going farther away from the house. When he could no longer be seen, he got up and began to trot across the field toward the gravel road leading to town.

On the road, the collie would turn from time to time as if wondering why Luke shuffled along, dragging his feet wearily, his head down. "I'm stumped, that's all Dan," Luke explained. "I can't seem to think of a place to take you."

When they were passing the Kemp place they saw the old 350 man sitting on the veranda, and Luke stopped. All he could

words for everyday use	**ex • ul • ta • tion** (eg' zəl tā shən) *n.*, triumph, excitement, joyousness. *The 4-H team's <u>exultation</u> over winning the fair was obvious.* **thwart** (thwart') *v.*, hinder, obstruct; defeat. *Sarah tried, unsuccessfully, to <u>thwart</u> my plans to get a puppy.*

think of was that Mr. Kemp had liked them both and it had been a pleasure to help him get the cows in the evening. Dan had always been with them. Staring at the figure of the old man on the veranda, he said in a worried tone, "I wish I could be sure of him, Dan. I wish he was a dumb, stupid man who wouldn't know or care whether you were worth anything. . . . Well, come on." He opened the gate bravely, but he felt shy and unimportant.

"Hello, son. What's on your mind?" Mr. Kemp called from the veranda. He was a thin, <u>wiry</u> man in a tan-colored shirt. He had a gray, untidy mustache, his skin was wrinkled and leathery, but his eyes were always friendly and amused.

"Could I speak to you, Mr. Kemp?" Luke asked when they were close to the veranda.

"Sure. Go ahead."

"It's about Dan. He's a great dog, but I guess you know that as well as I do. I was wondering if you could keep him here for me."

"Why should I keep Dan here, son?"

370 "Well, it's like this," Luke said, fumbling the words awkwardly: "My uncle won't let me keep him any more . . . says he's too old." His mouth began to tremble, then he blurted out the story.

"I see, I see," Mr. Kemp said slowly, and he got up and came over to the steps and sat down and began to stroke the collie's head. "Of course, Dan's an old dog, son," he said quietly. "And sooner or later you've got to get rid of an old dog. Your uncle knows that. Maybe it's true that Dan isn't worth his keep."

380 "He doesn't eat much, Mr. Kemp. Just one meal a day."

"I wouldn't want you to think your uncle was cruel and unfeeling, Luke," Mr. Kemp went on. "He's a fine man . . . maybe just a little bit too practical and straightforward."

"I guess that's right," Luke agreed, but he was really waiting and trusting the expression in the old man's eyes.

"Maybe you should make him a practical <u>proposition</u>."

MARK THE TEXT

Highlight or underline what Luke thinks about when he sees Mr. Kemp.

Use **THE STRATEGY**

MAKE PREDICTIONS. Predict whether Mr. Kemp will help Luke.

NOTE THE FACTS

What does Mr. Kemp say about Uncle Henry?

_____

_____

---

words for everyday use	**wir • y** (wīr′ ē) *adj.,* lean, sinewy, limber. *Jake's <u>wiry</u> body bounded past the other racers on the course.* **prop • o • si • tion** (prä pə zi′ shən) *n.,* proposal, something offered for consideration or acceptance. *In a formal <u>proposition</u>, the businesswoman listed her ideas for cutting costs.*

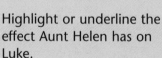

THINK AND REFLECT

Do you think Mr. Kemp's plan will work? Why? (Evaluate)

_____

_____

_____

"I—I don't know what you mean."

"Well, I sort of like the way you get the cows for me in the evenings," Mr. Kemp said, smiling to himself. "In fact, I

390 don't think you need me to go along with you at all. Now, supposing I gave you seventy-five cents a week. Would you get the cows for me every night?"

"Sure I would, Mr. Kemp. I like doing it, anyway."

"All right, son. It's a deal. Now I'll tell you what to do. You go back to your uncle, and before he has a chance to open up on you, you say right out that you've come to him with a business proposition. Say it like a man, just like that. Offer to pay him the seventy-five cents a week for the dog's keep."

400 "But my uncle doesn't need seventy-five cents, Mr. Kemp," Luke said uneasily.

"Of course not," Mr. Kemp agreed. "It's the principle of the thing. Be confident. Remember that he's got nothing against the dog. Go to it, son. Let me know how you do," he added, with an amused smile. "If I know your uncle at all, I think it'll work."

"I'll try it, Mr. Kemp," Luke said.
"Thanks very much." But he didn't have any confidence, for even though he knew that Mr. Kemp was a wise old

410 man who would not deceive him, he couldn't believe that seventy-five cents a week would stop his uncle, who was an important man. "Come on, Dan," he called, and he went slowly and <u>apprehensively</u> back to the house.

When they were going up the path, his aunt cried from the open window, "Henry, Henry, in heaven's name, it's Luke with the dog!"

"Oh. Oh, I see," Uncle Henry said, and gradually the color came back to his face. "You fished him out, eh?" he asked, still looking at the dog uneasily. "Well, you shouldn't have done

420 that. I told Sam Carter to get rid of the dog, you know."

"Just a minute, Uncle Henry," Luke said, trying not to falter. He gained confidence as Aunt Helen came out and

MARK THE TEXT

Highlight or underline the effect Aunt Helen has on Luke.

> **words for everyday use**
>
> ap • pre • hen • sive (ap′ rē hen′ siv) _adj.,_ uneasy, fearful. _I was <u>apprehensive</u> about performing in the big concert._ **apprehensively,** _adv._

stood beside her husband, for her eyes seemed to be gentle, and he went on bravely. "I want to make you a practical proposition, Uncle Henry."

"A what?" Uncle Henry asked, still feeling insecure, and wishing the boy and the dog weren't confronting him.

"A practical proposition," Luke blurted out quickly. "I know Dan isn't worth his keep to you. I guess he isn't
430 worth anything to anybody but me. So I'll pay you seventy-five cents a week for his keep."

"What's this?" Uncle Henry asked, looking bewildered. "Where would you get seventy-five cents a week, Luke?"

"I'm going to get the cows every night for Mr. Kemp."

"Oh, for heaven's sake, Henry," Aunt Helen pleaded, looking distressed, "let him keep the dog!" and she fled into the house.

"None of that kind of talk!" Uncle Henry called after her. "We've got to be sensible about this!" But he was shaken
440 himself, and overwhelmed with a distress that destroyed all his confidence. As he sat down slowly in the rocking chair and stroked the side of his big face, he wanted to say weakly, "All right, keep the dog," but he was ashamed of being so weak and sentimental. He stubbornly refused to yield to this emotion: he was trying desperately to turn his emotion into a bit of good, useful common sense, so he could justify his distress. So he rocked and pondered. At last he smiled. "You're a smart little shaver, Luke," he said slowly. "Imagine you working it out like this. I'm tempted
450 to accept your proposition."

"Gee, thanks, Uncle Henry."

"I'm accepting it because I think you'll learn something out of this," he went on <u>ponderously</u>.

"Yes, Uncle Henry."

"You'll learn that useless luxuries cost the smartest of men hard-earned money."

"I don't mind."

"Well, it's a thing you'll have to learn sometime. I think

NOTE THE FACTS

What is Luke's proposition?

_____

_____

NOTE THE FACTS

What does Uncle Henry want to say to Luke? Why doesn't he say it?

_____

_____

NOTE THE FACTS

What lesson does Uncle Henry want Luke to learn?

_____

_____

words for everyday use

pon • der • ous (pän' dər əs) *adj.,* heavy, unyielding. *The <u>ponderous</u> problem bothered Jowana day and night.* **ponderously,** *adv.*

460 practical streak in you. It's a streak I like to see in a boy.
O.K., son," he said, and he smiled with relief and went into
the house.

Turning to Dan, Luke whispered softly, "Well, what do
you know about that?"

As he sat down on the step with the collie beside him and
listened to Uncle Henry talking to his wife, he began to
glow with exultation. Then gradually his exultation began
to change to a vast wonder that Mr. Kemp should have had
such a perfect understanding of Uncle Henry. He began to
470 dream of someday being as wise as old Mr. Kemp and
knowing exactly how to handle people. It was possible, too,
that he had already learned some of the things about his
uncle that his father had wanted him to learn.

Putting his head down on the dog's neck, he vowed to
himself fervently that he would always have some money on
hand, no matter what became of him, so that he would be
able to protect all that was truly valuable from the practical
people in the world. ∎

NOTE THE FACTS

What is Luke's vow?

_____

_____

THINK AND REFLECT

What are some of the
valuable things you think
Luke would protect?
(Infer)

_____

_____

_____

Reflect ON YOUR READING

After Reading ➤ ASSESS YOUR PREDICTIONS

❑ Go through your completed Prediction Chart. Put a star next to each prediction that you were right about. Put a check next to each prediction where you changed your ideas from a previous prediction.
❑ Share your predictions with a partner. Talk about what clues in the story led you to make the predictions.

Reading Skills and Test Practice

IDENTIFY RELEVANT DETAILS

With your partner, discuss how to answer the following questions about relevant details. Use the Think-Aloud Notes to write down your reasons for eliminating the incorrect answers.

____1. How did Luke know he would need to rescue Dan?
    a. He heard Dan barking over the sound of the mill.
    b. The cigar gift to Sam made him suspicious.
    c. He refused to go on the errand without Dan.
    d. He heard the sound of rowing and turned around.

____2. Which of Uncle Henry's qualities allows him to accept Luke's proposition?
    a. his listening to his wife
    b. his respect for Mr. Kemp
    c. his practicality
    d. his emotion

How did using the reading strategy help you to answer the questions?

_____

_____

_____

_____

THINK-ALOUD NOTES

Investigate, Inquire, and Imagine

RECALL: GATHER FACTS
1a. What is Luke's vow?

→ INTERPRET: FIND MEANING
1b. Is Luke's vow practical or emotional? How does Luke's vow fit with the lesson Uncle Henry wants him to learn?

ANALYZE: TAKE THINGS APART
2a. Give examples from the story of the kind of person Luke wants to be when he grows up. How do his ideals shift or change throughout the story?

→ SYNTHESIZE: BRING THINGS TOGETHER
2b. What does Luke learn about his uncle? What does Luke learn about Mr. Kemp? How does what Luke learns about each man help him learn about himself?

PERSPECTIVE: LOOK AT OTHER VIEWS →
3a. View the struggle between Luke and Uncle Henry through the eyes of Aunt Helen. How would she explain why Luke and his uncle acted as they did?

EMPATHY: SEE FROM INSIDE
3b. How might Aunt Helen have reacted if Uncle Henry had not accepted Luke's proposition?

Literary Tools

PLOT AND CENTRAL CONFLICT. A **plot** is a series of events related to a *central conflict*, or struggle. What is the central conflict of the story? A plot includes the introduction of the conflict, its development, and its resolution. Complete the picture map below. Label the pictures that show the inciting incident, climax, resolution, and dénouement. For a review of these parts of a plot, see page 38 in the introduction to this unit.

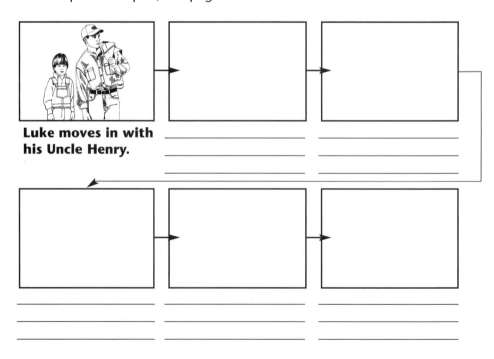

Luke moves in with his Uncle Henry.

WordWorkshop

SYNONYMS. Review the Words for Everyday Use from "Luke Baldwin's Vow." Then write on the line the letter of the word that is most nearly *the same* in meaning as the word listed.

_____1. **wiry**
   a. hyper
   b. sinewy
   c. connected
   d. husky

_____2. **methodical**
   a. belligerent
   b. confused
   c. timid
   d. orderly

_____3. **ponderous**
   a. heavy
   b. ethereal
   c. useless
   d. scholarly

_____4. **proposition**
   a. scandal
   b. suggestion
   c. boundary
   d. feeling

_____5. **exultation**
   a. bravado
   b. sorrow
   c. fearfulness
   d. joyousness

_____6. **furtive**
   a. trustworthy
   b. muscular
   c. sneaky
   d. decadent

_____7. **competent**
   a. capable
   b. competitive
   c. foolish
   d. bizarre

_____8. **aloof**
   a. high
   b. distant
   c. comical
   d. dangerous

_____9. **divert**
   a. distract
   b. tempt
   c. ignore
   d. falsify

_____10. **precise**
   a estimate
   b. short
   c. evade
   d. exact

Read-Write Connection

What do you think about the decisions Uncle Henry makes throughout the story? What do you think about Luke's decisions? Explain your responses.

_____

_____

Beyond the Reading

BRAINSTORMING ABOUT VALUES. In small groups, reread the last paragraph of "Luke Baldwin's Vow." Then brainstorm a list of things that are, in the opinion of you and your group members, valuable but not practical. When is it more important to choose valuable things instead of practical things? When should you choose practical things?

GO ONLINE. To find links and additional activities for this selection, visit the EMC Internet Resource Center at **emcp.com/languagearts** and click on Write-In Reader.

Unit 3 READING Review

Choose and Use Reading Strategies

Before reading the selection below, review with a partner how to use each of these reading strategies.

1. Read with a Purpose
2. Connect to Prior Knowledge
3. Write Things Down
4. Make Predictions
5. Visualize
6. Use Text Organization
7. Tackle Difficult Vocabulary
8. Monitor Your Reading Progress

Now apply at least two of these reading strategies as you read the excerpt from "Hollywood and the Pits" by Cherylene Lee. Use the margins and mark up the text to show how you are using the reading strategies to read actively.

When I was fifteen, the pit opened its secret to me. I breathed, ate, slept, dreamed about the La Brea Tar Pits. I spent summer days working the archaeological dig, and in dreams saw the bones glistening, the broken pelvises, the skulls, the vertebrae looped like a woman's pearls hanging on an invisible cord. I welcomed those dreams. I wanted to know where the next skeleton was, identify it, record its position, discover whether it was whole or not. I wanted to know where to dig in the coarse, black, gooey sand. I lost myself there and found something else.

My mother thought something was wrong with me. Was it good for a teenager to be fascinated by death? Especially animal death in the Pleistocene? Was it normal to be so obsessed by a sticky brown hole in the ground in the center of Los Angeles? I don't know if it was normal or not, but it seemed perfectly logical to me. After all, I grew up in Hollywood, a place where dreams and nightmares can often take the same shape. What else would a child actor do?

"Thank you very much, dear. We'll be letting you know. "

I knew what that meant. It meant I would never hear from them again. I didn't get the job. I heard that phrase a lot that year.

I walked out of the plush office, leaving behind the casting director, producer, director, writer, and whoever else came to listen to my reading for a semiregular role on a family sitcom. . . .

WordWorkshop

Unit 3 Words for Everyday Use

aloof, 86
apprehensive, 92
assess, 82
audacity, 60
billow, 44
burley, 81
competent, 88
concealment, 59
conceive, 55
cunning, 56
cynical, 47
derision, 60
dissimulate, 56
distinguish, 66
divert, 85

exultation, 90
furtive, 88
gaudy, 46
gesture, 47
guardian, 66
imposing, 89
irrational, 48
jostle, 46
malicious, 50
methodical, 84
ponderous, 93
precise, 81
proposition, 91
resourceful, 88
sagacity, 56

slow-witted, 86
stealthy, 58
stifle, 57
suave, 59
submerge, 44
supposition, 57
throng, 44
thwart, 90
transformation, 68
vapor, 67
vehement, 60
vex, 59
wiry, 91

Semantic Map. Work with a partner to fill in the Vocabulary Cluster with words from the list above. The categories have been labeled for you, and you may add circles wherever you like. Try to use as many words as possible. Be prepared to explain why you have placed the words in the various categories.

Literary Tools

Select the best literary element on the right to complete each sentence on the left. Write the correct letter in the blank.

_____1. Dikran is a main _____ in "The Hummingbird That Lived through Winter."

_____2. "The Tell-Tale Heart" is a story with a suspenseful _____.

_____3. Some of the _____ in "The Ground Is Always Damp" include "piñon wood smoke" and clear, empty, almost turquoise sky.

_____4. Acting on beliefs is a(n) _____ in "The Fan Club."

_____5. The ___ of "The Hummingbird That Lived through Winter" centers around saving a bird.

_____6. The struggle between Luke and Uncle Henry is the central ___ of "Luke Baldwin's Vow."

_____7. The ___ introduces the central conflict in a plot.

_____8. Luke saving Dan from drowning is the _____ of "Luke Baldwin's Vow."

_____9. The _____ of "The Tell-Tale Heart" is unreliable.

_____10. The _____ in "The Fan Club" is a high school.

a. character, 36, 65

b. climax, 38

c. conflict, 37

d. inciting incident, 38

e. mood, 37, 75, 78

f. narrator, 56, 63

g. plot, 37, 65, 83, 96

h. sensory details, 37

i. setting, 36, 65, 66, 71

j. theme, 39, 53

On Your Own

FLUENTLY SPEAKING. Think about a story from your own experience that you want to tell others. What tone do you want to use? What pace? What are the key details to include? With a group of your classmates, take turns telling your stories. Then discuss what you liked about each story and why.

PICTURE THIS. Choose one of the stories from this unit. Work with a partner to illustrate the story. In your artwork, shows the main events, people, objects, and themes of the story.

PUT IT IN WRITING. Write a short story of your own. Choose one of the elements of fiction, and concentrate on developing at least that one element as thoroughly as possible. For example, if you choose setting, work hard on creating a detailed setting that will make the reader feel as if he or she knows the place. You could also focus on character, plot, theme, or mood. Share your draft with a partner. Then revise the story and present a final copy to the class.

Unit FOUR

READING Poetry

POETRY

Defining the word *poetry* is difficult because poems take so many different forms. Poems do not have to be written down; some are chanted or sung. Some poems rhyme and have a consistent rhythm, but others do not.

Poetry differs from prose in that it packs more meaning into fewer words and often uses meter, rhyme, and rhythm more obviously. One thing that all poems have in common is that they use imaginative language carefully chosen and arranged to communicate experiences, thoughts, or emotions.

There are many different kinds of poetry. Some common kinds are listed below. The most common techniques of poetry involve imagery, shape, sound, and meaning. Each of these techniques is also discussed below.

Forms of Poetry

NARRATIVE POETRY. A **narrative poem** is a poem that tells a story. In this unit, Phil George's poem "Name Giveaway" is an example of a narrative poem.

DRAMATIC POETRY. A **dramatic poem** is a poem that relies heavily on dramatic elements such as monologue (speech by a single character) or dialogue (conversation involving two or more characters). Often dramatic poems tell stories like narrative poems. Naomi Shihab Nye's poem "The Lost Parrot" could be considered a dramatic poem.

LYRIC POETRY. A **lyric poem** is a highly musical verse that expresses the emotions of a speaker. Many of the poems in this unit are lyric poems, including Arnold Adoff's "Point Guard" and Maxine Kumin's "400-Meter Freestyle."

NOTE THE FACTS

How does poetry differ from prose?

_____

_____

_____

NOTE THE FACTS

What is a lyric poem?

_____

_____

_____

Techniques of Poetry: Imagery

An **image** is language that creates a concrete representation of an object or experience. An image is also the vivid mental picture created in the reader's mind by that language. For example, in the poem "The Women's 400 Meters," Lillian Morrison writes, "Skittish, / they flex knees, drum heels and / shiver at the starting line." The pictures you create in your mind of the women flexing their knees, drumming their heels, and shivering at the starting line are images. When considered in a group, images are called **imagery**. Poets use colorful, vivid language and figures of speech to create imagery. A **figure of speech** is language meant to be understood imaginatively instead of literally. The following are common figures of speech:

Figure of Speech	Definition	Example
metaphor	figure of speech in which one thing is written about as if it were another	"my heart was a tiger in full roar"
simile	comparison using *like* or *as*	"as if each leg were a loaded gun"
personification	figure of speech in which an idea, animal, or thing is described as if it were a person	a tree that can move and speak

Techniques of Poetry: Shape

The shape of a poem is how it looks on the page. Poems are often divided into stanzas, or groups of lines. The following are some common types of stanzas:

Stanza Name	Number of Lines
couplet	two
triplet or tercet	three
quatrain	four
quintain	five
sestet	six
heptastich	seven
octave	eight

A **concrete poem**, or **shape poem**, is one with a shape that suggests its subject.

Techniques of Poetry: Rhythm

The **rhythm** is the pattern of beats or stresses in a line. A regular rhythmic pattern is called a **meter**. Units of rhythm are called **feet**. A **foot** consists of some combination of weakly stressed (⌣) and strongly stressed (/) syllables, as follows:

Type of Foot	Pattern	Example
iamb, or **iambic foot**	⌣ /	a**fraid**
trochee, or **trochaic foot**	/ ⌣	**free**dom
anapest, or **anapestic foot**	⌣ ⌣ /	in a **flash**
dactyl, or **dactylic foot**	/ ⌣ ⌣	**fe**verish
spondee, or **spondaic foot**	/ /	**baseball**

The following terms are used to describe the number of feet in a line of poetry:

Term	# of Feet	Example
monometer	one foot	⌣ / To**day** ⌣ / We **play**
dimeter	two feet	/ ⌣ ⌣ / ⌣ **Fol**lowing | **close**ly
trimeter	three feet	⌣ / ⌣ / ⌣ / God **shed** | His **light** | on **thee**
tetrameter	four feet	/ ⌣ / ⌣ / ⌣ / ⌣ **In** the | **green**est | **of** our | **val**leys
pentameter	five feet	⌣ / ⌣ / ⌣ / A **vast** | re **pub** | lic **famed** | ⌣ / ⌣ / through **ev** | ry **clime**
hexameter or Alexandrine	six feet	⌣ / ⌣ / ⌣ / In **o** | ther's **eyes** | we **see** | ⌣ / ⌣ / ⌣ / our**selves** | the **truth** | to **tell**

THINK AND REFLECT

Create another example of an anapest, or anapestic foot. **(Apply)**

_____

_____

_____

THINK AND REFLECT

What term describes the number of feet in this example?

⌣ / ⌣ /
Before / sixteen? **(Apply)**

_____

_____

_____

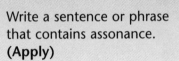

THINK AND REFLECT

Highlight or underline the alliteration in the following lines of poetry. **(Apply)**

"Before sixteen
I was fast
enough to fake
my shadow out."

NOTE THE FACTS

What is onomatopoeia?

_____

_____

_____

_____

Techniques of Poetry: Sound

RHYME. Rhyme is the repetition of sounds at the ends of words. **End rhyme** is rhyme that occurs at the ends of lines. **Internal rhyme** occurs within lines. **Sight rhyme** occurs when two words are spelled similarly but pronounced differently. **Rhyme scheme** is a pattern of end rhymes.

ALLITERATION. Alliteration is the repetition of initial consonant sounds. Galway Kinnell's "Blackberry Eating" contains three examples of alliteration: "in the _s_ilent, _s_tartled, icy, _bl_ack _l_anguage / of _bl_ackberry-eating in _l_ate September."

ASSONANCE. Assonance is the repetition of vowel sounds in stressed syllables that end with different consonant sounds as in "and I could read / every _crack_ and ripple / in that _patch_ of _asphalt_" in "First Love" by Carl Lindner.

CONSONANCE. Consonance is a kind of slant rhyme in which the ending consonant sounds match, but the preceding vowel sound does not, as in _find_ and _bound_.

ONOMATOPOEIA. Onomatopoeia is the use of words or phrases that sound like the things to which they refer, like _meow_, _buzz_, and _murmur_.

USING READING STRATEGIES WITH POETRY

Active Reading Strategy Checklists

The following checklists offer strategies for reading poetry.

1 READ WITH A PURPOSE. Before reading a poem, give yourself a purpose, or something to look for, as you read. Sometimes your teacher will set a purpose: "Pay attention to repeated words and phrases." Other times you can set your own purpose by previewing the title, the opening lines, and other information that are presented with the poem. Say to yourself

- ❑ I want to look for . . .
- ❑ I want to experience . . .
- ❑ I want to enjoy . . .
- ❑ I wonder . . .
- ❑ I want to see if . . .

2 CONNECT TO PRIOR KNOWLEDGE. Being aware of what you already know and thinking about it as you read can help you keep track of what's happening and will increase your knowledge. As you read, say to yourself

- ❏ I already know this about the poem's subject matter . . .
- ❏ This part of the poem reminds me of . . .
- ❏ I think this part of the poem is like . . .
- ❏ My experience tells me that . . .
- ❏ If I were the speaker, I would feel . . .
- ❏ I associate this image with . . .

3 WRITE THINGS DOWN. As you read poetry, write down how the poem helps you "see" what is described. Possible ways to write things down include

- ❏ Underline words and phrases that appeal to your five senses.
- ❏ Write down your questions and comments.
- ❏ Highlight figures of speech and phrases you enjoy.
- ❏ Create a graphic organizer to keep track of your responses.
- ❏ Use a code in the margin that shows how you respond to the poem.

4 MAKE PREDICTIONS. Before you read a poem, use information about the author, the subject matter, and the title to make a guess about what a poem may describe. As you read, confirm or deny your predictions, and make new ones based on how the poem develops. Make predictions like the following:

- ❏ The title tells me that . . .
- ❏ I predict that this poem will be about . . .
- ❏ This poet usually writes about . . .
- ❏ I think the poet will repeat . . .
- ❏ These lines in the poem make me guess that . . .

5 VISUALIZE. Visualizing, or allowing the words on the page to create images in your mind, is extremely important while reading poetry. In order to visualize the words, change your reading pace and savor the words. Allow the words to affect all of your senses. Make statements such as

- ❏ The words help me see . . .
- ❏ The words help me hear . . .
- ❏ The words help me feel . . .
- ❏ The words help me taste . . .
- ❏ The words help me smell . . .

Reading **TIP**

As you read the lines of a poem to yourself, pretend that you are the speaker.

Reading **TIP**

A simple code can help you remember your reactions to a poem. You can use
! for "This is like something I have experienced"
? for "I don't understand this"
✓ for "This seems important"

Reading **TIP**

Increase your enjoyment of poetry by reading it aloud.

6 USE TEXT ORGANIZATION. When you read a poem, pay attention to punctuation and line breaks. Learn to "chunk" the lines in a poem so they make sense. Try reading all the way to the end of the sentence rather than stopping at each line break. Punctuation, rhythm, repetition, and line length offer clues that help you vary your reading rate and word emphasis. Say to yourself

- ❑ The punctuation in these lines helps me . . .
- ❑ The writer started a new stanza here because . . .
- ❑ The writer repeats this line because . . .
- ❑ The rhythm of this poem makes me think of . . .
- ❑ These short lines affect my reading speed by . . .

7 TACKLE DIFFICULT VOCABULARY. Difficult words in a poem can get in the way of your ability to respond to the poet's words and ideas. Use context clues that the lines provide, consult a dictionary, or ask someone about words you do not understand. When you come across a difficult word in a poem, say to yourself

Reading ─TIP

If a poem has difficult vocabulary, read the poem, tackle the vocabulary you don't understand, and reread the poem.

- ❑ The lines near this word tell me that this word means . . .
- ❑ A definition provided with the poem shows that the word means . . .
- ❑ My work with the word before reading helps me know that the word means . . .
- ❑ A classmate said that the word means . . .

Fix-Up Ideas

- ■ Reread
- ■ Read in shorter chunks
- ■ Read aloud
- ■ Ask questions
- ■ Change your reading rate
- ■ Try a different reading strategy

8 MONITOR YOUR READING PROGRESS. All readers encounter difficulty when they read, especially if they don't choose the reading material themselves. When you have to read something, note problems you are having and fix them. The key to reading success is knowing when you are having difficulty. To fix problems, say to yourself

- ❑ Because I don't understand this part, I will . . .
- ❑ Because I'm having trouble staying connected to the ideas in the poem, I will . . .
- ❑ Because the words in the poem are too hard, I will . . .
- ❑ Because the poem is long, I will . . .
- ❑ Because I can't retell what the poem was about, I will . . .

Become an Active Reader

The instruction with the poems in this unit gives you an in-depth look at how to use one strategy for each poem. When you have difficulty, use fix-up ideas to fix a problem. For further information about the active reading strategies, see Unit 1, pages 4–15.

How to Use Reading Strategies with Poetry

Read the following excerpts to discover how you might use reading strategies as you read poetry.

Excerpt 1. Note how a reader uses active reading strategies while reading an excerpt from "The Listeners" by Walter de la Mare.

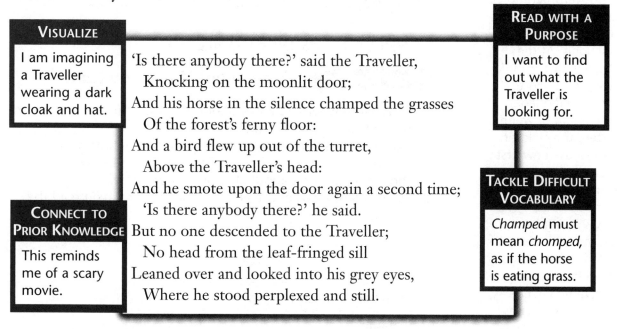

VISUALIZE

I am imagining a Traveller wearing a dark cloak and hat.

READ WITH A PURPOSE

I want to find out what the Traveller is looking for.

'Is there anybody there?' said the Traveller,
    Knocking on the moonlit door;
And his horse in the silence champed the grasses
    Of the forest's ferny floor:
And a bird flew up out of the turret,
    Above the Traveller's head:
And he smote upon the door again a second time;
    'Is there anybody there?' he said.
But no one descended to the Traveller;
    No head from the leaf-fringed sill
Leaned over and looked into his grey eyes,
    Where he stood perplexed and still.

CONNECT TO PRIOR KNOWLEDGE

This reminds me of a scary movie.

TACKLE DIFFICULT VOCABULARY

Champed must mean *chomped*, as if the horse is eating grass.

Excerpt 2. Note how a reader uses active reading strategies while reading this excerpt from "The Charge of the Light Brigade" by Alfred, Lord Tennyson.

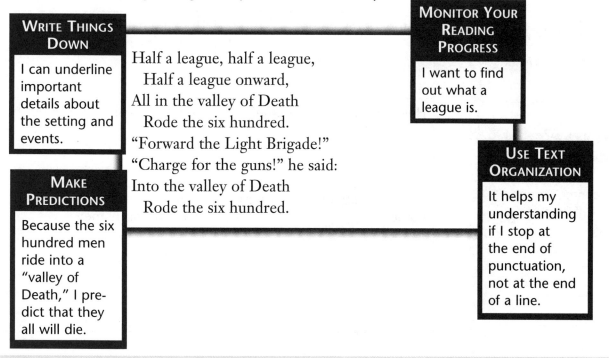

WRITE THINGS DOWN

I can underline important details about the setting and events.

MONITOR YOUR READING PROGRESS

I want to find out what a league is.

Half a league, half a league,
    Half a league onward,
All in the valley of Death
    Rode the six hundred.
"Forward the Light Brigade!"
"Charge for the guns!" he said:
Into the valley of Death
    Rode the six hundred.

MAKE PREDICTIONS

Because the six hundred men ride into a "valley of Death," I predict that they all will die.

USE TEXT ORGANIZATION

It helps my understanding if I stop at the end of punctuation, not at the end of a line.

Reader's resource

In the late 1800s and early 1900s, the government forced Native American parents to send their children away to boarding schools. At the schools, Native American children were required to conform to the language, dress, and religion of white people. Often, the children were forced to use new first and last names. Frequently, even the English translation of a Native American name was forbidden. Instead, government or church officials assigned Native American children English-sounding names. In **"Name Giveaway,"** poet Phil George discusses what happened to his own Native American name—Two Swans Ascending From Still Waters.

Word watch

PREVIEW VOCABULARY

ascend

Reader's journal

To what degree is your name part of who you are? Why?

_____

_____

_____

"Name Giveaway"

by Phil George

Active READING STRATEGY

CONNECT TO PRIOR KNOWLEDGE

Before Reading THINK ABOUT WHAT YOU KNOW

❑ Quickwrite what you know about your name in the first column of the Name Chart below.
❑ Explain who selected your name, provide any history your name has, describe how you feel about your name, and write down thoughts you have about changing your name.
❑ Fill in column two of the Name Chart below as you read the poem.

Graphic Organizer: Name Chart

Information about Names	
My Name	**The Speaker's Names**
Who selected my name:	Who selected the speaker's names:
History of my name:	How the names might have been chosen:
How I feel about my name:	How the speaker feels about his names:
How I feel about changing my name:	How the speaker feels about changing his name:

Phil George

That teacher gave me a new name . . . again.

She never even had feasts or a giveaway![1]

Still I do not know what "George" means;

and now she calls me: "Phillip."

TWO SWANS <u>ASCENDING</u> FROM STILL WATERS

must be a name too hard to remember. ∎

---

1. **giveaway**. A Native American ceremony in which a family gives gifts to honor a deserving family member

USE WHAT YOU KNOW AS YOU READ

❑ Listen as your teacher reads the poem aloud. As you listen, pretend you are the speaker.
❑ Reread the poem on your own. Record information about the speaker in your Name Chart.

WHAT DO YOU WONDER?

_____

_____

_____

_____

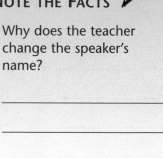

NOTE THE FACTS

Why does the teacher change the speaker's name?

_____

_____

_____

words for everyday use

as • cend (ə send′) v., move upward, rise. _The child watched as her balloon_ <u>_ascended_</u> _into the sky._ **ascending,** _adj._

Reflect ON YOUR READING

After Reading ▸ MAKE A CONNECTION

❑ In the space below, compare your feelings about your name with the speaker's feelings about his real name.
❑ How does the speaker react to the name change? Would you react in the same way if someone changed your name?

_____

_____

_____

_____

THINK-ALOUD
NOTES

_____

_____

_____

_____

_____

_____

_____

_____

_____

_____

_____

Reading Skills and Test Practice

IDENTIFY AN AUTHOR'S POINT OF VIEW

Discuss with a partner how to best answer these questions about an author's point of view. Use the Think-Aloud Notes to write down your reasons for eliminating the incorrect answers.

____1. The line "She never even had feasts or a giveaway!" suggests that the speaker
    a. feels punished by the teacher.
    b. is from a different culture than the teacher.
    c. communicates effectively with the teacher.
    d. understands the teacher's culture.

____2. What is the speaker's attitude toward his teacher?
    a. He is angry at his teacher and resents the teacher's stupidity.
    b. He feels superior to the teacher since she doesn't even have a giveaway.
    c. He is puzzled by her lack of observing traditions.
    d. He feels hurt because she ignores him.

How did using the reading strategy help you to answer the questions?

_____

_____

_____

_____

Investigate, Inquire, and Imagine

RECALL: GATHER FACTS
1a. In "Name Giveaway," what has the teacher done again?

→ INTERPRET: FIND MEANING
1b. How does the speaker feel about what the teacher has done?

ANALYZE: TAKE THINGS APART
2a. What evidence can you find that demonstrates the teacher's understanding of and feelings toward the speaker and his culture?

→ SYNTHESIZE: BRING THINGS TOGETHER
2b. Why does the teacher act in this way? Do you agree with the reason the speaker offers? Why, or why not? What might other possible reasons be?

EVALUATE: MAKE JUDGMENTS
3a. How well does "Name Giveaway" communicate the speaker's ideas and frustrations?

→ EXTEND: CONNECT IDEAS
3b. Compare your feelings to that of the speaker in the poem. What thoughts and emotions do you share?

Literary Tools

SPEAKER. The **speaker** is the voice that speaks, or narrates, a poem or story. What do you learn about the speaker in "Name Giveaway" by looking at his words? What thoughts and emotions does he show?

_____

_____

_____

Why do you think the speaker uses all capital letters for his real name?

_____

_____

_____

WordWorkshop

SYNONYMS. A **synonym** is a word that has the same meaning as another word. For example, *smile* and *grin* are synonyms. *Cry* and *weep* are also synonyms. Brainstorm a list of synonyms for the following words from "Name Giveaway." Then use a thesaurus to see if you can add more synonyms to your lists. Be sure to find synonyms for the words based on the definitions used in the poem.

1. new _____

   _____

2. feasts _____

   _____

3. giveaway _____

   _____

4. ascending _____

   _____

5. still _____

   _____

Read-Write Connection

How would you view a teacher who changed your name?

_____

_____

Beyond the Reading

POP CULTURE. Many well-known figures in sports, entertainment, politics, and other areas have changed their names or use stage names. Using magazines such as *People, Biography, Sports Illustrated*, and *Entertainment Weekly*, look for articles that feature celebrities. Write an essay about famous people who have modified or changed their names. What reasons do they give for doing so? Do you prefer the celebrity's original name or the professional name? If you became involved in sports or entertainment, would you consider changing your name? Why, or why not?

GO ONLINE. To find links and additional activities for this selection, visit the EMC Internet Resource Center at **emcp.com/languagearts** and click on Write-In Reader.

"FIRST LOVE" by Carl Lindner
and
"Point Guard" by Arnold Adoff

Active READING STRATEGY

READ WITH A PURPOSE

Before Reading ➤ DETERMINE THE SPEAKER'S TONE

❑ A speaker's **tone** is his or her attitude about a topic or event. As you read, look for things in each poem that help you determine each speaker's tone.

❑ Write the words that reveal each speaker's tone in the graphic organizer below.

Graphic Organizer: Speaker's Tone Chart

"First Love"	"Point Guard"
Words that reveal the speaker's tone	Words that reveal the speaker's tone
Summary of the speaker's tone	Summary of the speaker's tone

CONNECT

Reader's resource

In 1891, James Naismith, a physical education teacher in Springfield, Massachusetts, wanted to develop an indoor game that would be fun, easy to learn, and lively. An early version of his game had players throwing balls through large peach baskets. Naismith's game caught on. His new game became known as basketball.

As basketball developed, changes to the rules streamlined the game. Metal hoops took the place of baskets. Only five players per team were allowed on the floor at a time. Today, most teams have players who specialize in particular positions on the floor. A guard may be either a point guard, who runs the team's offense, or a shooting guard, who takes outside shots. The center usually stays near the basket, taking close shots and rebounding. Forwards play near the key, the painted free-throw area in front of each basket. Speakers in **"First Love"** and **"Point Guard"** describe the movements of modern players.

Reader's journal

What is your favorite sport to watch or play? What do you like most about that sport?

_____

_____

_____

MARK IMPORTANT WORDS

❏ Read along as your teacher reads the beginning stanza of "First Love" aloud. As you listen, mark words that help you determine the speaker's tone, or attitude, toward basketball.

❏ Read the rest of "First Love" on your own. Continue to mark words that indicate the speaker's tone.

❏ Read "Point Guard" on page 115. Mark words that indicate the speaker's tone.

MARK THE TEXT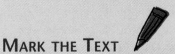

Underline or highlight what the speaker says he could do before he was sixteen.

FIX-UP IDEA

Read Aloud
If you are having trouble determining the speaker's tone in either poem, listen to a partner or your teacher read the poem aloud again. Then try reading the poem aloud yourself, using a tone of voice that expresses how the speaker feels. Remember to read to the end of thoughts, not to the end of lines.

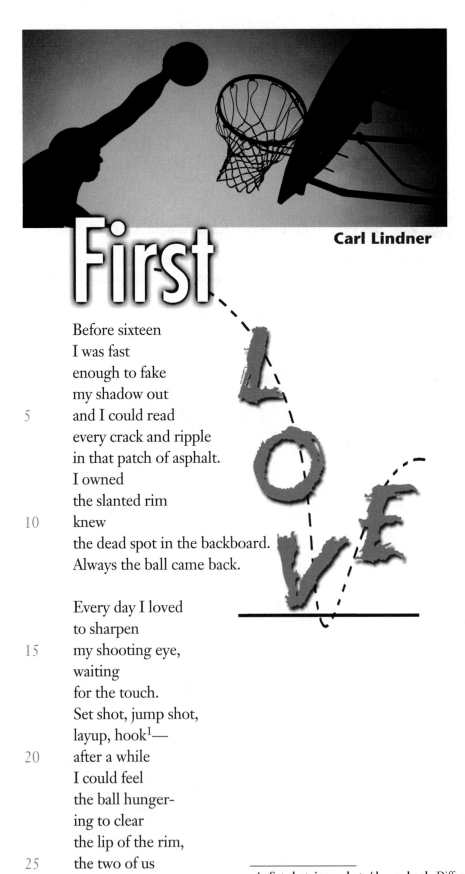

Carl Lindner

First LOVE

Before sixteen
I was fast
enough to fake
my shadow out
5 and I could read
every crack and ripple
in that patch of asphalt.
I owned
the slanted rim
10 knew
the dead spot in the backboard.
Always the ball came back.

Every day I loved
to sharpen
15 my shooting eye,
waiting
for the touch.
Set shot, jump shot,
layup, hook[1]—
20 after a while
I could feel
the ball hunger-
ing to clear
the lip of the rim,
25 the two of us
falling through. ■

---

1. **Set shot, jump shot, / layup, hook.** Different types of basketball shots

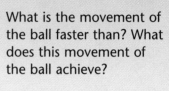

Arnold Adoff

You bring the ball down the court.
The pick[1] is set.
The play is set. The movement of
    the ball
        is faster
    than all
       the
          defensive
    hands and heads,
      and you
         get free.
You pass into the big girl
    at the key. She turns
        and
shoots and scores.
    The crowd roars. ■

---

1. **pick.** Strategy in which a player
legally blocks the movement of an
opponent

NOTE THE FACTS

What is the movement of
the ball faster than? What
does this movement of
the ball achieve?

_____

_____

_____

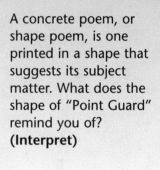

THINK AND REFLECT

A concrete poem, or
shape poem, is one
printed in a shape that
suggests its subject
matter. What does the
shape of "Point Guard"
remind you of?
(Interpret)

_____

_____

_____

DRAW A PICTURE

Draw a picture that shows
how the speaker feels.

Reflect ON YOUR READING

After Reading **REFLECT ON YOUR NOTES**

❑ With a partner, compare the parts of the poems you marked. Write these words in your Speaker's Tone Chart and fill in the rest of the chart.

❑ Discuss the tone of each speaker. How did marking important words help you determine each speaker's tone?

_____

_____

Reading Skills and Test Practice

IDENTIFY TONE

Discuss with your partner how best to answer the following questions about the tone of the poems. Use the Think-Aloud Notes to write down your reasons for eliminating the incorrect answers.

____1. What best expresses the speaker's attitude toward basketball in "First Love"?
   a. He respects the sport.
   b. He recommends it for everyone.
   c. He wants to be a professional player.
   d. He made it an important part of his life.

____2. What feature of basketball might the speaker in "Point Guard" most enjoy?
   a. the crowds
   b. the noise
   c. the action
   d. the sweat

How did using the reading strategy help you to answer the questions?

_____

_____

_____

_____

Investigate, Inquire, and Imagine

RECALL: GATHER FACTS
1a. What does the speaker in "First Love" do every day?

→ INTERPRET: FIND MEANING
1b. Why might the speaker have done this every day? What benefits could there have been?

ANALYZE: TAKE THINGS APART
2a. In "First Love," what words describe the speaker's views about his abilities as a young basketball player? What words indicate the speaker's views on the abilities of the offensive team in "Point Guard"?

→ SYNTHESIZE: BRING THINGS TOGETHER
2b. Summarize the speaker's main idea in "First Love." Summarize the speaker's main idea in "Point Guard."

EVALUATE: MAKE JUDGMENTS
3a. How well does "First Love" convey the sensations of playing or watching basketball? How well does "Point Guard" achieve the same?

→ EXTEND: CONNECT IDEAS
3b. What different but rewarding aspects of the game does each poem focus on? Which of these two poems most interests you? Why? What most appeals to you about this poem? How does it reflect an experience that you have had?

Literary Tools

TONE. **Tone** is a writer's or speaker's attitude toward a subject. Use your graphic organizer and the notes you took as you read to answer the following questions about the tone of each poem.

1. Describe the tone of "First Love" in your own words. How is the tone of the poem revealed?

_____

_____

_____

2. Describe the tone of "Point Guard" in your own words. How is the tone of the poem revealed?

_____

_____

_____

WordWorkshop

JARGON. **Jargon** is the specialized vocabulary members of a profession use. Often, it is difficult for people outside the profession to understand jargon. Use a dictionary or a book about basketball to define the following basketball jargon. Then create an illustration that further helps to define each word.

1. rim

2. backboard

3. hook shot

4. court

5. key

Read-Write Connection

Do you prefer quick movements and fast-paced games or slower games that perhaps involve specific strength, endurance, or in-depth thought? Explain your preference.

_____

_____

Beyond the Reading

RESEARCH THE HISTORY OF A SPORT. Research the history of a sport from its early invention to the present. Look for major changes and developments in the sport. Take notes as you do your research, and verify your findings using several sources. Then make a time line that highlights the developments you investigated. You may want to create your time line on a large roll of paper or on a series of poster boards so that you can display it in class. Sports to consider researching include basketball, baseball, cheerleading, wrestling, or soccer.

GO ONLINE. To find links and additional activities for this selection, visit the EMC Internet Resource Center at **emcp.com/languagearts** and click on Write-In Reader.

"400-METER FREESTYLE"
by Maxine Kumin

"The Women's 400 Meters"
by Lillian Morrison

Active READING STRATEGY

USE TEXT ORGANIZATION

Before Reading ➤ PREVIEW THE POEMS

❑ Read the Reader's Resource.
❑ Look over the shapes of the two poems.
❑ Look at the accompanying photographs and consider the titles. What do you expect each poem to be about?

Graphic Organizer: Pace and Motion Chart

Things That Set the Pace and Motion	
"400-Meter Freestyle"	"The Women's 400 Meters"

CONNECT

Reader's resource

Americans are fascinated with the drama of competitive sports. This obsession with sports is more than a love of competition or an appreciation for athletic ability. Sports encompass the full range of human struggle and emotion. In sports competition there is hope and disappointment, fear and joy, anticipation and achievement. Pay close attention to the struggles and emotions of the race participants in Maxine Kumin's **"400-Meter Freestyle"** and Lillian Morrison's **"The Women's 400 Meters."** The struggles and emotions of the athletes help readers experience two different kinds of races, one on land and the other in the water.

Word watch

PREVIEW VOCABULARY

careen	list
convert	skittish
expend	thrift
extravagance	

Reader's journal

What kind of competition have you experienced? How have you prepared for it?

_____

_____

USE A TEXT'S ORGANIZATION

❏ Read "400-Meter Freestyle" once, paying attention to the motion suggested by the shape of the poem. Think about how the shape and movement are related to the subject of the poem.

❏ Read the poem again. Mark places in the poem where you need to pause or stop to get a sense of the poem's meaning. Also mark places where you need to vary your volume, stress, and emotion. Make notes in your Pace and Motion Chart.

❏ Read the poem a third time, using the places you marked to help you create the feeling of witnessing a swimming race.

MARK THE TEXT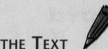

Underline or highlight how the swimmer moves forward.

FIX-UP IDEA

Listen to the Selection
If you have trouble understanding the poems, listen as they are read aloud by a partner. Pay attention to the words and the pace of the poem. Then practice reading the poems aloud yourself. Write down notes that help you understand what you are reading aloud.

400-METER FREESTYLE

Maxine Kumin

The gun full swing the swimmer catapults and cracks
        s
        i
        x

feet away onto that perfect glass he catches at
a
n
d

throws behind him scoop after scoop cunningly moving
        t
        h
        e

water back to move him forward. <u>Thrift</u> is his wonderful
s
e
c

5   ret; he has schooled out[1] all <u>extravagance</u>. No muscle
                                   r
                                   i
                                   p

ples without compensation wrist cock to heel snap to
h
i
s

mobile mouth that siphons in the air that nurtures

---

1. **schooled out.** Trained to eliminate

words for everyday use	**thrift** (thrift') *n.*, careful management of one's resources. *Her <u>thrift</u> enabled her to save enough money to retire early.* **ex • trav • a • gance** (ek strav' ə gəns) *n.*, unreasonable excess. *The house purchase was such an <u>extravagance</u> that the couple had no money left to buy furniture.*

          h
           i
            m
at half an inch above sea level so to speak.
T
h
e
astonishing whites of the soles of his feet rise
          a
          n
          d
10 salute us on the turns. He flips, <u>converts</u>, and is gone
a
l
l
in one. We watch him for signs. His arms are steady at
          t
          h
          e
catch, his cadent[2] feet tick in the stretch, they know
t
h
e
lesson well. Lungs know, too; he does not <u>list</u> for
          a
          i
          r
he drives along on little sips carefully <u>expended</u>
b
u
t
15 that plum red heart pumps hard cries hurt how soon
          i
          t
          s
near one more and makes its final surge   TIME 4:25:9 ■

---

2. **cadent.** Rhythmic

words for everyday use	**con • vert** (kən vərt′) *v.*, turn or change from one form to another. *When water freezes, it <u>converts</u> from a liquid to a solid.* **list** (list′) *v.*, tilt to one side. *The boat <u>listed</u> from side to side in the rough water.* **ex • pend** (ek spend′) *v.*, use or use up. *I have <u>expended</u> my energy cleaning.*

FIGURES OF SPEECH. **Figures of speech** are expressions that have more than one literal meaning. **Metaphor** and **personification** are two types of figures of speech. A **metaphor** is a figure of speech in which one thing is spoken or written about as if it were another. A metaphor invites the reader to make a comparison between the two things. "Love is a red, red rose" is an example of metaphor. **Personification** is a figure of speech in which an idea, animal, or thing is described as if it were a person. "Love reached out and bit me" is an example of personification. Look for metaphors and personification as you read "400-Meter Freestyle."

NOTE THE FACTS

What do the swimmer's feet know?

_____

_____

_____

WHAT DO YOU WONDER?

_____

_____

_____

Literary **TOOLS**

FIGURES OF SPEECH. "The Women's 400 Meters" contains two kinds of figures of speech. Look for **similes,** comparisons using *like* or *as,* and **metaphors,** comparisons in which one thing is spoken or written about as if it were another.

NOTE THE FACTS

What happens after the gun goes off?

_____

_____

_____

THINK AND REFLECT

What might the "bright tigers" in the last line represent? **(Interpret)**

_____

_____

_____

The Women's 400 METERS

Lillian Morrison

Skittish,

they flex knees, drum heels and

shiver at the starting line

waiting the gun

to pour them over the stretch

like a breaking wave.

Bang! they're off

careening down the lanes,

each chased by her own bright tiger. ∎

words for everyday use

skit • tish (skit ish) *adj.,* easily frightened; jumpy. *The skittish horse jumped backwards as the train roared by.*

ca • reen (kə rēn) *v.,* to lurch from side to side, especially while moving rapidly. *The spectators screamed when they saw the car careening down the racetrack.*

Reflect ON YOUR READING

After Reading ➤ DISCUSS ORGANIZATIONAL FEATURES

❏ Review your Pace and Motion Chart and discuss the organization of each poem.
❏ Write a set of tips that would help someone read each poem.

_____

_____

_____

_____

Reading Skills and Test Practice

IDENTIFY ORGANIZATIONAL PATTERNS

Discuss with your partner how best to answer the following questions about a text's organization. Use the Think-Aloud Notes to write down your reasons for eliminating the incorrect answers.

____1. Which line best represents the action suggested by the vertical lines connecting the horizontal lines of poetry in "400-Meter Freestyle"?

   a. "The gun full swing the swimmer catapults . . ."
   b. "No muscle ripples without compensation . . ."
   c. "He flips, converts, and is gone . . ."
   d. "he drives along on little sips . . ."

____2. What best represents where to pause in reading these lines from "The Women's 400 Meters"?

   waiting the gun
   to pour them over the stretch
   like a breaking wave.

   a. Readers should pause after *gun*, *stretch*, and *wave*.
   b. Readers should pause after *them*, *stretch*, and *wave*.
   c. Readers should pause after *gun* and *them*.
   d. Readers should pause after *stretch* and *wave*.

How did using the reading strategy help you to answer the questions?

_____

_____

_____

_____

_____

_____

_____

_____

_____

_____

_____

_____

_____

Investigate, Inquire, and Imagine

RECALL: GATHER FACTS
1a. How does the swimmer's body in "400-Meter Freestyle" feel near the end of the race?

→

INTERPRET: FIND MEANING
1b. How does the swimmer react to the physical pressure?

ANALYZE: TAKE THINGS APART
2a. What clues in the poem reveal the swimmer's thoughts and emotions?

→

SYNTHESIZE: BRING THINGS TOGETHER
2b. What is the swimmer's goal? How does he reach that goal?

EVALUATE: MAKE JUDGMENTS
3a. What elements of "400-Meter Freestyle" create the experience of witnessing a swimming race? Which elements are the most effective?

→

EXTEND: CONNECT IDEAS
3b. How does "The Women's 400 Meters" create a sense of anticipation and suspense? How does it make the reader feel like a witness to the event? How are the feelings of nervousness, suspense, and desire to win conveyed similarly in the two poems? How are they conveyed differently? What elements of "The Women's 400 Meters" mirror elements in "400-Meter Freestyle"? What elements of "The Women's 400 Meters" might make the reader think the poem is about swimming?

Literary Tools

FIGURES OF SPEECH. Figures of speech are expressions that have more than one literal meaning. A **simile** is a comparison using *like* or *as*. A **metaphor** is a figure of speech in which one thing is spoken or written about as if it were another. **Personification** is a figure of speech in which an idea, animal, or thing is described as if it were a person. Find examples of figures of speech in "400-Meter Freestyle" and "The Women's 400 Meters," and add them to the chart below.

Title of Poem	Simile	Metaphor	Personification
"400-Meter Freestyle"			
"The Women's 400 Meters"			

WordWorkshop

Visualize. Create a drawing that illustrates the meaning of each word below. Include a caption or title that explains each illustration. Be sure to illustrate the meanings of the words as they are used in the poems.

1. careen

2. expend

3. extravagance

4. list

5. skittish

Read-Write Connection

In what ways do you push yourself to the limit?

_____

_____

_____

Beyond the Reading

Read and Perform a Sports Poem. Find another sports poem you like. Practice reading the poem aloud. Then share it with a small group. Before sharing your poem, practice varying your pace, volume, stress, and tone so they fit the words in the poem. After your presentation, add your poem to a classroom bulletin board that displays everyone's poems.

Go Online. To find links and additional activities for this selection, visit the EMC Internet Resource Center at **emcp.com/languagearts** and click on Write-In Reader.

Reader's resource

Several varieties of blackberries grow in the United States. Some are native to North America and have grown wild for centuries. Others were transported from Europe, where they originally grew wild as well. Blackberries grow on vine-like bushes, many of which have sharp thorns. Berry breeders and farmers now cultivate many hybrid types of blackberries. These different varieties of blackberries ripen at different times, although many are ready to eat in late summer. In **"Blackberry Eating,"** Galway Kinnell writes about picking and eating blackberries.

Word watch

PREVIEW VOCABULARY

splurge

Reader's journal

Describe your favorite food and how you eat it.

_____

_____

_____

"Blackberry Eating"

by Galway Kinnell

Active READING STRATEGY

VISUALIZE

Before Reading ➡ **BEGIN TO VISUALIZE**

❑ Read the title and look at the image on page 127.
❑ Think about berries. What do you see? How do the berries feel? How do they taste and smell?
❑ Think about foods you associate with certain times of the year, special events, or holidays. Add these thoughts to the Association Chart below. Indicate holidays or events you associate with these foods.

Graphic Organizer: Association Chart

Foods I Eat in Different Seasons

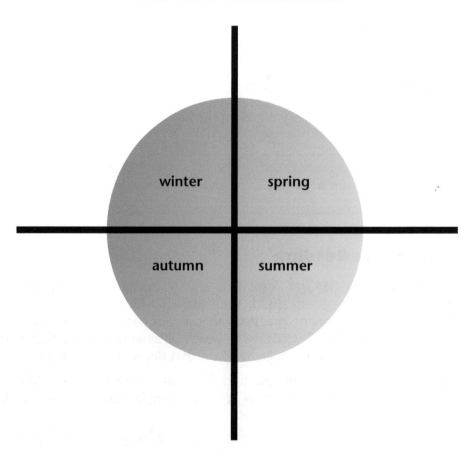

winter   spring

autumn   summer

BLACKBERRY Eating

Galway Kinnell

CREATE MIND PICTURES

❑ Listen as your teacher reads the poem aloud. As you listen, close your eyes and imagine that you are the speaker. Picture each thing the speaker describes.

❑ Read the poem a second time on your own. Keep a picture in your mind of the scene. Imagine the weather, the sounds, the smells, sights, tastes, and things the speaker touches. Repeat lines and phrases to help yourself fully imagine the scene.

I love to go out in late September

among the fat, overripe, icy, black blackberries

to eat blackberries for breakfast,

the stalks very prickly, a penalty

5   they earn for knowing the black art

of blackberry-making; and as I stand among them

lifting the stalks to my mouth, the ripest berries

fall almost unbidden[1] to my tongue,

as words sometimes do, certain peculiar words

10   like *strengths* or *squinched*,

many-lettered, one-syllabled lumps,

which I squeeze, squinch open, and <u>splurge</u> well

in the silent, startled, icy, black language

of blackberry-eating in late September. ■

---

1. **unbidden.** Not asked or invited

NOTE THE FACTS

What sometimes falls to the speaker's tongue like ripe berries?

_____

_____

_____

Literary TOOLS

ALLITERATION. Alliteration is the repetition of consonant sounds at the beginnings of syllables. Tongue twisters demonstrate an exaggerated use of alliteration, as in *She sells seashells by the seashore.* Underline or highlight examples of alliteration you find in the poem.

words for everyday use

splurge (splərj') *v.*, indulge oneself extravagantly or spend a lot of money. *When Dad got a raise, he <u>splurged</u> and took us all out for a fancy dinner.*

Reflect ON YOUR READING

After Reading ▸ **SUMMARIZE YOUR MIND PICTURES**

❑ Sketch or write a summary of the mind pictures you had as you listened to and reread "Blackberry Eating."

❑ Share your sketch or summary with a partner. Talk about details of berry eating that each of you imagined. Did you imagine similar berries and similar settings?

Reading Skills and Test Practice

IDENTIFY MAIN IDEAS

With your partner, discuss how to answer the questions about main ideas in the poem. Use the Think-Aloud Notes to write down your reasons for eliminating the incorrect answers.

_____1. How are the berries like some words?
   a. They are squishy.
   b. The speaker likes to move them around his or her mouth.
   c. They land unbidden on the speaker's tongue.
   d. They are sour.

_____2. How does the speaker feel about blackberry eating?
   a. It is a dreaded chore.
   b. The speaker is nonchalant about the activity.
   c. It is a yearly treat.
   d. The speaker's feelings are unclear.

How did using the reading strategy help you to answer the questions?

_____

_____

_____

_____

THINK-ALOUD NOTES

_____

_____

_____

_____

_____

_____

_____

_____

_____

_____

Investigate, Inquire, and Imagine

RECALL: GATHER FACTS
1a. What are the blackberries like in late September?

INTERPRET: FIND MEANING
1b. How would the fruit be different earlier in the year? What makes this time of year special for eating blackberries?

ANALYZE: TAKE THINGS APART
2a. Identify the author's descriptive words and phrases. Which words best describe what it is like to eat berries?

SYNTHESIZE: BRING THINGS TOGETHER
2b. Explain how the descriptions of blackberries could apply to the "language of blackberry eating" and to "certain peculiar words."

EVALUATE: MAKE JUDGMENTS
3a. Critique this poem's use of imagery. Explain whether the writer's descriptions capture the essence of "blackberry-eating in late September."

EXTEND: CONNECT IDEAS
3b. How could you communicate in writing about your own favorite food? What could you do to give readers a sense of how your favorite food tastes, smells, feels, looks, and sounds?

Literary Tools

ALLITERATION. **Alliteration** is the repetition of consonant sounds at the beginnings of syllables. Add examples of alliteration you find in the poem to the chart below. Write the consonants that are repeated in the second column.

Examples of Alliteration	Repeated Consonants

WordWorkshop

Using Figurative Language. Figurative language is language that appeals to the sense of sight, taste, touch, smell, or hearing. Poets use figurative language to help readers create strong mind pictures. Write a short poem about your favorite food. First make a list of words or images that come to mind when you think about your favorite food. Include words that describe the food's taste, smell, texture, sound, and image. Then use these words in a poem that describes the food. Use the word *splurge* somewhere in the title or body of your poem. Use your own paper as needed.

My favorite food: _____

Words that describe my favorite food:

My poem:

Read-Write Connection

What is your favorite season of the year, and why?

_____

_____

_____

Beyond the Reading

Find a Poem with Onomatopoeia. Onomatopoeia is the use of words or phrases like *boom, pow,* or *achoo* that sound like what they name. In "Blackberry Eating," words like *squinch* and *squeeze* are fun because they bring out the full flavor of words. Such words also make the meaning of the word much easier to understand because an example is built right into the word. Find another poem that contains several words of onomatopoeia. Make a copy of the poem and highlight or underline the words that show onomatopoeia.

Go Online. To find links and additional activities for this selection, visit the EMC Internet Resource Center at **emcp.com/languagearts** and click on Write-In Reader.

"THE LOST PARROT"

by Naomi Shihab Nye

Active READING STRATEGY

WRITE THINGS DOWN

Before Reading ➤ **LOOK FOR WORDS THAT DESCRIBE A SPEAKER'S FEELINGS**

❑ Write down words and phrases that a speaker might use in a poem about a lost parrot.

_____

_____

❑ As you read, add words and phrases from "The Lost Parrot" to the Word Chart below.

Graphic Organizer: Word Chart

Words that convey anxiety	Words that convey loss	Words that convey sadness

"The Lost Parrot"

Reader's resource

Author Naomi Shihab Nye wrote "**The Lost Parrot**" about a real boy named Carlos. She was teaching third graders how to write a "dream-poem." A dream-poem, Nye says, is "one in which a writer follows images that first come to him or her through dreaming—whether while sleeping or during a wakeful state." Carlos had trouble with Nye's assignment. Nye wanted the class to "experiment with as many images as they could," but Carlos could write about only one image. As you read, picture how Carlos and the teacher interact. Think about gestures they make, their facial expressions, and how they speak.

READ ALOUD

Read the following words aloud before you begin reading.
Na • o • mi Shi • hab Nye (nā ō′ mē shē′ häb nī′) *n.*
Car • los (car′ lōs) *n.*
San An • to • ni • o (san an tō′ nyō) *n.*
mangoes (man gōs) *n.*

Reader's journal

Have you ever lost someone or something you cared about? Describe your experience.

_____

_____

GATHER INFORMATION

❑ Listen as your teacher reads the first two lines of the poem. Identify words and phrases that convey anxiety, loss, or sadness. Add these words to the appropriate column of your Word Chart.

❑ Continue reading the poem on your own. Stop after each stanza to identify the speaker's emotions. Add words and phrases that express these emotions to your chart.

FIX-UP IDEA

Use Context Clues
Dialogue between Carlos and his teacher is indented, but you cannot tell who is speaking by the indentions. Pay attention to the context around the indentions to help you determine who is speaking in each line. In the white space next to each line in the second and third indented stanzas, write down who is speaking.

NOTE THE FACTS

What are the only words that Carlos can write?

_____

_____

_____

The LOST PARROT

Naomi Shihab Nye

Carlos bites the end of his pencil
He's trying to write a dream-poem, but waves at me, frowning

      I had a parrot

He talks slowly, like his voice travels far
5   to get out of his body

      A dream-parrot?
      No, a real parrot!
      Write about it

He squirms, looks nervous, everyone else is almost finished
10   and he hasn't started

      It left
      What left?
      The parrot

He hunches over the table, pencil gripped in fist,
15   shaping the heavy letters
Days later we will write story-poems, sound-poems,
but always the same subject for Carlos

      It left

He will insist on reading it and the class will look puzzled
20   The class is tired of the parrot

Write more, Carlos
I can't

Why not?

I don't know   where   it went

25   Each day when I leave he stares at the ceiling
       Maybe he is planning an expedition
       into the back streets of San Antonio[1]
       armed with nets and ripe mangoes[2]
       He will find the parrot nesting in a rain gutter
30   This time he will guard it carefully, make sure it stays

       Before winter comes and his paper goes white
       in all directions

       Before anything else he loves
       gets away ■

---

1. **San Antonio.** City in southern Texas
2. **mangoes.** A yellow-red, oblong tropical fruit

MARK THE TEXT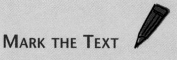

Underline or highlight why Carlos can't write more about the parrot.

DRAW A PICTURE

Draw a picture that shows how Carlos feels.

Reflect ON YOUR READING

After Reading SUMMARIZE THE SPEAKER'S FEELINGS

❑ Review the words in your Word Chart.
❑ Write a paragraph that summarizes the speaker's feelings.

_____

_____

_____

_____

_____

**THINK-ALOUD
NOTES**

_____

_____

_____

_____

_____

_____

_____

_____

_____

_____

_____

Reading Skills and Test Practice

ANALYZE A CHARACTER

READ, THINK, AND EXPLAIN. Read the following advice and answer the
questions that follow.

If you love something, set it free.

1. Would Carlos agree with this advice? How might he respond if
someone suggested that losing his parrot was for the best?

_____

_____

_____

2. What is your opinion of the advice?

_____

_____

REFLECT ON YOUR RESPONSE. Compare your response with that of a partner.
Were your responses similar? How did using the reading strategy help
you answer the questions? What advice would you give to someone who
lost something?

_____

_____

_____

Investigate, Inquire, and Imagine

RECALL: GATHER FACTS
→
1a. What is Carlos trying to write a poem about? What are the only words Carlos is able to write?

INTERPRET: FIND MEANING
1b. Why is Carlos unable to write more?

ANALYZE: TAKE THINGS APART
→
2a. Identify the words and phrases that describe Carlos. What does he do? How does he act?

SYNTHESIZE: BRING THINGS TOGETHER
2b. Describe Carlos in your own words. What do you think prevents Carlos from writing more?

PERSPECTIVE: LOOK AT OTHER VIEWS
→
3a. Why is the parrot so important to Carlos?

EMPATHY: SEE FROM INSIDE
3b. What do you think will happen to Carlos if he never finds the parrot? How might his teacher and classmates help him?

Literary Tools

DIALOGUE. "The Lost Parrot" contains **dialogue**, or conversation involving two or more people or characters, but it does not look like the dialogue you normally see in a story. The dialogue in this poem is not separated from the rest of the text by punctuation or by tag lines, lines that identify who is speaking. Using the dialogue in this poem, rewrite the conversation between the speaker and Carlos. Use quotation marks and tag lines to indicate who is speaking. Be creative with your tag lines—for example, instead of writing "he said," write "he whined."

_____

_____

_____

_____

_____

WordWorkshop

HOMONYMS. **Homonyms** are words that are spelled and pronounced alike but have different meanings. The following words in "The Lost Parrot" are homonyms that can be used as both a noun and a verb. Identify how each word below acts as a noun and a verb by providing dictionary definitions that illustrate two different parts of speech. Put a check mark next to the definition used in the poem.

1. **hunch:** noun _____

   verb _____

2. **parrot:** noun _____

   verb _____

3. **voice:** noun _____

   verb _____

4. **wave:** noun _____

   verb _____

5. **bite:** noun _____

   verb _____

Read-Write Connection

At the end of the poem, what would you do if you were Carlos?

Beyond the Reading

READ ABOUT BIRDS. Using the library or the Internet, find more information about parrots or some other bird. Research the bird's physical description, habitat, diet, and population status. Write a report that answers the following questions: What does the bird look like? Where does it live? What does it eat? Is it endangered?

GO ONLINE. To find links and additional activities for this selection, visit the EMC Internet Resource Center at **emcp.com/languagearts** and click on Write-In Reader.

"The Charge of the Light Brigade"

by Alfred, Lord Tennyson

Active READING STRATEGY

WRITE THINGS DOWN

Before Reading ➤ **FILL IN A CHART**

❑ Read the Reader's Resource.
❑ Read the poem. As you read, highlight or underline words and phrases that describe the poem's setting, main characters, and important conflicts and outcomes.
❑ After you finish reading, add the underlined or highlighted words and phrases to the Literary Elements Chart below.

Graphic Organizer: Literary Elements Chart

Setting
Main Characters
Conflicts
The Outcome

CONNECT

Reader's resource

Alfred, Lord Tennyson was the poet laureate, or most honored poet, of England in the late 1850s. His poem, **"The Charge of the Light Brigade,"** recalls the Battle of Balaklava, fought on October 25, 1854, during the Crimean War. In the battle, a small force of sword-carrying British soldiers on horseback attacked a strong line of Russian troops armed with cannons and guns. Of the 673 British soldiers who fought in the Light Brigade, only 195 survived.

Word watch

PREVIEW VOCABULARY

blunder   reel
dismay   sunder
plunge

Reader's journal

How would you react if you were required to face a situation that might cost you your life?

_____

_____

_____

_____

The Charge of the Light Brigade

Alfred, Lord Tennyson

1

Half a league,[1] half a league,
　Half a league onward,
All in the valley of Death
　Rode the six hundred.
5　"Forward, the Light Brigade!"
"Charge for the guns!" he said:
Into the valley of Death
　Rode the six hundred.

2

"Forward, the Light Brigade!"
10　Was there a man <u>dismay'd</u>?
Not tho' the soldier knew
　Someone had <u>blunder'd</u>:
Theirs not to make reply,
Theirs not to reason why,
15　Theirs but to do and die:
Into the valley of Death
　Rode the six hundred.

3

Cannon to right of them,
Cannon to left of them,
20　Cannon in front of them
　Volley'd and thunder'd;
Storm'd at with shot and shell,
Boldly they rode and well,

---

1. **league.** Unit of distance

words for everyday use	
	dis • may (dis mā') v., unnerve; deter by arousing fear. *The amount of work <u>dismayed</u> Sam, and he gave up.* **dismayed,** *adj.*
	blun • der (blun' dər) v., make a mistake. *I could have scored a goal, but I <u>blundered</u> and shot the puck over the goal.*

Into the jaws of Death,
25   Into the mouth of Hell
    Rode the six hundred.

4

Flash'd all their sabres[2] bare,
Flash'd as they turn'd in air,
Sabring the gunners there,
30   Charging an army, while
    All the world wonder'd:
<u>Plunged</u> in the battery-smoke
Right thro' the line they broke;
Cossack[3] and Russian
30   <u>Reel'd</u> from the sabre stroke
    Shatter'd and <u>sunder'd</u>.
Then they rode back, but not
    Not the six hundred.

5

Cannon to right of them,
40   Cannon to left of them,
Cannon behind them
    Volley'd and thunder'd;
Storm'd at with shot and shell,
While horse and hero fell,
45   They that had fought so well
Came thro' the jaws of Death
Back from the mouth of Hell,
All that was left of them,
    Left of six hundred.

6

50   When can their glory fade?
O the wild charge they made!
    All the world wondered.
Honor the charge they made,
Honor the Light Brigade,
55   Noble six hundred. ■

---

2. **sabres.** Cavalry swords
3. **Cossack.** Member of the Southern Russian cavalry

words for everyday use	**plunge** (plunj') v., enter quickly into something. *I plunged into the book as soon as I got home from the library.* **reel** (rēl') v., waver or fall back as from a blow. *Glen reeled when the door flew open and hit him.* **sunder** (sun' dər) v., break apart or become disunited. *Our group would sunder if we were caught by a violent storm.*

MARK THE TEXT

Underline or highlight what happened to the Light Brigade as they rode back.

Literary TOOLS

REPETITION. **Repetition** is more than one use of a sound, word, or phrase. Highlight or underline examples of repetition Tennyson uses in the poem.

WHAT DO YOU WONDER?

_____
_____
_____
_____

Reflect ON YOUR READING

After Reading ➤ SUMMARIZE THE SPEAKER'S FEELINGS

❑ Review your completed Literary Elements Chart.
❑ In your own words, describe the setting, main characters, what they did, and what happened to them.

_____

_____

_____

_____

_____

_____

_____

_____

_____

_____

_____

_____

_____

_____

_____

Reading Skills and Test Practice

IDENTIFY MAIN IDEAS

Discuss with a partner how best to answer the following questions about the main ideas in "The Charge of the Light Brigade." Use the Think-Aloud Notes to write down your reasons for eliminating the incorrect answers.

_____1. What does the speaker say is the soldier's duty?
a. to follow his own best judgment
b. to avoid blunders
c. to protect the captain
d. to follow orders

_____2. How does the speaker describe the valley where the battle takes place?
a. It is a frightening place.
b. It is a beautiful place until the battle begins.
c. It is a heavenly place even during the battle.
d. There is no description of the valley.

How did using the reading strategy help you to answer the questions?

_____

_____

_____

_____

Investigate, Inquire, and Imagine

RECALL: GATHER FACTS
1a. What does the speaker say about the orders given to the soldiers?

INTERPRET: FIND MEANING
1b. Why would the soldiers charge knowing that the command is a mistake?

ANALYZE: TAKE THINGS APART
2a. Compare and contrast stanzas 4 and 6. What technique is the poet using? Which lines are different, and which lines are the same?

SYNTHESIZE: BRING THINGS TOGETHER
2b. Rewrite in your own words the section of the story found in each of these stanzas. How does the poet's technique emphasize these two parts of the story?

EVALUATE: MAKE JUDGMENTS
3a. How well does this poem tell the story of the Battle of Balaklava? What parts of the story could be missing? How well does the poem recreate the setting and mood, or atmosphere, of a horrible battle scene?

EXTEND: CONNECT IDEAS
3b. Using what you know about war and military capabilities today, explain how a modern battle scene might differ from the battle described in this poem.

Literary Tools

REPETITION. **Repetition** is more than one use of a sound, word, or phrase. Tennyson uses literary techniques in this poem such as repetition and details that create strong emotions to create *suspense*, a feeling of expectation, anxiousness, or curiosity. Review the examples of repetition that you marked in the poem. Which uses of repetition help to build suspense?

_____

_____

WordWorkshop

ANTONYMS. **Antonyms** are words with opposite meanings. Find antonyms for the words below. Then write a new poem that uses the antonyms. Use your own paper as needed.

1. blunder _____

2. dismay _____

3. plunge _____

4. reel _____

5. sunder _____

Read-Write Connection

What would you have done if you believed the orders to charge were a mistake?

_____

_____

_____

_____

_____

_____

_____

_____

_____

_____

Beyond the Reading

READ ABOUT THE CRIMEAN WAR. Using the library or the Internet, find more information about the Crimean War. Why was Russia so interested in controlling the Black Sea? Why were England, France, and Sardinia interested in stopping Russia from doing so? What were some major events in the war? What was the outcome of the war? Prepare a graphic aid such as a map, chart, or table that explains your findings.

GO ONLINE. To find links and additional activities for this selection, visit the EMC Internet Resource Center at **emcp.com/languagearts** and click on Write-In Reader.

Unit 4 READING Review

Choose and Use Reading Strategies

Before reading the poem below, review and discuss with a partner how to use reading strategies with poetry.

1. Read with a Purpose
2. Connect to Prior Knowledge
3. Write Things Down
4. Make Predictions
5. Visualize
6. Use Text Organization
7. Tackle Difficult Vocabulary
8. Monitor Your Reading Progress

Poet A. E. Housman was interested in appealing to readers' emotions. His poems often assume that evil outweighs good and that negative conditions and outcomes are the norm. Use the margins and mark up Housman's "I to My Perils" below. Show how you use reading strategies to read actively. After you finish reading, summarize the speaker's ideas in two or three sentences.

> I to my <u>perils</u>
>   Of cheat and charmer
>   Came clad in armour
>   By stars <u>benign</u>.
> Hope lies to mortals
>   And most believe her,
>   But man's deceiver
>   Was never mine.
> The thoughts of others
>   Were light and fleeting,
>   Of lovers' meeting
>   Or luck or fame.
> Mine were of trouble,
>   And mine were steady,
>   So I was ready
>   When trouble came.

per • il (per' əl) n., exposure to the risk of being hurt; danger. *The excitement of mountain climbing outweighs the <u>perils</u>.*

be • nign (bi nīn') *adj.,* kindly; nonthreatening. *I was scared to go to the new school, but the <u>benign</u> atmosphere made it easy to relax and meet people.*

Literary Tools

Select the literary element from the column on the right that best completes each sentence on the left. Write the correct letter in the blank.

_____1. "Half a league, half a league, / half a league onward" includes an example of _____.

_____2. A(n) _____ is a figure of speech in which one thing is spoken or written of as if it were another.

_____3. A(n) _____ is a figure of speech in which an idea, animal, or thing is described as if it were a person.

_____4. The voice that narrates a poem can be called the _____.

_____5. In poetry, _____ is not always indicated by quotation marks or tag lines like "she said."

_____6. A(n) _____ is a figure of speech that makes a comparison using _like_ or _as_.

_____7. _Peter picked a peck of pickled peppers_ is an example of _____.

_____8. A writer's or speaker's _____ expresses an attitude toward a subject.

_____9. A(n) _____ is a statement that has more than a straightforward, literal meaning.

a. personification, 102, 121, 124

b. figure of speech, 102, 121, 122, 124

c. speaker, 111

d. tone, 113, 117

e. simile , 102, 121, 124

f. metaphor, 102, 121, 122, 124

g. alliteration, 104, 127, 129

h. repetition, 139, 141

i. dialogue, 135

WordWorkshop

UNIT 4 WORDS FOR EVERYDAY USE

ascend, 109	expend, 121	skittish, 122
blunder, 138	extravagance, 120	sunder, 139
careen, 122	list, 121	thrift, 120
convert, 121	plunge, 139	splurge, 127
dismay, 138	reel, 139	

CREATE CONTEXT CLUES. Create sentences for ten of the Words for Everyday Use listed above. Your sentences should include context clues that help readers understand the meanings of the words as they are used in the poems in this unit. Unit 2, pages 20–21, provides examples of context clues you can use in your sentences: *comparison, contrast, restatement, examples,* and *cause and effect.*

1. _____

_____

2. _____

_____

3. _____

_____

4. _____

_____

5. _____

_____

6. _____

_____

7. _____

_____

8. _____

_____

9. _____

_____

10. _____

_____

On Your Own

Look through poetry collections and search the Internet until you find a poem that you like. Then complete one of the following activities using the poem you have found.

FLUENTLY SPEAKING. Pretend that you are a poet giving a reading at a local bookstore. Practice reading your poem aloud to discover how the poem sounds best. Then read your poem to a small group of four or five classmates. If possible, make an audio or video recording of your reading to share with the rest of the class.

PICTURE THIS. Create a drawing that illustrates images and ideas presented throughout your poem. Include a copy of the poem with your drawing. Try typing your copy of the poem using a font, or print style, that matches the poem's images and ideas.

PUT IT IN WRITING. Write a letter to persuade a friend to read the poem you have selected. Discuss any lines, images, or figures of speech that you especially like. Tell what you think the poem means, and why. Include a copy of the poem that includes additional handwritten notes for your friend.

Unit FIVE

READING Folk Literature

FOLK LITERATURE

Human beings are storytelling creatures. Long before people invented writing, they were telling stories about the lives of their gods and heroes. The best of their stories were passed by word of mouth from generation to generation, from folk to folk. These early stories were told in the form of poems, songs, and what we would now call prose tales.

Stories, poems, and songs passed by word of mouth from person to person are important elements of a group's culture. Eventually, many of these verbally transmitted stories, poems, and songs were written down. **Folk literature** is the written versions of these stories, poems, and songs. Folk literature is full of literary devices that helped storytellers remember the stories. These devices include the use of repetition, common phrases such as "once upon a time" and "they lived happily ever after," and familiar characters and events. Some common types of folk literature are defined below.

Types of Folk Literature

MYTHS. **Myths** are stories that explain objects or events in the natural world as resulting from the action of some supernatural force or entity, most often a god. Every early culture around the globe has produced myths. In this unit, you will read four myths from different parts of the world. The play *Persephone* in Unit 6 is based on a Greek myth.

FOLK TALES. **Folk tales** are brief stories passed by word of mouth from generation to generation in a particular culture. **Fairy tales** are folk tales that contain supernatural beings, such as fairies, dragons, ogres, and animals with human qualities. **Tall tales** are colorful stories that depict the exaggerated wild adventures of North American folk heroes. Many of these heroes and stories revolve around the American frontier and the Wild West.

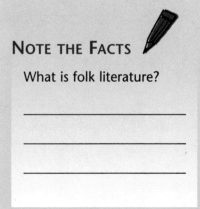

NOTE THE FACTS

What is folk literature?

_____

_____

_____

MARK THE TEXT

Highlight or underline eight types of folk literature. Start here and continue on the next page.

Persephone and Demeter are two mythological figures. What others can you think of? (Extend)

_____

_____

_____

PARABLES. **Parables** are very brief stories told to teach a moral lesson. Some of the most famous parables are those told by Jesus in the Bible.

FABLES. **Fables** are brief stories, often with animal characters, told to express a moral. Famous fables include those of Æsop and Jean de La Fontaine.

FOLK SONGS. **Folk songs** are traditional or composed songs typically made up of stanzas, a refrain, and a simple melody. They express commonly shared ideas or feelings and may be narrative (telling a story) or lyrical (expressing an emotion). Traditional folk songs are anonymous songs that have been transmitted orally. "Song of the Thunders" and "Song of the Crows" in this unit are two folk songs from the Anishinabe people.

LEGENDS. **Legends** are stories that have been passed down through time. These stories are often believed to be based on history but without evidence that the events occurred.

USING READING STRATEGIES WITH FOLK LITERATURE

Active Reading Strategy Checklists

In the stories, poems, and songs that are a part of folk literature, storytellers want to entertain their audiences and to pass along cultural ideas and beliefs. The following checklists offer strategies for reading folk literature.

1 READ WITH A PURPOSE. Give yourself a purpose, or something to look for, as you read. Often, you can set a purpose for reading by previewing the title, the opening lines, and instructional information. Other times, a teacher may set your purpose: "Notice how the character of Amaterasu is developed." To read with a purpose, say to yourself

❑ I want to look for . . .
❑ I will keep track of . . .
❑ I want to find out what happens to . . .
❑ I want to understand how . . .
❑ The message of this selection is . . .

Reading TIP

One purpose for reading myths is to understand what it might have been like to live in a culture long ago.

2 **CONNECT TO PRIOR KNOWLEDGE.** Connect to what you already know about a particular culture and its storytelling traditions. To connect to prior knowledge, say to yourself

- ❏ I know that this type of folk literature has . . .
- ❏ The events in this selection remind me of . . .
- ❏ Something similar I've read is . . .
- ❏ I like this part of the selection because . . .

3 **WRITE THINGS DOWN.** Create a written record of the cultural ideas and beliefs that a storyteller passes along. To keep a written record

- ❏ Underline characters' names.
- ❏ Write down your thoughts about the storyteller's ideas and beliefs.
- ❏ Highlight the most exciting, funniest, or most interesting parts of the tale.
- ❏ Create a graphic organizer to keep track of the sequence of events.
- ❏ Use a code to respond to what happens.

4 **MAKE PREDICTIONS.** Use information about the title and subject matter to guess what a folk literature selection will be about. Confirm or deny your predictions, and make new ones based on what you learn. To make predictions, say to yourself

- ❏ The title tells me that the selection will be about . . .
- ❏ I predict that this character will . . .
- ❏ Tales from this cultural tradition usually . . .
- ❏ The conflict between the characters will be resolved by . . .
- ❏ I think the selection will end with . . .

5 **VISUALIZE.** Visualizing, or allowing the words on the page to create images in your mind, helps you understand a storyteller's account. In order to visualize what happens in a folk literature selection, imagine that you are the storyteller. Read the words in your head with the type of expression and feeling that the storyteller might use with an audience. Make statements such as

- ❏ I imagine the characters sound like . . .
- ❏ My sketch of what happens includes . . .
- ❏ I picture this sequence of events . . .
- ❏ I envision the characters as . . .

Reading **TIP**

Instead of writing down a short response, use a symbol or a short word to indicate your response. Use codes like the ones listed below.

+	I like this.
−	I don't like this.
√	This is important.
Yes	I agree with this.
No	I disagree with this.
?	I don't understand this.
!	This is like something I know.
ᕽ	I need to come back to this later.

Reading **TIP**

Sketching story events helps you remember and understand them.

6 **USE TEXT ORGANIZATION.** When you read folk literature, pay attention to transition or signal words such as *first*, *if/then*, and *on the other hand*. These words identify important ideas and text patterns. Stop occasionally to retell what you have read. Say to yourself

- ❑ What happens first is . . .
- ❑ There is a conflict between . . .
- ❑ The high point of interest is . . .
- ❑ I can summarize this section by . . .
- ❑ The message of this selection is that . . .

7 **TACKLE DIFFICULT VOCABULARY.** Difficult words can hinder your ability to understand folk literature. Use context, consult a dictionary, or ask someone about words you do not understand. When you come across a difficult word, say to yourself

- ❑ The words around the difficult word tell me it must mean . . .
- ❑ A dictionary definition shows that the word means . . .
- ❑ My work with the word before reading helps me know that the word means . . .
- ❑ A classmate said that the word means . . .

8 **MONITOR YOUR READING PROGRESS.** All readers encounter difficulty when they read, especially if they are reading assigned material and not something they have chosen on their own. When you are assigned to read folk literature, note the problems you are having and fix them. The key to reading success is knowing when you are having difficulty. To fix problems, say to yourself

- ❑ Because I don't understand this part, I will . . .
- ❑ Because I'm having trouble staying connected, I will . . .
- ❑ Because the words are hard, I will . . .
- ❑ Because this selection is long, I will . . .
- ❑ Because I can't retell what this section was about, I will . . .

Become an Active Reader

The instruction with the folk literature in this unit gives you an in-depth look at how to use one strategy with each folk literature selection. Learn how to combine several strategies to ensure your complete understanding of what you are reading. When you have difficulty, use fix-up ideas to fix a problem. For further information about the active reading strategies, including the fix-up ideas, see Unit 1, pages 4–15.

Reading **TIP**

If the words in a selection are difficult to pronounce, practice saying them aloud before you read.

FIX-UP IDEAS

Whenever you feel your attention is failing, or if you do not understand what you are reading, use a fix-up idea.

- ■ Reread
- ■ Ask a question
- ■ Read in shorter chunks
- ■ Read aloud
- ■ Retell
- ■ Work with a partner
- ■ Unlock difficult words
- ■ Vary your reading rate
- ■ Choose a new reading strategy
- ■ Create a mnemonic device

How to Use Reading Strategies with Folk Literature

Use the following excerpts to discover how you might use reading strategies as you read folk literature.

Excerpt 1. Note how a reader uses active reading strategies while reading this excerpt from "The Epic of Gilgamesh," retold by Christina Kolb.

TACKLE DIFFICULT VOCABULARY

Oppress might mean "keep down" because it contains the word part *press*.

MONITOR YOUR READING PROGRESS

I will stop after each paragraph to summarize what it says.

Gilgamesh, king of Uruk in southern Babylonia, was two-thirds divine and one-third human. He himself built the great city of Uruk. He was like a wild bull—powerful, bold, and able to best any man in combat. Perhaps because he was so very powerful, Gilgamesh was also arrogant. He drove the people of Uruk too hard, oppressing even the weak. Eventually the people of Uruk, weighed down by their heavy burdens, prayed to the gods for relief. The gods granted the people's prayers and created Enkidu.

WRITE THINGS DOWN

I can write down the names of characters and a brief description of who each is.

MAKE A PREDICTION

I predict Gilgamesh will have to learn to be less arrogant.

Excerpt 2. Note how a reader uses active reading strategies while reading this excerpt from "The Secret Name of Ra," retold by Geraldine Harris.

CONNECT TO PRIOR KNOWLEDGE

I associate ancient Egypt with mummies and pyramids. I wonder if any of those things will appear in this myth.

READ WITH A PURPOSE

I want to find out what Ra's secret name is and why it is kept secret.

Ra, the Sole Creator was visible to the people of Egypt as the disc of the sun, but they knew him in many other forms. He could appear as a crowned man, a falcon or a man with a falcon's head and, as the scarab beetle[1] pushes a round ball of dung in front of it, the Egyptians pictured Ra as a scarab pushing the sun across the sky. In caverns deep below the earth were hidden another seventy-five forms of Ra: mysterious beings with mummified bodies and heads consisting of birds or snakes, feathers or flowers. The names of Ra were as numerous as his forms; he was the Shining One, The Hidden One, The Renewer of the Earth, The Wind in the Souls, The Exalted One, but there was one name of the Sun God which had not been spoken since time began. To know this secret name of Ra was to have power over him and over the world that he had created.

---

1. **scarab beetle.** Black-winged beetle sacred to ancient Egyptians

VISUALIZE

Picturing Ra pushing the sun across the sky helps me understand how Egyptians imagined Ra.

USE TEXT ORGANIZATION

The last sentence hints that someone will gain power over Ra by finding out his secret name.

Reader's resource

The Anishinabe are a group of American Indians who live primarily in Minnesota, Wisconsin, and Canada. They are sometimes called Ojibway people, and they used to be called Chippewa by the government. **"Song of the Thunders"** and **"Song of the Crows"** are Anishinabe dream songs. Dream songs are made up in a dream or just after waking up from one. For Anishinabe people, dreams have a spiritual meaning and are often interpreted as advice to the dreamer. Most dream songs are about animals or nature. In them, the dreamer's *manidó,* or spirit, becomes the animal or natural occurrence.

Word watch

PREVIEW VOCABULARY

pity

Reader's journal

Describe a dream you have had that was especially vivid and memorable.

_____

_____

_____

_____

"SONG OF THE THUNDERS" and
"SONG OF THE CROWS"

from *Chippewa Customs* by Frances Densmore

Active READING STRATEGY

VISUALIZE

Before Reading ➤ **BEGIN VISUALIZING**

❑ Read the Reader's Resource and respond to the Reader's Journal question.
❑ Close your eyes and think of a time you heard thunder. On your own paper, describe the sound and the scene.
❑ Visualize a crow. What words would you use to describe the sight and sound of a crow?
❑ Preview the Sensory Details Chart below. In this chart, you will jot down words that describe your visualizations as you read.

Graphic Organizer: Sensory Details Chart

Sight	Sound	Touch	Taste	Smell

SONG OF THE THUNDERS

Sung by Gágandac'

Na´nǐngo´dinunk	Sometimes
ninbaba´cawen´dan	I go about <u>pitying</u>
Niyau´	Myself
Baba´maciyan´	While I am carried by the wind
Gicǐguñ´	Across the sky ■

VISUALIZE

❑ Listen as your teacher reads aloud "Song of the Thunders." As you listen, make a picture in your mind. Then use the Sensory Details Chart to record details about your mind picture.

❑ Repeat this process for "Song of the Crows."

FIX-UP IDEA

Refocus

If you are having trouble visualizing, use these questions to refocus. What do you think of when you hear the word *pity?* What sound would a self-pitying person make? Think about how thunder would look if you could see it. For the second song, think about what the crow does. Why might this be important? How might the crow's action change how you see the crow? Try visualizing again after you refocus.

words for everyday use

pi • ty (pi´tē) *v.*, feel compassion or sympathy for (someone or something). *After Virginia lost her purse, my mother <u>pitied</u> her and bought her a new one.*

Sung by Henry Selkirk

Be´bani´gani´ . . . . The first to come
Nin´digog´ . . . . I am called
Binĕ´siwûg´ . . . . Among the birds
Nin´wĕndjigi´miw´ûñ´ . . . . I bring the rain
Andeg´nindigo´ . . . . Crow is my name ■

Reflect ON YOUR READING

❑ Use the space below to sketch an image of one of your visualizations or to write a short paragraph describing what you saw.

❑ Discuss your sketch or paragraph with a partner. Ask each other the following questions: How did your visualization for each song make you feel? What new images do you have of thunder and crows after reading these songs?

Reading Skills and Test Practice

COMPARE AND CONTRAST

Discuss with a partner how best to answer the following questions about comparing and contrasting. Use the Think-Aloud Notes to write down your reasons for eliminating the incorrect answers.

____1. In "Song of the Thunders," thunder is compared to a
   a. crow.
   b. sad person.
   c. mighty wind.
   d. booming noise.

____2. What makes a crow different from other birds?
   a. It has a spirit and can sing a song.
   b. It has a name.
   c. It brings the rain.
   d. It comes when called.

How did using the reading strategy help you to answer the questions?

_____

_____

THINK-ALOUD NOTES

_____

_____

_____

_____

_____

_____

_____

_____

_____

_____

_____

Investigate, Inquire, and Imagine

RECALL: GATHER FACTS
1a. In "Song of the Thunders," how does the speaker sometimes feel? What is the crow in "Song of the Crows" called to do?

INTERPRET: FIND MEANING
1b. Who is the speaker of "Song of the Thunders"? How does "Song of the Crows" change the crow's reputation?

ANALYZE: TAKE THINGS APART
2a. Identify how the dreamer of each dream song becomes something or someone else.

SYNTHESIZE: BRING THINGS TOGETHER
2b. How does this help the dreamer to understand nature better?

PERSPECTIVE: LOOK AT OTHER VIEWS
3a. Judging from these two songs, how do the Anishinabe people feel about nature?

EMPATHY: SEE FROM INSIDE
3b. How might the dreamers of these two songs feel about such environmental problems as pollution and the destruction of forests?

Literary Tools

PERSONIFICATION. Personification is a figure of speech in which something not human is described as if it were human.

Whom does the dreamer become in each of these songs? Explain how these songs are examples of personification.

_____

_____

_____

_____

_____

WordWorkshop

HOMOPHONES. A **homophone** is a word that has the same pronunciation as another word but a different meaning, origin, and usually, spelling. The words *their, there,* and *they're* are homophones. For each word below, write at least one homophone and a simple definition for each word.

EXAMPLE
their: belonging to them
there: a place, usually distant from the person speaking
they're: shortened form of *they are*

1. hour _____

   _____

2. rain _____

   _____

3. witch _____

   _____

4. hole _____

   _____

5. bear _____

   _____

Read-Write Connection

Describe the thoughts and emotions you might have if you were a storm cloud. Use your own paper as needed.

_____

_____

Beyond the Reading

READ NATIVE AMERICAN FOLKLORE. Read at least two myths or legends from the Native American oral tradition. Many examples can be found on the Internet and in collections at the library. Then choose the story you like best, and create a children's book that retells it. Include illustrations to show what is happening.

GO ONLINE. To find links and additional activities for this selection, visit the EMC Internet Resource Center at **emcp.com/languagearts** and click on Write-In Reader.

Reader's resource

"The Epic of Gilgamesh" originated as stories that were passed down orally. Eventually, these stories became an epic poem. An **epic** is a long story, often told in verse, that tells of a culture's heroes and gods and reveals its beliefs, values, and way of life. In this case, the epic presents a pessimistic, or gloomy, worldview. Although Gilgamesh is the greatest of heroes, he is unable to bring his fellow humans the one thing he thinks is most important. The most complete version of this epic was found carved into twelve stone tablets. This retelling of the story summarizes the main points of the original epic.

Word watch

PREVIEW VOCABULARY

cower
demur
ebb
intolerable
oppress
strew

talon
tempestuous
transgressor
vain
wrest

Reader's journal

Why do you think humans fear aging and death?

_____

_____

_____

"THE EPIC OF GILGAMESH"

Retold by Christina Kolb

Active READING STRATEGY

WRITE THINGS DOWN

Before Reading ➤ **UNDERSTAND CHRONOLOGICAL ORDER**

❑ **Chronological order** is the order in which events occur in time. The events in "The Epic of Gilgamesh" are mostly told in chronological order, but there is one **flashback**, or part of the story that presents events that happened at an earlier time.
❑ Read the background information in the Reader's Resource.
❑ Preview the two Time Lines below. As you read, you will record the most important events from the story on the appropriate Time Line. Use the first Time Line to record events from Gilgamesh's life and the second Time Line to record events from Utnapishtim's story from an earlier time. You might need to continue the Time Lines on your own paper.

Graphic Organizer: Time Lines

Gilgamesh

Utnapishtim

THE EPIC OF GILGAMESH

Retold by Christina Kolb

Gilgamesh, king of Uruk in southern Babylonia, was two-thirds divine and one-third human. He himself built the great city of Uruk. He was like a wild bull—powerful, bold, and able to best any man in combat. Perhaps because he was so very powerful, Gilgamesh was also arrogant. He drove the people of Uruk too hard, <u>oppressing</u> even the weak. Eventually the people of Uruk, weighed down by their heavy burdens, prayed to the gods for relief. The gods granted the people's prayers and created Enkidu.

Enkidu was a wild man, all covered with hair, and he dwelled with the animals. Enkidu was tamed by a priestess who then urged him to strive against Gilgamesh. Enkidu challenged Gilgamesh and the two wrestled like bulls.

10

During Reading

MAKE A TIME LINE

- ❑ Many of the names in this epic seem hard to pronounce. However, they are all pronounced just as you would expect the letters to sound. Practice reading aloud the names in the Read Aloud box. Being able to say the names in your head will help you read more smoothly.
- ❑ Listen as your teacher reads the first three paragraphs of the epic aloud. As you listen, record events on the Gilgamesh Time Line.
- ❑ Continue to read on your own. As you read, use your Time Lines to write down key events in the order in which they happened. Be sure to notice the flashback to Utnapishtim's story.

READ ALOUD

Gilgamesh (gil' gə mesh)
Enkidu (en' kē dū)
Anu (ä' nū)
Ishtar (ish' tär)
Utnapishtim
  (ùt na pish' təm)
Urshanabit
  (ər shan' ə bət)
Shamash (shä' mesh)

NOTE THE FACTS

What reason does Gilgamesh give for rejecting Ishtar? What does Ishtar, in her anger, insist that Anu do? How does she get him to do it?

_____

_____

_____

_____

Use THE STRATEGY

WRITE THINGS DOWN. What do Enkidu and Gilgamesh do to the Bull of Heaven? How does Ishtar react? Record your answers on your Time Line.

Their fight was long and terrible, but in the end Gilgamesh conquered Enkidu the wild man. From this contest and struggle of bodies emerged the bond of friendship. Together the two brave companions set out seeking adventure. In the cedar forest to the west, they killed Huwawa, a terrible monster who guarded the forest for Enlil, Lord of the Storm.

20

Ishtar saw Gilgamesh's strength and courage, fell in love with him, and asked him to marry her. Gilgamesh, however, slighted the advances of the <u>tempestuous</u> goddess of love and war, saying that Ishtar was never loyal and faithful to those whom she loved. Enraged, Ishtar flew to the heavens to see her father, Anu. She demanded that Anu make a Bull of Heaven to destroy Gilgamesh. Anu <u>demurred</u>, saying that the Bull of Heaven would cause a seven-year period of drought. Ishtar replied, "If you will not make the Bull of Heaven, I will smash the gates to the underworld, and the dead will devour the living."

30

Knowing that Ishtar did not make <u>vain</u> threats, Anu created the Bull of Heaven. Ishtar drove the Bull of Heaven down to Uruk. At the river near the city, the bull snorted, and a hole in the earth opened up and swallowed two hundred men. The bull snorted again, and another two hundred men fell into a chasm[1] in the earth. The bull snorted a third time, and Enkidu seized the horns of the Bull of Heaven. Gilgamesh took his sword and struck the Bull of Heaven in the neck. He slew the bull and then made of it an offering to Shamash.

40

Ishtar mourned the death of the Bull of Heaven and cursed Gilgamesh. Enkidu seized the thigh bone of the bull and threw it in Ishtar's face. Ishtar and the women of her temple gathered to wail over the thigh bone of the Bull of Heaven.[2]

---

1. **chasm.** Deep split in the earth
2. **Ishtar . . . Bull of Heaven.** Ishtar was also sometimes portrayed as a goddess of mourning.

> **words for everyday use**
> tem • pes • tu • ous (tem pes′ chü əs) *adj.,* violent; stormy. *The boat was tossed about by the <u>tempestuous</u> sea.*
> de • mur (di mər′) *v.,* hesitate because of doubts. *We asked him to state his opinion, but he <u>demurred</u>, saying that he had not yet decided how he felt.*
> vain (vān′) *adj.,* without force or effect. *Because Josh did not help Jeremy as he had promised, Jeremy wondered if all Josh's promises were <u>vain</u>.*

The next day, Enkidu told Gilgamesh that he had a
dream. He said, "I dreamed that the gods were in council
50 and Anu said that because we two have killed Huwawa and
the Bull of Heaven, one of us must die. Enlil then said,
'Enkidu must die. Gilgamesh shall not die.' Shamash tried
to save me, but in vain."

Then Enkidu fell down in sickness. Gilgamesh sat by his
sick friend's side. Enkidu's sickness was long. Finally, he
told Gilgamesh, "I dreamed Anzu,[3] who has the paws of a
lion and the <u>talons</u> of an eagle, seized me and overpowered
me. He carried me down to Erkalla's[4] house of darkness,
the house where one goes in and never comes back out, the
60 house of death. I won't die gloriously in battle but in
sickness and in shame." Soon after this dream, Enkidu died.

Gilgamesh wept over Enkidu. Before this time Gilgamesh
had not worried about death, but the passing of Enkidu
made death real and terrifying for him. Gilgamesh cried
out, "My friend, my younger brother, what sleep is this that
has seized you? You have become dark, and you cannot
hear me."

Gilgamesh touched his friend's heart, but it was still.
Gently, Gilgamesh covered his friend's face as if he were a
70 bride. Then Gilgamesh roared with rage, tearing off his
finery. Gilgamesh was like a madman in his grief. He wept
by Enkidu's side for seven days and nights, but his
mourning could not bring Enkidu back to life.

Finally, Gilgamesh got up and began wandering. He
longed to speak with Utnapishtim, his ancestor who
survived the flood and death itself, Utnapishtim who had
been granted eternal life by the gods. Gilgamesh wandered
to the mountains where the sun sets, followed the passage
between the mountains where the sun travels at night, and
80 came at last to a gate. There stood two terrible scorpions.

One scorpion said to the other, "This one is two-thirds god."

---

3. **Anzu.** In Mesopotamian mythology, a terrifying monster
4. **Erkalla.** Another name for Ereshkigal, the queen of the underworld

**words
for
everyday
use**   tal • on (tal' ən) *n.,* claw of a bird of prey. *The eagle seized its prey with its talons.*

Reading STRATEGY
REVIEW

VISUALIZE. Create a mind
movie of what happens
in lines 56–73. What
happens to Enkidu?
How does Gilgamesh feel
about it?

_____

_____

_____

Literary TOOLS

CENTRAL CONFLICT. A **central
conflict** is the main problem
or struggle in the plot of a
poem, story, or play. A
conflict can pit one character
against another character or
against himself or herself. A
character can also come into
conflict with society or with
nature. As you read, try to
identify the central conflict
of "The Epic of Gilgamesh."

His mate answered, "But one-third man."

The first scorpion asked Gilgamesh, "Why have you
journeyed thus far to us?"

Gilgamesh said, "I have come to see my ancestor
Utnapishtim. My friend Enkidu has died, the common lot[5]
of man has claimed him. Men say that Utnapishtim has
found everlasting life."

90 The scorpion said, "No mortal man has journeyed
beyond these mountains. There is only death and darkness
beyond—you will learn nothing and only come to grief."

"I have already known grief," Gilgamesh said. "I will go
on. Open the gate to the mountains!"

The scorpions opened the gate, and Gilgamesh entered
the dark. At long last, he came to the valley of the gods. It
was lovely, full of fruit and <u>strewn</u> with jewels, and
Gilgamesh was overcome by pain, wishing that Enkidu
could see what he was seeing. There, Gilgamesh wept,
crying "Enkidu, Enkidu."

100 Shamash came to Gilgamesh and said, "You will never
find the eternal life for which you are searching."
Gilgamesh, however, would not give up.

Siduri came to Gilgamesh and said, "Gilgamesh, where
are you wandering? You will never find the life you seek.
When the gods created humans, they let death be man's
share and kept life for themselves. Gilgamesh, fill your
belly. Make merry. Dance and feast by day and night. Wear
fresh clothes and bathe in sweet water. Look at the child
who holds your hand, and make your wife happy in your
110 embrace. This is the fitting concern of man."

Gilgamesh said, "How can I give up when Enkidu is dust
and I too shall die and be laid in the ground?"

Siduri then sent Gilgamesh to Urshanabit, the boatman,
who carried Gilgamesh across the sea to Utnapishtim.

"Utnapishtim, my ancestor, I have crossed mountains and
seas to see you. In my heart, my friend has died many

---

5. **lot.** One's fortune in life

**words
for
everyday
use** strew (strü') v., spread by scattering. *The squirrels eat the nuts and <u>strew</u> the shells
across the lawn.* **strewn,** *adj.*

times, but he still seems alive to me. He became dust so suddenly. Is there something more than death? I am so tired, so very tired."

120   Utnapishtim touched Gilgamesh's shoulder. "There is nothing everlasting. Houses fall and floods <u>ebb</u>. The sleeping and the dead are alike—death comes to all, master and servant alike. Only the day of a human's death is unknown."

    Gilgamesh then asked, "If this is so, how did you come to gain eternal life?"

    Utnapishtim began his story. "I lived in Shurrupak, on the banks of the Euphrates.[6] The city was old, and its gods grew old—Anu, the father; Enlil; Ishtar; Ea; and the rest. People were numerous, and they raised noise that disturbed
130 the gods. The gods met in council. Enlil, Lord of the Storm, said, 'The noise raised by these humans is <u>intolerable</u>. Sleep is no longer possible.' Enlil planned to release a mighty flood, and the other gods consented.

    "Ea could not warn mankind, but he whispered to the reeds of the river, and the reeds whispered to me in my sleep. In my dreams, I heard Ea's voice, saying, 'Tear down your house and build a ship. Into the ship, bring the seed of all living creatures.'

    "Who am I to disobey a god? I built an enormous ship,
140 according to Ea's measurements. After six days of working, I completed my ship on the seventh day. I took my family, the seeds of all living animals, and my possessions, and went into the ship. Soon, the tempest roared, and the land was shattered. Even the gods <u>cowered</u> and wept at the storm's fury. Ishtar cried out, 'Why did I cry out for battle in the council of the gods? I have cried out for the destruction of my people, the people to whom I myself gave birth.' The gods sat together and wept, but still the storm raged for six days and seven nights.

150   "On the seventh day, I opened the window of the ship, and light fell on my face. The world was covered with

THINK AND REFLECT

Summarize what the gods and Utnapishtim tell Gilgamesh in answer to his search. **(Synthesize)**

_____

_____

_____

NOTE THE FACTS

Why do the gods plan a flood?

_____

_____

---

6. **Euphrates.** River flowing from Turkey southward to Syria and Iraq

words for everyday use	**ebb** (eb') v., flow back; recede. _When the tide <u>ebbs</u>, we can hunt for shells along the shore._ **in • tol • er • a • ble** (in täl' ər ə bəl) adj., unbearable; too severe or painful to be endured. _We thought that Jessica's rudeness to the new students was <u>intolerable</u>._ **cow • er** (kou' ər) v., crouch or huddle. _The tiny kitten <u>cowered</u> before the barking, snarling dog._

FIX-UP IDEA

Use the Margin Questions

If you are having trouble with your Time Lines, try using the margin questions. These questions will guide you to many of the key events in the story. Then, once you know the answers to the margin questions, reread the epic and fill in additional events.

NOTE THE FACTS

What test does Utnapishtim suggest to Gilgamesh? How does Gilgamesh do on the test?

_____

_____

_____

water, and humanity was dust. There, for a time, I wept. Then I looked for shore. Finally, the ship ran aground against the mountain Nisir. To see if the waters were receding, I sent a dove which returned to me, seeing no place to stand. Then I sent a swallow out to fly. It also returned. Finally, I sent a crow, which saw that the waters had receded and did not return. In gratitude, I made sacrifice to the gods. Ishtar and the other gods approached
160   the offering.

"When Enlil came, he was furious, saying, 'Has life escaped? No humans were to live through this devastation!' Ninurta then blamed Ea for my escape.

"Ea said, 'You sent the flood senselessly, without thinking it through. You should punish evildoers alone. Let the punishment fit the crime. Do not drive the <u>transgressor</u> too hard. Rather than the flood, you should have let lions, wolves, famine, or plague strike down the people. I did not reveal the secret of our council. Utnapishtim received a vision.'
170   "Then Enlil picked up my wife and me, touched our foreheads, and blessed us, saying, 'Before now these have been humans. Now, Utnapishtim and his wife are transformed, being like us gods.' Enlil took us away to live here at the source of the rivers.

"So, Gilgamesh," Utnapishtim concluded. "Who will assemble the gods for you, to grant you eternal life? It is not to be repeated."

Gilgamesh bowed his head.

"If you wish," Utnapishtim said, "you may test yourself.
180   Prevail against sleep for six days and nights." While Gilgamesh sat there, sleep immediately drifted over him like wet fog. Utnapishtim laughed to his wife, "Look at this hero who seeks everlasting life! Sleep steals over him like mist even now!"

Each day that Gilgamesh slept, Utnapishtim's wife placed a fresh loaf of bread by his side. On the seventh day, Utnapishtim touched Gilgamesh and he came alive.

words for everyday use

trans • gres • sor (trans gres' sər) *n.*, one who breaks a law or commandment. *The Code of Hammurabi calls for harsh punishments for <u>transgressors</u> of Mesopotamian laws.*

Gilgamesh protested, "I was barely asleep when you woke me!"

Utnapishtim said, "Come on, Gilgamesh. Count these loaves and discover how many days you have slept. Your first loaf is dry, the second leathery, the third soggy, the fourth white with mold, the fifth gray with mildew, the sixth rotten, and the seventh—you woke."

Gilgamesh said, "What shall I do? Where shall I go? Death is a thief that steals over me. Death is wherever I set my feet."

Utnapishtim took Gilgamesh to Urshanabit, the boatman, to lead him back to his own land. Just as Gilgamesh was leaving, Utnapishtim called out, "You have toiled and worn yourself out, so I will give you a gift to carry back to your own country. I shall reveal to you a great secret. Under the water there grows a plant with deep roots. It will prick your hand like a thorn, but hold on to it. If you succeed in getting that plant, you will have eternal life."

Gilgamesh dove under the waters for the plant and <u>wrested</u> it from the bottom of the sea. Gilgamesh called the plant "The-Old-Man-Will-Be-Made-Young," and he planned to give it to the elders of Uruk and then eat it himself. Once on land, Gilgamesh journeyed for several leagues,[7] making his way toward Uruk. He saw a pool of cool water, and he went down to the water to bathe. A snake smelled the plant and rose out of the water and carried the plant away to eat it. As the snake turned to go back to the water, it shed its skin. Ever since that time, snakes have been able to cast off their skin and become young again, but death has remained the lot of humans.

Gilgamesh cried, "For whom have I labored? For whom has my heart's blood dried? I have not brought a blessing on myself. I did the lowly snake a good service."

Gilgamesh sat down and wept bitter tears. ■

NOTE THE FACTS

What gift does Gilgamesh receive from Utnapishtim? What happens to this gift?

_____

_____

_____

---

7. **leagues.** Units of measure

words for everyday use

wrest (rest') v., pull or force away violently with a twisting motion. *The small child finally <u>wrested</u> his favorite toy away from the other child.*

Reflect ON YOUR READING

After Reading ➤ **REVIEW WHAT YOU WROTE**

❏ Look back over your Time Lines. Cross out any events that you no longer think are significant. Circle two or three events that you think are most important to the story.
❏ Discuss your Time Lines with a partner. If you circled different events, explain to your partner why you chose the events you did. Then listen to your partner's explanation.

Reading Skills and Test Practice

PUT EVENTS IN SEQUENCE

Discuss with a partner how best to answer the following questions about the organization of the selection. Use the Think-Aloud Notes to write down your reasons for eliminating the incorrect answers.

____1. At what point does Shamash tell Gilgamesh that he will never find eternal life?
    a. after Gilgamesh speaks with Utnapishtim
    b. before Enkidu dies
    c. after Gilgamesh enters the gate between the mountains
    d. before Gilgamesh falls asleep

____2. What does Ishtar do after Gilgamesh refuses to marry her?
    a. sends a flood to destroy all human beings
    b. makes a beast to kill Gilgamesh
    c. wanders in the wilderness
    d. demands that a bull be made to destroy Gilgamesh

How did using the reading strategy help you to answer the questions?

_____

_____

THINK-ALOUD NOTES

Investigate, Inquire, and Imagine

RECALL: GATHER FACTS →
1a. Who is Utnapishtim, and what unusual quality does he possess? What two challenges does he give Gilgamesh?

INTERPRET: FIND MEANING
1b. How is Gilgamesh successful or unsuccessful in meeting Utnapishtim's challenges? What does his success or failure suggest about human beings?

ANALYZE: TAKE THINGS APART →
2a. What errors or impulsive actions do Gilgamesh and Enkidu commit, and why? What are the consequences of these actions?

SYNTHESIZE: BRING THINGS TOGETHER
2b. What natural phenomenon does this story express? What view of humans does this story express? How would you describe the gods in this story?

EVALUATE: MAKE JUDGMENTS →
3a. Shamash states that the "fitting concern of" humans is to "fill your belly. Make merry. Dance and feast by day and night. Look at the child who holds your hand, and make your [partner] happy. . . ." Do you agree? In other words, do you think the role of humans is simply to enjoy life on earth? What other purposes, if any, do you think humans should strive to fulfill?

EXTEND: CONNECT IDEAS
3b. Medical science has enabled humans to live longer lives. Do you think we should use technology to extend our lives forever, if that becomes a possibility? Why, or why not? What might society be like if we all had eternal life? What would be the advantages and disadvantages of immortality?

Literary Tools

CENTRAL CONFLICT. A **central conflict** is the main problem or struggle in the plot of a poem, story, or play. A conflict can pit one character against another character or against him or herself. A character can also come into conflict with society or with nature. What is the central conflict of "The Epic of Gilgamesh"? What event introduces this conflict? How is this conflict resolved?

_____

_____

_____

_____

WordWorkshop

CLASSIFYING VOCABULARY WORDS. One way to learn and remember vocabulary words is to classify them, or sort them into groups based on some shared characteristic. Below is a list of words from "The Epic of Gilgamesh." Review the meaning of each word by finding it in context in the story or by looking it up in a dictionary. Then sort the words into categories. You can add more categories if you need them. Finally, label each category with a name.

combat	mortal	talon
cower	mourn	tempest
demur	oppress	tempestuous
devour	prevail	transgressor
divine	recede	vain
ebb	slight	wrest
intolerable	strew	

Read-Write Connection

Imagine that you lived at the time of this story. How would you feel about the gods?

_____

_____

_____

_____

_____

_____

Beyond the Reading

COMPARE STORIES. You might have noticed that the story Utnapishtim tells Gilgamesh is similar to the story of Noah and the ark. Scholars have long discussed the similarities and differences between these stories. Find a version of the story of Noah in the Bible or elsewhere. Read the story. Then write an essay comparing and contrasting Utnapishtim's experience to Noah's. For example, you might consider how each character finds out about the flood, what the purpose of the flood is in each case, what the characters must do in response, how long the flood lasts, and how they find out that dry land has surfaced.

GO ONLINE. To find links and additional activities for this selection, visit the EMC Internet Resource Center at **emcp.com/languagearts** and click on Write-In Reader.

"The Secret Name of Ra"

Retold by Geraldine Harris

Active READING STRATEGY

MAKE PREDICTIONS

Before Reading ➤ **GATHER INFORMATION**

❏ Read the title and look at the image on page 170.
❏ Read the background information in the Reader's Resource, and respond to the Reader's Journal question.
❏ Preview the Predictions Chart below. Using the information you gathered from the other Before Reading activities, make a prediction about what will happen in this story. Write your predictions and the clues you used to make them in the chart.

Graphic Organizer: Predictions Chart

Predictions	Clues	Adjustments to Predictions

CONNECT

Reader's resource

Like the Mesopotamians, the Egyptians worshiped many gods. Many gods of Egyptian myths either die or come close to death even though they are immortal. This might seem impossible, but ancient Egyptians were used to accepting many different explanations of things as equally true and possible. For example, they believed that the pharaoh was the son of Ra, the sun god and king of all the gods. They also believed, however, that the pharaoh was the reincarnation of Horus, the son of Isis and Osiris. In this retelling of **"The Secret Name of Ra,"** you will discover how Horus became linked to Ra.

Word watch

PREVIEW VOCABULARY

abyss	exalt
cunning	quiver
deity	sole
drivel	summon
envoy	virile

Reader's journal

When, if ever, is tricking someone acceptable?

_____

_____

_____

_____

During Reading

MAKE PREDICTIONS

- ❏ Listen as your teacher reads the first two paragraphs of the myth aloud. Think about how the information in these paragraphs affects your first prediction. Adjust the prediction as necessary, or make a new prediction.
- ❏ Take turns reading the rest of the selection with a partner. Pause after each paragraph to adjust predictions and make new ones. You may discuss your predictions with your partner as you go.

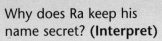

THINK AND REFLECT

Why does Ra keep his name secret? **(Interpret)**

_____

_____

_____

The SECRET Name of Ra

Retold by Geraldine Harris

Ra, the <u>Sole</u> Creator was visible to the people of Egypt as the disc of the sun, but they knew him in many other forms. He could appear as a crowned man, a falcon or a man with a falcon's head and, as the scarab beetle[1] pushes a round ball of dung in front of it, the Egyptians pictured Ra as a scarab pushing the sun across the sky. In caverns deep below the earth were hidden another seventy-five forms of Ra: mysterious beings with mummified bodies[2] and heads consisting of birds or snakes, feathers or flowers. The names of Ra were as numerous as his forms; he was the Shining One, The Hidden One, The Renewer of the Earth, The Wind in the Souls, The <u>Exalted</u> One, but there was one name of the Sun God which had not been spoken since time began. To know this secret name of Ra was to have power over him and over the world that he had created.

Isis longed for such a power. She had dreamed that one day she would have a marvellous falcon-headed son called Horus and she wanted the throne of Ra to give to her child. Isis was the Mistress of Magic, wiser than millions of men, but she

10

20

---

1. **scarab beetle.** Black-winged beetle held sacred by ancient Egyptians
2. **mummified bodies.** Bodies that have been preserved by removing the internal organs and adding a special substance to keep the body from disintegrating

words for everyday use

sole (sōl') adj., only. *Fishing was Lucrecia's sole interest.*
ex • alt (eg zôlt') v., praise; glorify; worship. *People in ancient Babylon exalted their city-god Marduk.*

knew that nothing in creation was powerful enough to harm
its creator. Her only chance was to turn the power of Ra
against himself and at last Isis thought of a cruel and <u>cunning</u>
plan. Every day the Sun God walked through his kingdom,
30   attended by a crowd of spirits and lesser <u>deities</u>, but Ra was
growing old. His eyes were dim, his step no longer firm and
he had even begun to <u>drivel</u>.

One morning Isis mingled with a group of minor goddesses
and followed behind the King of the Gods. She watched the
face of Ra until she saw his saliva drip onto a clod of earth.
When she was sure that no-one was taking any notice of her,
she scooped up the earth and carried it away. Isis mixed the
earth with the saliva of Ra to form clay and modelled a
wicked-looking serpent. Through the hours of darkness she
40   whispered spells over the clay serpent as it lay lifeless in her
hands. Then the cunning goddess carried it to a crossroads on
the route which the Sun God always took. She hid the
serpent in the long grass and returned to her palace.

The next day Ra came walking through his kingdom with
the spirits and lesser deities crowding behind him. When
he approached the crossroads, the spells of Isis began to
work and the clay serpent <u>quivered</u> into life. As the Sun
God passed, it bit him in the ankle and crumbled back into
earth. Ra gave a scream that was heard through all creation.
50   His jaws chattered and his limbs shook as the poison
flooded through him like a rising Nile. "I have been wounded
by something deadly," whispered Ra. "I know that in my
heart, though my eyes cannot see it. Whatever it was, I, the
Lord of Creation, did not make it. I am sure that none of you
would have done such a terrible thing to me, but I have never
felt such pain! How can this have happened to me? I am the
Sole Creator, the child of the watery <u>abyss</u>. I am the god with
a thousand names, but my secret name was only spoken once,
before time began. Then it was hidden in my body so that

words for everyday use

cun • ing (kun′ iŋ) _adj._, clever; sly; crafty. _Foxes are known for their <u>cunning</u> ability to escape from hunters._

de • i • ty (dē′ ə tē) _n._, god or goddess. _Isis was one of the <u>deities</u> worshiped by the ancient Egyptians._

driv • el (driv′ əl) _v._, drool. _When our dog knows it is dinnertime, he hungrily <u>drivels</u>._

qui • ver (kwiv′ ər) _v._, shake or tremble. _The thought of going up to the attic alone made the small child <u>quiver</u> with fear._

a • byss (ə bis′) _n._, anything too deep for measurement; ocean depths. _The hole was so deep it seemed a bottomless <u>abyss</u>._

FIX-UP IDEA

Tackle Difficult Vocabulary

If you are having trouble understanding the myth, try tackling difficult vocabulary. Use the definitions in Words for Everyday Use, but also try to figure out word meanings from familiar word parts and context clues. For example, look at the word *Ennead* in line 66. How do the sentences that follow explain the meaning of that unfamiliar word?

Use THE STRATEGY

MAKE PREDICTIONS. What offer does Isis make to Ra? Predict what will happen as a result. Don't turn the page until you have written a new prediction.

60 no-one should ever learn it and be able to work spells against me. Yet as I walked through my kingdom something struck at me and now my heart is on fire and my limbs shake. Send for the Ennead! Send for my children! They are wise in magic and their knowledge pierces heaven."

Messengers hurried to the great gods and from the four pillars of the world came the Ennead: Shu and Tefenet, Geb and Nut, Seth and Osiris, Isis and Nephthys. <u>Envoys</u> traveled the land and the sky and the watery abyss to <u>summon</u> all the deities created by Ra. From the marshes came frog-headed

70 Heket, Wadjet the cobra goddess and the fearsome god, crocodile-headed Sobek. From the deserts came fiery Selkis, the scorpion goddess, Anubis the jackal, the guardian of the dead and Nekhbet the vulture goddess. From the cities of the north came warlike Neith, gentle cat-headed Bastet, fierce lion-headed Sekhmet and Ptah the god of crafts. From the cities of the south came Onuris, the divine huntsman and ram-headed Khnum with Anukis his wife and Satis his daughter. Cunning Thoth and wise Seshat, goddess of writing; <u>virile</u> Min and snake-headed Renenutet, goddess of

80 the harvest, kindly Meskhenet and monstrous Taweret, goddesses of birth—all of them were summoned to the side of Ra.

The gods and goddesses gathered around the Sun God, weeping and wailing, afraid that he was going to die. Isis stood among them beating her breast and pretending to be as distressed and bewildered as all the other frightened deities.

"Father of All," she began, "whatever is the matter? Has some snake bitten you? Has some wretched creature dared to strike at his Creator? Few of the gods can compare with me

90 in wisdom and I am the Mistress of Magic. If you will let me help you, I'm sure that I can cure you."

Ra was grateful to Isis and told her all that had happened. "Now I am colder than water and hotter than fire," complained the Sun God. "My eyes darken. I cannot see the sky and my body is soaked by the sweat of fever."

words for everyday use

en • voy (än′ voi′) *n.*, messenger. *The <u>envoy</u> delivered the king's message to the ruler of the distant land.*
sum • mon (sum′ ən) *v.*, call together; order to appear. *The sick man <u>summoned</u> a doctor to his home.*
vir • ile (vir′ əl) *adj.*, having strength; forceful. *Neo is so <u>virile</u> in* The Matrix *movies that he can fight many opponents at once.*

"Tell me your full name," said cunning Isis. "Then I can use it in my spells. Without that knowledge the greatest of magicians cannot help you."

"I am the maker of heaven and earth," said Ra. "I made the heights and the depths, I set horizons at east and west and established the gods in their glory. When I open my eyes it is light; when I close them it is dark. The mighty Nile floods at my command. The gods do not know my true name but I am the maker of time, the giver of festivals. I spark the fire of life. At dawn I rise as Khepri, the scarab and sail across the sky in the Boat of Millions of Years. At noon I blaze in the heavens as Ra and at evening I am Ra-atum, the setting sun."

"We know all that," said Isis. "If I am to find a spell to drive out this poison, I will have to use your secret name. Say your name and live."

"My secret name was given to me so that I could sit at ease," moaned Ra, "and fear no living creature. How can I give it away?"

Isis said nothing and knelt beside the Sun God while his pain mounted. When it became unbearable, Ra ordered the other gods to stand back while he whispered his secret name to Isis. "Now the power of the secret name has passed from my heart to your heart," said Ra wearily. "In time you can give it to your son, but warn him never to betray the secret!"

Isis nodded and began to chant a great spell that drove the poison out of the limbs of Ra and he rose up stronger than before. The Sun God returned to the Boat of Millions of Years and Isis shouted for joy at the success of her plan. She knew now that one day Horus her son would sit on the throne of Egypt and wield the power of Ra. ■

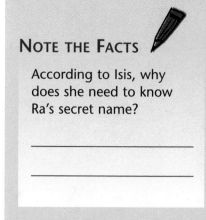

NOTE THE FACTS

According to Isis, why does she need to know Ra's secret name?

_____

_____

THINK AND REFLECT

Why does Isis cure Ra rather than let him die? **(Synthesize)**

_____

_____

_____

Reflect ON YOUR READING

After Reading ➤ ASSESS YOUR PREDICTIONS

❑ Review your list of predictions. Put a star next to every prediction you were right about. Put a check next to every prediction in which you changed your ideas from a previous prediction.

❑ Discuss your chart with a partner. Talk about which clues in the story led you to make the predictions.

Reading Skills and Test Practice

IDENTIFY MAIN IDEAS

Discuss with a partner how best to answer the following questions about main ideas. Use the Think-Aloud Notes to write down your reasons for eliminating the incorrect answers.

_____1. Why did Isis want to know Ra's secret name?
    a. She wanted his power for herself.
    b. She wanted to destroy him.
    c. She needed to know it to save her own life.
    d. She wanted his power for her son.

_____2. Why did Ra reveal his secret name?
    a. His children demanded to know.
    b. He thought he was dying.
    c. He was delirious.
    d. He never revealed it.

How did using the reading strategy help you to answer the questions?

_____

_____

Investigate, Inquire, and Imagine

RECALL: GATHER FACTS
1a. What are some of the forms and names Ra took? What is the one thing that could take away this god's power? What is beginning to happen to Ra?

INTERPRET: FIND MEANING
1b. Is Ra a powerful god? Why, or why not?

ANALYZE: TAKE THINGS APART
2a. What human qualities do Ra and Isis have? What godlike qualities do they have?

SYNTHESIZE: BRING THINGS TOGETHER
2b. What effect do you think seeing a god at his or her weakest, or most human, had on his or her worshipers? Explain.

EVALUATE: MAKE JUDGMENTS
3a. Evaluate how Isis went about getting what she wanted. Do you think her actions are understandable? Are they acceptable? Why, or why not?

EXTEND: CONNECT IDEAS
3b. What other ways might Isis have gone about getting what she wanted?

Literary Tools

MOTIVE. A **motive** is a reason for acting in a certain way. What was Isis's motive for offering to heal Ra?

_____

_____

_____

What was Ra's motive in refusing to tell his secret name?

_____

_____

_____

WordWorkshop

WRITING ABOUT VOCABULARY WORDS. Writing and thinking about the concepts behind vocabulary words can help you remember the words and their meanings. Answer the following questions. Make sure your answers show your understanding of the meaning of the italicized words.

1. Describe a *cunning* act by you or someone you know.

   _____

   _____

2. If someone calls your ideas *drivel,* what are they really saying? Explain.

   _____

3. Why might the notion of an *abyss* make someone *quiver?*

   _____

4. Can a person have more than one *sole* passion? Explain why or why not.

   _____

   _____

5. Of the gods and goddesses you have learned about so far in this unit, who would you say is the most *virile?* Why?

   _____

Read-Write Connection

How might people today have a "secret name"? In other words, is there any essential part of each person that he or she cannot give away? Explain.

_____

_____

Beyond the Reading

READ ABOUT ANCIENT EGYPT. Find a book about ancient Egypt. You might choose to read nonfiction about pyramids, mythology, or mummies, or you might find a book of historical fiction set in Egypt long ago. Write a synopsis, or summary, of the book, and share your findings with the class.

GO ONLINE. To find links and additional activities for this selection, visit the EMC Internet Resource Center at **emcp.com/languagearts** and click on Write-In Reader.

"Why the Sky Is Far Away from the Earth"

Retold by Fitzgerald Iyamabo

Active READING STRATEGY

USE TEXT ORGANIZATION

Before Reading ➡ **UNDERSTAND CAUSE-AND-EFFECT ORGANIZATION**

❏ "Why the Sky Is Far Away from the Earth" is a Yoruban myth. A **myth** is a story that explains the beginnings of things in the natural world. Myths generally use cause-and-effect organization because they deal with how things came to be the way they are, in other words, what caused certain natural phenonena. As you read this myth, you should watch for signal words such as *why, then, even worse, caused, as a result,* and *because,* which signal causes and effects.

❏ Read the background information in the Reader's Resource.

❏ Preview the Actions and Consequences Chart below. As you read, you will use this chart to track the people's actions and the consequences of those actions.

Graphic Organizer: Actions and Consequences Chart

Actions	Consequences

CONNECT

Reader's resource

The Yoruba people are the second largest ethnic group in Nigeria, a West African nation. They have lived in that region since prehistoric times. According to Yoruban mythology, the people were descended from a creator god named Oduduwa. By the 1600s, the Yoruba had developed a vast empire covering hundreds of miles. Slavery and the influence of British colonists in Africa brought down this empire, but 17 million Yorubans still live in and around Nigeria. The Yoruban culture is known for its artwork and rich, complex oral tradition. **"Why the Sky Is Far Away from the Earth"** is a myth from that tradition.

Reader's journal

What does greed mean to you? Write a definition of greed and give examples.

_____

_____

_____

_____

_____

_____

_____

_____

USE TEXT ORGANIZATION

❑ Listen as your teacher reads the first two paragraphs of the myth aloud. Write actions that people take in the left column of your chart. Write consequences of these actions in the right column.

❑ Read the third paragraph aloud. Underline signal words, and then record actions and consequences in your chart.

❑ Read the rest of the selection on your own. Watch for signal words, and stop after each paragraph to record actions and consequences in your chart.

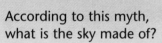

NOTE THE FACTS

According to this myth, what is the sky made of?

_____

_____

READ ALOUD

Read aloud the highlighted paragraph. What is the worst thing the people did?

_____

_____

WHY the Sky is far away from the earth

Retold by Fitzgerald Iyamabo

L et me tell you a story my grandfather told me. It is a story his grandfather told him, and his own grandfather before him. Back in those days, in the ancient kingdom of Benin in present-day Nigeria, the sky wasn't far away from the earth. If an adult stood up straight and stretched his hand, he could touch the sky. Why, you ask? Well, the sky was made of the sweetest food you ever imagined. It tasted something like the sweetest croissant with honey baked into it, only better. And it was very light

10 and fluffy.

Anyway, people did not need to go looking for food every day because the sky was there, so of course there were no hunters or farmers back then. Then, however, people started to get greedy and wasteful. Often they cut off more of the sky than they needed. The sylphs and fairies that tended the sky warned them not to do so, but no one listened. They warned them that if they kept wasting the food, a day would come when the Owner of the sky would take back His gift. But still no one listened.

20 Even worse, people also started to kill the innocent animals that lived in the forest. They had gotten tired of eating the sky every day, and they decided that they wanted meat. The gnomes that worked in the forest were distressed. They warned the people to stop killing Osanobua's[1] creatures, but they continued killing and

_____

1. **Osanobua.** Almighty God

eating the animals. Worse yet, they also wasted the meat. They would kill an antelope, for instance, eat a little bit of it, and throw the rest away or let it go bad. So the poor creature would lose its life for nothing.

30   One day a hunter (and there were now hunters among the Binis[2]) was returning from a hunt. Listen to this. He had an elephant on his back, an antelope in his bag, and a rabbit in each hand. When he heard a small cricket chirping in the sand, he wanted that as well! He started digging for it with his big toe. This was too much for Eshu,[3] the mischievous one. He caused the hunter to stumble and fall under the weight of the elephant. He was crushed by the elephant and died immediately. The people were frightened by this, which was a lesson that greed can

40   get you in trouble.

But you see, people forget things quickly. Very soon, they had gone back to their old ways. Osanobua, the patient One, watched sadly as the people continued to disobey Him. But even the patient will one day lose his patience. One day a pregnant woman cut off a large piece of the sky. When she took it into her house, her husband warned her that she might not be able to eat the whole thing, but she reminded him that she was pregnant and eating for two. After a while, she realized that she would not be able to eat

50   everything. She called her husband, and he started to help, but they still couldn't finish it. Frightened, they called their neighbors to help. It seemed that the more food they ate, the more remained. Very soon the whole village was eating, but they soon knew it would be impossible to finish the food.

By this time it was night, so they went into the bush and quietly buried what was left. They thought that in this way they would not be found out, as if you can hide from the all-seeing Eye of Osanobua! Anyway, they woke up the next

60   morning relieved that nothing seemed to have gone wrong. The pregnant woman was the first to go outside her house. Her husband was still inside when he heard her shriek loudly. He rushed outside, and what he saw made his heart

---

2. **Binis.** Traditional name for Edo people
3. **Eshu.** Messenger and trickster god

FIX-UP IDEA

Retell
If you have trouble identifying the actions and consequences in this myth, stop at the end of each paragraph and retell the information you just read in your own words. If you can't retell the information from the paragraph, go back and reread it. Once you can retell the paragraph without leaving out important information, identify the actions in the paragraph. Then identify the consequences, if any, of those actions. Write both in your chart.

THINK AND REFLECT

Why are the people afraid? (Interpret)

_____

_____

start pounding in fear. The sky was no longer there. Then he looked upward, and many, many miles away, he saw the sky. They both started crying loudly, along with the other people who had gathered there, but it was too late.

70   Then a loud Voice boomed from above: "For years you have enjoyed the many gifts that I gave to you, but you did not think you had to obey my instructions on how to enjoy these gifts. I will still bless you with food, but now you will have to work for it. Because you did the opposite of my will, instead of getting food from above, you will get it from below. You will till the ground until your body aches, before I permit any food to appear. So shall it be from this day forth."

The people cried bitterly, but it was too late. And from that day forth, my friends, the sky has remained far from us, and we have had to depend on the soil for our food. So

80   now you know. Greed will always bring grief, whether it concerns food, riches, attention from others, or anything else. We are allowed only our fair share and no more. ■

Reflect ON YOUR READING

❑ Share your chart with a partner. What does the myth explain?
❑ On the lines below, write a summary of the explanation in this myth. Use details from the myth to support your answer.

_____

_____

_____

_____

Reading Skills and Test Practice

IDENTIFY CAUSE AND EFFECT

READ, THINK, AND EXPLAIN. Discuss with a partner how best to answer the following questions about cause and effect. Use the Think-Aloud Notes to write down your ideas before drafting your answers.

1. What characteristic of people does the narrator say caused their misfortune? Give examples from the text that demonstrate this characteristic.

_____

_____

_____

_____

2. Why do the people have to get food from below instead of above?

_____

_____

_____

REFLECT ON YOUR RESPONSE. Compare your answer to that of your partner or another student. How did using the reading strategy help you to answer these questions?

_____

_____

THINK-ALOUD NOTES

_____

_____

_____

_____

_____

_____

_____

_____

_____

_____

Investigate, Inquire, and Imagine

RECALL: GATHER FACTS   →   INTERPRET: FIND MEANING
1a. What happens to the hunter in this myth, and why?

1b. What explanation does this story offer of the origins of hunting and farming?

ANALYZE: TAKE THINGS APART   →   SYNTHESIZE: BRING THINGS TOGETHER
2a. Order the crimes of the people of Benin from least harmful to worst, according to how they are presented in the story.

2b. What punishment do the people receive for their crimes? What lesson does this story teach?

EVALUATE: MAKE JUDGMENTS   →   EXTEND: CONNECT IDEAS
3a. Do you agree with the story's interpretation of each crime's seriousness? Which crime do you think is the worst, and why?

3b. Do you think the lesson of this story is still valuable in our society today? If so, why? Where do you see people making the same mistake as the people of Benin? What are the consequences of their actions?

Literary Tools

MOTIF. A **motif** is anything that appears repeatedly in one or more works of literature, art, or music. One of the most common motifs in mythology involves a golden age ruined by human wickedness. What golden age is described in this Yoruban myth, and how is it ruined?

_____

_____

Can you think of other stories that share this motif?

_____

_____

WordWorkshop

WORD ORIGINS. Words have come into the English language from many other languages. Use a dictionary to find the language that gave English each of the following words from "Why the Sky Is Far Away from the Earth." Then write a paragraph that uses all of the words.

1. croissant: _____

2. sylph: _____

3. antelope: _____

4. elephant: _____

5. village: _____

_____

_____

_____

_____

_____

_____

Read-Write Connection

Why do you think the people in this story take more than they need?

_____

_____

_____

_____

Beyond the Reading

READ AFRICAN FOLK LITERATURE. Read several myths, legends, or folk tales from African cultures. Pick one tale that you especially like. Practice telling the story out loud, using gestures, facial expressions, and tone of voice to make the retelling fun. Then, with your classmates, organize an African storytelling festival for younger children in your school district.

GO ONLINE. To find links and additional activities for this selection, visit the EMC Internet Resource Center at **emcp.com/languagearts** and click on Write-In Reader.

Reader's resource

In Shinto, the ancient native religion of Japan, Amaterasu is the goddess of the sun. Until 1946, all emperors of Japan were considered to be gods descended from Amaterasu. It is said that when the first emperor, Jimmu, took power in 660 BC, Amaterasu gave him her mirror as proof that he was divine. Today, the mirror is believed to be in Amaterasu's shrine, or the place where she is worshiped. In this retelling of "**Amaterasu,**" you will learn about the origin of this mirror.

Reader's journal

When you are afraid or upset, do you prefer to be alone or with others? Explain.

_____

_____

_____

_____

_____

_____

_____

"Amaterasu"

Retold by Carolyn Swift

Active READING STRATEGY

READ WITH A PURPOSE

Before Reading ▶ **SET A PURPOSE**

❏ Read the background information in the Reader's Resource.
❏ Your purpose for reading this myth will be to learn about the character of the goddess Amaterasu.
❏ Preview the Cluster Chart below. In this chart, you will record details about Amaterasu from the myth. Look for what the narrator tells you about Amaterasu, what you learn about her from other characters, and what you can infer from her actions and the things she says. You may add as many circles as you need.

Graphic Organizer: Cluster Chart

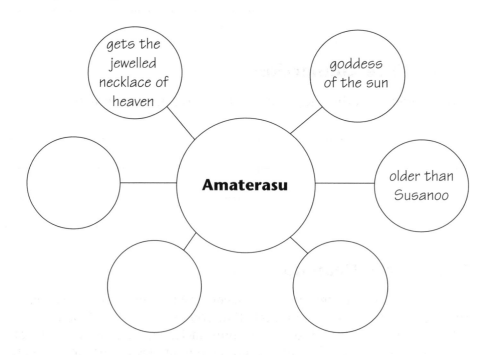

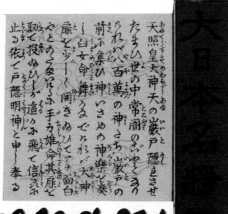

Amaterasu

Retold by Carolyn Swift

During Reading

READ WITH A PURPOSE

- ❑ Listen as your teacher reads the first five paragraphs of the myth aloud. Record information about Amaterasu in your Cluster Chart.
- ❑ Read the rest of the selection on your own. Keep track of details and ideas about Amaterasu in your chart.

Back in the mists of time there lived a boy called Susanoo. His father and mother were the first people on earth, but then his father became Lord of the Heavens and his mother Lady of the Underworld.

Susanoo himself lived with his brothers and sisters on the bridge which linked heaven and earth, but he was always complaining. He complained about not being able to visit his mother, even though his father explained to him that if he once went to the underworld he would never be able to

10 come back, and he complained even more when his sister Amaterasu was given the jewelled necklace of heaven and made goddess of the sun, while he was given only corals and made god of the sea. Finally his father became sick of his constant moanings and groanings.

"I don't want to see your face around Heaven any more," he told him. "You have the whole earth and sea to play around in so there's no need for you to make all our lives a misery up here."

"Oh, all right," Susanoo grumbled, "but first I must say

20 goodbye to Amaterasu."

So off he stumped to look for her. Being in a bad mood, he shook every mountain he passed so that rocks crashed down the slopes, and he stamped his feet so that the earth quaked. Hearing all the noise, Amaterasu was frightened. She took up her bow and arrow so that, when her younger brother arrived, he found himself facing the drawn bow of a fierce-looking warrior.

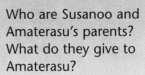

NOTE THE FACTS

Who are Susanoo and Amaterasu's parents? What do they give to Amaterasu?

_____

_____

NOTE THE FACTS

What physical effects did Susanoo's mood have on the world around him? How did Amaterasu look when he found her?

_____

_____

"You can put that thing down," he told her. "I come in peace."

30 "Prove it," she said suspiciously, not taking her eyes off him.

Susanoo handed her his sword. She took it from him and broke it into three pieces. Then, before he could complain, she blew on them and turned them into three beautiful little girls.

"One day these three little daughters of mine will bring new life into the world," she told him, "while your sword could only have brought death."

"I can do better than that!" Susanoo boasted. "Give me 40 the necklaces you're wearing."

So Amaterasu unclasped the five necklaces and gave them to her brother. Then he blew on them and turned them into five little boys.

"Now I have five sons," he said.

"They were made out of my necklaces so they should be my sons!" Amaterasu snapped.

"But your daughters were made from my sword," Susanoo argued.

"That's different!" Amaterasu told him.

50 At that Susanoo lost his temper. He tore up all the rice fields that Amaterasu had been carefully ripening and caused such destruction that the frightened goddess ran and hid in a cave, blocking the entrance with a large stone.

Because Amaterasu was the sun goddess, this meant that the world was suddenly plunged into darkness. Without the sun's heat the land became very cold and nothing grew in field or forest. Worse still, the evil spirits took advantage of the darkness to get up to all sorts of wickedness. It was a disaster. Something had to be done, so all the good spirits 60 gathered together in a dry river bed to try to decide what to do.

"We must tempt Amaterasu to come out of the cave," said one.

"And block up the entrance the minute she does, so she can't go back into it again," added another.

"But what would tempt her to come out?" asked a third.

"We must put everything she likes most outside," replied the first.

"And what does she like most?" the third asked.

70 "Seeing her sunny face reflected in the lake," answered a fourth.

"But we can't bring the lake up to the cave!" objected the third.

"Then we must make something that will reflect her face the way the lake does and put that outside the cave," suggested a fifth.

"I don't know what we could make that would do that," the third grumbled, "and anyway, how will she know it's there unless we can get her to come out of the cave in the

80 first place?"

At that they all looked thoughtful. No one spoke for a while.

"I know!" the second suddenly shouted in triumph. "She always used to come out every morning as soon as she heard the cock crow. We must get all the cocks to crow outside the cave."

So they all put their heads together to try to think what would reflect the sun like the waters of the lake. After trying all sort of things in vain, they finally managed to

90 invent a mirror, or looking-glass. This they hung from the branch of a japonica tree[1] immediately opposite the cave and, knowing Amaterasu's fondness for jewellery, they hung jewelled necklaces from the other branches.

When all was ready, they gathered outside the cave with every cock they could find. First they chanted prayers. Then they gave the signal and all the cocks began to crow. Not satisfied with that, everyone present began to sing and dance, led by the goddess Ama no Uzume[2] doing a tap-dance on an upturned tub.

100 Wondering what all the noise was about, Amaterasu peeped out of the cave and at once saw her own face reflected in the mirror. She had never seen a looking-glass before, so she thought the people must have found another sun to replace her and ran from the cave in a rage. The others immediately stretched ropes across the mouth of the cave to stop her from going back into it again, but there

---

1. **japonica tree.** Any tree, shrub, or plant associated with the Far East
2. **Ama no Uzume.** Goddess of dawn and mirth

Use THE STRATEGY

READ WITH A PURPOSE. What does Amaterasu like more than anything? What does this tell you about her character? Record your answers in the Cluster Chart.

FIX-UP IDEA

Refocus
If you are having trouble focusing on the character of Amaterasu, try refocusing on the conflict of the story. Review the definition of *central* on page 162. Then, as you read, look for the conflict. How is it introduced? How is it resolved?

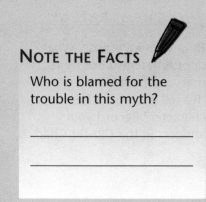

110 was no need. By then she had discovered that it was her own shining face looking back at her. She was delighted by this and by the necklaces, as well as the singing and dancing for, truth to tell, she had begun to feel lonely in her cave. So once more the sun's bright rays lit the earth and the trees and flowers and rice began to grow again in its heat. Then everyone suddenly remembered the cause of all the trouble.

"If Susanoo had stayed out of heaven when his father told him to, this would never have happened!" they shouted angrily, and went off in a body to look for him. When they found him, they cut off his pigtail as punishment and threw him out of heaven by force. ■

Reflect ON YOUR READING

After Reading ➤ SUMMARIZE WHAT YOU LEARNED

❑ Review your Cluster Chart.
❑ Work with a partner to answer the following questions: What kind of person is Amaterasu? How can you tell? Make notes about your answers on the lines below.

_____

_____

_____

_____

Reading Skills and Test Practice

ANALYZE CHARACTER

READ, THINK, AND EXPLAIN. Discuss with a partner how best to answer the following question about character. Use the Think-Aloud Notes to write down your ideas before drafting your answers.

Discuss the shortcomings or character flaws shown by Amaterasu. Use details and information from the story to support your ideas.

_____

_____

_____

_____

_____

_____

REFLECT ON YOUR RESPONSE. How did using the reading strategy help you to answer this question?

_____

_____

Investigate, Inquire, and Imagine

RECALL: GATHER FACTS
1a. Why does Amaterasu hide in the cave? What plan do the good spirits develop to draw her out?

INTERPRET: FIND MEANING
1b. Why are the good spirits so concerned about Amaterasu staying in the cave? Does Amaterasu mind being tricked? How can you tell?

ANALYZE: TAKE THINGS APART
2a. What does Susanoo do when he is angry? What happens when Amaterasu goes into the cave? What natural occurrences might cause these results?

SYNTHESIZE: BRING THINGS TOGETHER
2b. What might this story be trying to explain about the natural world?

EVALUATE: MAKE JUDGMENTS
3a. Do you agree with the spirits who blamed the trouble on Susanoo? Why, or why not?

EXTEND: CONNECT IDEAS
3b. In what other ways might Susanoo have dealt with his feelings?

Literary Tools

CHARACTERIZATION. Characterization is the act of creating a character. Writers create characters by showing what characters say, do, and think; by showing what other characters (and the narrator) say about them; and by showing what physical features, dress, and personality the characters display. In your Cluster Chart for this selection, you recorded the characterization of Amaterasu. How would you describe Susanoo's character?

_____

_____

_____

_____

What details led you to this description?

_____

_____

_____

_____

WordWorkshop

USING WORDS AS DIFFERENT PARTS OF SPEECH. Many words can be used as more than one part of speech. For example, the word *chant* is used as a verb in "Amaterasu," but it can also be used as a noun meaning "a simple song or melody." For each of the following words, write two sentences using the word as two different parts of speech. For each sentence, label which part of speech the word is.

1. mist: _____

    _____

2. bridge: _____

    _____

3. moan: _____

    _____

4. slope: _____

    _____

5. mirror: _____

    _____

Read-Write Connection

Can you recall a time when you felt, like Susanoo, that you had been treated unfairly by your parents or felt that your sibling was favored over you? How did you handle the situation?

_____

_____

_____

_____

Beyond the Reading

READ ABOUT SUN GODS AND GODDESSES. Locate and read another myth about a sun god. Then make a chart that compares Amaterasu to the god or goddess in the story you read.

GO ONLINE. To find links and additional activities for this selection, visit the EMC Internet Resource Center at **emcp.com/languagearts** and click on Write-In Reader.

Unit 5 READING Review

Choose and Use Reading Strategies

Before reading an excerpt from "The Instruction of Indra," retold by Joseph Campbell (with Bill Moyers), review with a partner how to use reading strategies with folk literature.

1. Read with a Purpose
2. Connect to Prior Knowledge
3. Write Things Down
4. Make Predictions
5. Visualize
6. Use Text Organization
7. Tackle Difficult Vocabulary
8. Monitor Your Reading Progress

Next, apply at least two of these reading strategies as you read the excerpt below. Use the margins and mark up the text to show how you are using the reading strategies to read actively. You may find it helpful to choose a graphic organizer from Appendix B to gather information as you read the excerpt, or use the Summary Chart on page B-13 to create a graphic organizer that summarizes the excerpt.

There is a wonderful story in one of the Upanishads[1] about the god Indra.[2] Now, it happened at this time that a great monster had enclosed all the waters of the earth, so there was a terrible drought, and the world was in a very bad condition. It took Indra quite a while to realize that he had a box of thunderbolts and that all he had to do was drop a thunderbolt on the monster and blow him up. When he did that, the waters flowed, and the world was refreshed and Indra said, "What a great boy am I."

So, thinking, "What a great boy am I," Indra goes up to the cosmic mountain, which is the central mountain of the world, and decides to build a palace worthy of such as he. The main carpenter of the gods goes to work on it, and in very quick order he gets the palace into pretty good condition.

---

1. **Upanishads.** Indian philosophical and religious writings
2. **Indra.** Chief god of the early Aryan religion, later absorbed into Hinduism

But every time Indra comes to inspect it, he has bigger ideas about how splendid and grandiose the palace should be. Finally, the carpenter says, "My god, we are both immortal, and there is no end to his desires. I am caught for eternity." So he decides to go to Brahma, the creator god, and complain.

WordWorkshop

Unit 5 Words for Everyday Use

abyss, 171
cower, 163
cunning, 171
deity, 171
demur, 160
drivel, 171
ebb, 163
envoy, 172

exalt, 170
intolerable, 163
oppress, 159
pity, 153
quiver, 171
sole, 170
strew, 162

summon, 172
talon, 161
tempestuous, 160
transgressor, 164
vain, 160
virile, 172
wrest, 165

Synonyms. Synonyms are words or expressions that mean the same or nearly the same thing. For each word below, list two synonyms.

1. wrest _____

2. summon _____

3. vain _____

4. deity _____

5. exalt _____

6. tempestuous _____

7. stress _____

8. cunning _____

9. quiver _____

10. drivel _____

Literary Tools

Select the literary element from the column on the right that best completes each sentence on the left. Write the correct letter in the blank.

_____1. To discuss the feelings of a tree is to use _____.

_____2. The golden age of the past is a common _____ in literature.

_____3. Description of Isis's physical appearance, accounts of her actions, and things that she says contribute to Geraldine Harris's _____ of the goddess.

_____4. The _____ in a story is the main problem or struggle.

_____5. A character's reason for acting in a certain way is called that character's _____.

a. characterization, 190

b. central conflict, 162, 167

c. motif, 182

d. motive, 171, 176

e. personification, 156

On Your Own

FLUENTLY SPEAKING. Find a folk tale or legend, and make arrangements to read it aloud to a group of elementary school children. Practice reading the tale aloud until you can do it smoothly and without errors. You might want to record your reading to see how you sound. When you present the tale, make sure you use lots of expression in your voice to help younger readers understand what is happening.

PICTURE THIS. Choose a folk tale, myth, fairy tale, or legend, and make it into a comic book for friends and classmates. Your drawings should help readers understand what kind of people the characters are and what is happening in the story.

PUT IT IN WRITING. Choose a folk tale, myth, fairy tale, or legend and rewrite it as a short drama. You may add scenes to your drama that show what might have happened after the selection you read ended. Act out your drama for the class.

Unit SIX

READING Drama

DRAMA

A **drama,** or *play*, is a story told through characters played by actors. Early groups of people around the world enacted ritual scenes related to hunting, warfare, or religion. From these, drama arose. Western drama as we know it first began in ancient Greece.

Elements of Drama

THE PLAYWRIGHT AND THE SCRIPT. The author of a play is the **playwright.** A playwright has limited control in deciding how his or her work is presented. Producers, directors, set designers, and actors all interpret a playwright's work and present their interpretations to the audience.

A **script** is the written text from which a drama is produced. Scripts are made up of stage directions and dialogue. Scripts may be divided into long parts called acts and short parts called scenes. In this unit, you will read *Persephone*, a one-act play written by Claire Boiko and based on a Greek myth.

STAGE DIRECTIONS. **Stage directions** are notes included in a play to describe how something should look, sound, or be performed. Stage directions can describe lighting, costumes, music, sound effects, or other elements of a play. They can also describe entrances and exits, gestures, tone of voice, or other elements related to the acting of a play. Stage directions sometimes provide historical or background information. In stage directions, the parts of the stage are described from the actors' point of view, as shown in the diagram on the next page. As you read the selection from the play, pay attention to the suggestions the playwright has given for the set, the lighting, and props.

NOTE THE FACTS

What do stage directions describe?

_____

_____

_____

Up Right	Up Center	Up Left
Right Center	Center	Left Center
Down Right	Down Center	Down Left

Reading STRATEGY
REVIEW

VISUALIZE. Using the Parts of a Stage diagram, mark where characters would go if stage directions told them to *cross down center.*

DIALOGUE. The speech of the actors in a play is called **dialogue.** A speech given by one character is called a **monologue.** In a play, dialogue appears after the names of characters.

ACTS AND SCENES. An **act** is a major part of a play. One-act, three-act, and five-act plays are all common. A **scene** is a short section of a literary work, one that happens in a single place and time. There may be any number of scenes in each act, and the number of scenes may vary from act to act.

SPECTACLE. The **spectacle** includes all the elements of the drama that are presented to the audience's senses. The set, props, special effects, lighting, and costumes are all part of the spectacle.

USING READING STRATEGIES WITH DRAMA

Active Reading Strategy Checklists

When reading drama, be aware of the plot (what happens), the setting, the characters, the dialogue (what the characters say), and the stage directions (how the characters say their lines and the actions they take onstage). The following checklists offer things to consider as you read drama.

1 **READ WITH A PURPOSE.** Before reading drama, give yourself a purpose, or something to look for, as you read. Sometimes your teacher will give you a purpose: "As you read the play, look for how the seasons of the year came to be." Other times you can set your own purpose by previewing the opening lines and instructional information. Say to yourself

- ❑ I want to look for . . .
- ❑ I need to learn what happens to . . .
- ❑ I want to experience how . . .
- ❑ I want to understand why . . .
- ❑ I want to figure out what causes . . .

2 **CONNECT TO PRIOR KNOWLEDGE.** Being aware of what you already know and thinking about it as you read can help you understand the characters and events. As you read, say to yourself

- ❑ The setting is a lot like . . .
- ❑ What happens here is similar to what happens in . . .
- ❑ This character is like . . .
- ❑ The ending reminds me of . . .
- ❑ I like this description because . . .

3 **WRITE THINGS DOWN.** As you read drama, write down important ideas that the author is sharing with readers. Possible ways to write things down include

- ❑ Underline important information in the stage directions.
- ❑ Write down things you want to remember about how the characters might say their lines.
- ❑ Highlight lines you want to read aloud.
- ❑ Create a graphic organizer to keep track of people and events.
- ❑ Use a code in the margin that shows how you respond to the action.

4 **MAKE PREDICTIONS.** As you read drama, use information in the stage directions and the dialogue to make guesses about what will happen next. Make predictions like the following:

- ❑ The title makes me predict that . . .
- ❑ The stage directions make me think that . . .
- ❑ I think the selection will end with . . .
- ❑ I think there will be a conflict between . . .
- ❑ The dialogue makes me guess that . . .

Reading TIP

Become an actor! Practice reading parts of the play aloud using a voice that expresses what the characters feel.

USE A CODE

Here's a way to code the text.
- +   I like this
- –   I don't like this
- √   This is important
- Yes I agree with this
- No I disagree with this
- ?   I don't understand this
- W I wonder . . .
- !   This is like something I know
- ↶ I need to come back to this later

Create additional code marks to note other reactions you have.

Reading TIP

Sketch what the setting and the characters look like. The sketch will help you envision the action.

5 VISUALIZE. Visualizing, or allowing the words on the page to create images in your mind, helps you understand the action and how the characters may say their lines. In order to visualize the setting, the characters, and the action, make statements such as

- ❑ The setting and props . . .
- ❑ This character speaks . . .
- ❑ This character's movements are . . .
- ❑ This character wears . . .
- ❑ Over the course of the play, this character's behavior . . .
- ❑ The words help me see, hear, feel, smell, taste . . .

6 USE TEXT ORGANIZATION. When you read drama, pay attention to the dialogue, the characters, and the action. Learn to stop occasionally and retell what you have read. Say to yourself

- ❑ The stage directions help me pay attention to . . .
- ❑ The exposition, or introduction, is about . . .
- ❑ The conflict centers on . . .
- ❑ The climax, or high point of interest, occurs when . . .
- ❑ The resolution, or the outcome, of the play is that . . .
- ❑ My summary of this scene is . . .

Reading TIP

Insert synonyms for difficult words as you read. If you are unsure about a synonym that will work, ask a classmate about the synonym he or she would use.

7 TACKLE DIFFICULT VOCABULARY. Difficult words in drama can get in the way of your ability to understand the characters and events. Use context, consult a dictionary, or ask someone about words you do not understand. When you come across a difficult word in a drama, say to yourself

- ❑ The lines near this word tell me that this word means . . .
- ❑ A dictionary definition shows that the word means . . .
- ❑ My work with the word before reading helps me know that the word means . . .
- ❑ A classmate said that the word means . . .
- ❑ This word is pronounced . . .

8 MONITOR YOUR READING PROGRESS. All readers encounter difficulty when they read, especially if the reading material is not self-selected. When you have to read something, note problems you are having and fix them. The key to reading success is knowing when you are having difficulty. To fix problems, say to yourself

- ❑ Because I don't understand this part, I will . . .
- ❑ Because I'm having trouble staying connected to what I'm reading, I will . . .

- ❏ Because the words in the play are too hard, I will . . .
- ❏ Because the play is long, I will . . .
- ❏ Because I can't retell what happened here, I will . . .

Become an Active Reader

The instruction with the drama selection in this unit gives you an in-depth look at how to use one strategy. Brief margin notes guide your use of additional strategies. Using one active reading strategy will greatly increase your reading success and enjoyment. Use the white space in the margins to add your own comments and strategy ideas. Learn how to use several strategies in combination to ensure your complete understanding of what you are reading. When you have difficulty, try a fix-up idea. For further information about the active reading strategies, see Unit 1, pages 4–15.

FIX-UP IDEAS

- ■ Reread
- ■ Ask a question
- ■ Read in shorter chunks
- ■ Read aloud
- ■ Retell
- ■ Work with a partner
- ■ Unlock difficult words
- ■ Vary your reading rate
- ■ Choose a new reading strategy
- ■ Create a mnemonic device

How to Use Reading Strategies with Drama

Note how a reader uses active reading strategies while reading this excerpt from *Persephone*.

READ WITH A PURPOSE

I will keep reading to find out how winter ended.

CONNECT TO PRIOR KNOWLEDGE

I have heard other stories about Hades, the god of the underworld.

TACKLE DIFFICULT VOCABULARY

I know what the word *urge* means, so I can use that word part to understand *urgently*.

MONITOR YOUR READING PROGRESS

Reading the lines aloud and changing my voice for each character helps me understand what the characters are saying.

VISUALIZE

I can picture Demeter's tears turning to drops of ice.

USE TEXT ORGANIZATION

The stage directions help me understand what would be happening on stage.

MAKE PREDICTIONS

I predict that spring will come when Demeter gets Persephone back.

WRITE THINGS DOWN

I can underline the lines that talk about the seasons.

SHEPHERD: Mighty Demeter! I have seen the Princess Persephone.

DEMETER [*Urgently*]: Where is she, shepherd boy? Tell me!

SHEPHERD: Lord Hades has taken her to the underworld.

DEMETER [*Upset*]: No! It can't be! [*Crosses down center shouting, shaking her fists*] Hades, hear me! Until Persephone returns to me, the sun will not shine in the heavens. [*Lights dim.*] No tree will bear fruit. No flower will bloom. Not a single blade of grass will grow upon the earth. [CHORUS *makes the sound of wind.*] And it will be winter—winter—winter! Forever! [DEMETER *moves left, sits on ground and weeps.*]

CHORUS: Winter . . . winter . . . winter. Forever. [1ST NARRATOR *enters right.*]

1ST NARRATOR: Demeter wept. So bitterly cold it was that her tears froze to drops of ice. And all the people in the hills and valleys of Greece wept for her, for they were cold and hungry. [SHEPHERD *rises, rubbing his arms and shivering. He exits right.*]

Persephone

by Claire Boiko

Active READING STRATEGY

READ WITH A PURPOSE

Before Reading ➤ **SET A PURPOSE**

❑ Respond to the Reader's Journal question, and discuss your ideas with the class.

❑ As you read this selection, your purpose will be to notice the relationship between the mother and daughter in this play and to understand how that relationship affects the seasons of the year.

❑ Read the Reader's Resource to gather background information about the mother, the daughter, and the story behind this play.

❑ Preview the Seasons Chart below. In this chart, you will record details about each season mentioned in the play. You should also record what causes each season to occur.

Graphic Organizer: Seasons Chart

Summer	Winter	Spring

CONNECT

Reader's resource

The one-act play *Persephone* is based on a Greek myth about Demeter, the goddess of harvest and grain, and her daughter, Persephone, who becomes the goddess of the seasons. **Myths** are stories that explain things in the natural world. Before modern science, people depended on myths to answer basic questions such as how the world was created, what happens to people when they die, and why the seasons change. This myth focuses on the origin of the seasons. The playwright of this humorous, dramatic version of the myth is Claire Boiko, who has turned many well-known stories into plays.

Word watch

PREVIEW VOCABULARY

airy	modesty
desolate	plaintive
disclose	quandary
distraught	relent
fickle	smug
grimace	vigorous
haughty	waver

Reader's journal

How much freedom is appropriate for someone your age? At what point should a parent or guardian step in to protect you?

READ WITH A PURPOSE

❑ With your class, practice pronouncing the names in the Read Aloud section below.

❑ From the list of characters, choose a part to read. Your teacher will be the 1st Narrator. Listen as your teacher reads aloud the italicized stage directions and the first two speeches by the 1st Narrator.

❑ Read the rest of the selection aloud with your class. As you read the lines, use your voice to express the emotion or tone identified by the stage directions. Pause occasionally to fill in your Seasons Chart.

READ ALOUD

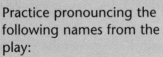

Practice pronouncing the following names from the play:
Demeter (di mē' tər)
Persephone (Pər se' fō nē)
Hades (hā' dēz)
Zeus (zōōs)
Hermes (hər' mēz)
Chorus (kôr' is)
Mount Olympus
  (mount ō lim' pis)

Persephone
Claire Boiko

CHARACTERS
1ST NARRATOR
2ND NARRATOR
DEMETER
PERSEPHONE
MOTH FROM UNDERWORLD
SHEPHERD BOY
HADES
1ST BAT
2ND BAT
ZEUS
HERMES
CHORUS OF AT LEAST SIX, EXTRAS

SCENE 1

TIME: *Long ago.*
PLACE: *Ancient Greece.*

Greek music is heard, as 1ST NARRATOR *enters down right, in front of curtain.*

1ST NARRATOR: Spring, fall, summer, winter. How did the seasons come to be? The Greeks had an explanation for it. Eons and eons ago, before your great-grandfather's great-grandfather was born, gods and goddesses lived on earth. [*Curtain opens.*]

10   *Demeter's garden. Backdrop of snowcapped mountains and*
blazing sun. At center is Demeter's temple. At right, pillars with
a bench in front, on which the CHORUS, *in blue and white tunics*
and floral, sits, facing audience. Down left is a grape arbor. All
hold positions as 1ST NARRATOR *speaks.*

1ST NARRATOR [*Looking around, then continuing*]: In this
very garden lived the goddess of summer and harvest,
Demeter. [DEMETER *enters right, dressed in flowing green*
robe, sandals, and wearing a diadem of silver wheat stalks. She
carries a cornucopia of fruit on a tray, which she places in front of
20   CHORUS. *Music fades out.*]
DEMETER: Children of the earth, I bring you rosy apples,
plump figs, ripe olives and purple grapes. A horn of plenty!
CHORUS: Thank you, Demeter. You are most generous. [*All*
pose as 2ND NARRATOR *enters.*]
2ND NARRATOR: And so it went, eon after eon. It was
always summer in the land of legend, and there was always
more than enough food and drink. But alas . . .
CHORUS [*Sighing*]: Alas . . .
2ND NARRATOR: Demeter had a lovely daughter—Princess
30   Persephone, the goddess of spring and flowers.
[PERSEPHONE *enters left, scattering flower petals from a basket.*
She crosses to DEMETER, *who embraces her.*] Persephone was
as unpredictable as spring. She was beautiful but willful,
<u>fickle</u>, and just a little bit naughty.
1ST NARRATOR: Demeter loved Persephone—not wisely,
but too well. [MOTH *from Underworld enters down left, hides*
in grape arbor, listening intently.]
DEMETER [*To* CHORUS, *proudly*]: Look, children of the
earth. Feast your eyes on my beautiful Princess
40   Persephone!
CHORUS [*Shaking heads*]: Careful, Demeter—
DEMETER [*Pointing out* PERSEPHONE'S *features*]: Look at
these sparkling eyes. That silken hair.
CHORUS: Speak no more, Demeter.

**words
for
everyday
use**
fi • ckle (fi′ kəl) *adj.,* prone to changing one's mind often. *One girl was so <u>fickle</u>*
that she went through five different boyfriends in less than a week.

NOTE THE FACTS

What time of year is it? What
is unusual about "the land of
legend"? Record your answers
in your Seasons Chart.

THINK AND REFLECT

What does it mean that
Demeter loved
Persephone "not wisely,
but too well"? (**Interpret**)

_____

_____

_____

CHORUS. A **chorus** is a person or group of people who speaks directly to the audience to convey the author's viewpoint or to introduce story details. As you read, think about the purpose served by the Chorus. In this scene, why might the Chorus cry "Danger!"?

_____

_____

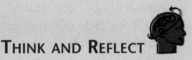

THINK AND REFLECT

Reread lines 59–77. What do you learn about the relationship between Demeter and Persephone from this conversation? What do you learn about Persephone's personality? **(Infer)**

_____

_____

_____

Reading TIP

Zeus is the god of thunder and the leader of the gods and goddesses. His seat of government is Mount Olympus.

DEMETER [*Delighted*]: She is more beautiful than Aphrodite.

CHORUS [*Alarmed*]: Stop. Please stop!

DEMETER: Wiser than Athena.

CHORUS [*Urgently*]: Danger! Danger!

DEMETER [*Excitedly*]: She is a princess fit for a god!

50 [CHORUS *gasps.*]

PERSEPHONE [*With false modesty*]: Oh, Mother.

2ND NARRATOR [*Pointing to* MOTH, *who crosses down left to apron[1]*]: Do you see that gray moth? He is a messenger for Hades, the god of the underworld.[2]

MOTH [*With evil laugh*]: A princess fit for a god, to be sure, and I know which god… Hades! I will lead this beautiful girl to him. And then [*Rubs hands together gleefully*]—ha! ha! How he will reward me! [*Returns to hiding place in grape arbor*]

DEMETER [*Warmly*]: Have you eaten yet this morning, my

60 beloved daughter? What would you like?

PERSEPHONE [*In a bored tone*]: I would really like a pomegranate,[3] Mother.

DEMETER: Persephone, dearest, you ate all the pomegranates yesterday.

PERSEPHONE [*Sighing*]: You never grow enough pomegranates!

DEMETER: I'll grow more, just for you. [*Trumpet blares off-stage.*] Oh, that is the trumpet of Zeus, calling us to Mount Olympus. I must go. [*Shakes her finger at*

70 PERSEPHONE] While I am gone, promise me you will not leave this garden.

PERSEPHONE: But, Mother, I'm old enough to explore the world myself. [*Thunder is heard off.*]

DEMETER [*Alarmed*]: Thunder! I'd better hurry. [*Sternly*] Persephone, you must promise me not to leave.

PERSEPHONE: Oh, if I must, I must. [*Reluctantly*] I promise not to leave the garden.

---

1. **apron.** The front part of the stage between the curtain and the edge
2. **the underworld.** The realm of the dead, ruled by the god Hades
3. **pomegranate.** Fruit with bright red skin, a thick cluster of tiny seeds, and sweet, red fruit

words for everyday use

mo • de • sty (mä′ də stē) *n.,* freedom from arrogance or conceitedness. *His modesty prevented him from taking credit for the accomplishment.*

DEMETER [*Relieved*]: Good. Now, I can go in peace. [*Exits quickly.* MOTH *flutters on and circles* PERSEPHONE.]

80 **PERSEPHONE** [*Trying to shoo* MOTH *away; irritated*]: Go away, moth. You are a creature of the night. What are you doing here in the sunshine?

MOTH [*Slyly*]: Persephone, aren't you hungry?

PERSEPHONE: Hungry? Hm-m. Well, yes.

MOTH: I've heard you're very fond of pomegranates. Rich, red, juicy pomegranates.

PERSEPHONE [*Clapping her hands*]: Oh yes, I adore pomegranates! But they're all gone.

MOTH: I know where there are some delicious
90 pomegranates. [MOTH *beckons her.*] Come with me. It's not far. [PERSEPHONE *hesitates.*] You'll be back before your mother misses you.

PERSEPHONE [*Wavering*]: Not far, you say?

MOTH [*Moving to exit left*]: Only twenty steps. Follow me. [*She follows; they exit. Thunder is heard, as curtain closes.*]

SCENE 2

SHEPHERD BOY *enters, carrying crook; a water flask hangs at his waist. He sits on edge of stage, puts down crook, and begins to play* plaintive *melody on flute, as* CHORUS *moves backdrop depicting rugged, bare mountains onto stage in front of curtain. There is a*
100 *cleft in the mountains, center, where the curtain's opening is.*

SHEPHERD [*Looking around, uncomfortably*]: This place seems strange to me. [*Shudders*] As soon as I find my lost lamb, I will go home. [*He rises and calls sheep.*] Ba-a-a. Ba-a! Where are you, little lamb? [MOTH *flutters on left, followed by* PERSEPHONE. SHEPHERD *bows to* PERSEPHONE, *who nods her head at him,* haughtily. MOTH *flutters to center.* SHEPHERD *addresses audience in an aside.*] By all the gods on Olympus!

Reading STRATEGY REVIEW

MAKE PREDICTIONS. Where do you think Moth is leading Persephone? What clues in the play lead you to this prediction?

_____

_____

_____

_____

Literary TOOLS

ASIDE. An **aside** is a statement made by a character in a play and meant to be heard by the audience but not by the other characters. In lines 107–109, underline or highlight the words the Shepherd says in an aside. Why do you think he makes this an aside?

_____

_____

_____

_____

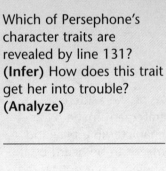

THINK AND REFLECT

Which of Persephone's
character traits are
revealed by line 131?
(Infer) How does this trait
get her into trouble?
(Analyze)

_____

_____

_____

_____

That is Princess Persephone. But why is she here, in this
barren desert? [*Bows again to* PERSEPHONE] Good day,
110   Princess. May I help you in some way?

PERSEPHONE [*Grandly*]: How very nice of you. Perhaps you
can tell me where the pomegranate tree is? I can't seem to
find it, and I'm exceedingly hungry and thirsty.

SHEPHERD [*Astonished*]: A pomegranate tree? Here? Why,
not even a blade of grass could grow here. [*Holds water flask
out to* PERSEPHONE] But if you are thirsty, please take some
of my water.

PERSEPHONE [*Crossing to* SHEPHERD]: Oh, thank you. [*He
hands her flask and she drinks. While they are occupied with their
120   backs to center stage,* MOTH *calls into opening between mountains.*]

MOTH [*Urgently*]: Lord Hades! Come quickly. I have
brought you a princess! [Hades *enters through opening,
followed by* BATS.] Look there, my Lord! [MOTH *points
excitedly at* PERSEPHONE. *Thunder rolls loudly, as lights flash.*]

HADES [*Staring at* PERSEPHONE; *overwhelmed*]: She is more
beautiful than Aphrodite. [*To* MOTH] Well done, my small
servant!

MOTH [*Crossing to* PERSEPHONE, *eagerly*]: Pretty Persephone,
come this way. I have a surprise for you. [SHEPHERD *sees*
130   HADES, *gasps.*]

PERSEPHONE [*Excitedly*]: A surprise? I love surprises! [*As she
turns,* SHEPHERD *grabs her hand.*]

SHEPHERD [*Fearfully*]: It's Hades, lord of the underworld.
You must not go! I won't let him take you. [HADES *runs to*
PERSEPHONE *and takes her hand. She screams as they pull her
in opposite directions. Thunder rolls.* HADES *waves to* BATS, *who
surround* SHEPHERD, *flapping wings. He drops* PERSEPHONE'S
hand as he tries to fight them off. HADES *laughs evilly and pulls*
PERSEPHONE *though center opening.* BATS *and* MOTH *follow*
140   *them off.* SHEPHERD *picks up crook, runs offstage left. After a
moment,* CHORUS *enters and removes backdrop.*]

• • • • •

Demeter's garden. CHORUS *members have removed wreaths,
now wear gray robes and sit somberly with heads bowed.*
DEMETER, *also wearing long gray robe, paces upstage.* MOTH
flutters right and hides.

DEMETER [*Wringing her hands, distraught*]: Where can my beloved Persephone be? Where has she gone? She promised not to leave the garden.

CHORUS [*Whispering eerily*]: Persephone. Persephone.
150 Persephone.

DEMETER: She could be anywhere. Lost. Frightened. Alone. [SHEPHERD *runs on left, thrown himself at* DEMETER'S *feet.*]

SHEPHERD: Mighty Demeter! I have seen the Princess Persephone.

DEMETER [*Urgently*]: Where is she, shepherd boy? Tell me!

SHEPHERD: Lord Hades has taken her to the underworld.

DEMETER [*Upset*]: No! It can't be! [*Crosses down center shouting, shaking her fists*] Hades, hear me! Until Persephone returns to
160 me, the sun will not shine in the heavens. [*Lights dim.*] No tree will bear fruit. No flower will bloom. Not a single blade of grass will grow upon the earth. [CHORUS *makes the sound of wind.*] And it will be winter—winter—winter! Forever! [DEMETER *moves left, sits on ground and weeps.*]

CHORUS: Winter . . . winter . . . winter. Forever. [1ST NARRATOR *enters right.*]

1ST NARRATOR: Demeter wept. So bitterly cold it was that her tears froze to drops of ice. And all the people in the hills and valleys of Greece wept for her, for they were cold
170 and hungry. [SHEPHERD *rises, rubbing his arms and shivering. He exits right.*]

CHORUS [*Hands outstretched, pleading*]: Mother Demeter, feed us. We are hungry. Send the sun to warm us. We are cold. Cold. Cold. [*They shiver.*]

1ST NARRATOR: At last Demeter would stand it no more. For the children of earth belonged to her, too. She called out to the greatest god of them all—Zeus. [*Exits*]

DEMETER [*Rising and stretching her arms out to heaven*]: Father Zeus, hear me. Bring back my daughter! Bring back
180 Persephone! [*Trumpet is heard off. Lights flash.* ZEUS, *followed by* HERMES, *enters left.*]

Use **THE STRATEGY**

READ WITH A PURPOSE. What threat involving the seasons does Demeter make? Record your answer in the proper column of your Seasons Chart.

DRAW A PICTURE

NOTE THE FACTS

What must Persephone not do if she is to be returned to her mother?

_____

_____

Reading TIP

Hermes is the messenger of the gods as well as the god of mischief.

ZEUS: I hear you, Demeter. [DEMETER *runs to* ZEUS.] If I bring Persephone back, will the sun shine once again?

DEMETER [*Nodding*]: Yes.

ZEUS: Will there be olives and grapes and roses for the children of the earth?

DEMETER [*Eagerly*]: Yes. Oh, yes!

ZEUS: Then, I will bring her back. But hear me! Persephone must not have eaten one meal in the 190 underworld. If any food passes her lips, she must stay with Lord Hades forever.

DEMETER: I'm sure she will not eat. She is most particular about her food. Oh, please bring her to me swiftly, Father Zeus!

ZEUS [*To* HERMES]: Hermes, fly to the underworld. Tell Lord Hades I order him to release Princess Persephone. Then bring her back here to Demeter's garden.

DEMETER: Oh, thank you!

MOTH [*Crossing downstage; aside*]: Oh no! I must warn Lord 200 Hades! [*Exits left*]

HERMES: Yes, Zeus. I am on my way. [*He mimes flying off right.*]

ZEUS: A bit of advice, Demeter: Don't boast about your child again. And try to keep her close to you.

DEMETER: I'll promise never to boast, though she is the most beautiful, the cleverest—

ZEUS [*Frowning*]: Demeter!

DEMETER [*Lamely*]: I mean, Persephone is nice enough—if you like princesses.

ZEUS: That's better. [*Curtain closes.*]

SCENE 3

210 SETTING: *Hades' palace, a cavern in shades of black and gray, with stalactites hanging from ceiling. Down center are two Stalagmites cut into rough thrones.* HADES *is seated on one throne, watching* PERSEPHONE, *who sits on other, wailing loudly.* BATS *hover near her.* 1ST BAT *offers her a huge handkerchief.* 2ND BAT *has tray of food.*

1ST BAT [*Pleadingly*]: Dry your tears, Princess Persephone.

2ND BAT: And you must eat. You haven't touched any food since Lord Hades brought you here.

PERSEPHONE [*Waving them away*]: I don't want any food. I
hope to starve. [*To* HADES] Then you'll be sorry. Aren't you
tired of hearing me cry? Don't you want to send me home?
[2ND BAT *puts down tray behind throne.*]

HADES [*Smiling*]: Never. You will stay with me forever.
Your tears are like a refreshing spring shower.

PERSEPHONE [*Aside, frustrated*]: The worse I behave, the
better Hades seems to like me! [*To* HADES, *meanly*] I am not
charming. Look. [*She makes a face at him.* HADES *laughs
heartily.*]

2ND BAT [*to* 1ST BAT, *shocked*]: Look! Lord Hades is
laughing.

1ST BAT: He never even smiled before. Things are
certainly upside down in the underworld.

PERSEPHONE: I can be even uglier. [*She grimaces at him.*
HADES *doubles up with laughter.*] Now, will you send me
home?

HADES: Never, never, never. You make me laugh. Nobody
ever made me laugh before.

PERSEPHONE: I will become a statue. Nobody laughs at
statues. [*She folds her arms, closes her eyes, and freezes.* BATS,
alarmed, fan her vigorously.]

2ND BAT: Lord Hades, what shall we do? She won't move.

HADES [*Rising, speaking dramatically*]: Oh, Princess
Persephone. You are lost to me forever. [Hades *motions to*
BATS, *who cross down center with him.*] Don't worry. I know
how to deal with my proud princess. Whatever I ask her to
do—she will do the opposite. Watch. [BATS *follow* HADES,
who crosses behind PERSEPHONE.] Persephone, you may
remain a statue as long as you like. [*Sternly*] But whatever
you do, don't sing. I repeat: Do not sing one of those sickly
sweet songs your mother taught you. [HADES *smiles slyly and
returns to his throne.* PERSEPHONE *rises haughtily and crosses
downstage.*]

220

230

240

250

THINK AND REFLECT

Why does Hades move
down center in line 244?
(Infer) How does he trick
Persephone? **(Synthesize)**

_____

_____

_____

_____

**words
for
everyday
use**

gri • mace (grĭ′ məs) *n.*, a facial expression, usually of disgust or disapproval.
I can't help grimacing every time I have to pull off an adhesive bandage.
vig • or • ous (vĭ′ gə rəs) *adj.*, forceful or energetic. *Should your exercise be so
vigorous that you can't even speak while you're on the treadmill?* **vigorously,** *adv.*

STAGE DIRECTIONS. Stage directions are notes to describe how something should look, sound, or be performed. How do the stage directions in line 258 help you understand the true meaning of what Hades says?

_____

_____

PERSEPHONE: You don't like sweet songs, Lord Hades? Then I shall sing the sweetest song I know. [*Music begins, and she sings song about spring, as* HADES *blissfully conducts an imaginary orchestra. After song,* PERSEPHONE *sits.*] There. I hope you hated that.

HADES [*Beaming*]: Oh, yes. I hated it. It was dreadful.

PERSEPHONE [*Hopefully*]: Was it dreadful enough to send me home?

260

HADES: From what I hear you weren't very nice to your mother. You disobeyed her.

PERSEPHONE [*Plaintively*]: I was wrong to disobey her. If you let me go, I'll apologize to her. Please.

HADES: No, Persephone.

PERSEPHONE: Let me go, or I'll hold my breath until I expire! [*She inhales, blowing out her cheeks.*]

HADES [*Turning to her with great interest*]: Will you? How fascinating. I've never seen anyone expire. [*As he stares at*

270

her, she exhales and wrinkles her nose in disgust.]

PERSEPHONE: You don't amuse me.

HADES: I know. But you amuse me. That is why I will never let you go. [MOTH *flutters onstage, followed by* CHORUS.] Ah-h, here is my messenger and the shadows from the upper world. Welcome, my friends. This is Persephone. [*Indicating her*] Have you ever seen such a beautiful girl? [*She makes a face at him.*]

CHORUS [*Sighing sadly*]: Ah-h, Persephone. Poor Persephone.

MOTH [*Pulling urgently at* HADES' *sleeve*]: Lord Hades, I

280

have something of great importance to tell you. [*Pulls him down right*]

HADES: Well, what it is?

MOTH: Zeus is sending Hermes to take Persephone back to the earth. He'll be here any minute.

HADES: No! [*Folding arms stubbornly*] I won't give her back.

MOTH: You will have to. Zeus is stronger than you are.

HADES: True. True. But—there must be a way to keep her here.

MOTH: There is. Has Persephone eaten anything?

290

HADES: Not a bite.

MOTH: Zeus says that if she eats anything in the underworld, she must stay here with you forever.

HADES [*Eagerly*]: Then, bring me something for Princess Persephone to eat. Something she cannot resist!

MOTH [*Excitedly*]: I know the very thing! [MOTH *flutters quickly off left and returns with pomegranate on tray. Pomegranate can be opened to* <u>disclose</u> *large red seeds.* MOTH *presents tray to* HADES, *who crosses to* PERSEPHONE, *thrusting tray under her nose.* PERSEPHONE *closes her eyes and turns away.*]

300   **HADES** [*Kindly*]: Please, princess. Have a morsel of food.

PERSEPHONE: No. [CHORUS *gathers around her throne, anxiously.*]

CHORUS [*Sotto voce*]:[4] Do not eat, Persephone. Do not eat anything.

HADES [*Opening pomegranate, inhaling its fragrance*]: M-m-m. There is no aroma as sweet as a fresh, juicy pomegranate. [PERSEPHONE *sniffs, smiles.*]

PERSEPHONE [*Pushing it away*]: No, I will eat nothing here.

HADES [*With cunning*]: Very well. Then there will be more
310   for me. [*Pretending to eat*] M-m-m. Sweet, juicy seeds. [*As* PERSEPHONE *reaches for pomegranate*, HADES *snatches it away.*] Now, now. You had your chance.

PERSEPHONE [*Pulling pomegranate toward her*]: It isn't polite to offer a person something and then take it away. Besides, I'm *so* hungry.

CHORUS [*Louder*]: No, Persephone, no!

HADES, BATS, *and* **MOTH** [*Sweetly*]: Eat, Persephone, eat!

PERSEPHONE [*Pulling out three seeds*]: Just three little seeds. One . . . [*Thunder rolls after she eats each seed.*] Two . . .
320   Three . . .

CHORUS: Woe. Oh, woe. What have you done, Persephone? What have you done? [*Trumpet sounds.* HERMES *runs on, carrying a scroll. He crosses center, unrolls scroll.*]

HERMES [*Reading*]: Hear the command of Zeus, Lord Hades. The Princess Persephone is to return to her mother, Demeter, immediately. [*Rerolls scroll*]

---

4. **Sotto voce.** Very quietly; under one's breath

**words
for
everyday
use**

   dis • close (dis klōz′) *v.*, reveal; make known. *Reporters often count on inside tips from people who are willing to <u>disclose</u> the secrets of their fellow government officials.*

NOTE THE FACTS

How does Hades plan to keep Persephone in the underworld?

_____

_____

THINK AND REFLECT

What mistake has Persephone made? How is this related to the other mistakes she has made in this play? **(Analyze)**

_____

_____

_____

_____

_____

PERSEPHONE [*Running to* HERMES]: I'm going home? [*To* CHORUS, *jubilantly*] Did you hear? I'm going home! [*To* HADES, *airily*] Goodbye, Lord Hades. [HADES *takes* PERSEPHONE'S *hand and leads her back to throne.*]

HADES: Sit down, Persephone. You are not leaving me—ever!

HERMES [*Sternly, wagging a finger*]: Zeus will be angry. You dare not disobey Zeus!

HADES [*Unconcerned*]: I would not dream of disobeying Zeus. But is there not another line in that proclamation? Something about Persephone's eating?

HERMES [*Alarmed, to* PERSEPHONE]: Persephone—answer me truthfully. Did you eat while you were here in the underworld?

PERSEPHONE: Well, I ate only three little pomegranate seeds. [HADES *smiles broadly.*]

HERMES: This is most serious. You should not have eaten anything. Now, I must leave you here. [PERSEPHONE *wails and runs to* HERMES, *clinging to his arm.*]

PERSEPHONE [*Panicky*]: No, no! Take me home. Take me to my mother!

HERMES: Quiet! Let me think. [*To* HADES] Lord Hades, I must take up this matter with Zeus.

HADES [*Smugly*]: Do so, of course. [HERMES *starts off right.* PERSEPHONE *clings tightly to his arm.*]

PERSEPHONE [*Pleadingly*]: You can't go without me. You must take me home.

HADES [*Relenting*]: Very well. Let's all go to Demeter's garden and straighten out this whole matter. [HADES *takes* PERSEPHONE'S *free arm.*] Zeus will hear both sides of the question, and naturally I will win. Princess Persephone will be mine forever!

PERSEPHONE [*Whimpering*]: Forever is much too long! [*Curtain closes.*]

330

340

350

360

Literary TOOLS

PARODY. A **parody** is a literary work that imitates another work for humorous purposes. Myths are typically retold in a serious way. As you read, think about what makes this version of the myth a parody. In other words, what makes the play humorous?

---

words for everyday use

air • y (ā′ rē) *adj.,* proud. *"I won't be needing your help anymore," declared the woman in an airy tone.* **airily,** *adv.*

smug (sməg) *adj.,* highly self-satisfied. *After winning the final round of the debate tournament, Kevin and Charon looked quite smug as they walked onto the stage.* **smugly,** *adv.*

re • lent (rē lent′) *v.,* give in. *Mom finally relented to our begging and pleading and took us out to dinner.* **relenting,** *adj.*

SCENE 4

SETTING: *Demeter's garden, dimly lit.*

DEMETER *stands down left, still wearing gray robe.* CHORUS, *also in gray, is down right, huddled on benches, shivering. They make sounds of a* <u>desolate</u> *wind. Floral wreaths for each member of* CHORUS *are hidden under bench.*

DEMETER [*Calling out, mournfully*]: Persephone . . .

CHORUS [*Echoing*]: Persephone . . . [*They make more wind*
370 *sounds until trumpet blares off. Lights flash and stage brightens.* ZEUS *enters.*]

ZEUS: Mother Demeter—

DEMETER: Father Zeus! [*Rushes to him, eagerly*] But where is Persephone? You promised me Persephone!

ZEUS [*Clearing his throat*]: Ah, yes, Persephone. We must discuss the matter of Persephone. [*Trumpet sounds again.* HERMES *enters, with* PERSEPHONE *clutching his arm.* HADES *follows, holding her other hand.* PERSEPHONE *breaks away from them, runs to* DEMETER, *and embraces her.*]

380 **PERSEPHONE**: Mother! Oh, I am so sorry. I will never disobey you again! Will you ever forgive me?

DEMETER [*Joyfully*]: My dear, dear child. Of course, I forgive you. Welcome home. [*As she spies* HADES, *he bows mockingly to her.*] Lord Hades, why are you here? [*She stands in front of* PERSEPHONE, *guarding her.*]

ZEUS: It seems, Demeter, there is a misunderstanding. Persephone was to be returned to you only if she had not eaten in the underworld. However, it seems that while she was with Lord Hades, she ate—

390 **PERSEPHONE** [*Interrupting*]: Only three tiny pomegranate seeds.

DEMETER: Three pomegranate seeds. That's very little.

HADES [*Nonchalantly*]: But the fact is—she did eat something. So, she belongs to me. [*He starts toward* DEMETER, *who holds her hand out warningly.*]

---

words for everyday use

des • o • late (de' sə lət) *adj.,* deserted; gloomy. *Many people feel <u>desolate</u> when the chaos and company of the holidays fades into a quiet, more solitary January.*

FIX-UP IDEA

Refocus
If you are having trouble understanding how Persephone's relationship to Demeter impacts the seasons, try refocusing your reading on the stage directions. Using clues from the stage directions, make a note in the margin when the season changes. Then figure out what has happened in the relationship to make that change occur. Record your findings in the Seasons Chart.

ASK A QUESTION

_____

_____

_____

_____

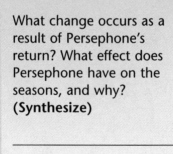

THINK AND REFLECT

What change occurs as a result of Persephone's return? What effect does Persephone have on the seasons, and why? (Synthesize)

_____

_____

_____

_____

DEMETER: Take one step toward my daughter, and I will blow you back to the underworld. [*As she gestures,* CHORUS *howls like a strong wind.*]

PERSEPHONE: I was tricked. I didn't know I wasn't to eat

400   anything.

ZEUS: This is a <u>quandary</u>. Quiet, everyone, while I think. [*He puts hands to head, closes eyes. All are quiet until* ZEUS *opens his eyes and smiles.*] I have the solution. Persephone will remain with Demeter for nine months of the year. But, for each pomegranate seed she ate, she must spend one month with Hades.

HADES [*Philosophically*]: It's not what I hoped for. But, three months with Persephone are better than no months with Persephone.

410   DEMETER [*Coldly*]: I promise you, Hades, every one of those months she spends with you will be winter, cold and gloomy.

ZEUS: So be it! [*Turns to* DEMETER] Now, Demeter. Will you please do as you promised and bring back the sun, the fruit, and the flowers?

DEMETER [*Beaming*]: I promise. [DEMETER *and* CHORUS *remove robes.* CHORUS *puts on wreaths.* DEMETER *puts on diadem.[5] She waves her hand.*] Bring on the sunshine. [*Lights come up full.*] Enter blossoms, flowers, and fruit.

420   HADES [*Waving airily*]: Farewell, Persephone. I shall expect you in nine months. [*He exits.*]

DEMETER [*To* CHORUS]: Come, children of earth. Spring has returned! [*To audience*] Come, everyone. Eat, drink, sing, dance! Let the music begin! [*Music is heard. All on stage may sing and dance as curtain closes.*]

THE END

---

5. **diadem.** Crown

words for everyday use

quan • da • ry (kwän′ drē) *n.*, state of confusion or doubt. *Torn between doing what his mother asked and what his friends wanted, Geoff found himself in a <u>quandary</u>.*

Reflect ON YOUR READING

After Reading ➤ ## SUMMARIZE YOUR FINDINGS

❑ Review the information in your chart. Then, with a partner, take turns summarizing for each other the ancient Greek explanation for the change of seasons.

❑ Write a paragraph explaining how, according to Greek myth, the relationship between Demeter, Persephone, and Hades impacts the seasons. Use details from the play to support your answer.

_____

_____

_____

_____

_____

_____

_____

_____

Reading Skills and Test Practice
EVALUATE CAUSE AND EFFECT

Discuss with a partner how best to answer the following questions about cause and effect. Use the Think-Aloud Notes to write down your reasons for eliminating the incorrect answers.

_____1. According to the play *Persephone*, winter is caused by
   a. Persephone's anger at her mother, Demeter.
   b. Demeter's grief at the loss of her daughter, Persephone.
   c. Zeus's anger at the pride of the other gods.
   d. Hermes's failure to deliver an important message.

_____2. Which of the following is *not* a cause of Persephone's abduction?
   a. Persephone's greed and selfishness
   b. Demeter's excessive pride in her daughter
   c. Persephone's disobedience of her mother
   d. Demeter's role as goddess of summer

How did using the reading strategy help you to answer the questions?

_____

_____

THINK-ALOUD NOTES

_____

_____

_____

_____

_____

_____

_____

_____

_____

_____

_____

Investigate, Inquire, and Imagine

RECALL: GATHER FACTS
1a. Excluding the gods, which two creatures in this play are associated with the underworld?

→ **INTERPRET: FIND MEANING**
1b. Why might these creatures be appropriate for the underworld?

ANALYZE: TAKE THINGS APART
2a. List at least three times Persephone is tricked in this play. What mistake does Demeter make?

→ **SYNTHESIZE: BRING THINGS TOGETHER**
2b. How would you describe Persephone's character? What is Demeter's character flaw?

EVALUATE: MAKE JUDGMENTS
3a. Evaluate the usefulness of this myth in explaining the seasons. In what ways does it make sense or fail to make sense?

→ **EXTEND: CONNECT IDEAS**
3b. What other myths do you know that explain natural phenomena?

WordWorkshop

SEMANTIC FAMILY: TONES OF VOICE. A **semantic family** is a group of words related by meaning. In the stage directions for this play, you saw many words that describe tones of voice. Read the sentences in the right column aloud, trying different tones of voice. Then match each tone of voice to the statement on the left that would most likely be said in that tone. You will use each tone only once. Be prepared to explain your choices.

_____1. haughty

_____2. plaintive

_____3. airy

_____4. urgent

_____5. smug

_____6. alarmed

_____7. stern

_____8. sly

_____9. astonished

_____10. distraught

a. "I'm only going to tell you this once, son. Don't go near the well when I'm not with you. Understand?"

b. "Oh, woe is me. My life is so hard!"

c. "Hurry! We've got to catch the next bus!"

d. "What? I had no idea you were planning on going to Europe!"

e. "Oh, you don't want me to play? Well, no problem. I've never been interested in such foolish games anyway."

f. "You? Why would I want to talk to such a lowly, pathetic creature as you?"

g. "Heh, heh, come with me, children. I have a wonderful surprise for you."

h. "Oh, no! The electricity just went out, and I've lost the paper I've worked on all day!"

i. "Yes, I'm more than pleased with my performance in the race. I'm the best!"

j. "It's getting dark! What if we can't find our way home?"

Literary Tools

ASIDE. An **aside** is a statement, made by a character in a play, that is meant to be heard by the audience but not by the other characters. List three times characters speak in asides in *Persephone.* Also explain why the character uses an aside rather than allowing other characters to hear.

_____

_____

_____

_____

_____

_____

What is the value of an aside for the audience?

_____

_____

_____

Read-Write Connection

What do you think Hades' underworld is like? Describe what it might be like to spend a day there.

_____

_____

_____

_____

Beyond the Reading

PERFORM A ONE-ACT PLAY. Find a book of one-act plays in your classroom, school, or community library. With a small group, find a play that you like, and prepare to perform it for the class. If you don't have as many group members as there are parts, you can read more than one part. You don't need to memorize your lines, but you should rehearse the play until you can read the lines fluently and with expression. If you like, create props and costumes to enhance your performance.

GO ONLINE. To find links and additional activities for this selection, visit the EMC Internet Resource Center at **emcp.com/languagearts** and click on Write-In Reader.

Unit 6 READING Review

Choose and Use Reading Strategies

Before reading an excerpt from *The Miracle Worker* by William Gibson, review with a partner how to use reading strategies with drama.

1. Read with a Purpose
2. Connect to Prior Knowledge
3. Write Things Down
4. Make Predictions
5. Visualize
6. Use Text Organization
7. Tackle Difficult Vocabulary
8. Monitor Your Reading Progress

Next, apply at least two of these reading strategies as you read the excerpt below, which is about six-year-old Helen Keller, who is both deaf and blind, and two other children. The children are playing with paper dolls. Use the margins and mark up the text to show how you are using the reading strategies to read actively. You may find it helpful to choose a graphic organizer from Appendix B to gather information as you read the excerpt, or use the Summary Chart on page B-13 to create a graphic organizer that summarizes the excerpt.

Martha [*Snipping*]: First I'm gonna cut off this doctor's legs, one, two, now then—

Percy: Why you cuttin' off that doctor's legs?

Martha: I'm gonna give him a operation. Now I'm gonna cut off his arms, one, two. Now I'm gonna fix up—

[*She pushes* Helen's *hand away from her mouth.*]

You stop that.

Percy: Cut off his stomach, that's a good operation.

Martha: No, I'm gonna cut off his head first, he got a bad cold.

Percy: Ain't gonna be much of that doctor left to fix up, time you finish all them opera—

[*But* Helen *is poking her fingers inside his mouth, to feel his tongue; he bites at them, annoyed, and she jerks them away.* Helen *now fingers her own lips, moving them in imitation, but soundlessly.*]

Martha: What you do, bite her hand?

Percy: That's how I do, she keep pokin' her fingers in my mouth, I just bite 'em off.

Martha: What she tryin' do now?

Percy: She tryin' talk. She gonna get mad. Looka her tryin' talk.

[Helen *is scowling, the lips under her fingertips moving in ghostly silence, growing more and more frantic, until in a bizarre rage she bites at her own fingers. This sends* PERCY *off into laughter, but alarms* Martha.]

Martha: Hey, you stop now.

[*She pulls* Helen's *hand down.*]

You just sit quiet and—

[*But at once* Helen *topples* Martha *on her back, knees pinning her shoulders down, and grabs the scissors.* Martha *screams.* Percy *darts to the bell string on the porch, yanks it, and the bell rings. . . .*]

WordWorkshop

UNIT 6 WORDS FOR EVERYDAY USE

airy, 212
desolate, 213
disclose, 211
distraught, 207
fickle, 203

grimace, 209
haughty, 205
modesty, 204
plaintive, 205
quandary, 214

relent, 212
smug, 212
vigorous, 209
waver, 205

WRITE ABOUT VOCABULARY WORDS. Writing about and discussing vocabulary words will help you remember them. On your own paper, respond to each of the following prompts about the concepts behind the vocabulary words in this unit. Make sure that your answers show your understanding of the italicized words.

1. Describe a time when you *wavered* about something. Were you in a *quandary?* Explain why, or why not.

2. Explain the difference between *modesty* and *smugness*.

3. Name a situation that might cause you to *grimace*, and explain why you might react that way.

4. Why might it be difficult to be around someone who is *fickle*?

5. Describe someone behaving *haughtily*. Might this person's words be described as *airy?* Why, or why not?

Literary Tools

Select the literary element from the column on the right that best completes each sentence on the left. Write the correct letter in the blank.

_____ 1. A(n) ___ is a group of people who speaks directly to the audience to convey the author's viewpoint or to introduce story details.

_____ 2. A remark meant for the audience but not the other characters to hear is called a(n) ___.

_____ 3. ___ are usually italicized and help readers visualize what would be happening on stage.

_____ 4. A(n) ___ is a major section of a play. There are often one, three, or five of these in a dramatic work.

_____ 5. Because Claire Boiko wrote *Persephone*, she could be called a(n) ___.

_____ 6. The words characters say to each other can be called ___.

_____ 7. The written version of a play is called its ___.

_____ 8. A short part of a play that happens in a single time and place is called a(n) ___.

_____ 9. In a(n) ___, a story is told through characters played by actors.

_____ 10. A speech given by one character is called a(n) ___.

a. act, 196

b. aside, 205, 217

c. chorus, 204

d. dialogue, 196

e. drama, 195

f. monologue, 196

g. playwright, 195

h. scene, 196

i. script, 195

j. stage directions, 210

On Your Own

FLUENTLY SPEAKING. Look through an anthology of plays, and find a monologue, or long speech by a single character, to perform for your class or another group. Prepare an introduction to this monologue to let your listeners know what the play is about and how this monologue fits into it. Practice reading the speech aloud until you can present it smoothly and with appropriate feeling.

PICTURE THIS. Draw a cartoon of one of the most memorable scenes from *Persephone*. Add cartoon bubbles to show the characters expressing thoughts that were not in the original selection.

PUT IT IN WRITING. If the play *Persephone* had continued rather than ending where it did, what do you think Demeter and Persephone would have said to each other? Write an imaginary dialogue between mother and daughter. You might also have them talk to Hades and tell them how they feel about him. Try to make the characters speak and act as they did in Claire Boiko's play.

Unit SEVEN

READING Nonfiction

NONFICTION

Nonfiction is writing about real people, places, things, and events. It can also explore thoughts and ideas. Categories of nonfiction writing follow.

Forms of Nonfiction

ARTICLE. An **article** is a brief work of nonfiction on a specific topic. You can find articles in encyclopedias, newspapers, and magazines.

AUTOBIOGRAPHY. An **autobiography** is the story of a person's life told by that person. Consequently, autobiographies are told from the first-person point of view.

BIOGRAPHY. A **biography** is the story of a person's life told by another person. Although biographies are told from a third-person point of view, autobiographical excerpts such as **letters**, **diaries**, and **journals** may be included.

DOCUMENTARY WRITING. **Documentary writing** is writing that records an event or subject in accurate detail. A profile of the Jazz Age or a report on human rights abuses in China would be examples of documentary writing.

ESSAY. An **essay**, originally meaning "a trial or attempt," is a short nonfiction work that explores a single subject and is typically a more lasting work than an article. Among the many types of essays are personal and expository essays. A **personal**, or **expressive, essay** deals with the life or interests of the writer. Personal essays are often, but not always, written in the first person. "The Price of Freedom" in this unit is an example of an expressive essay. An **expository essay** features the developed ideas of the writer on a certain topic, usually expressing an author's opinion. "Appearances Are Destructive" is an example of an expository essay.

Reading TIP

You will often read nonfiction to learn or to read for information. The purpose of this type of reading is to gain knowledge.

NOTE THE FACTS

What kind of essay deals with the life or interests of the writer?

_____

_____

_____

CONNECT TO PRIOR
KNOWLEDGE. What types of
histories have you read in
social studies class?

_____

_____

_____

_____

THINK AND REFLECT

Write another example of
how-to writing. (Apply)

_____

_____

_____

Reading TIP

A nonfiction work can have
more than one purpose. For
example, in a memoir a writer
could entertain with a story,
then persuade the reader to
take action.

HISTORY. A **history** is an account of past events. To write histories, writers may use **speeches, sermons, contracts, deeds, constitutions, laws, political tracts,** and other types of public records. "The *Challenger* Disaster" is an example of a speech, that is now read to show the history of that event.

HOW-TO WRITING. **How-to writing** is writing that explains a procedure or strategy. A manual that explains how to operate a DVD player is an example of how-to writing.

MEMOIR. A **memoir** is a nonfiction narration that tells a story autobiographically or biographically. Memoirs are based on a person's experiences and reactions to events. "The Green Mamba" by Roald Dahl is an example of an autobiographical memoir. "Roberto Clemente: A Bittersweet Memoir" by Jerry Izenberg is an example of a biographical memoir.

SPEECH. A **speech** is a public address that was originally delivered orally. "The *Challenger* Disaster" given by President Reagan is an example of a speech.

Purposes and Methods of Writing in Nonfiction

PURPOSE. A writer's **purpose**, or aim, is a writer's reason for writing. The following chart classifies modes, or categories, of prose writing by purpose.

Modes and Purposes of Writing		
Mode	Purpose	Writing Forms
personal/ expressive writing	to reflect	diary entry, memoir, personal letter, autobiography, personal essay
imaginative/ descriptive writing	to entertain, to describe, to enrich, and to enlighten	poem, character sketch, play, short story
narrative writing	to tell a story, to narrate a series of events	short story, biography, legend, myth, history
informative/ expository writing	to inform, to explain	news article, research report, expository essay, book review
persuasive/ argumentative writing	to persuade	editorial, petition, political speech, persuasive essay

Types of Nonfiction Writing

In order to write effectively, a writer can choose to organize a piece of writing in different ways. The following chart describes types of writing that are commonly used in nonfiction, as well as tells how they are organized.

Type of Writing	Description
narration	Narrative writing tells a story or describes events. It may use chronological, or time, order.
dialogue	Dialogue reveals people's actual speech, which is set off with quotation marks.
description	Descriptive writing tells how things look, sound, smell, taste, or feel, often using spatial order.
exposition	Expository writing presents facts or opinions and is sometimes organized in one of these ways: ■ **Analysis** breaks something into its parts and shows how the parts are related. ■ **Classification** places subjects into categories according to what they have in common. ■ **Comparison-and-contrast order** presents similarities as it compares two things and differences as it contrasts them. ■ **How-to writing** presents the steps in a process or directions on how to do something.

NOTE THE FACTS

What type of exposition presents similarities as it compares two things and differences as it contrasts them?

_____

_____

_____

Active Reading Strategy Checklists

When reading nonfiction, it is important to know that the author is telling you about true events. The following checklists offer things to consider when reading nonfiction selections.

1 READ WITH A PURPOSE. Before reading nonfiction, give yourself a purpose, or something to look for, as you read. Sometimes your teacher will give you a purpose: "Find out what the author experienced on her trip to Arkansas." Other times you can set your own purpose by previewing the title, the opening lines, and instructional information. Say to yourself

❑ This selection will be about . . .
❑ I will keep track of . . .
❑ The author wants readers to know . . .
❑ The author wrote this to . . .

2 CONNECT TO PRIOR KNOWLEDGE. Being aware of what you already know and calling it to mind as you read can help you understand a writer's views. As you read, say to yourself

❑ I already know this about the author's ideas . . .
❑ These things in the selection are similar to something I have experienced . . .
❑ Something similar I've read is . . .
❑ I agree with this because . . .

3 WRITE THINGS DOWN. As you read nonfiction, write down or mark important points that the author makes. Possible ways to keep a written record include

❑ Underline the author's key ideas.
❑ Write down your thoughts about the author's ideas.
❑ Highlight the author's main points and supporting details.
❑ Create a graphic organizer to keep track of ideas.
❑ Use a code to respond to the author's ideas.

Reading TIP

Read nonfiction carefully the first time through. Take notes as you read. After you finish reading, reread your notes. Mark them up and make additions or corrections. Rereading your notes and clarifying them helps you remember what you've read.

Reading TIP

To **connect to your prior knowledge,** compare what you are reading to

■ things you have read before
■ things you have experienced
■ things you know about the topic

Reading TIP

A simple code can help you remember your reactions to what you are reading. You can use

! for "This is like something I have experienced"
? for "I don't understand this"
✓ for "This seems important"

4 **MAKE PREDICTIONS.** Before you read a nonfiction selection, use information about the author, the subject matter, and the title to guess what the selection will be about. Make predictions like the following:

- ❑ What will come next is . . .
- ❑ The author will support ideas by . . .
- ❑ I think the selection will end with . . .
- ❑ The title tells me that the selection will be about . . .

5 **VISUALIZE.** Visualizing, or allowing the words on the page to create images in your mind, helps you understand the author's message. In order to visualize what a selection is about, imagine that you are the narrator. Read the words in your head with the type of expression that the author means to put behind them. Make statements such as

- ❑ This parts helps me envision how . . .
- ❑ My sketch of this part would include . . .
- ❑ This part helps me see how . . .
- ❑ This part changes my views on . . .
- ❑ The author connects ideas by . . .

6 **USE TEXT ORGANIZATION.** When you read nonfiction, pay attention to the main idea and supporting details. Learn to stop occasionally and retell what you have read. Say to yourself

- ❑ The writer's main point is . . .
- ❑ The writer supports the main point by . . .
- ❑ In this section, the writer is saying that . . .
- ❑ I can summarize this section by . . .
- ❑ I can follow the events because . . .

7 **TACKLE DIFFICULT VOCABULARY.** Difficult words can hinder your ability to understand a writer's message. Use context, consult a dictionary, or ask someone about words you do not understand. When you come across a difficult word in nonfiction, say to yourself

- ❑ The lines near this word tell me that this word means . . .
- ❑ A dictionary definition shows that the word means . . .
- ❑ My work with the word before reading helps me know that the word means . . .
- ❑ A classmate said that the word means . . .

Reading **TIP**

Skim a selection before you read it. Make a list of words that might slow you down, and write *synonyms*, words that have the same or nearly the same meaning, for each in the margins. As you read, use the synonyms in place of the words.

8 MONITOR YOUR READING PROGRESS. All readers encounter difficulty when they read, especially if they do not choose the reading material themselves. When you have to read something, take note of problems you are having and fix them. The key to reading success is knowing when you are having difficulty. To fix problems, say to yourself

- ❏ Because I don't understand this part, I will . . .
- ❏ Because I'm having trouble staying connected to the ideas in the selection, I will . . .
- ❏ Because the words in the selection are too hard, I will . . .
- ❏ Because the selection is long, I will . . .
- ❏ Because I can't retell what the selection was about, I will . . .

Become an Active Reader

The instruction with the nonfiction selections in this unit gives you an in-depth look at how to use one strategy. Learning how to use several strategies in combination will ensure your complete understanding of what you are reading. When you have difficulty, use active reading solutions to fix a problem. For further information about the active reading strategies, see Unit 1, pages 4–15.

How to Use Reading Strategies with Nonfiction

The following excerpts illustrate how a reader might use active reading strategies with nonfiction.

Excerpt 1. Note how a reader uses reading strategies while reading this excerpt from "The Green Mamba" by Roald Dahl.

READ WITH A PURPOSE

I want to learn what is going to happen with the green mambas.

CONNECT TO PRIOR KNOWLEDGE

This reminds me of the garter snakes I caught as a kid.

"OH, THOSE SNAKES! How I hated them! They were the only fearful thing about Tanganyika, and a newcomer very quickly learnt to identify most of them and to know which were deadly and which were simply poisonous. The killers, apart from the black mambas, were the green mambas, the cobras and the tiny little puff adders that looked very much like small sticks lying motionless in the middle of a dusty path, and so easy to step on."

VISUALIZE

I am imagining several snakes. All of them look menacing and are slithering through the grass—soundlessly.

MAKE PREDICTIONS

I am guessing that a green mamba might attack someone.

Excerpt 2. Note how a reader uses active reading strategies while reading this excerpt from Peggy Noonan's speech for President Reagan "The *Challenger* Disaster."

WRITE THINGS DOWN

I can highlight all the sections that compare past and present events.

TACKLE DIFFICULT VOCABULARY

Since the word *coincidence* comes from the word *coincide*, or to occur at the same time, the phrase "There's a coincidence today" refers to two things occurring.

"We've grown used to the idea of space, and perhaps we forget that we've only just begun. We're still pioneers. They, the members of the *Challenger* crew, were pioneers.

And I want to say something to the schoolchildren of America who were watching the live coverage of the shuttle's takeoff. I know it is hard to understand, but sometimes painful things like this happen. It's all part of taking a chance and expanding man's horizons. The future doesn't belong to the fainthearted; it belongs to the brave. The *Challenger* crew was pulling us into the future, and we'll continue to follow them. . . .

There's a coincidence today. On this day 390 years ago, the great explorer Sir Francis Drake died aboard ship off the coast of Panama. In his lifetime the great frontiers were the oceans, and a historian later said, "He lived by the sea, died on it, and was buried in it."

MONITOR YOUR READING PROGRESS

I don't understand this part—I'll work with a partner and answer the margin questions.

USE TEXT ORGANIZATION

Noonan compares past and present events several times. This makes it easier for me to see the big picture of exploration.

"The Green Mamba"
by Roald Dahl

Word watch

PREVIEW VOCABULARY

arc	manipulate
forlorn	unruffled
malevolent	wheedling

Reader's journal

What would you do if someone told you a deadly snake had just entered your house?

_____

_____

_____

Active READING STRATEGY

VISUALIZE

Before Reading → ### CREATE A MIND PICTURE FROM A MEMORY

❑ With a partner, describe your favorite place—do not tell the name of this place. Be sure that both of you have your eyes closed so that you can both visualize the picture being created. Then ask your partner to guess the name of the place you have described.
❑ Share your mind pictures with the class.
❑ As you read the selection, try to visualize the place, as well as the characters and their actions. Then make sketches of your visualizations in the chart below.

Graphic Organizer: Visualization Chart

Page #	Sketch
Page 1	

The GREEN Mamba

Roald Dahl

VISUALIZE THE CHARACTERS

❑ Your teacher will read the first page of the story. Listen closely and create mind pictures. As you are listening, sketch what you are seeing in your Visualization Chart.

❑ Begin reading where your teacher left off. Visualize what you are reading about. Notice the setting, characters, and descriptions.

❑ Each time you stop to visualize, add to your Visualization Chart.

O H, THOSE SNAKES! How I hated them! They were the only fearful thing about Tanganyika, and a newcomer very quickly learnt to identify most of them and to know which were deadly and which were simply poisonous. The killers, apart from the black mambas, were the green mambas, the cobras and the tiny little puff adders that looked very much like small sticks lying motionless in the middle of a dusty path, and so easy to step on.

10   One Sunday evening I was invited to go and have a sundowner[1] at the house of an Englishman called Fuller who worked in the Customs office[2] in Dar es Salaam. He lived with his wife and two small children in a plain white wooden house that stood alone some way back from the road in a rough grassy piece of ground with coconut trees scattered about. I was walking across the grass towards the house and was about twenty yards away when I saw a large green snake go gliding straight up the veranda[3] steps of Fuller's house and in through the open front door. The

20   brilliant yellowy-green skin and its great size made me certain it was a green mamba, a creature almost as deadly as the black mamba, and for a few seconds I was so startled and dumbfounded and horrified that I froze to the spot. Then I pulled myself together and ran round to the back of the house shouting, "Mr Fuller! Mr Fuller!"

    Mrs Fuller popped her head out of an upstairs window. "What on earth's the matter?" she said.

READ ALOUD

Read aloud lines 19–23. Why is the narrator horrified?

_____

_____

_____

Reading TIP

Note that British punctuation does not use a period after abbreviations of titles such as Mr. or Mrs.

---

1. **sundowner.** An evening refreshment
2. **Customs office.** Government agency that controls taxes on imports and exports
3. **veranda.** Open-air porch area, usually with a roof

"You've got a large green mamba in your front room!" I shouted. "I saw it go up the veranda steps and right in 30   through the door!"

"Fred!" Mrs Fuller shouted, turning round. "Fred! Come here!"

Freddy Fuller's round red face appeared at the window beside his wife. "What's up" he asked.

"There's a green mamba in your living-room!" I shouted.

Without hesitation and without wasting time with more questions, he said to me, "Stay there. I'm going to lower the children down to you one at a time." He was completely cool and <u>unruffled</u>. He didn't even raise his 40   voice.

A small girl was lowered down to me by her wrists and I was able to catch her easily by the legs. Then came a small boy. Then Freddy Fuller lowered his wife and I caught her by the waist and put her on the ground. Then came Fuller himself. He hung by his hands from the window-sill and when he let go he landed neatly on his two feet.

We stood in a little group on the grass at the back of the house and I told Fuller exactly what I had seen.

The mother was holding the two children by the hand, 50   one on each side of her. They didn't seem to be particularly alarmed.

"What happens now?" I asked.

"Go down to the road, all of you," Fuller said. "I'm off to fetch the snake-man." He trotted away and got into his small ancient black car and drove off. Mrs Fuller and the two small children and I went down to the road and sat in the shade of a large mango tree.

"Who is this snake-man?" I asked Mrs Fuller.

"He is an old Englishman who has been out here for 60   years," Mrs Fuller said. "He actually *likes* snakes. He understands them and never kills them. He catches them and sells them to zoos and laboratories all over the world.

words for everyday use

un • ruf • fled (un ru' fəld) *adj.*, poised; calm. *Despite the hubbub, our teacher remained <u>unruffled</u>.*

Every native for miles around knows about him and whenever one of them sees a snake, he marks its hiding place and runs, often for great distances, to tell the snake-man. Then the snake-man comes along and captures it. The snake-man's strict rule is that he will never buy a captured snake from the natives."

"Why not?" I asked.

70   "To discourage them from trying to catch snakes themselves," Mrs Fuller said. "In his early days he used to buy caught snakes, but so many natives got bitten trying to catch them, and so many died, that he decided to put a stop to it. Now any native who brings in a caught snake, no matter how rare, gets turned away."

"That's good," I said.

"What is the snake-man's name?" I asked.

"Donald Macfarlane," she said. "I believe he's Scottish."

"Is the snake in the house, Mummy?" the small girl asked.

80   "Yes, darling. But the snake-man is going to get it out."

"He'll bite Jack," the girl said.

"Oh, my God!" Mrs Fuller cried, jumping to her feet. "I forgot about Jack!" She began calling out, "Jack! Come here, Jack! Jack! . . . Jack! . . . Jack!"

The children jumped up as well and all of them started calling to the dog. But no dog came out of the open front door.

"He's bitten Jack!" the small girl cried out. "He must have bitten him!" She began to cry and so did her brother, who

90 was a year or so younger than she was. Mrs Fuller looked grim.

"Jack's probably hiding upstairs," she said. "You know how clever he is."

Mrs Fuller and I seated ourselves again on the grass, but the children remained standing. In between their tears they went on calling to the dog.

"Would you like me to take you down to the Maddens' house?" their mother asked.

"No!" they cried. "No, no, no! We want Jack!"

100   "Here's Daddy!" Mrs Fuller cried, pointing at the tiny black car coming up the road in a swirl of dust. I noticed a long wooden pole sticking out through one of the car windows.

NOTE THE FACTS

How do the children and Mrs. Fuller react when they realize the dog is still in the house?

_____

_____

THINK AND REFLECT

What role does the dog play in this story? **(Interpret)**

_____

_____

_____

Literary TOOLS

SUSPENSE. Suspense is a feeling of expectation, anxiety, or curiosity created by questions raised in the mind of a reader. As the story unfolds, readers fear that someone will be bitten by the green mamba. This fear is reinforced by the author's attention to *sensory details,* which carefully describe things that can be seen, tasted, touched, heard, or smelled. As you read, underline or highlight the words that create a suspenseful mood.

Use THE STRATEGY

VISUALIZE. Remember to stop, close your eyes, and see the picture that the words create.

The children ran to meet the car. "Jack's inside the house and he's been bitten by the snake!" they wailed. "We know he's been bitten! He doesn't come when we call him!"

Mr Fuller and the snake-man got out of the car. The snake-man was small and very old, probably over seventy. He wore leather boots made of thick cowhide and he had long gauntlet-type gloves[4] on his hands made of the same
110   stuff. The gloves reached above his elbows. In his right hand he carried an extraordinary implement, an eight-foot-long wooden pole with a forked end. The two prongs of the fork were made, so it seemed, of black rubber, about an inch thick and quite flexible, and it was clear that if the fork was pressed against the ground the two prongs would bend outwards, allowing the neck of the fork to go down as close to the ground as necessary. In his left hand he carried an ordinary brown sack.

Donald Macfarlane, the snake-man, may have been old
120   and small but he was an impressive-looking character. His eyes were pale blue, deep-set in a face round and dark and wrinkled as a walnut. Above the blue eyes, the eyebrows were thick and startlingly white, but the hair on his head was almost black. In spite of the thick leather boots, he moved like a leopard, with soft slow cat-like strides, and he came straight up to me and said, "Who are you?"

"He's with Shell,"[5] Fuller said. "He hasn't been here long."

"You want to watch?" the snake-man said to me.

"Watch?" I said, wavering. "Watch? How do you mean
130   watch? I mean where from? Not in the house?"

"You can stand out on the veranda and look through the window," the snake-man said.

"Come on," Fuller said. "We'll both watch."

"Now don't do anything silly," Mrs Fuller said.

The two children stood there <u>forlorn</u> and miserable, with tears all over their cheeks.

---

4. **gauntlet-type gloves.** Protective gloves
5. **Shell.** Shell Oil, the company Dahl flew for

| words for everyday use | for • lorn (for lorn') *adj.*, sad, lonely, hopeless. *The <u>forlorn</u> puppy must have been lost or abandoned.* |

The snake-man and Fuller and I walked over the grass towards the house, and as we approached the veranda steps the snake-man whispered, "Tread softly on the wooden boards or he'll pick up the vibration. Wait until I've gone in, then walk up quietly and stand by the window."

140

The snake-man went up the steps first and he made absolutely no sound at all with his feet. He moved soft and catlike on to the veranda and straight through the front door and then he quickly but very quietly closed the door behind him.

I felt better with the door closed. What I mean is I felt better for myself. I certainly didn't feel better for the snake-man. I figured he was committing suicide. I followed Fuller on to the veranda and we both crept over to the window. The window was open, but it had a fine mesh mosquito-netting all over it. That made me feel better still. We peered through the netting.

150

The living-room was simple and ordinary, coconut matting on the floor, a red sofa, a coffee-table and a couple of armchairs. The dog was sprawled on the matting under the coffee-table, a large Airedale with curly brown and black hair. He was stone dead.

The snake-man was standing absolutely still just inside the door of the living-room. The brown sack was now slung over his left shoulder and he was grasping the long pole with both hands, holding it out in front of him, parallel to the ground. I couldn't see the snake. I didn't think the snake-man had seen it yet either.

160

A minute went by . . . two minutes . . . three . . . four . . . five. Nobody moved. There was death in that room. The air was heavy with death and the snake-man stood as motionless as a pillar of stone, with the long rod held out in front of him.

And still he waited. Another minute . . . and another . . . and another.

170

And now I saw the snake-man beginning to bend his knees. Very slowly he bent his knees until he was almost squatting on the floor, and from that position he tried to peer under the sofa and the armchairs.

FIX-UP IDEA

Reread
If you find it difficult to picture things as you read, try refocusing on the highlighted passage on this page. Reread the passage carefully. Imagine you were there. How would the man move? What would you hear? How would you feel watching him? Write a description of what you see, hear, and feel. Add details using your own words.

NOTE THE FACTS

Who sees the snake first?
What does he do?

_____

_____

_____

_____

Reading STRATEGY
REVIEW

USE PRIOR KNOWLEDGE. As you
read the selection think about
what you know about snakes.
Use this information to
predict what will happen
next in the selection.

And still it didn't look as though he was seeing
anything.

Slowly he straightened his legs again, and then his head
began to swivel around the room. Over to the right, in the
180 far corner, a staircase led up to the floor above. The snake-
man looked at the stairs, and I knew very well what was
going through his head. Quite abruptly, he took one step
forward and stopped.

Nothing happened.

A moment later I caught sight of the snake. It was lying
full-length along the skirting[6] of the right-hand wall, but
hidden from the snake-man's view by the back of the sofa.
It lay there like a long, beautiful, deadly shaft of green
glass, quite motionless, perhaps asleep. It was facing away
190 from us who were at the window, with its small triangular
head resting on the matting near the foot of the stairs.

I nudged Fuller and whispered, "It's over there against the
wall." I pointed and Fuller saw the snake. At once, he
started waving both hands, palms outward, back and forth
across the window, hoping to get the snake-man's attention.
The snakeman didn't see him. Very softly, Fuller said,
"Pssst!" and the snake-man looked up sharply. Fuller
pointed. The snake-man understood and gave a nod.

Now the snake-man began working his way very very
200 slowly to the back wall of the room so as to get a view of
the snake behind the sofa. He never walked on his toes as
you or I would have done. His feet remained flat on the
ground all the time. The cowhide boots were like
moccasins, with neither soles nor heels. Gradually, he
worked his way over to the back wall, and from there he
was able to see at least the head and two or three feet of the
snake itself.

But the snake also saw him. With a movement so fast it
was invisible, the snake's head came up about two feet off
210 the floor and the front of the body arched backwards, ready
to strike. Almost simultaneously, it bunched its whole body
into a series of curves, ready to flash forward.

The snake-man was just a bit too far away from the snake

---

6. **skirting.** Baseboard

to reach it with the end of his pole. He waited, staring at the snake, and the snake stared back at him with two small <u>malevolent</u> black eyes.

Then the snake-man started speaking to the snake. "Come along, my pretty," he whispered in a soft <u>wheedling</u> voice. "There's a good boy. Nobody's going to hurt you.
220 Nobody's going to harm you, my pretty little thing. Just lie still and relax . . ." He took a step forward towards the snake, holding the pole out in front of him.

What the snake did next was so fast that the whole movement couldn't have taken more than a hundredth of a second, like the flick of a camera shutter. There was a green flash as the snake darted forward at least ten feet and struck at the snake-man's leg. Nobody could have got out of the way of that one. I heard the snake's head strike against the thick cowhide boot with a sharp little crack, and then at
230 once the head was back in that same deadly backward-curving position, ready to strike again.

"There's a good boy," the snake-man said softly. "There's a clever boy. There's a lovely fellow. You mustn't get excited. Keep calm and everything's going to be all right." As he was speaking, he was slowly lowering the end of the pole until the forked prongs were about twelve inches above the middle of the snake's body. "There's a lovely fellow," he whispered. "There's a good kind little chap. Keep still now, my beauty. Keep still, my pretty. Keep quite
240 still. Daddy's not going to hurt you."

I could see a thin dark trickle of venom running down the snake-man's right boot where the snake had struck.

The snake, head raised and <u>arcing</u> backwards, was as tense as a tight-wound spring and ready to strike again. "Keep still, my lovely," the snake-man whispered. "Don't move now. Keep still. No one's going to hurt you."

Then *wham*, the rubber prongs came down right across the snake's body, about midway along its length, and pinned

words for everyday use	**ma • lev • o • lent** (mə lev′ və lənt) *adj.,* having or showing hatred. *The young man's <u>malevolent</u> gesture revealed his anger.* **whee • dling** (hwēd liŋ) *adj.,* coaxing; flattering. *The girl spoke with a pleading, <u>wheedling</u> tone when she wanted a treat.* **arc** (ärk) *v.,* follow a curved course. *The rainbow <u>arced</u> over the horizon.*

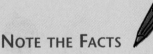

NOTE THE FACTS

What does the snake-man
do once the prongs are
just behind the snake's
head?

_____

_____

_____

it to the floor. All I could see was a green blur as the snake
thrashed around furiously in an effort to free itself. But the
snake-man kept up the pressure on the prongs and the
snake was trapped.

What happens next? I wondered. There was no way he
could catch hold of that madly twisting flailing length of
green muscle with his hands, and even if he could have
done so, the head would surely have flashed around and
bitten him in the face.

Holding the very end of the eight-foot pole, the snake-
man began to work his way round the room until he was at
the tail end of the snake. Then, in spite of the flailing and
the thrashing, he started pushing the prongs forward along
the snake's body towards the head. Very very slowly he did
it, pushing the rubber prongs forward over the snake's
flailing body, keeping the snake pinned down all the time
and pushing, pushing, pushing the long wooden rod
forward millimetre[7] by millimetre. It was a fascinating and
frightening thing to watch, the little man with white
eyebrows and black hair carefully <u>manipulating</u> his long
implement and sliding the fork ever so slowly along the
length of the twisting snake towards the head. The snake's
body was thumping against the coconut matting with such
a noise that if you had been upstairs you might have
thought two big men were wrestling on the floor.

Then at last the prongs were right behind the head itself,
pinning it down, and at that point the snake-man reached
forward with one gloved hand and grasped the snake very
firmly by the neck. He threw away the pole. He took the
sack off his shoulder with his free hand. He lifted the great,
still twisting length of the deadly green snake and pushed
the head into the sack. Then he let go the head and
bundled the rest of the creature in and closed the sack. The
sack started jumping about as though there were fifty angry

250

260

270

280

---

7. **millimetre.** British spelling of *millimeter,* a Metric unit of measure

words for everyday use	ma • nip • u • late (mə niˈ pyə lāt) v., treat or operate with the hands in a skillful manner. *Gina carefully <u>manipulated</u> the tangled necklaces until she got them apart.*

rats inside it, but the snake-man was now totally relaxed and he held the sack casually in one hand as if it contained no more than a few pounds of potatoes. He stooped and picked up his pole from the floor, then he turned and looked towards the window where we were peering in.

"Pity about the dog," he said. "You'd better get it out of the way before the children see it." ■

NOTE THE FACTS

What are the snake-man's final instructions to the two men watching him?

_____

_____

_____

Reflect ON YOUR READING

After Reading ▶ **REFLECT ON YOUR PICTURES**

❑ Share the pictures in your Visualization Chart with a partner.
❑ Compare the similarities and the differences between the sketches that each of you drew. Analyze the reasons for the differences. Record them below.

_____

_____

_____

_____

THINK-ALOUD NOTES

_____

_____

_____

_____

_____

_____

_____

_____

_____

_____

_____

Reading Skills and Test Practice

DRAWING CONCLUSIONS

Discuss with your partner how best to answer the following questions about the story. Use the Think-Aloud Notes to write down your reasons for eliminating the incorrect answers.

____1. Based on the following passage, what can you conclude about the snake-man?

The snake-man was small and very old, probably over seventy. He wore leather boots made of thick cowhide and he had long gauntlet-type gloves on his hands made of the same stuff.

a. He is uncertain what to do.
b. He is prepared and capable.
c. He is too old to be catching snakes.
d. He is incapable of catching a snake.

____2. Which word or phrase best describes the snake-man in the following passage?

"Keep still, my lovely," the snake-man whispered. "Don't move now. Keep still. No one's going to hurt you."

a. petrified
b. calm
c. nervous
d. a beginner

Investigate, Inquire, and Imagine

RECALL: GATHER FACTS →
1a. How does Mr. Fuller respond to the news that a green mamba has entered his living room? What does he do? How does he act?

INTERPRET: FIND MEANING
1b. Based on Mr. Fuller's actions and reactions, how do you think he feels about the snake?

ANALYZE: TAKE THINGS APART →
2a. What words and phrases does the narrator use to describe the green mamba and its actions? What words and phrases does he use to describe the snake-man and his actions?

SYNTHESIZE: BRING THINGS TOGETHER
2b. In your own words, summarize the narrator's characterization of both the green mamba and the snake-man.

EVALUATE: MAKE JUDGMENTS →
3a. How effective is the snake-man's method of dealing with the green mamba? How else might he handle the situation?

EXTEND: CONNECT IDEAS
3b. What might the snake-man tell his old friends from Scotland about this experience? How might his old Scottish friends react?

Literary Tools

SUSPENSE. **Suspense** is a feeling of expectation, anxiety, or curiosity created by questions raised in the mind of a reader. Look back at the sensory details the author used to build suspense that you highlighted as you read the selection. Write each sensory detail in the following chart beneath the sense to which it appeals.

Sensory Details				
Sight	**Sound**	**Touch**	**Taste**	**Smell**

Discuss with your classmates how Roald Dahl builds suspense in "The Green Mamba." In what ways did you wonder what would happen next? Note the points in the story where you felt the suspense increase.

_____

_____

_____

WordWorkshop

VOCABULARY IN CONTEXT. Fill in each blank below with the most appropriate vocabulary word from "The Green Mamba." You may have to change the tense of the word.

unruffled	forlorn	malevolent
wheedling	arc	manipulate

1. Ignoring his student's_____ voices begging him to put off the test to another day, Mr. Atkinson called for silence and passed out the test.

2. When the thunderstorm struck, the _____ campers huddled miserably in their tents.

3. When the boat began to take on water, the _____ guide calmly directed everyone to put on life preservers and bail.

4. The balloonist easily _____ the ropes and valves to guide the hot-air balloon over the green fields and low hills.

5. The mob boss faced his enemy with a(n) _____ stare.

Read-Write Connection

If you were the narrator, would you want to watch the snake-man? Why, or why not?

_____

_____

_____

Beyond the Reading

RESEARCH POISONOUS SNAKES. Using the library or the Internet, look up information on the green mamba, the black mamba, the cobra, the puff adder, or another poisonous snake. Research the snake's physical description, habitat, diet, and population status (is it endangered?). Try to answer most of the following questions about the snake. Where does it live? Is it extremely or only mildly venomous? What does it eat? Does its venom have medical uses? Report your finding to the class.

GO ONLINE. To find links and additional activities for this selection, visit the EMC Internet Resource Center at **emcp.com/languagearts** and click on Write-In Reader.

Roberto Clemente:

"A Bittersweet Memoir"

by Jerry Izenberg

Active READING STRATEGY

USE TEXT ORGANIZATION

Before Reading ➤ **PREVIEW TEXT ORGANIZATION**

❏ Notice that this selection is not divided into sections with titles.
❏ Writing down suggested titles of sections will be your task. The sections may be short (a few paragraphs) or long (more than a page in length). You will need to use text organization to decide when one section ends and another begins.
❏ Preview the Organization Chart below.
❏ As you read, you will write down a suggested title for a section in the margin. Then add it to the left column of the Organization Chart. In the right column, you will take notes on details that you think are important.

Graphic Organizer: Organization Chart

Section Title	Details
Career Records	3,000 career hits 9,454 at bats 1,205 runs

CONNECT

Reader's resource

"Roberto Clemente: A Bittersweet Memoir" tells of the greatness of one man—Roberto Clemente. He was born and discovered to have remarkable baseball talent in Carolina, Puerto Rico. From there, he moved to the United States to play professional baseball. In 1954, he began playing for the Pittsburgh Pirates—he was thought to be one of the greatest baseball players in the world. He played baseball for another 18 years, breaking record after record. To the world's stunned surprise, he was killed in 1972 while flying much needed supplies to earthquake victims in Nicaragua, Central America.

Word watch

PREVIEW VOCABULARY

conjecture

Reader's journal

Whom from the past or present do you most admire, and why?

_____

_____

_____

_____

WRITE DOWN TOPICS AND DETAILS

❑ Read the first page and decide where the first section might end. Give this first section a title and write it in the margin. Then write down two or three important details in your Organization Chart.

❑ Keep reading and adding section titles and details to the text and to your chart.

Reading TIP

A **memoir** is a nonfiction narration that tells a story. A memoir can be autobiographical (about one's own life) or biographical (about someone else's life). Memoirs are based on a person's experiences and reactions to historical events. "Roberto Clemente: A Bittersweet Memoir" is a biographical memoir.

READ ALOUD

Read aloud the highlighted text (lines 13–33). What won't the record books tell you?

_____

_____

_____

Roberto Clemente: A Bittersweet Memoir

Jerry Izenberg

I saw him play so often. I watched the grace of his movements and the artistry of his reflexes from who knows how many press boxes. None of us really appreciated how pure an athlete he was until he was gone. What follows is a personal retracing of the steps that took Roberto Clemente from the narrow, crowded streets of his native Carolina to the local ball parks in San Juan and on to the major leagues. But it is more. It is a remembrance formed as I stood at the water's edge in Puerto Rico and stared at daybreak into the waves that killed him. It is all the people I met
10 *in Puerto Rico who knew him and loved him. It is the way an entire island in the sun and a Pennsylvania city in the smog took his death. . . .*

The record book will tell you that Roberto Clemente collected 3,000 hits during his major-league career. It will say that he came to bat 9,454 times, that he drove in 1,305 runs, and played 2,433 games over an eighteen-year span.

But it won't tell you about Carolina, Puerto Rico; and the old square; and the narrow, twisting streets; and the roots
20 that produced him. It won't tell you about the Julio Coronado School and a remarkable woman named María Isabella Casares, whom he called "Teacher" until the day he died and who helped to shape his life in times of despair and depression. It won't tell you about a man named Pedron Zarrilla who found him on a country softball team and put him in the uniform of the Santurce club and who

nursed him from promising young athlete to major-league superstar.

And most of all, those cold numbers won't begin to delineate[1] the man Roberto Clemente was. To even begin to understand what this magnificent athlete was all about, you have to work backward. The search begins at the site of its ending.

The car moves easily through the predawn streets of San Juan. A heavy all-night rain has now begun to drive, and there is that post-rain sweetness in the air that holds the promise of a new, fresh, clear dawn. This is a journey to the site of one of Puerto Rico's deepest tragedies. This last says a lot. Tragedy is no stranger to the sensitive emotional people who make this island the human place it is.

Shortly before the first rays of sunlight, the car turns down a bumpy secondary road and moves past small shantytowns, where the sounds of the children stirring for the long walk toward school begin to drift out on the morning air. Then there is another turn, between a brace[2] of trees and onto the hardpacked dirt and sand, and although the light has not yet quite begun to break, you can sense the nearness of the ocean. You can hear its waves pounding harshly against the jagged rocks. You can smell its saltiness. The car noses to a stop, and the driver says, "From here you must walk. There is no other way." The place is called Puente Maldonado and the dawn does not slip into this angry place. It explodes in a million lights and colors as the large fireball of the sun begins to nose above the horizon.

"This is the nearest place," the driver tells me. "This is where they came by the thousands on that New Year's Eve and New Year's Day. Out there," he says, gesturing with his right hand, "out there, perhaps a mile and a half from where we stand. That's where we think the plane went down."

The final hours of Roberto Clemente were like this. Just a month or so before, he had agreed to take a junior-league baseball team to Nicaragua and manage it in an all-star game in Managua. He had met people and made friends there. He was not a man who made friends casually. He had always said that the people you wanted to give your friendship to were

---
1. **delineate.** Describe
2. **brace.** Grove that provides shelter from wind

30

40

50

60

Literary TOOLS

ANECDOTE. An **anecdote** is a brief story, usually told to make a point. Within this memoir, a number of people who knew Robert Clemente offer anecdotes about the kind of person he was and the things he did. These anecdotes help create a more complete picture of Roberto Clemente, both as a baseball player and as a human being.

NOTE THE FACTS

What happened out in the ocean?

_____

_____

_____

MARK THE TEXT

Highlight or underline what happened two weeks after Clemente left Nicaragua.

the people for whom you had to be willing to give something in return—no matter what the price.

Two weeks after he returned from that trip, Managua, Nicaragua exploded into flames. The earth trembled and people died. It was the worst earthquake anywhere in the Western Hemisphere in a long, long time.

Back in Puerto Rico, a television personality named Luis Vigereaux heard the news and was moved to try to help the victims. He needed someone to whom the people would listen, someone who could say what had to be said and get the work done that had to be done and help the people who had to be helped.

"I knew," Luis Vigereaux said, "Roberto was such a person, perhaps the only such person who would be willing to help."

And so the mercy project, which would eventually claim Roberto's life, began. He appeared on television. But he needed a staging area. The city agreed to give him Sixto Escobar Stadium.

"Bring what you can," he told them. "Bring medicine . . . bring clothes . . . bring food . . . bring shoes . . . bring yourself and help us load. We need so much. Whatever you bring, we will use."

And the people of San Juan came. They walked through the heat and they drove cars and battered little trucks, and the mound of supplies grew and grew. Within two days, the first mercy planes left for Nicaragua.

Meanwhile, a ship had been chartered and loaded. And as it prepared to steam away, unhappy stories began to drift back from Nicaragua. Not all the supplies that had been flown in, it was rumored, were getting through. Puerto Ricans who had flown the planes had no passports, and Nicaragua was in a state of panic.

"We have people there who must be protected. We have black-market types that must not be allowed to get their hands on these supplies," Clemente told Luis Vigereaux. "Someone must make sure—particularly before the ship gets there. I'm going on the next plane."

The plane they had rented was an old DC-7. It was scheduled to take off at 4:00 P.M. on December 31, 1972. Long before take-off time, it was apparent that the plane needed more work. It had even taxied onto the runway and then turned back. The trouble, a mechanic who was at the airstrip that day <u>conjectured</u>, had to do with both port [left side] engines. He worked on them most of the afternoon.

The departure time was delayed an hour, and then two, and then three. Across town, a man named Rudy Hernandez, who had been a teammate of Roberto's when they were rookies in the Puerto Rican League and who had later pitched for the Washington Senators, was trying to contact Roberto by telephone. He had just received a five-hundred-dollar donation, and he wanted to know where to send it. He called Roberto's wife, Vera, who told him that Roberto was going on a trip and that he might catch him at the airport. She had been there herself only moments before to pick up some friends who were coming in from the States, and she had left because she was fairly sure that the trouble had cleared and Roberto had probably left already.

"I caught him at the airport and I was surprised," Rudy Hernandez told me. "I said I had this money for Nicaraguan relief and I wanted to know what to do with it. Then I asked him where he was going."

"Nicaragua," Clemente told him.

"It's New Year's Eve, Roberto. Let it wait."

"Who else will go?" Roberto told him. "Someone has to do it."

At 9 P.M., even as the first stirrings of the annual New Year's Eve celebration were beginning in downtown San Juan, the DC-7 taxied onto the runway, received clearance, rumbled down the narrow concrete strip, and pulled away from the earth. It headed out over the Atlantic and banked toward Nicaragua, and its tiny lights disappeared on the horizon.

Just ninety seconds later, the tower at San Juan International Airport received this message from the pilot: "We are coming back around."

Just that.

Nothing more.

And then there was a great silence.

words for everyday use	**con • jec • ture** (kən jek′ chər) v., predict; guess. *Bob <u>conjectures</u> that the Sluggers will win the championship this year.*

USE TEXT ORGANIZATION. Breaking down the text into smaller sections helps you to remember the main points. As you read, identify the main idea of each section and add it to your Organization Chart.

NOTE THE FACTS

Why did Clemente believe he had to go to Nicaragua even though it was New Year's Eve?

_____

_____

_____

NOTE THE FACTS

What did people begin to do when they heard the news? Why?

_____

_____

_____

_____

"It was almost midnight," recalls Rudy Hernandez, a former teammate of Roberto's. "We were having this party in my restaurant, and somebody turned on the radio and the announcer was saying that Roberto's plane was feared missing. And then, because my place is on the beach, we saw these giant floodlights crisscrossing the waves, and we heard the sound of the helicopters and the little search planes."

150 Drawn by a common sadness, the people of San Juan began to make their way toward the beach, toward Puente Maldonado. A cold rain had begun to fall. It washed their faces and blended with the tears.

They came by the thousands and they watched for three days. Towering waves boiled up and made the search virtually impossible. The U.S. Navy sent a team of expert divers into the area, but the battering of the waves defeated them too. Midway through the week, the pilot's body was found in the swift-moving currents to the north. On Saturday bits of the cockpit were sighted.

160 And then—nothing else.

"I was born in the Dominican Republic," Rudy Hernandez said, "but I've lived on this island for more than twenty years. I have never seen a time or a sadness like that. The streets were empty, the radios silent, except for the constant bulletins about Roberto. Traffic? Forget it. All of us cried. All of us who knew him and even those who didn't, wept that week.

"Manny Sanguillen, the Pittsburgh catcher, was down here playing winter ball, and when Manny heard the news
170 he ran to the beach and he tried to jump into the ocean with skin-diving gear. I told him, man, there's sharks there. You can't help. Leave it to the experts. But he kept going back. All of us were a little crazy that week.

"There will never be another like Roberto."

Who was he . . . I mean really?

Well, nobody can put together all the pieces of another man's life. But there are so many who want the world to know that it is not as impossible a search as you might think.

He was born in Carolina, Puerto Rico. Today the town
180 has about 125,000 people, but when Roberto was born there in 1934, it was roughly one-sixth its current size.

María Isabella Casares is a schoolteacher. She has taught

Reading TIP

Note that the author's method of organization is not always chronological. Rather, he begins at the end of Clemente's life, then goes back to the beginning, and finally finishes with the details of Clemente's death.

the children of Carolina for thirty years. Most of her teaching has been done in tenth-grade history classes. Carolina is her home and its children are her children. And among all of those whom she calls her own (who are all the children she taught), Roberto Clemente was something even more special to her.

190   "His father was an overseer on a sugar plantation. He did not make much money," she explained in an empty classroom at Julio Coronado School. "But then, there are no rich children here. There never have been. Roberto was typical of them. I had known him when he was a small boy because my father had run a grocery store in Carolina, and Roberto's parents used to shop there."

    There is this thing that you have to know about María Isabella Casares before we hear more from her. What you have to know is that she is the model of what a teacher should be. Between her and her students even now, as back

200 when Roberto attended her school, there is this common bond of mutual respect. Earlier in the day, I had watched her teach a class in the history of the Abolition Movement in Puerto Rico. I don't speak much Spanish, but even to me it was clear that this is how a class should be, this is the kind of person who should teach, and these are the kinds of students such a teacher will produce.

    With this as a background, what she has to say about Roberto Clemente carries much more impact.

    "Each year," she said, "I let my students choose the seats

210 they want to sit in. I remember the first time I saw Roberto. He was a very shy boy and he went straight to the back of the room and chose the very last seat. Most of the time he would sit with his eyes down. He was an average student. But there was something very special about him. We would talk after class for hours. He wanted to be an engineer, you know, and perhaps he could have been. But then he began to play softball, and one day he came to me and said, 'Teacher, I have a problem.'

    "He told me that Pedron Zarrilla, who was one of our

220 most prominent baseball people, had seen him play, and that Pedron wanted him to sign a professional contract with the Santurce Crabbers. He asked me what he should do.

    "I have thought about that conversation many times. I

NOTE THE FACTS

What does the speaker say it is important to understand about María Isabella Casares?

_____

_____

_____

ASK A QUESTION

_____

_____

_____

_____

MARK THE TEXT

Underline or highlight the advice Clemente's teacher gives him.

believe Roberto could have been almost anything, but God gave him a gift that few have, and he chose to use that gift. I remember that on that day I told him, 'This is your chance, Roberto. We are poor people in this town. This is your chance to do something. But if in your heart you prefer not to try, then Roberto, that will be your problem—

230 and your decision.' "

There was and there always remained a closeness between this boy-soon-to-be-a-man and his favorite teacher.

"Once, a few years ago, I was sick with a very bad back. Roberto, not knowing this, had driven over from Rio Piedras, where his house was, to see me.

"Where is the teacher?" Roberto asked Mrs. Casares' stepdaughter that afternoon.

"Teacher is sick, Roberto. She is in bed."

"Teacher," Roberto said, pounding on the bedroom door,

240 "get up and put on your clothes. We are going to the doctor whether you want to or not."

"I got dressed," Mrs. Casares told me, "and he picked me up like a baby and carried me in his arms to the car. He came every day for fifteen days, and most days he had to carry me, but I went to the doctor and he treated me. Afterward, I said to the doctor that I wanted to pay the bill.

"'Mrs. Casares,' he told me, 'please don't start with that Clemente, or he will kill me. He has paid all your bills, and don't you dare tell him I have told you.'

250 "Well, Roberto was like that. We had been so close. You know, I think I was there the day he met Vera, the girl he later married. She was one of my students, too. I was working part-time in the pharmacy and he was already a baseball player by then, and one day Vera came into the store.

"'Teacher,' Roberto asked me, 'who is that girl?'

"'That's one of my students,' I told him. 'Now don't you dare bother her. Go out and get someone to introduce you. Behave yourself.'

"He was so proper, you know. That's just what he did, and

260 that's how he met her, and they were married here in Carolina in the big church on the square."

On the night Roberto Clemente's plane disappeared, Mrs. Casares was at home, and a delivery boy from the pharmacy stopped by and told her to turn on the radio and sit down.

"I think something has happened to someone who is very close with you, Teacher, and I want to be here in case you need help."

María Isabella Casares heard the news. She is a brave woman, and months later, standing in front of the empty crypt in the cemetery at Carolina where Roberto Clemente 270 was to have been buried, she said, "He was like a son to me. This is why I want to tell you about him. This is why you must make people—particularly our people, our Puerto Rican children—understand what he was. He was like my son, and he is all our sons in a way. We must make sure that the children never forget how beautiful a man he was."

The next person to touch Roberto Clemente was Pedron Zarrilla, who owned the Santurce club. He was the man who discovered Clemente on the country softball team, and he was the man who signed him for a four-hundred-dollar bonus.

280 "He was a skinny kid," Pedron Zarrilla recalls, "but even then he had those large powerful hands, which we all noticed right away. He joined us, and he was nervous. But I watched him, and I said to myself, 'this kid can throw and this kid can run, and this kid can hit. We will be patient with him.' The season had been through several games before I finally sent him in to play."

Luis Olmo remembers that game. Luis Olmo had been a major-league outfielder with the Brooklyn Dodgers. He had been a splendid ballplayer. Today he is in the insurance 290 business in San Juan. He sat in his office and recalled very well that first moment when Roberto Clemente stepped up to bat.

"I was managing the other team. They had a man on base and this skinny kid comes out. Well, we had never seen him, so we didn't really know how to pitch to him. I decided to throw him a few bad balls and see if he'd bite.

"He hit the first pitch. It was an outside fast ball, and he never should have been able to reach it. But he hit it down the line for a double. He was the best bad-ball hitter I have ever seen, and if you ask major-league pitchers who are 300 pitching today, they will tell you the same thing. After a while it got so that I just told my pitchers to throw the ball down the middle because he was going to hit it no matter where they put it, and at least if he decided not to swing we'd have a strike on him.

FIX-UP IDEA

Read Aloud/Think Aloud
If you are having trouble completing the Organization Chart, work with a partner to do a read aloud/think aloud. Read two or three paragraphs aloud. Stop and think aloud with your partner about the section you read. Identify the main idea of the section and your response to what you read. Then have your partner read the next two or three paragraphs. Again, stop to think aloud. Continue this way until you have completed the selection.

NOTE THE FACTS

What did Olmo tell his pitchers?

_____

_____

_____

VISUALIZE. Take the time to associate new words with an image. This will increase your ability to understand and remember what you read.

NOTE THE FACTS

What did Pedron Zarrilla know about Clemente?

_____

_____

_____

MARK THE TEXT

A **metaphor** is a figure of speech in which one thing is spoken or written about as if it were another. This figure of speech invites the reader to make a comparison between the two things. Underline or highlight the sentence that uses a metaphor to describe Clemente.

"I played in the big leagues. I know what I am saying. He was the greatest we ever had . . . maybe one of the greatest anyone ever had. Why did he have to die?"

Once Pedron Zarrilla turned him loose, there was no stopping Roberto Clemente. As Clemente's confidence grew, he began to get better and better. He was the one the crowd came to see out at Sixto Escobar Stadium.

"You know, when Clemente was in the lineup," Pedron Zarrilla says, "there was always this undercurrent of excitement in the ball park. You knew that if he was coming to bat, he would do something spectacular. You knew that if he was on first base, he was going to try to get to second base. You knew that if he was playing right field and there was a man on third base, then that man on third base already knew what a lot of men on third base in the major were going to find out—you don't try to get home against Roberto Clemente's arm."

"I remember the year that Willie Mays came down here to play in the same outfield with him for the winter season. I remember the wonderful things they did and I remember that Roberto still had the best of it.

"Sure I knew we were going to lose him. I knew it was just a matter of time. But I was only grateful that we could have him if only for that little time."

The major-league scouts began to make their moves. Olmo was then scouting, and he tried to sign him for the Giants. But it was the Dodgers who won the bidding war. The Dodgers had Clemente, but in having him, they had a major problem. He had to be hidden.

This part takes a little explaining. Under the complicated draft rules that baseball used at that time, if the Dodgers were not prepared to bring Clemente up to their major-league team within a year (and because they were winning with proven players, they couldn't), then Clemente could be claimed by another team.

They sent him to Montreal with instructions to the manager to use him as little as possible, to hide him as much as possible, and to tell everyone he had a sore back, a sore arm, or any other excuse the manager could give. But how do you hide a diamond when he's in the middle of a field of broken soda bottles?

310

320

330

340

In the playoffs that year against Syracuse, they had to use Clemente. He hit two doubles and a home run and threw a man out at home the very first try.

The Pittsburgh Pirates had a man who saw it all. They drafted him at the season's end.

350   And so Roberto Clemente came to Pittsburgh. He was the finest prospect the club had had in a long, long time. But the Pirates of those days were spectacular losers and even Roberto Clemente couldn't turn them around overnight.

"We were bad, all right," recalls Bob Friend, who later became a great Pirate pitcher. "We lost over a hundred games, and it certainly wasn't fun to go to the ball park under those conditions. You couldn't blame the fans for being noisy and impatient. Branch Rickey, our general manager, had promised a winner. He called it his five-year

360   plan. Actually, it took ten."

When Clemente joined the club, it was Friend who made it his business to try to make him feel at home. Roberto was, in truth, a moody man, and the previous season hadn't helped him any.

"I will never forget how fast he became a superstar in this town," says Bob Friend. "Later he would have troubles because he was either hurt or thought he was hurt, and some people would say that he was loafing. But I know he gave it his best shot and he helped make us winners."

370   The first winning year was 1960, when the Pirates won the pennant and went on to beat the Yankees in the seventh game of the World Series. Whitey Ford, who pitched against him twice in that Series, recalls that Roberto actually made himself look bad on an outside pitch to encourage Whitey to come back with it. "I did," Ford recalls, "and he unloaded. Another thing I remember is the way he ran out a routine ground ball in the last game and when we were a little slow covering, he beat it out. It was something most people forget but it made the Pirates'

380   victory possible."

The season was over. Roberto Clemente had hit safely in every World Series game. He had batted over .300. He had been a superstar. But when they announced the Most Valuable Player Award voting, Roberto had finished a distant third.

NOTE THE FACTS

What kind of a team were the Pirates when Clemente joined?

_____

_____

_____

MAKE A NOTE

_____

_____

_____

_____

"I really don't think he resented the fact that he didn't win it," Bob Friend says. "What hurt—and in this he was right—was how few votes he got. He felt that he simply wasn't being accepted. He brooded about that a lot. I think his attitude became one of 'Well, I'm going to show them

390 from now on so that they will never forget.'

"And you know, he sure did."

Roberto Clemente went home and married Vera. He felt less alone. Now he could go on and prove what it was he had to prove. And he was determined to prove it.

"I know he was driven by thoughts like that," explains Buck Canel, a newspaper writer who covers all sports for most of the hemisphere's Spanish language papers. "He would talk with me often about his feelings. You know, Clemente felt strongly about the fact that he was a Puerto

400 Rican and that he was a black man. In each of these things he had pride.

"On the other hand, because of the early language barriers, I am sure that there were times when he _thought_ people were laughing at him when they were not. It is difficult for a Latin-American ballplayer to understand everything said around him when it is said at high speed, if he doesn't speak English that well. But, in any event, he wanted very much to prove to the world that he was a superstar and that he could do things that in his heart he

410 felt he had already proven."

In later years, there would be people who would say that Roberto was a hypochondriac (someone who _imagined_ he was sick or hurt when he was not). They could have been right, but if they were, it made the things he did even more remarkable. Because I can testify that I saw him throw his body into outfield

420 fences, teeth first, to make remarkable plays. If he thought he was hurt at the time, then the act was even more courageous.

His moment finally came. It took eleven years for the Pirates to win a World Series berth again, and when they did in 1971, it was Roberto Clemente who led the way. I will never forget him as he was during that 1971 series with the Orioles, a Series that the Pirates figured to lose, and in which they, in fact, dropped the first two games down in Baltimore.

When they got back to Pittsburgh for the middle slice of the tournament, Roberto Clemente went to work and led this team. He was a superhero during the five games that followed. He was the big man in the Series. He was the MVP.[3] He was everything he had ever dreamed of being on a ball field.

Most important of all, the entire country saw him do it on network television, and never again—even though nobody knew it would end so tragically soon—was anyone ever to doubt his ability.

The following year, Clemente ended the season by collecting his three-thousandth hit. Only ten other men had ever done that in the entire history of baseball.

"It was a funny thing about that hit," Willie Stargell, his closest friend on the Pirates, explains. "He had thought of taking himself out of the lineup and resting for the playoffs, but a couple of us convinced him that there had to be a time when a man had to do something for himself, so he went on and played and got it. I'm thankful that we convinced him, because, you know, as things turned out, that number three thousand was his last hit.

"When I think of Roberto now, I think of the kind of man he was. There was nothing phony about him. He had his own ideas about how life should be lived, and if you didn't see it that way, then he let you know in so many ways, without words, that it was best you each go your separate ways.

"He was a man who chose his friends carefully. His was a friendship worth having. I don't think many people took the time and the trouble to try to understand him, and I'll admit it wasn't easy. But he was worth it.

---

3. **MVP.** Most valuable player

NOTE THE FACTS

What happened during Clemente's second World Series?

_____

_____

_____

MARK THE TEXT

Underline or highlight the words that show what kind of man and friend Clemente was.

THINK AND REFLECT

In what ways was
Clemente a role model?
(Interpret)

_____

_____

_____

"The way he died, you know, I mean on that plane carrying supplies to Nicaraguans who'd been dying in that earthquake, well, I wasn't surprised he'd go out and do something like that. I wasn't surprised he'd go. I just never thought what happened could happen to him.

"But I know this. He lived a full life. And if he knew at that moment what the Lord had decided, well, I really believe he would have said, 'I'm ready.'"

470

He was thirty-eight years old when he died. He touched the hearts of Puerto Rico in a way that few people ever could. He touched a lot of other hearts, too. He touched hearts that beat inside people of all colors of skin.

He was one of the proudest of The Proud People. ∎

THINK AND REFLECT

Which seem to have been
Clemente's best years in
baseball? Why? (Analyze)

_____

_____

_____

Roberto Clemente's Career Statistics with the Pittsburgh Pirates

Year	G	AB	R	H	2B	3B	HR	RBI	AVG
1955	124	474	48	121	23	11	5	47	.255
1956	147	543	66	169	30	7	7	60	.311
1957	111	451	42	114	17	7	4	30	.253
1958	140	519	69	150	24	10	6	50	.289
1959	105	432	60	128	17	7	4	50	.296
1960	144	570	89	179	22	6	16	94	.314
1961	146	572	100	201	30	10	23	89	*.351
1962	144	538	95	168	28	9	10	74	.312
1963	152	600	77	192	23	8	17	76	.320
1964	155	622	95	*211	40	7	12	87	*.339
1965	152	589	91	194	21	14	10	65	*.329
1966	154	638	105	202	31	11	29	119	.317
1967	147	585	103	*209	26	10	23	110	*.357
1968	132	502	74	146	18	12	18	57	.291
1969	138	507	87	175	20	*12	19	91	.345
1970	108	412	65	145	22	10	14	60	.352
1971	132	522	82	178	29	8	13	86	.341
1972	102	378	68	118	19	7	10	60	.312
Total	2433	9454	1416	3000	440	166	240	1305	.317

G=games played   H=base hits   HR=home runs
AB=official at bats   2B=second-base hits   RBI=runs batted in
R=runs   3B=third-base hits   AVG=batting average

(Batting average is figured by dividing a player's hits by his official at bats. Example: 3000 ÷ 9454 = 0.3173259995769, which rounds off to .317. Batting averages over .300 are considered excellent.) *=led the National League with this statistic

Reflect ON YOUR READING

❏ With a partner, compare what you wrote in your Organization Chart.
❏ Work together to write a one-paragraph summary of the selection.

_____

_____

_____

_____

_____

_____

Reading Skills and Test Practice

ANALYZE CHARACTER

Discuss with your partner how best to answer the following questions
about the selection. Use the Think-Aloud Notes to write down your
reasons for eliminating the incorrect answers.

_____1. What does Clemente's last action tell you about his character?
   a. He was most concerned with his baseball stats.
   b. He wanted to earn a lot of money.
   c. He was a great humanitarian.
   d. He cared deeply for his teacher, María Isabella Casares.

_____2. What did María Isabella Casares encourage Clemente to do?
   a. She encouraged him to do his best in school.
   b. She encouraged him to marry Vera.
   c. She wanted him to play for Zarrilla.
   d. She encouraged him to make his own decision.

How did using the reading strategy help you to answer the questions?

_____

_____

_____

_____

THINK-ALOUD NOTES

_____
_____
_____
_____
_____
_____
_____
_____
_____
_____
_____
_____

Investigate, Inquire, and Imagine

RECALL: GATHER FACTS
1a. How did Roberto Clemente die? Where was he traveling? Why was he going there?

➔ **INTERPRET: FIND MEANING**
1b. What did the final actions of Clemente's life reveal about his character? Why did people gather by the thousands at Puente Maldonado?

ANALYZE: TAKE THINGS APART
2a. Examine the kinds of relationships Clemente formed with people. What did friendship mean to him? In what ways do his close friends describe him? How do those descriptions differ from the views of people who did not know him personally?

➔ **SYNTHESIZE: BRING THINGS TOGETHER**
2b. Summarize Roberto Clemente's character. In forming your answers, consider the priorities in Clemente's life and what he considered less important. Finally, conclude by considering what aspect of Clemente's character you will remember most after reading about him.

EVALUATE: MAKE JUDGMENTS
3a. How well does "Roberto Clemente: A Bittersweet Memoir" achieve the goal of giving readers an understanding about who Clemente was and his impact on the world? Explain your answer.

➔ **EXTEND: CONNECT IDEAS**
3b. How does your new knowledge about Clemente's well-rounded life (that included more than just a love a baseball) give you insight to other famous athletes? Explain your answer.

Literary Tools

ANECDOTE. An **anecdote** is a brief story, usually told to make a point. Copy the graphic organizer below to examine the anecdotes in "Roberto Clemente: A Bittersweet Memoir." Fill out a graphic organizer for each person who offers information about Clemente. Then summarize their anecdotes about him. How well do the anecdotes complement each other? Which offers the most insight into Clemente as a baseball player? Which offers the most insight into Clemente the person? One example has been done for you.

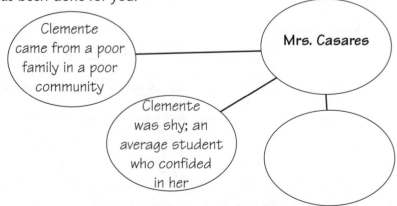

WordWorkshop

WORD ORIGINS. The origin of a word can be traced back to where it came from—Middle English, Latin, French, or another language. Find a dictionary that gives word origins. Then find the word origin for each of the following words. Finally, use each one in a sentence (many dictionaries will also give you an example of the word used in a sentence).

EXAMPLE
memoir
word origin: from Middle French *memoire* (memory), from the Latin word *memoria*
sentence: *My grandmother wrote a memoir about her journey to the United States.*

statistic
word origin:_____

sentence: _____

prospect
word origin:_____

sentence: _____

franchise
word origin:_____

sentence: _____

league
word origin:_____

sentence: _____

uniform
word origin:_____

sentence: _____

Read-Write Connection

Why do you think Roberto Clemente "touched the hearts" of so many people?

Beyond the Reading

SHOWCASE A GREAT ATHLETE. Research an athletic "great." Then write a short article about the person you selected. Finally, as a class, put these all together into a class book.

GO ONLINE. To find links and additional activities for this selection, visit the EMC Internet Resource Center at **emcp.com/languagearts** and click on Write-In Reader.

Reader's resource

On January 28, 1986, with millions of people watching, the space shuttle *Challenger* exploded less than two minutes after take off. Inside the *Challenger* were six astronauts and one teacher. It was the most serious accident ever in the history of the U.S. space program. Speechwriter Peggy Noonan wrote **"The *Challenger* Disaster"** speech, which President Ronald Reagan gave to the nation shortly after the explosion.

Reader's journal

If a national tragedy occurred, would you want to talk about it with your family and friends? Why, or why not?

_____

_____

_____

_____

_____

"The *Challenger* Disaster"

by Peggy Noonan

Active READING STRATEGY

CONNECT TO PRIOR KNOWLEDGE

Before Reading ➤ THINK ABOUT WHAT YOU KNOW

❑ Respond in writing to the Reader's Journal question.
❑ Discuss your response with a few of your classmates.
❑ Preview the FQR (Fact/Question/Response) Chart below. As you read "The *Challenger* Disaster," put any facts you learn in the first column. In the middle column, write down questions that come up as you are reading. In the last column, react or respond to the selection.

Graphic Organizer: Fact/Question/Response Chart

Fact	Question	Response

The Challenger DISASTER

Peggy Noonan

Nineteen years ago, almost to the day, we lost three astronauts in a terrible accident on the ground.[1] But we've never lost an astronaut in flight; we've never had a tragedy like this. And perhaps we've forgotten the courage it took for the crew of the shuttle; but they, the *Challenger* Seven, were aware of the dangers, but overcame them and did their jobs brilliantly. We mourn seven heroes: Michael Smith, Dick Scobee, Judith Resnik, Ronald McNair, Ellison Onizuka, Gregory Jarvis, and Christa McAuliffe. We mourn their loss as a nation together.

For the families of the seven, we cannot bear, as you do, the full impact of this tragedy. But we feel the loss, and we're thinking about you so very much. Your loved ones were daring and brave, and they had that special grace, that special spirit that says, "Give me a challenge and I'll meet it with joy." They had a hunger to explore the universe and discover its truths. They wished to serve, and they did. They served all of us.

10

---

1. **lost three astronauts . . . on the ground.** On January 27, 1967, a flash fire occurred on *Apollo I* during a launch pad test. All three crew members died.

During Reading →

USE WHAT YOU KNOW AS YOU READ

❏ Listen as your teacher reads the first paragraph of the selection aloud. What is the purpose of this speech? What affect does the opening of the speech have on you? How do you think you would feel upon hearing these words if you had witnessed this tragedy?

❏ Continue reading the selection on your own. Keep thinking about the effect the words have on you and what effect they might have if you had witnessed this tragedy.

❏ As you read, fill in your FQR Chart, noting the facts in the selection and your questions and responses.

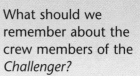

NOTE THE FACTS

What should we remember about the crew members of the *Challenger*?

_____

_____

MARK THE TEXT

Highlight or underline what the crew members hungered to do.

Fix-Up Idea

Listen to the Selection
If you are having trouble connecting to the selection, try listening to the selection. How does listening to a speech have a different effect than reading a speech?

_____

_____

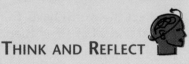

Think and Reflect

How were the crew members like Sir Frances Drake? (Interpret)

_____

_____

_____

Literary Tools

Diction. Diction, when applied to writing, refers to word choice. Diction can be formal (*Sir. Please move your car.*) Or it can be very informal (*Yo!—move da car.*) It can be simple or complex, ordinary or unusual. The purpose and audience determines the diction—the word choices the writer makes. As you read, think about the diction the writer uses in this speech.

We've grown used to wonders in this century. It's hard to dazzle us. But for twenty-five years the United States space program has been doing just that. We've grown used to the idea of space, and perhaps we forget that we've only just begun. We're still pioneers. They, the members of the *Challenger* crew, were pioneers.

And I want to say something to the schoolchildren of America who were watching the live coverage of the shuttle's takeoff. I know it is hard to understand, but sometimes painful things like this happen. It's all part of the process of exploration and discovery. It's all part of taking a chance and expanding man's horizons. The future doesn't belong to the fainthearted; it belongs to the brave. The *Challenger* crew was pulling us into the future, and we'll continue to follow them. . . .

There's a coincidence today. On this day 390 years ago, the great explorer Sir Francis Drake[2] died aboard ship off the coast of Panama. In his lifetime the great frontiers were the oceans, and a historian later said, "He lived by the sea, died on it, and was buried in it." Well, today we can say of the *Challenger* crew: Their dedication was, like Drake's, complete.

The crew of the space shuttle *Challenger* honored us by the manner in which they lived their lives. We will never forget them, nor the last time we saw them, this morning, as they prepared for the journey and waved goodbye and "slipped the surly bonds of earth" to "touch the face of God."[3] ∎

---

2. **Sir Francis Drake.** English admiral (*circa* 1540–1596); first Englishman to sail around the world

3. **slipped the surly bonds . . . face of God.** Lines from John Magee's poem "High Flight"

Reflect ON YOUR READING

After Reading ➤ **REFLECT ON WHAT YOU LEARNED**

❑ Think about what you know about the space program. Look over the questions on your FQR Chart. How did your background knowledge affect your reading of the selection?

❑ With your group from the Before Reading activity, discuss the effect of the speech. Compare and contrast it to speeches you have heard about disasters or tragedies you have seen.

_____

_____

_____

_____

Reading Skills and Test Practice

RECOGNIZE THE AUTHOR'S PURPOSE

With your group, discuss how to answer these questions about the speech. Use the Think-Aloud Notes to write down your reasons for eliminating the incorrect answers.

_____1. Why does Noonan compare the *Challenger* crew to Sir Francis Drake?
   a. She wants to show that they were completely dedicated to their task.
   b. She wants to demonstrate how safe they were.
   c. She wants to prove they were well trained and prepared for their task.
   d. She wants to honor them for the way they lived their lives.

_____2. Which is a purpose of the speech?
   a. to describe the history of the space program
   b. to show that Sir Francis Drake was a brave explorer
   c. to promote the study of science, with a special emphasis on space studies
   d. to honor the astronauts who died

How did using the reading strategy help you to answer the questions?

_____

_____

THINK-ALOUD NOTES

_____

_____

_____

_____

_____

_____

_____

_____

_____

_____

Investigate, Inquire, and Imagine

RECALL: GATHER FACTS
1a. What had the U.S. space program been doing for twenty-five years?

INTERPRET: FIND MEANING
1b. What could the space program's activities have left people thinking?

ANALYZE: TAKE THINGS APART
2a. What words does the speaker use to describe the crew members throughout the speech?

SYNTHESIZE: BRING THINGS TOGETHER
2b. How do these descriptions help form the speaker's main message? What is that message?

EVALUATE: MAKE JUDGMENTS
3a. How well does the speaker get across the main message? How well do you think the speaker's words echoed the thoughts of the American public? In what ways might the speaker's message have been different from the thoughts of the American public?

EXTEND: CONNECT IDEAS
3b. How well does the message in the speech parallel your own thoughts and feelings about the *Challenger* disaster? Explain your answer.

Literary Tools

DICTION. **Diction,** when applied to writing, refers to word choice. Does the speaker of this speech use formal or informal language? How complex are the speaker's sentences? How did the intended audience and the intent of the speech affect the diction (word choice)? Can you think of another example of this type of writing (diction)?

_____

_____

_____

_____

_____

_____

_____

WordWorkshop

IRREGULAR VERBS—PAST AND PRESENT. Most present tense verbs can be changed to the past tense by adding *–ed.* For example, with the regular present tense verb *fix* becomes *fixed,* and *walk* becomes *walked.* Irregular verbs are different. Adding *–ed* will not work, the entire word changes. Write the present tense for each of the present tense verbs listed. See the example below. A dictionary or thesaurus can help.

EXAMPLE	**Present tense**	**Irregular past tense**
	lose	lost

Present tense	**Irregular past tense**
is	_____
take	_____
go	_____
fly	_____
begin	_____
buy	_____
catch	_____
hear	_____

Read-Write Connection

Have you ever heard of the saying, "Sometimes bad things happen to good people?" Have you ever witnessed this kind of occurrence or experienced it yourself? If so, what were the circumstances? How does this saying relate to the speech and the circumstances of the *Challenger* disaster?

_____

_____

_____

_____

Beyond the Reading

EXPLORE A FAMOUS SPEECH. Research a different famous American speech involving a major event. While researching, keep in mind the following questions: What are some of the memorable lines and images from? How are they alike or different from "The *Challenger* Disaster"? How were the speeches received by their intended audiences?

GO ONLINE. To find links and additional activities for this selection, visit the EMC Internet Resource Center at **emcp.com/languagearts** and click on Write-In Reader.

Reader's resource

A **persuasive essay** tries to influence the opinion of the reader. In **"Appearances Are Destructive,"** South African author Mark Mathabane tries to persuade his audience about the value of school uniforms. To write a persuasive essay, the writer carefully considers his or her audience, clearly states his or her opinion on the subject, and then supports that opinion with evidence reasons and examples.

Word watch

PREVIEW VOCABULARY

curtail	distraught
derail	infringe
diminution	meretricious

READ ALOUD

Practice pronouncing the following words aloud before reading the selection.

Ma • tha • ba • ne
(mä tä bä′ nā)
apart • heid
(ä pär′ tāt, ä pär′ tīt)
Shan • gri-La (shaŋ gri lä′)
Faulk • ner (fôk′ nər)

Reader's journal

When have you attempted to persuade someone to do something? What methods of persuasion did you use? Were you successful? Why, or why not?

"Appearances Are Destructive"

by Mark Mathabane

Active READING STRATEGY

TACKLE DIFFICULT VOCABULARY

Before Reading ➤ **PREVIEW VOCABULARY AND FOOTNOTES**

❑ With a partner, review the Words for Everyday Use at the bottom of the selection pages.
❑ Read each word, its definition, and the sentence in which it is used. Copy the words and their definitions into your Word Study Notebook, using the format below.
❑ Choose a word, and have your partner use it in a sentence of his or her own. Then have your partner choose a word for you to use in a sentence of your own. Continue taking turns until you have covered all of the words.

Graphic Organizer: Word Study Notebook

Word:_____

Pronunciation:_____
_____

Definition: _____

Sentence: _____
_____

Drawing:

Appearances are Destructive

Mark Mathabane

A s public schools reopen for the new year, strategies to
curb school violence will once again be hotly debated.
Installing metal detectors and hiring security guards will
help, but the experience of my two sisters makes a
compelling case for greater use of dress codes as a way to
protect students and promote learning.

Shortly after my sisters arrived here from South Africa I
enrolled them at the local public school. I had great
expectations for their educational experience. Compared
with black schools under apartheid, American schools are
Shangri-Las,[1] with modern textbooks, school buses,
computers, libraries, lunch programs and dedicated teachers.

But despite these benefits, which students in many parts
of the world only dream about, my sisters' efforts at
learning were almost <u>derailed</u>. They were constantly

10

---

1. **Shangri-Las.** Remote, beautiful, imaginary places where life approaches perfection

---

**words
for
everyday
use**

de • rail (dē rāl′) v., hinder or impede the progress of. *Her plans to join the track
team were temporarily <u>derailed</u> when she broke her leg.*

During Reading

UNLOCK WORDS AS YOU READ

- Follow along in your
  textbook as your teacher
  reads the first page
  aloud. If you come across
  words that you don't
  know, add them to your
  word study notebook.
- When your teacher has
  finished reading, review
  the words you listed and
  try to determine their
  meanings by using
  context clues.
- Continue reading the
  selection on your own.
  Jot down unfamiliar
  words, and try to define
  them by using context
  clues. If the context clues
  do not provide the
  meaning, try analyzing
  the word parts—prefixes,
  roots, and suffixes—to
  determine meaning. If
  that strategy fails, consult
  a dictionary. Record the
  definitions in your
  notebook.

NOTE THE FACTS

What do American schools
have that South African
schools don't?

_____

_____

MARK THE TEXT

Underline or highlight the frustrations teachers have shared with the author.

Literary TOOLS

OPINION. An **opinion** is a statement that cannot be proven. It expresses an attitude, a feeling, or a wish. It does not express a fact about the world. The sentence "This is a beautiful holiday song" expresses an opinion. The sentence "This is a holiday song" is a fact. A persuasive essay attempts to take the strong opinion of the author and back it up with facts to get the reader to agree. Preview the Fact and Opinion Chart in Literary Tools on page 269. As you read, add any facts learned in the first column. Add opinions in the right column.

taunted for their homely outfits. A couple of times they came home in tears. In South Africa students were required to wear uniforms, so my sisters had never been preoccupied with clothes and jewelry.

20   They became so <u>distraught</u> that they insisted on transferring to different schools, despite my reassurances that there was nothing wrong with them because of what they wore.

I have visited enough public schools around the country to know that my sisters' experiences are not unique. In schools in many areas, Nike, Calvin Klein, Adidas, Reebok and Gucci are more familiar names to students than Zora Neale Hurston, Shakespeare and Faulkner.[2] Many students seem to pay more attention to what's on their bodies than
30   in their minds.

Teachers have shared their frustrations with me at being unable to teach those students willing to learn because classes are frequently disrupted by other students ogling themselves in mirrors, painting their fingernails, combing their hair, shining their gigantic shoes or comparing designer labels on jackets, caps and jewelry.

The fiercest competition among students is often not over academic achievements, but over who dresses most expensively. And many students now measure parental love
40   by how willing their mothers and fathers are to pamper them with money for the latest fads in clothes, sneakers and jewelry.

Those parents without the money to waste on such <u>meretricious</u> extravagances are considered uncaring and cruel. They often watch in dismay and helplessness as their children become involved with gangs and peddle drugs to raise the money.

When students are asked why they attach so much importance to clothing, they frequently reply that it's the

---

2. **Zora Neale Hurston, Shakespeare and Faulkner.** All highly acclaimed authors

words for everyday use	**dis • traught** (dis trät') adj., agitated; troubled. *The bird was <u>distraught</u> over the loss of her nest.* **mer • e • tri • cious** (mer ə tri' shəs) adj., falsely attractive, pretentious, superficially significant. *People who don't know Jim well admire him for his <u>meretricious</u> attributes, but I value his kindness and generosity.*

50 cool thing to do, that it gives them status and earns them respect. And clothes are also used to send sexual messages, with girls thinking that the only things that make them attractive to boys are skimpy dresses and gaudy looks, rather than intelligence and academic excellence.

The argument by civil libertarians[3] that dress codes <u>infringe</u> on freedom of expression is misleading. We observe dress codes in nearly every aspect of our lives without any <u>diminution</u> of our freedoms—as demonstrated by flight attendants, bus drivers, postal employees, high
60 school bands, military personnel, sports teams, Girl and Boy Scouts, employees of fast-food chains, restaurants, and hotels.

In many countries where students outperform their American counterparts academically, school dress codes are observed as part of creating the proper learning environment. Their students tend to be neater, less disruptive in class and more disciplined, mainly because their minds are focused more on learning and less on materialism. It's time Americans realized that the benefits
70 of safe and effective schools far outweigh any perceived <u>curtailment</u> of freedom of expression brought on by dress codes. ∎

---

3. **civil libertarians.** Supporters of freedom from government interference

Do you think some students attach too much importance to what they wear? Why, or why not? **(Evaluate)**

_____

_____

_____

READ ALOUD

Read aloud the high-lighted text. What does the author say Americans should realize? Is this a fact or an opinion? **(Analyze)**

_____

_____

_____

_____

Reading **STRATEGY**
REVIEW

CONNECT TO PRIOR KNOWLEDGE. Does your school require students to wear uniforms? If not, what changes would your school go through if school uniforms were required? How do you feel about school uniforms? Do a quickwrite on the topic. Compare your ideas to those presented by the author, Mark Mathabane.

words for everyday use

in • fringe (in frinj') *v.*, trespass on, intrude on, overstep the bounds of. *Yolanda infringed on her older sister's privacy when she read her sister's diary.*
dim • i • nu • tion (di mə nü' shən) *n.*, act or process of diminishing. *At the end of the sale, the shopkeepers were pleased by the diminution of goods.*
cur • tail (kər tāl') *v.*, make less. *The mayor hoped that more police officers on the streets would help to curtail crime.* **curtailment,** *n.*

Reflect ON YOUR READING

After Reading ▶ **REVIEW AND PRACTICE WORDS**

❑ Compare your list of words in your Word Study Notebook with those of a classmate.
❑ Then work together to write a sentence of your own for each of the listed words. Make sure your sentences show that you understand the definition of the word.

THINK-ALOUD NOTES

_____

_____

_____

_____

_____

_____

_____

_____

_____

_____

_____

_____

Reading Skills and Test Practice

USE CONTEXT CLUES

With a partner, discuss how to answer the following vocabulary questions. Read the following passages and mark the letter of the best meaning for the underlined word. Use the Think-Aloud Notes to write down your reasons for eliminating the incorrect answers.

_____1. "They became so <u>distraught</u> that they insisted on transferring to different schools, despite my reassurances that there was nothing wrong with them because of what they wore."
  a. loud
  b. upset
  c. determined
  d. disorganized

_____2. "The argument by civil libertarians that dress codes <u>infringe</u> on the freedom of expression is misleading."
  a. support
  b. confuse
  c. clarify
  d. trespass on

How did using the reading strategy help you to answer the questions?

_____

_____

_____

_____

Investigate, Inquire, and Imagine

RECALL: GATHER FACTS →
1a. What initial expectations does the author have for his sister's education?

INTERPRET: FIND MEANING
1b. Why does he have these expectations?

ANALYZE: TAKE THINGS APART →
2a. List the five reasons the author gives to support his position on school dress codes.

SYNTHESIZE: BRING THINGS TOGETHER
2b. Respond to each of the author's reasons with your own opinion. Then summarize your opinion on school dress code in general.

EVALUATE: MAKE JUDGMENTS →
3a. Is the author able to persuade the reader to agree with his point of view on school dress codes? Why, or why not? Which of his reasons most strongly supports his argument? Why? Which of his reasons is the weakest? How effective would this be in persuading parents or teachers to take the author's view on school dress codes?

EXTEND: CONNECT IDEAS
3b. Whether or not you agree with the author's opinion about school dress codes, think about some of the points he makes in his essay. Which of his statements do you find hold true in your own school? Does your opinion change when you consider this issue from the author's point of view?

Literary Tools

OPINION. An **opinion** is a statement that cannot be proven. It expresses an attitude, a feeling, or a wish. It does not express a fact about the world. A persuasive essay attempts to take the strong opinion of the author and back it up with facts to get the reader to agree. Review the facts and opinions you noted during reading in the Fact and Opinion Chart below.

Fact	Opinion

In this essay does the author do a good job supporting his opinions with facts? Explain your answer.

_____

_____

WordWorkshop

VOCABULARY IN CONTEXT. Fill in each blank below with the most appropriate vocabulary word from "Appearances Are Destructive." You may have to change the tense of the word.

curtail	derail	diminution
distraught	infringe	meretricious

1. She became _____ when her mother cancelled the party.

2. The police force was proud to report a recent _____ in crime.

3. Paulette realized she'd have to _____ her socializing and concentrate on studying.

4. Too many people focus on such _____ goals as wearing expensive clothes.

5. She was careful not to _____ on her friend's rights.

Read-Write Connection

How do you think the author's sisters might have been treated at your school? Why?

_____

_____

_____

_____

_____

_____

Beyond the Reading

TAKE A STAND ON SCHOOL UNIFORMS. Write a persuasive essay of your own in response to Mark Mathabane's. Take a position on whether school uniforms should be required. Then support it with facts. Do your research carefully.

GO ONLINE. To find links and additional activities for this selection, visit the EMC Internet Resource Center at **emcp.com/languagearts** and click on Write-In Reader.

"The Price of Freedom"

by Cassandra M. Vanhooser

Active READING STRATEGY

READ WITH A PURPOSE

Before Reading ▶ **PREVIEW THE AUTHOR'S PURPOSE**

❏ Preread the first and last paragraph of "The Price of Freedom." What one emotion does the author share in each of the two paragraphs? Keep this emotion in mind as you continue reading.

❏ Preview the Main Idea Chart below. As you read "The Price of Freedom," write down the main idea of each paragraph in the first column and details connected to it in the last column. An example has been done for you.

Graphic Organizer: Main Idea Chart

	Main Idea	Details Connected to the Main Idea
Paragraph 1	emotions of author	trying not to cry
Paragraph 2		
Paragraph 3		
Paragraph 4		
Paragraph 5		
Paragraph 6		
Paragraph 7		
Paragraph 8		
Paragraph 9		
Paragraph 10		
Paragraph 11		
Paragraph 12		

CONNECT

Reader's resource

"The Price of Freedom" by Cassandra M. Vanhooser is an example of expressive writing. An author's purpose in expressive writing is to think about and share an experience, an issue, or an emotion. "The Price of Freedom" is about the powerful feelings the author experienced when she visited the National Prisoner of War Museum in Andersonville, Georgia.

Word watch

PREVIEW VOCABULARY

indignity   solely
permeate

Reader's journal

What experiences have you had that were different from your expectations?

_____

_____

_____

_____

_____

_____

IDENTIFY THE AUTHOR'S PURPOSE

❑ Read the first page. What is the main point the author makes? Keep this point in mind as you read the rest of the essay.

❑ As you read the rest of the essay, underline or highlight where you think the author is making an important point related to her main idea. Then make a note in your Main Idea Chart.

Use **THE STRATEGY**

READ WITH A PURPOSE. Predict the author's purpose. After reading the selection, check your prediction and revise it if necessary.

_____

_____

NOTE THE FACTS

What did the author expect at the museum?

_____

_____

The Price of FREEDOM

Cassandra M. Vanhooser

The nation pays tribute to American prisoners of war who purchased our freedom by sacrificing their own. As hard as I try, I can't stop the hot, salty tears that spill down my cheeks.

I came to the National Prisoner of War Museum in Andersonville, Georgia, expecting to wade through musty memorabilia and obscure statistics. Instead, I hear the voices and see the faces of America's POWs. Now I understand what my freedom—indeed, the independence of every

10 American—truly cost.

From the Revolution to the Gulf War, more than 800,000 men, women, and children have been held captive by enemy forces. Other military museums touch on the subject, but this is the first memorial dedicated <u>solely</u> to the plight of American prisoners of war. Its location—on the very site of the Andersonville Prison Camp where 45,000 Union soldiers were incarcerated[1]—seems fitting.

20 As I wander through the museum, I get only a tiny taste of <u>indignities</u> prisoners of war endured. I feel gut-wrenching terror when I walk into a darkened room and suddenly face a wall of weapons pointed at me. As I watch interviews with family members, I imagine waiting years for a loved one's return. I look inside the prison door at the simulated Hanoi Hilton[2] and pray I'll never know the mind-numbing experience of being shackled in a tiny cell. In my heart, I bend down to kiss the American soil with each returning soldier.

That I can experience this part of history is in large part thanks to the POWs themselves. The American Ex-
30 Prisoners of War, a veterans group of more than 30,000 members, teamed with the National Park Service to raise the money needed to build the museum. Their influence <u>permeates</u> the project, especially in the commemorative courtyard.

"The prisoner of war story is cruel," says Bill Fornes, an ex-POW who spent 12 years working on the project. "It's hard. It's emotional. We wanted a place where, after that, visitors could reflect, ease themselves, and realize the world's not all bad." It's here I meet Lloyd Diehl from New
40 Jersey, an ex-POW.

"I'm here to try to heal a little bit from what I experienced and what I still experience," says Lloyd, who was captured on December 19, 1944, in Belgium during the Battle of the Bulge. He spent four months in Stalag 9B, a German prison camp.

"I don't feel shame anymore. I did at first. It's like saying I gave up," he says, his voice quivering with emotion. "You

---

1. **incarcerated.** Put in prison
2. **simulated Hanoi Hilton.** Copy of a Vietnamese wartime prison

words for everyday use	**sole • ly** (sō′ lē) *adv.*, only. *Juana decided to enter the race solely for the fun of it.* **in • dig • ni • ty** (in dig′ nə tē) *n.*, insult; humiliating treatment. *We are lucky to have never experienced the indignities that those hostages suffered.* **per • me • ate** (pər′ mē āt) *v.*, spread through or penetrate something. *The smoke permeated the air.*

FIX-UP IDEA

Read Aloud/Think Aloud
If you are having trouble flagging important points, work with a partner to do a read and think aloud. Read two or three paragraphs aloud. Stop and think aloud with your partner about the section you read. Identify the main idea of the section and your response to what you read. With your partner, decide whether to flag the passage.

MARK THE TEXT

Underline or highlight the sentence that tells who raised the money to build the museum.

Reading STRATEGY REVIEW

CONNECT TO PRIOR KNOWLEDGE. Have you ever done anything like what the author writes about? How did it feel?

_____

_____

_____

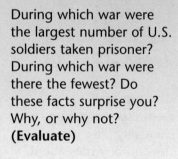

NOTE THE FACTS

What emotion did many POWs experience?

_____

_____

_____

THINK AND REFLECT

Why does the speaker thank Lloyd? **(Interpret)**

_____

_____

_____

THINK AND REFLECT

During which war were the largest number of U.S. soldiers taken prisoner? During which war were there the fewest? Do these facts surprise you? Why, or why not? **(Evaluate)**

_____

_____

_____

just don't do that. It wasn't in my vocabulary, or I didn't think it was. Then to do it, to surrender—I think we all felt shame.

"We were reduced to the existence of a dog," he continues. "But we knew that when we got liberated[3]—and we all expected to get liberated—that it was only up from that point."

Lloyd was burying a fellow POW in a prison graveyard when liberation finally came. "An American plane flew over and strafed[4] us, and all we could do was crouch down," he remembers. "He missed us the first time, but he went around and did it again. That time he came in over the top of us and not in front of us, and we waved as he flew by. The third time he went by, he wiggled his wings like he recognized us; then we went out and finished burying this guy."

As Lloyd shares his story, he lays his head on my shoulder and begins to weep, the wounds deep and painful even now, after more than 50 years have passed—I cradle this man—a complete stranger—in my arms and whisper the only words worthy of his sacrifice.

"Thank you," I tell him. ∎

---

3. **liberated.** Freed
4. **strafed.** Fired at

American POWs			
War	Number of prisoners	POW deaths	Death rate
American Revolution (1775–1783)	20,000	8,500	43%
War of 1812	5,000	252	5%
Spanish-American War (1898)	12	0	0%
Civil War (1861–1865)	346,950	49,102	14%
World War I (1914–1918)	4,120	147	4%
World War II Europe (1939–1945)	95,532	1,124	1%
World War II Pacific (1941–1945)	34,648	12,935	37%
Korean War (1950–1953)	7,140	2,701	38%
Vietnam War (1959–1975)	766	114	15%
Persian Gulf War (1991)	23	0	0%

Reflect ON YOUR READING

REFLECT ON YOUR READING

After Reading ▶ **REVIEW THE AUTHOR'S PURPOSE**

❑ Go back and look at the passages you flagged and the Main Idea Chart that you filled out.

❑ What is the main idea in "The Price of Freedom"? How do other parts of the essay support the main idea?

Reading Skills and Test Practice

IDENTIFY THE AUTHOR'S PURPOSE

READ, THINK, AND EXPLAIN. What is the author's purpose? How is her encounter with Lloyd Diehl related to her purpose?

_____

_____

_____

_____

_____

_____

_____

_____

REFLECT ON YOUR RESPONSE. Compare your response with that of your partner. How did the information you wrote down while reading help you form your response?

_____

_____

_____

_____

_____

_____

_____

_____

_____

_____

_____

_____

_____

_____

_____

Investigate, Inquire, and Imagine

RECALL: GATHER FACTS
1a. What does the speaker experience as she wanders through the museum?

→ INTERPRET: FIND MEANING
1b. How do these experiences affect her?

ANALYZE: TAKE THINGS APART
2a. Identify the emotions the speaker describes in the essay.

→ SYNTHESIZE: BRING THINGS TOGETHER
2b. How do these emotions combine to give the reader a sense of the speaker's reaction to visiting this place? How do they contribute to the speaker's message?

EVALUATE: MAKE JUDGMENTS
3a. In your opinion, how does the speaker view war? How has this visit affected her? How many of her thoughts and viewpoints on these subjects have changed as a result of this visit?

→ EXTEND: CONNECT IDEAS
3b. How might the speaker describe her experience to a visitor from a different country? How would that description be different from or similar to the essay you read?

Literary Tools

UNITY. **Unity** in a piece of writing is the use of details related to the main idea, or theme. An essay with unity is one in which all the parts help to support the thesis statement, or main idea. Do you think Vanhooser achieves unity in her essay? Explain your answer using details from the selection.

_____

_____

_____

_____

_____

_____

_____

WordWorkshop

DESCRIPTIVE COMPOUNDS. **Descriptive compounds** are words that have been combined to describe an experience. In "The Price of Freedom," the author uses descriptive compounds like *mind-numbing* and *gut-wrenching*. Other compounds include *stomach-churning, tear-jerking,* and *head-spinning*. On your own, write down as many compounds as you can come up with.

_____

_____

_____

_____

_____

Read-Write Connection

What sacrifices have you made for another person? Why did you make them?

_____

_____

_____

_____

_____

_____

_____

_____

Beyond the Reading

WRITE A LETTER. Work with a partner and write a letter of thanks and support to former prisoners of war for their sacrifices. Send your letter to the National Prisoners of War Museum (use the Internet to research the mailing address).

GO ONLINE. To find links and additional activities for this selection, visit the EMC Internet Resource Center at **emcp.com/languagearts** and click on Write-In Reader.

Unit 7 READING Review

Choose and Use Reading Strategies

Before reading the excerpt below, review with a partner how to use each of these reading strategies.

1. Read with a Purpose
2. Connect to Prior Knowledge
3. Write Things Down
4. Make Predictions
5. Visualize
6. Use Text Organization
7. Tackle Difficult Vocabulary
8. Monitor Your Reading Progress

Now apply at least two of these reading strategies as you read the following excerpt from "Ships in the Desert" by Al Gore. Use the margins and mark up the text to show how you are using the reading strategies to read actively. You may find it helpful to choose a graphic organizer from Appendix B to gather information as you read the excerpt, or use the Summary Chart on page B-13 to create a graphic organizer that summarizes the excerpt.

I was standing in the sun on the hot steel deck of a fishing ship capable of processing a fifty-ton catch on a good day. But it wasn't a good day. We were anchored in what used to be the most productive fishing site in all of central Asia, but as I looked out over the bow, the prospects of a good catch looked bleak. Where there should have been gentle blue-green waves lapping against the side of the ship, there was nothing but hot dry sand—as far as I could see in all directions. The other ships of the fleet were also at rest in the sand, scattered in the dunes that stretched all the way to the horizon.

Oddly enough, it made me think of a fried egg I had seen back in the United States on television the week before. It was sizzling and popping the way a fried egg should in a pan, but it was in the middle of a sidewalk in downtown Phoenix. I guess it sprang to mind because, like the ship on which I was standing, there was nothing wrong with the egg itself. Instead, the world beneath it had changed in an unexpected way that made the egg seem—

through no fault of its own—out of place. It was illustrating the newsworthy point that at the time Arizona wasn't having an especially good day, either, because for the second day in a row temperatures had reached a record 122 degrees.

WordWorkshop

UNIT 7 WORDS FOR EVERYDAY USE

arc, 235	forlorn, 232	permeate, 273
conjecture, 245	indignity, 273	solely, 273
curtail, 267	infringe, 267	unruffled, 230
derail, 265	malevolent, 235	wheedling, 235
diminution, 267	manipulate, 236	
distraught, 266	meretricious, 266	

CREATE A CROSSWORD PUZZLE. In a small group, put together a list of words to include in a crossword puzzle. Your list should contain ten of the Unit 7 Words for Everyday Use from the above list and ten words that everybody knows. Use as many of the words as you can from your list (you may not be able to use all of them). Use your own paper for the CLUES ACROSS and CLUES DOWN. Refer to the Crossword Puzzle activity in Appendix A on page A-3 for examples. After you fill in your puzzle and finish your clues, make another blank numbered puzzle. Exchange blank puzzles and clues with another group. See which group can solve their puzzle first.

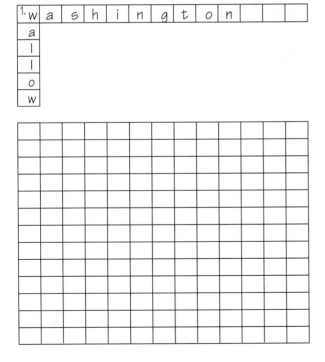

Literary Tools

Select the best literary element on the right to complete each sentence on the left. Write the correct letter in the blank.

_____ 1. A note to your friend would be an example of informal _____.

_____ 2. Writers often use sensory details to create in the reader a feeling of expectation, anxiety, or curiosity known as _____.

_____ 3. In Roberto Clemente's memoir, people who knew him tell _____ about the kind of person he was and the things he did.

_____ 4. The use of details related to the main idea or theme creates _____ in a piece of writing.

_____ 5. The sentence "It's a beautiful day" expresses a(n) _____.

a. anecdote, 243, 256

b. diction, 260, 262

c. opinion, 269

d. suspense, 232, 239

e. unity, 276

On Your Own

FLUENTLY SPEAKING. Memorize a 100–150-word passage from a selection in this unit. Have a partner help you memorize the passage by chunking it (breaking it down into smaller sections). Memorize short sections at a time, and work up to repeating the whole selection from memory.

PICTURE THIS. Review the Unit 7 Words for Everyday Use listed in the WordWorkshop on page 279. Choose a word and look up the definition on the page listed. Then, draw a sketch to help you remember this word. See Unit 9, page 334 for an example.

PUT IT IN WRITING. Review the definition for *anecdote* in Literary Tools on pages 243 and 256. Write an anecdote about someone who is important to you. Your anecdote should help the reader to understand the kind of person he or she is and why he or she is important to you.

Unit EIGHT

READING
Informational
and Visual Media

INFORMATIONAL AND VISUAL MEDIA

Learning how to read online and print reference works, graphic aids, and other visuals will help you access, process, and think about the vast amount of information available to you.

Informational Media

Media are channels or systems of communication, information, or entertainment. *Mass media*, designed to reach the mass of the people, refers specifically to means of communication, such as newspapers, radio, or television. *Journalism* is the gathering, evaluating, and spreading, through various media, of news and facts of current interest. Journalism has expanded from printed matter (newspapers and periodicals) to include radio, television, documentary films, the Internet, and computer news services.

Newspapers, issued on a daily or weekly basis, report the news, provide commentary on the news, advocate various public policies, and furnish special information and advice to readers.

Periodicals, released at regular intervals, are publications that include journals, magazines, or newsletters. They feature material of special interest to particular audiences.

Technical writing refers to scientific or process-oriented instructional writing that is of a technical or mechanical nature, such as **instruction manuals**, **how-to instructional guides**, and **procedural memos**. In this unit, "How to Chop an Onion in Four Easy Steps" provides a step-by-step procedure for chopping an onion.

NOTE THE FACTS

What are three examples of mass media?

_____

_____

_____

Reading TIP

When reading technical writing, look for words such as *first, second, then, next, before,* and *after.* These transition words help you understand the sequence of steps or events.

Technical writing may also include diagrams or pictures to help you identify parts or understand difficult instructions.

Icons may alert you to safety issues, optional steps, or other special features in the directions.

Reading TIP

Editorials and commentaries present opinions. The opinions are often supported by facts, but you need to pay attention to what is fact and what is opinion.

THINK AND REFLECT

Based on the title "Getting into Web Development," what can you infer about the people who were interviewed? **(Infer)**

_____

_____

_____

_____

Reading STRATEGY
REVIEW

CONNECT TO PRIOR KNOWLEDGE. Give an example of a multimedia application you have used. How did it help you?

_____

_____

_____

_____

Elements of Informational Media

NEWS ARTICLES. News articles are informational pieces of writing about a particular topic, issue, event, or series of events. They can be found in newspapers, periodicals, and Internet sites such as news groups or information services.

EDITORIALS AND COMMENTARIES. An **editorial** is an article in a newspaper or periodical that gives the opinions of the editors or publishers. A **commentary** is a report of an event that expresses the opinion of a participant or observer.

ESSAYS. An **essay** is a brief work of prose nonfiction. It usually is not a complete or in-depth treatment of a subject.

INTERVIEWS. An **interview** is a question and answer exchange between a reporter who wants precise information from a reliable source and the person who has that information. "Getting into Web Development" is an example of an interview in this unit.

REVIEWS. A **review**, or *critique*, is a critical evaluation of a work, such as a book, play, movie, or musical performance or recording.

Electronic Media

Electronic media includes online magazines and journals, known as **webzines** or **e-zines**, **computer news services**, and many **web-based newspapers** that are available on the **Internet**. In addition to handling web documents, the Internet also allows people to send e-mail, access archives of files, and participate in discussion groups.

Multimedia is the presentation of information using the combination of text, sound, pictures, animation, and video. Common multimedia computer applications include **game**s, **learning software**, **presentation software**, **reference materials**, and **web pages**. Using multimedia can provide a varied and informative interactive experience.

Elements of Electronic Media

ELECTRONIC MAIL. Electronic mail, or **e-mail**, is used to send written messages between individuals or groups on the Internet. E-mail messages tend to be more informal and conversational in style than letters.

WEB PAGES. A **web page** is an electronic "page" on the World Wide Web or Internet that may contain text, pictures, and sometimes animations related to a particular topic. A *website* is a collection of pages grouped together to organize the information offered by the person, company, or group that owns it.

NEWSGROUPS. Another use of e-mail is listservs, in which discussions on a particular subject are grouped together into **newsgroups** on a wide range of subjects. Messages to a newsgroup are accessible in the form of a list on a local news server that has a worldwide reach. Users can choose which messages they want to read and reply by posting messages to the newsgroup.

INFORMATION SERVICES. Information services, or *news services*, provide electronic news, information, and e-mail services.

BULLETIN BOARD SYSTEMS. A **bulletin board system**, or BBS, is an online service that allows users to post and read messages on a particular topic, converse in a *chat room*, play games with another person, and copy, or download, programs to their personal computers.

WEBZINES OR E-ZINES. Webzines or **e-zines** are periodicals that are available online. They may be available only online, or they may also be available in a magazine distributed by traditional methods.

ONLINE NEWSPAPERS. Major newspapers are now available online. Past editions of the paper are usually accessible through an online archive.

Visual Media

Many books and news media rely on **visual arts**, such as **fine art**, **illustrations**, and **photographs**, to convey ideas. Critically viewing a painting or photograph can add meaning to your understanding of a text.

Elements of Visual Media

GRAPHIC AIDS. Graphic aids are visual materials with information such as **drawings**, **illustrations**, **diagrams**, **charts**, **graphs**, **maps**, and **spreadsheets**. Variations in Vital Signs by Age is an example of a chart in this unit.

PHOTOGRAPHS. Photographs can accompany news stories or historical documents, serve as scientific evidence or works of art, and record everyday life. See pages 300–301 for examples of historical photographs in this unit. New photographic technology allows for digital formats to be stored on disk and downloaded to computers.

NOTE THE FACTS

What is the difference between a web page and a website?

_____

_____

_____

THINK AND REFLECT

What is the difference between informational media and electronic media? **(Compare and Contrast)**

_____

_____

_____

Reading STRATEGY
REVIEW

CONNECT TO PRIOR KNOWLEDGE. Give an example of a time when you used a graphic aid. How did you use it?

_____

_____

_____

THINK AND REFLECT

How does photography as a visual art differ from photography as photojournalism? (Compare and Contrast)

_____

_____

_____

DIGITAL PHOTOGRAPHY. With **digital photography**, images are converted into a code of ones and zeroes that a computer can read. Digital photographs can be manipulated into new images.

PHOTOJOURNALISM. **Photojournalism** is documentary photography that tells a particular story in visual terms. Photojournalists, who usually work for newspapers and periodicals, cover cultural and news events in areas such as politics, war, business, sports, and the arts.

VISUAL ARTS. The **visual arts** include painting, sculpture, drawing, printmaking, collage, photography, video, and computer-assisted art. With art, the artist tries to communicate with viewers, who may have different ideas about how to interpret the work. Learning about the location and time period of an artwork can contribute to a better understanding of it.

USING READING STRATEGIES WITH INFORMATIONAL AND VISUAL MEDIA

Active Reading Strategy Checklists

When reading informational and visual media, you will need to identify how the text is structured. Scan the material first. Headings, pictures, and directions will reveal what the selection wants to communicate. Use the following checklists when you read informational and visual media.

1 READ WITH A PURPOSE. Before reading informational and visual media, give yourself a purpose, or something to look for, as you read. Know why you are reading and what information you seek. Sometimes your teacher will give you a purpose: "Keep track of the steps in the process." Other times you can set your own purpose by previewing the title, the opening and closing paragraphs, and instructional information. Say to yourself

❑ I need to look for . . .
❑ I must keep track of . . .
❑ I need to understand the writer's views on . . .
❑ It is essential that I figure out how . . .
❑ I want to learn what happened when . . .

Reading TIP

Scan the first and last paragraphs, or any headings, pictures, and graphs, before you read. This will give you a quick picture of what the writer wants you to understand.

2 **CONNECT TO PRIOR KNOWLEDGE.** Connect to information you already know about the writer's topic. As you read, build on what you know. Say to yourself

- ❏ I know this about the topic already . . .
- ❏ Other information I've read about this topic said . . .
- ❏ I've used similar visual aids by . . .
- ❏ I did something similar when . . .
- ❏ This information is like . . .

3 **WRITE THINGS DOWN.** As you read informational and visual media, write down or mark ideas that help you understand the writer's views. Possible ways to keep a written record include

- ❏ Underline information that answers a specific question.
- ❏ Write down steps in a process.
- ❏ Highlight conclusions the writer draws.
- ❏ Create a graphic organizer that shows how to do something.
- ❏ Use a code to respond to the writer's ideas.

4 **MAKE PREDICTIONS.** Before you read informational and visual media, use the title and subject matter to guess what the selection will be about. As you read, confirm or deny your predictions, and make new ones based on what you learn. Make predictions like the following:

- ❏ The title tells me that the selection will be about . . .
- ❏ Graphic aids show me that . . .
- ❏ I predict that the writer will want me to . . .
- ❏ This selection will help me . . .
- ❏ This writer will conclude by . . .

5 **VISUALIZE.** Visualizing, or allowing the words on the page to create images in your mind, helps you understand what informational and visual media is trying to communicate. In order to visualize what an informational and visual media selection is communicating, you need to picture the people, events, or procedure that a writer describes. Make statements such as

- ❏ I imagine these people will . . .
- ❏ A drawing of this part would include . . .
- ❏ I picture that this is happening in this section . . .
- ❏ I envision the situation as . . .

Reading **TIP**

Instead of writing down a short response, use a symbol or a short word to indicate your response.
+   I like this
–   I don't like this
√   This is important
Yes I agree with this
No I disagree with this
?   I don't understand this
!   This is like something I know
〰 I need to come back to this later

Reading **TIP**

Make a visual diagram of a procedure. You will remember the procedure longer and it will be easier to review.

6 **USE TEXT ORGANIZATION.** When you read informational and visual media, pay attention to the text's structure. Learn to stop occasionally and retell what you have read. Say to yourself

- ❑ The title, headings, and pictures tell me this selection will be about . . .
- ❑ The writer's directions . . .
- ❑ There is a pattern to how the writer presents . . .
- ❑ The writer presents the information by . . .
- ❑ The writer includes helpful sections that . . .

7 **TACKLE DIFFICULT VOCABULARY.** Difficult words can hinder your ability to understand informational and visual media. Use context, consult a dictionary, or ask someone about words you do not understand. When you come across a difficult word in the selection, say to yourself

- ❑ The writer defines this word by . . .
- ❑ A dictionary definition shows that the word means . . .
- ❑ My work with the word before reading helps me know that the word means . . .
- ❑ A classmate said that the word means . . .

8 **MONITOR YOUR READING PROGRESS.** All readers encounter difficulty when they read, especially if they haven't chosen the reading material. When you have to read something, note problems you are having and fix them. The key to reading success is knowing when you are having difficulty. To fix problems, say to yourself

- ❑ Because I don't understand this part, I will . . .
- ❑ Because I'm having trouble staying connected to the ideas in the selection, I will . . .
- ❑ Because the words in the selection are too hard, I will . . .
- ❑ Because the selection is long, I will . . .
- ❑ Because I can't retell what the selection was about, I will . . .

Become an Active Reader

Active reading strategy instruction in this unit gives you an in-depth look at how to use one active reading strategy with each selection. Learning how to use several strategies in combination increases your chances of success even more. Use the questions and tips in the margins to keep your attention focused on reading actively. Use the white space in the margins to jot down responses that your reading generates. For more information about the active reading strategies, see Unit 1, pages 4–15.

Reading TIP

Difficult words are usually crucial to understanding informational and visual media. If words are not defined in the text, look up the meanings in a dictionary, and write them down.

Fix-Up Ideas

- ■ Reread
- ■ Ask a question
- ■ Read in shorter chunks
- ■ Read aloud
- ■ Retell
- ■ Work with a partner
- ■ Unlock difficult words
- ■ Vary your reading rate.
- ■ Choose a new reading strategy
- ■ Create a mnemonic device

How to Use Reading Strategies with Informational and Visual Media

To see how readers use active reading strategies, look over the responses one reader has while reading a poster that uses informational and visual media. As you look over the reader's responses, underline or highlight responses that demonstrate that the reader is reading actively.

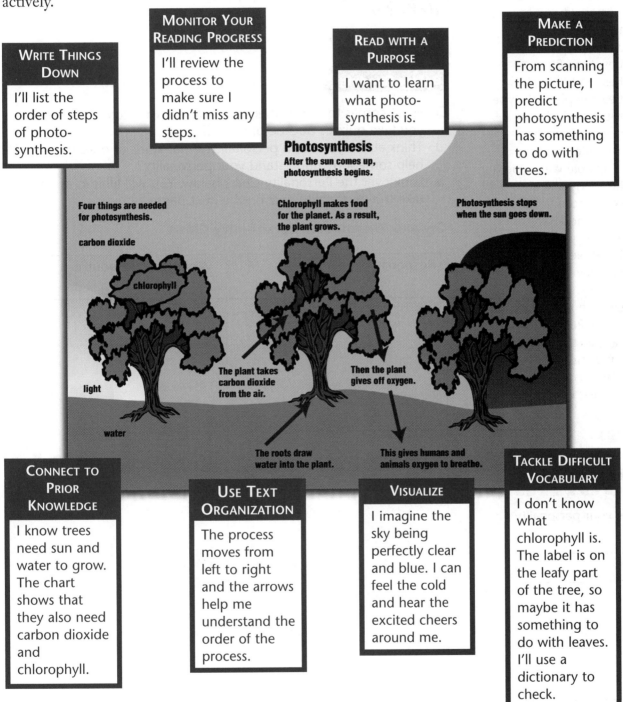

WRITE THINGS DOWN

I'll list the order of steps of photo-synthesis.

MONITOR YOUR READING PROGRESS

I'll review the process to make sure I didn't miss any steps.

READ WITH A PURPOSE

I want to learn what photo-synthesis is.

MAKE A PREDICTION

From scanning the picture, I predict photosynthesis has something to do with trees.

Photosynthesis
After the sun comes up, photosynthesis begins.

Four things are needed for photosynthesis.

carbon dioxide

chlorophyll

light

water

Chlorophyll makes food for the planet. As a result, the plant grows.

The plant takes carbon dioxide from the air.

Then the plant gives off oxygen.

The roots draw water into the plant.

This gives humans and animals oxygen to breathe.

Photosynthesis stops when the sun goes down.

CONNECT TO PRIOR KNOWLEDGE

I know trees need sun and water to grow. The chart shows that they also need carbon dioxide and chlorophyll.

USE TEXT ORGANIZATION

The process moves from left to right and the arrows help me understand the order of the process.

VISUALIZE

I imagine the sky being perfectly clear and blue. I can feel the cold and hear the excited cheers around me.

TACKLE DIFFICULT VOCABULARY

I don't know what chlorophyll is. The label is on the leafy part of the tree, so maybe it has something to do with leaves. I'll use a dictionary to check.

Reader's resource

Psychologists have developed a variety of ways to define different personality types. One of the most basic theories defines type A personalities, type B personalities, and type C personalities. People with type A personalities typically are more competitive, more rushed, time oriented, and aggressive. People with type B personalities generally are more relaxed, more flexible, more passive, and less stressed. Type C people seem like type B people on the surface, but they tend to suppress feelings of stress and to put their own needs last. **"What Is Your Personality Type?"** is a quiz that helps classify your personality in a different way—as a be-er, a do-er, or somewhere in between.

Reader's journal

Describe your personality.

_____

_____

_____

_____

_____

_____

_____

"What Is Your Personality Type?"

Active READING STRATEGY

CONNECT TO PRIOR KNOWLEDGE

Before Reading ➤ THINK ABOUT WHAT YOU KNOW

❑ What comes to mind when you hear the word *quiz?* Where do you take quizzes outside of school?

❑ Think about your own personality. What kinds of questions would help somebody understand your personality?

❑ Look over the Personality Chart below. You will fill it in as you take the personality quiz on the next page.

Graphic Organizer: Personality Chart

Response	What it says about my personality

What is your *personality* type?

____1. Before going to bed on a school night, I:
   A. make sure my homework is done and my clothes are set out for the morning.
   B. watch my favorite show on television.
   C. spend an hour on the phone with a friend, planning a weekend outing.

____2. I make my bed:
   A. perfectly—every day.
   B. in a passable way—most of the time.
   C. only when forced to do it.

____3. During vacations, I prefer to:
   A. relax and enjoy the free time.
   B. get a job to make money.
   C. join a club or a sports team, attend events, go on excursions with family or friends.

____4. Given free time in class, I:
   A. spend it doing homework for other classes.
   B. work ahead in my textbook.
   C. read for fun, draw, or chat with friends.

____5. I worry about having enough time in the day to accomplish all I need to do.
   A. true
   B. false

____6. After a great day, I feel as if I have:
   A. done something helpful.
   B. accomplished a lot of work.
   C. discovered something beautiful.

____7. My favorite shoes:
   A. are comfortable.
   B. look great.
   C. are practical.

During Reading

THINK ABOUT WHAT YOU KNOW

❑ Follow along in the text as your teacher reads the first quiz question and the possible responses aloud. Think about which answer applies to you. Write the response in the left column of the graphic organizer.

❑ Think about what your responses say about your personality. For example, if you choose "A" for question 1, it might mean you like to be prepared. Write the meaning of your response in the right column of the graphic organizer.

❑ Keep filling in the graphic organizer as you read the rest of the quiz.

_____

_____

_____

What Your Score Means:

10–24 points—Be-er
Be-ers tend to be more relaxed and less judgmental. They think it is more important to "be" than to "do." They tend to appreciate beauty and nature. They often accept what comes their way. They tend to live in the moment rather than focus on the future.

25–38 points—Be-er/Do-er
Be-er/do-ers have some characteristics of be-ers and some of do-ers. They may show characteristics of be-ers in some situations and characteristics of do-ers in other situations. Be-er/do-ers tend to be relaxed, though they are usually more excitable than be-ers. They tend to make plans but are flexible if plans don't go their way.

39–48 points—Do-er
Do-ers tend to be very active and goal-oriented. They tend to work hard to achieve their goals. They are usually practical. They tend to be more prone to stress than be-ers. Do-ers prefer to be busy.

____**8.** I would spend an unexpected inheritance on:
   A. a new bike or scooter.
   B. a new pet.
   C. investments.

____**9.** If a friend betrays my trust, I:
   A. never speak to him or her again.
   B. confront him or her immediately, expressing my anger.
   C. wait a day and then ask the friend why he or she did such a thing.

10. Which of the following situations would likely make you mad? (Check all that apply.)
_____ A waiter is rude to you.
_____ A teacher criticizes a paper on which you worked very hard.
_____ Your brother borrows your bicycle without asking.
_____ A parent makes a negative remark about your clothes or hair.
_____ A friend cancels his or her plans with you to do something with another friend instead.
_____ The computer you are using malfunctions, causing you to lose your nearly completed research paper.

Scoring:
1. A=4, B=0, C=2
2. A=4, B=2, C=0
3. A=0, B=4, C=2
4. A=2, B=4, C=0
5. A=4, B=0
6. A=2, B=4, C=0
7. A=0, B=2, C=4
8. A=2, B=2, C=4
9. A=2, B=4, C=0
10. 2 points for each item checked

Reflect ON YOUR READING

❏ When you have finished taking the quiz, add up your score and see how the quiz describes your personality. Do you agree or disagree with the assessment?

❏ Meet with two or three classmates to discuss your quiz results and whether they were accurate. Write a paragraph that evaluates the accuracy of the quiz.

Reading Skills and Test Practice

DRAW CONCLUSIONS

Discuss with a group how best to answer questions that require you to draw conclusions. Use the Think-Aloud Notes to write down your reasons for eliminating the incorrect answers.

_____1. Based on the explanation of be-ers and do-ers at the end of the quiz, which would a be-er be most likely to do?
   a. spend Saturday morning running errands
   b. volunteer once a week at an animal shelter
   c. research and plan a trip for friends
   d. watch the clouds go by and daydream

_____2. Based on the explanation of be-ers and do-ers at the end of the quiz, which would a do-er on a student activities committee be most likely to do?
   a. delegate jobs to others on a committee
   b. decide that things will probably get done somehow
   c. encourage others to get involved with student activities
   d. plan and run activities and be involved in several others

How did using the reading strategy help you to answer the questions?

_____

_____

_____

_____

THINK-ALOUD NOTES

_____

_____

_____

_____

_____

_____

_____

_____

_____

_____

_____

_____

Investigate, Inquire, and Imagine

RECALL: GATHER FACTS
1a. What is the purpose of this personality quiz?

INTERPRET: FIND MEANING
1b. Why might taking this quiz be helpful?

ANALYZE: TAKE THINGS APART
2a. Explain what each of your quiz responses suggests about your personality.

SYNTHESIZE: BRING THINGS TOGETHER
2b. Overall, describe your personality based on your responses to the quiz.

EVALUATE: MAKE JUDGMENTS
3a. Evaluate whether a quiz like this can effectively identify a person's personality.

EXTEND: CONNECT IDEAS
3b. What other questions would you ask to determine somebody's personality?

Literary Tools

QUIZ. A **quiz** is a short test. You may have taken quizzes in school. That kind of quiz is generally designed to show how much you have learned about a certain subject. What is the purpose of this quiz? How does it differ from quizzes you take at school? What other kinds of quizzes can you think of?

_____

_____

_____

_____

_____

_____

_____

WordWorkshop

Semantic Map. Work with a partner to fill in the Vocabulary Cluster below. The categories have been labeled for you, and you may add circles wherever you like. Add words that describe each personality type. Use the Reader's Resource on page 288 to get started. Then add words of your own.

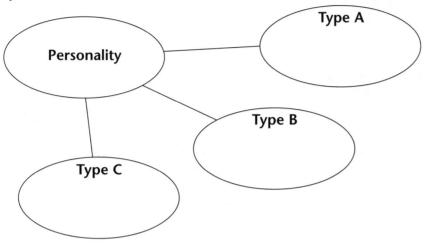

Read-Write Connection

Which questions in the quiz do you think reveal the most about your personality? Why?

_____

_____

_____

_____

Beyond the Reading

Explore Other Personality Types. Use the Internet to research other personality tests, such as the Myers-Briggs personality-type indicator. Take another personality test. Write a report about the results and how accurate you think they are, based on your own assessment of your personality.

Go Online. To find links and additional activities for this selection, visit the EMC Internet Resource Center at **emcp.com/languagearts** and click on Write-In Reader.

Vital signs are used to monitor the functions of the body. They include body temperature, pulse, respiration, and blood pressure. *Body temperature* is the balance between the heat produced by the body and the heat lost by the body. *Pulse* is a wave of blood created by the contraction of the left ventricle of the heart. In a healthy person, the pulse reflects the heartbeat. *Respiration* is the act of breathing. Resting respirations are measured in breaths per minute. *Blood pressure* is the measure of the pressure the blood exerts as it moves through the arteries. Blood pressure includes systolic and diastolic pressure. *Systolic* pressure measures the contraction pressure of the ventricles. *Diastolic* pressure is the pressure when the ventricles are at rest and is lower than systolic pressure. The **chart** on the next page shows changes in vital signs by age.

Reader's journal

When do you like to work with numbers? When do you find such work difficult?

_____

_____

_____

VARIATIONS IN VITAL SIGNS BY AGE

Active READING STRATEGY

WRITE THINGS DOWN

Before Reading ▶ START A K-W-L CHART

❏ Prepare to track unfamiliar facts and terms in the K-W-L Chart as you read.
❏ Before you read, write down what you know about body temperature, pulse rate, breathing rate, and blood pressure. Write your notes in the "What I Know" column.
❏ Write down anything you want to know in the "What I Want to Learn" column.

Graphic Organizer: K-W-L Chart

What I *Know*	What I *Want* to Learn	What I Have *Learned*

VARIATIONS IN VITAL SIGNS BY AGE

Age	Average temperature	Resting pulse rate/min Average	Range	Respiratory rate/minute	Mean blood pressure
Newborn	36.1–37.7°C 97.0–100.0°F	125	70–190	30–80	78 systolic 42 diastolic
1 year	37.7°C 99.7°F	120	80–160	20–40	96 systolic 65 diastolic
2 years	37.2°C 98.9°F	110	80–130	20–30	100 systolic 63 diastolic
4 years	37.2°C 98.9°F	100	80–120	20–30	97 systolic 64 diastolic
6 years	37.0°C 98.6°F	100	75–115	20–25	98 systolic 65 diastolic
8 years	37.0°C 98.6°F	90	70–110	20–25	106 systolic 70 diastolic
10 years	37.0°C 98.6°F	90	70–110	17–22	110 systolic 72 diastolic
12 years	37.0°C 98.6°F	male: 85 female: 90	65–105 70–110	17–22	116 systolic 74 diastolic
14 years	37.0°C 98.6°F	male: 80 female: 85	60–100 65–105		120 systolic 76 diastolic
16 years	37.0°C 98.6°F	male: 75 female: 80	55–95 60–100	15–20	123 systolic 76 diastolic
18 years	37.0°C 98.6°F	male: 70 female: 75	50–90 55–95	15–20	126 systolic 79 diastolic
Adult	37.0°C 98.6°F	male: 70 female: 75	50–90 55–95	15–20	120 systolic 80 diastolic
>70 years	36.0°C 96.8°F	male: 70 female: 75	50–90 55–95	15–20	may increase

Data from *Nelson Textbook of Pediatrics, Growth and Development of Children, Pediatrics* (May 1977), National Heart, Lung, and Blood Institute, Task Force on Blood Pressure Control in Children: Report of the Task Force on Blood Pressure Control in Children.

TAKE NOTES

❑ As you study the chart, note in the "What I Have Learned" column of your K-W-L Chart what you learned about body temperature, pulse rate, breathing rate, and blood pressure.

❑ What other questions do you have about body temperature, pulse rate, breathing rate, and blood pressure? Write these in the "What I Want to Learn" column.

NOTE THE FACTS

A 12-year-old boy has a pulse rate of 107. Does his pulse fall in the normal or abnormal range for his age?

_____

_____

THINK AND REFLECT

In your own words, explain what *vital signs* are. **(Summarize)**

_____

_____

Reflect ON YOUR READING

After Reading **REFLECT ON YOUR CHART**

❑ How did keeping a K-W-L Chart help your reading?
❑ How could you find answers to the questions in the "What I Want to Learn" column?

THINK-ALOUD NOTES

_____
_____
_____
_____
_____
_____
_____
_____
_____
_____
_____

Reading Skills and Test Practice

INTERPRET INFORMATION

Discuss with a partner how to answer questions that require you to interpret information in a chart. Use the Think-Aloud Notes to write down your reasons for eliminating the incorrect answers.

_____1. Occupations that would need the information in this chart would include
    a. flight attendants.
    b. rescue personnel.
    c. veterinary assistants.
    d. teacher's aides.

_____2. According to the chart, what happens to resting pulse as people age?
    a. It drops.
    b. It remains constant.
    c. It rises.
    d. It depends on gender.

How did using the reading strategy help you to answer the questions?

_____

_____

_____

_____

Investigate, Inquire, and Imagine

RECALL: GATHER FACTS
1a. Which column gives you information on the normal range of pulse rates?

→ INTERPRET: FIND MEANING
1b. How can you expect your pulse rate to change when you are 16?

ANALYZE: TAKE THINGS APART
2a. According to this chart, newborn babies and the elderly are alike in one way and different in another. Explain how they are alike and how they are different.

→ SYNTHESIZE: BRING THINGS TOGETHER
2b. In general, does pulse rate and blood pressure follow a similar pattern over the years? Explain your answer.

EVALUATE: MAKE JUDGMENTS
3a. What do the terms *average*, *normal*, and *abnormal* mean? What does it mean to be out of the average range?

→ EXTEND: CONNECT IDEAS
3b. Who might use a chart like this? Why might they use it?

Literary Tools

TABLE. A **table** is a type of chart, also called a matrix chart, in which data is placed by matching it with vertical and horizontal categories. Data in a table are read in rows, which extend horizontally across the table, and columns, which run vertically down the table. The top row (and sometimes the left column) normally has headings that indicate the type of data shown in each corresponding cell, or square that holds data. In what ways do tables make it easier to read and interpret the data presented?

_____

_____

_____

_____

WordWorkshop

Word Origins: Science Terms. Use a dictionary to find the word origin of each of the following words. List the word origin. Then use each word in a sentence.

1. **temperature**

   word origin: _____

   sentence: _____

2. **pulse**

   word origin: _____

   sentence: _____

3. **diastolic**

   word origin: _____

   sentence: _____

4. **systolic**

   word origin: _____

   sentence: _____

5. **Fahrenheit**

   word origin: _____

   sentence: _____

6. **Celsius**

   word origin: _____

   sentence: _____

Read-Write Connection

Which system of measurement do you think is better—the metric system or the U.S. measure system? Write your response on a separate piece of paper. Support your answer with a solid argument.

Beyond the Reading

Creating a Health Guide. Use the Internet and other sources to find information about healthy living. For example, include information about healthy eating and exercise. Include the information from the vital signs chart and other visual aids. Prepare your own health guide. You might present your information in a poster, booklet, or website.

Go Online. To find links and additional activities for this selection, visit the EMC Internet Resource Center at **emcp.com/languagearts** and click on Write-In Reader.

Historical Photographs

by Arthur Rothstein

Active READING STRATEGY

READ WITH A PURPOSE

Before Reading ➤ READ ABOUT AIM

- ❑ Like a writer, a photographer has an aim. An **aim** is the writer's or photographer's purpose or goal. Writers or photographers may have these aims: to inform, to tell a story, to reflect, to entertain or share a perspective, or to persuade readers or viewers to think or see something in a certain way.
- ❑ As you look at the photographs, think about Rothstein's aim and the effect of the photographs on you, the viewer. Take notes in the Aim Chart below.

Graphic Organizer: Aim Chart

Photograph	Aim	Effect
Farmer and Sons Walking in the Face of a Dust Storm		
Farmer Pumping Water from a Well		
Dust Bowl Farmer Raising a Fence to Keep It from Being Buried under Drifting Sand		

CONNECT

Reader's resource

The **historical photographs** you are about to view were taken by Arthur Rothstein in 1936. The Farm Security Administration assigned him to photograph the Oklahoma Dust Bowl. The dust bowl affected large parts of the Midwest in the 1930s. Drought dried up already scant crops and caused dust storms to take over fields and gardens. Although many of Rothstein's photographs appear to be unposed, Rothstein often set them up to achieve a special effect.

Reader's journal

How do you face difficulties in your life? What strategies do you use?

_____

_____

_____

_____

_____

LOOK AT THE PHOTOGRAPHS

❏ Look at the first photograph. What do you think the photographer's aim is? What effect does it have on you? Jot down your thoughts in the Aim Chart.

❏ Look at the other two photographs. Again, try to determine Rothstein's aim and write down your ideas in the chart.

THINK AND REFLECT

What similarities and differences do you see in the two photographs on this page? (Compare and Contrast)

_____

_____

_____

FIX-UP IDEA

Use Text Organization
Examine the caption of each photograph. How does looking at the caption help you understand the photograph?

_____

_____

Historical Photographs

Arthur Rothstein

Farmer and Sons Walking in the Face of a Dust Storm,
1936. Arthur Rothstein.

Farmer Pumping Water from a Well,
1936. Arthur Rothstein.

Dust Bowl Farmer Raising a Fence to Keep It from Being Buried under Drifting Sand, 1936. Arthur Rothstein.

Critical Viewing

• Describe the scene in the top left image on page 300. What is happening? Where are the people going? What do you notice about the door?

• What is happening in the bottom left image on page 300? What is the man doing? What is he looking at?

• What is the man doing in the above photograph? What is the boy doing? What do you think is buried where the man is digging? How would you describe the photograph?

NOTE THE FACTS

What is the farmer doing in the photograph on this page?

_____

_____

Reading STRATEGY
REVIEW

WRITE THINGS DOWN. Writing things down can help you understand how to "read" a photograph. Use the space around each photograph to jot down thoughts you have as you view the photo, including questions you have or things you notice.

THINK AND REFLECT

How would you feel if you were the farmer in the photograph on this page? **(Empathize)**

_____

_____

Reflect ON YOUR READING

After Reading ➤ REVIEW PURPOSE

❑ Review the notes you made in your Aim Chart about the photographer's aim and the effect of each photograph.
❑ Which of the photographs do you find most effective in achieving the photographer's purpose? Why? Discuss these questions with a partner.

Reading Skills and Test Practice

INTERPRET VISUAL MEDIA
With a partner, discuss how to answer questions about the photographs. Use the Think-Aloud Notes to write down your reasons for eliminating the incorrect answers.

_____1. What seems difficult about the man's job in *Dust Bowl Farmer Raising a Fence to Keep It from Being Buried under Drifting Sand?*
    a. There are endless numbers of fence posts.
    b. His shovel looks too large for him to use.
    c. The boy doesn't seem to be helping.
    d. The number of cows to fence in is large.

_____2. What effect do the three images have on the viewer?
    a. They make life during the Dust Bowl look easy.
    b. They show people doing extraordinary things.
    c. They capture the problems faced by people during the Dust Bowl.
    d. They portray leisure activities in harsh settings in order to be ironic.

How did using the reading strategy help you to answer the questions?

_____

_____

_____

_____

THINK-ALOUD NOTES

Investigate, Inquire, and Imagine

RECALL: GATHER FACTS
1a. What is the man doing in the second photograph?

→ INTERPRET: FIND MEANING
1b. How does the man seem to view his circumstances and his task?

ANALYZE: TAKE THINGS APART
2a. What do these three images have in common? How do they differ from one another?

→ SYNTHESIZE: BRING THINGS TOGETHER
2b. What message do these photographs have for the viewer? What emotion do they convey?

EVALUATE: MAKE JUDGMENTS
3a. How effective are the photographs in conveying an idea? How well do they speak to the viewer? Which of the three is the most powerful? Why?

→ EXTEND: CONNECT IDEAS
3b. Think about a photograph you have seen of a recent event. What was the purpose of the photograph? How did it affect you?

Literary Tools

AIM. A writer's **aim** is his or her purpose or goal. Like writers, many photographers work to achieve specific purposes. Rothstein posed his subjects in many of the photographs he took. What do you think he achieved by asking the people to pose in a certain way? How would the photographs have been different if he had simply taken them while people were working and going about everyday life? What was Rothstein's aim?

_____

_____

_____

WordWorkshop

WORD PARTS. The word *photograph* is made up of two parts: *photo,* meaning light, and *graph,* meaning something written or drawn. Use word parts to determine the meaning of the following words. If necessary, check your guess in a dictionary. Then use each word in a sentence.

1. **photokinesis**

   meaning:_____

   sentence:_____

2. **photophobia**

   meaning:_____

   sentence:_____

3. **photosensitive**

   meaning:_____

   sentence:_____

4. **monograph**

   meaning:_____

   sentence:_____

5. **graphology**

   meaning:_____

   sentence:_____

Read-Write Connection

What emotions do these photographs evoke? What are your impressions about the people in the photographs?

Beyond the Reading

TELLING A STORY. Choose one of the photographs from this selection. Think about the people pictured, their surroundings, and what they are doing. If you wish, do some research about the Dust Bowl to help you understand what life was like then. Write a story about the people in the photograph and their experiences. Share your story with some of your classmates.

GO ONLINE. To find links and additional activities for this selection, visit the EMC Internet Resource Center at **emcp.com/languagearts** and click on Write-In Reader.

"How to Chop an Onion in Four Easy Steps"

by Ken Haedrich

Active READING STRATEGY

READ WITH A PURPOSE

Before Reading ▶ SET A PURPOSE

- ❑ From the title of this piece, you know that this is a "how-to" piece. The purpose of reading is to learn how to chop an onion.
- ❑ What are some of the things you can do while reading to help you achieve your purpose?
- ❑ Preview the "How-To" Chart below. You will complete this after you read.

Graphic Organizer: "How-To" Chart

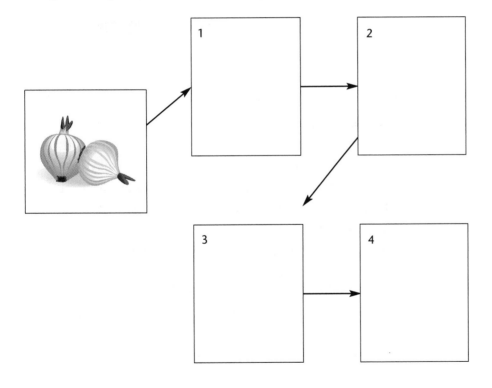

CONNECT

Reader's resource

Onions come in many varieties, shapes, sizes, and tastes. Cutting onions often causes people to cry. One possible reason is that cutting releases chemicals from within the onion that irritate the eyes. To lessen this effect, experts recommend chilling or soaking the onion before chopping it. **"How to Chop an Onion in Four Easy Steps"** gives more tips on cutting onions.

Word watch

PREVIEW VOCABULARY

glance
intact
perpendicular

Reader's journal

Do you like to prepare foods from scratch? Why, or why not?

_____

_____

_____

_____

_____

READ TO LEARN

❑ Preview the selection. The title says the process involves four easy steps. You will notice four numbered steps in the selection. Read the first step.

❑ Read the next three steps. After each step, pause and think about whether you understand what you are supposed to do. If not, reread the step.

NOTE THE FACTS ✏

Why should you pull off the hairy roots?

_____

_____

Reading TIP

When reading directions, it is a good idea to read through them once before you begin using them. That way you can make sure you have all materials on hand, allow enough time for the project, and follow steps in the correct order. Then, after you have read through the steps once, reread them, highlighting any key information or steps. Then read again, pausing after each step to complete it before reading the next step.

How to Chop an Onion

in Four Easy Steps
Ken Haedrich

1 Select a sharp chef's knife. Before you begin, peel off as many layers of papery skin as you can, the better to make your first cut without your knife <u>glancing</u> off the surface. Pull off any hairy roots, too. They have an unappetizing way of ending up where they shouldn't. Place the onion on its side on a chopping board. Hold your knife comfortably, with your forefinger running down one side of the blade and your thumb pressed against the opposite side. With one fell swoop,[1] slide the knife down and away from you, slicing off the top half inch of the onion. (If your knife isn't particularly sharp, first pierce the surface of the onion with the tip of your knife so the blade has a starting notch.)

10

---

1. **one fell swoop.** All at once

words for everyday use	**glance** (glants') *v.*, strike awkwardly so as to slide off or be deflected. *The dart glanced the edge of the board and fell to the floor.*

2 Turn the onion so it rests on the newly cut flat surface. Starting at the center of the root end, slice the onion in half. Peel off any remaining skin.

3 Rest half the onion on its largest flat surface, root end pointing away from you. Working from the far edge of the onion toward your body, slice down through the onion, leaving about 1/2 inch between each cut. Do not, however, slice through the onion at the root end. (An <u>intact</u> root end keeps the onion from falling apart.)

4 Rotate the onion so the end cut faces your knife blade. Then make 1/2-inch cuts <u>perpendicular</u> to the first set of cuts. The onion will fall apart into neat, 1/2-inch dice. Discard root. Repeat with the other half. ■

20

FIX-UP IDEA

Visualize
Think about peeling, chopping, smelling, and eating onions. Try to imagine what you feel and smell, and whether your eyes water. As you read the selection, keep a picture in your mind of the scene. Try to imagine the sounds, the smells, the sights, and the things you touch.

NOTE THE FACTS

Which end of the onion should you not slice through?

_____

_____

_____

THINK AND REFLECT

What could you do with an onion once you have chopped it? **(Extend)**

_____

_____

_____

words for everyday use

in • tact (in takt′) *adj.*, untouched; entire. *The violent storm ripped the roof from the old cabin but left everything inside <u>intact</u>.*
per • pen • dic • u • lar (pər pən di′ kyə lər) *adj.*, being at right angles to a given line or plane. *Oak Street runs <u>perpendicular</u> to Main Street.*

Reflect ON YOUR READING

After Reading ➤ REVIEW WHAT YOU LEARNED

❑ Illustrate the four steps of the process, using the "How-To" Chart on page 305.

❑ Evaluate the selection. Are these good directions? What would you add or do differently?

_____

_____

_____

_____

THINK-ALOUD NOTES

_____

_____

_____

_____

_____

_____

_____

_____

_____

_____

Reading Skills and Test Practice

UNDERSTAND SEQUENCE

Discuss with a partner how to answer questions about sequence. Use the Think-Aloud Notes to write down your reasons for eliminating the incorrect answers.

_____1. According to the directions, what should you do to the onion before you cut it?
   a. wash it
   b. peel off outer layers
   c. dry the onion
   d. roll it on the cutting board

_____2. Why do you peel the onion?
   a. so that the blade doesn't slide off the onion
   b. to protect your eyes from too many juices
   c. the outer layers taste very bitter
   d. so that the skin doesn't get into what you're cooking

How did using the reading strategy help you to answer the questions?

_____

_____

_____

_____

Investigate, Inquire, and Imagine

RECALL: GATHER FACTS
1a. How do you rest the onion before slicing, according to both steps 2 and 3?

INTERPRET: FIND MEANING
1b. What purpose does this serve?

ANALYZE: TAKE THINGS APART
2a. Look at each step of the onion-chopping process. Do any of the four steps contain extra information that you don't need? Could any steps be combined?

SYNTHESIZE: BRING THINGS TOGETHER
2b. Summarize, in your own words, Ken Haedrich's steps for chopping an onion.

EVALUATE: MAKE JUDGMENTS
3a. Does this process describe the best possible way to chop an onion? Why, or why not?

EXTEND: CONNECT IDEAS
3b. How would you modify the onion-chopping directions so they would apply to chopping another ingredient, such as tomatoes or chile peppers?

Literary Tools

CHRONOLOGICAL ORDER. Chronological order is the arrangement of details in the order in which they occur. Writing that describes processes, events, and cause-and-effect relationships often uses chronological order. What words does the author use to clarify the order of steps in the process? Why is chronological order important in directions?

_____

_____

_____

_____

_____

WordWorkshop

UNDERSTANDING COOKING TERMS. Cooking, like many other activities, has its own terminology. Use cookbooks, a dictionary, or cooking websites to find the meaning of each of the following cooking terms. If the word has a meaning not related to cooking, note that, too.

1. **cream** *(v.)*

    cooking meaning: _____

    other meaning: _____

2. **zest**

    cooking meaning: _____

    other meaning: _____

3. **blanch**

    cooking meaning: _____

    other meaning: _____

4. **baste**

    cooking meaning: _____

    other meaning: _____

5. **fold**

    cooking meaning: _____

    other meaning: _____

Read-Write Connection

Have you ever chopped an onion or another vegetable? Describe the process you used.

_____

_____

Beyond the Reading

FOLLOWING A RECIPE. Recipes are a type of direction writing. You can find recipes in cookbooks, in magazines, and online. Find a recipe that appeals to you. Follow the directions. When you are done, comment on how hard or easy the recipe was to follow, whether you were happy with the results, and if you would recommend the recipe to somebody else.

GO ONLINE. To find links and additional activities for this selection, visit the EMC Internet Resource Center at **emcp.com/languagearts** and click on Write-In Reader.

"Getting into Web Development"

Interview with Dave Schaller and Susan Nagel

Active READING STRATEGY

USE TEXT ORGANIZATION

Before Reading ➤ **PREVIEW ORGANIZATION**

❑ Read the Reader's Resource. Look at the title and photograph on page 312. Scan the rest of the text.
❑ What do you learn about the text from titles and headings?
❑ An **interview** is a question and answer exchange between a reporter who wants precise information from a reliable source and the person who has that information. Notice how the questions and answers are formatted differently in the text.
❑ Prepare to use the organizational clues to fill in the Organization Chart as you read.

Graphic Organizer: Organization Chart

Organizational Feature	Information
Title	
Photograph	

CONNECT

Reader's resource

Many organizations and individuals have websites. Web developers create websites for themselves or others. They think about what text, graphics, video, and sound should be used and how it should all fit together. **"Getting into Web Development"** is an interview with Dave Schaller and Susan Nagel of Educational Web Adventures LLP, who have created many websites.

Reader's journal

Do you enjoy using the Internet? Why do you use it?

_____

_____

_____

_____

_____

USE THE TEXT'S
ORGANIZATIONAL
FEATURES

❑ Read the title and the
first paragraph. Use the
Organization Chart to
keep track of some of the
organizational features.
For example, in the
"Information" column
next to Title, write what
you learn about the
selection from the title.
Then add what you learn
from the photograph.

❑ As you read, continue
filling in the chart. Add
other forms of
organization and how
they help you understand
the text.

NOTE THE FACTS

How did Dave Schaller
and Susan Nagel get
involved with designing
websites?

_____

_____

Getting into Web Development

Web developers **Dave Schaller** and **Susan Nagel**, of **Educational Web Adventures LLP,** have created a variety of interactive Internet sites for young people.

Here they answer a few questions about their work.

How did you become involved in designing web sites?
We've both been interested in education for a long time, but we worked in different settings—Susan was an art teacher, and Dave was a writer and museum exhibit developer. When the Web appeared in the mid-1990s, we realized that it could be a great new medium for education. We didn't see any companies focusing on educational Web development, so we formed one ourselves. Our specialty is developing educational games and simulations for museums, distance learning programs, and corporations.

What do you like best about your work?
We both like learning new things, and now that's our job! We've done projects about art, history, ecology, space exploration, and many other subjects, and for each one, one of the best parts has been learning about the subject. It's also challenging and fun to make each project take shape.

Web sites are getting more and more complex, and we've got to make sure that all the pieces—the text, graphics, programming, and everything else—fit together just like (or even better than) we'd planned. But watching each site come together is really exciting.

What is the hardest thing about this kind of work?

Neither of us ever expected to run a business, so that part—accounting, marketing, and such—was all new to us. It's been a challenge, but if you love what you're doing, even the hard parts usually feel like fun.

How do you decide what works and what doesn't work so well in a web site?

Partly, we draw on our previous experience teaching and writing museum exhibits. And we've developed so many games and activities that we have a decent feel for what works and what doesn't. But we still bring in kids to test our projects. We always find things to change and improve after watching them and talking with them. There's nothing better than watching kids grin as they play a game we developed—and nothing more enlightening than watching them frown from frustration or confusion! And, of course, kids and teachers around the world send us their thoughts and suggestions by e-mail!

Here are a few of Dave Schaller and Susan Nagel's recent projects:

FUN ONLINE AT THE CHILDREN'S MUSEUM OF INDIANAPOLIS

Create a puppet show, solve some geo-mysteries, design a space station, and more!
http://www.childrensmuseum.org/

LEONARDO'S WORKSHOP: AN ARTEDVENTURE WITH CARMINE CHAMELEON

Travel back in time to Leonardo da Vinci's workshop to solve this interactive mystery.
http://www.sanford-artedventures.com/

BUILD-A-PRAIRIE

Can you turn a barren plain into a healthy prairie? Choose the right species and watch the prairie come to life!
http://www.umn.edu/bellmuse/mnideals/prairie

Find their latest projects on their web site:
http://www.eduweb.com/adventure.html

FIX-UP IDEA

Partnered Read Aloud
If you have difficulty following the text, read aloud with a partner. One person should read the interviewer's questions (in bold type) and the other should read the responses (plain type).

MARK THE TEXT

Highlight or underline the hardest part of the job for Schaller and Nagel.

Reading STRATEGY
REVIEW

SET A PURPOSE. Setting a purpose for reading can help you stay focused on your reading. Before looking at one of the websites designed by Schaller and Nagel, set a purpose. For example, you might read to find clues to the mystery on Leonardo's Workshop, or you might read to evaluate how informative and entertaining one of the sites is.

THINK AND REFLECT

Which of the websites listed sound most interesting to you? Why? (Evaluate)

_____

_____

_____

Reflect ON YOUR READING

After Reading ➤ ANALYZE THE TEXT'S ORGANIZATIONAL FEATURES

❑ In a short paragraph, identify the text's organizational features and describe why this is a good (or bad) way to organize the text. Explain how the organization helped or hindered your understanding.
❑ When finished, share and discuss your essay with a partner.

Reading Skills and Test Practice

RECOGNIZE MAIN IDEAS

READ, THINK, AND EXPLAIN. Discuss with your group how to answer the following question that asks you to recognize main ideas. Use the Think-Aloud Notes to jot down ideas.

Explain what Dave Schaller and Susan Nagel like about their work as web developers. Based on what you read, would you be interested in a job in web development? Why, or why not? What other questions would you want answered to help you decide?

_____

_____

_____

_____

_____

_____

_____

REFLECT ON YOUR RESPONSE. Compare your response to those of your group. How were you able to recognize main ideas?

_____

_____

_____

_____

Investigate, Inquire, and Imagine

RECALL: GATHER FACTS
1a. What is the specialty of Educational Web Adventures LLP?

→ **INTERPRET: FIND MEANING**
1b. Why did Schaller and Nagel choose this focus for their business?

ANALYZE: TAKE THINGS APART
2a. List three projects Dave Schaller and Susan Nagel have designed.

→ **SYNTHESIZE: BRING THINGS TOGETHER**
2b. How might these projects be related to the work Schaller and Nagel did before they became web designers?

EVALUATE: MAKE JUDGMENTS
3a. Schaller and Nagel think that the Internet is a great medium for education. Do you agree? Why?

→ **EXTEND: CONNECT IDEAS**
3b. What is your favorite website? What do you like about it?

Literary Tools

INTERVIEW. An **interview** is a question and answer exchange between a reporter who wants precise information from a reliable source and the person who has that information. What information did the interviewer want? Why were Schaller and Nagel good sources?

WordWorkshop

ELECTRONIC MEDIA WORD SORT. There are many words related to the Internet and other electronic media. First brainstorm a list of electronic media words; there are some listed below to get you started. Make a vocabulary card for each word. Include the word, the meaning, and a contextual sentence. Then do a word sort for these words. You might sort by words with similar word parts ("web" words, "net" words, "e–" words, etc.) or by words with similar meanings or functions (searching and browsing, communicating, electronic media, etc.).

Brainstorm electronic media words:
website
e-mail
cyberspace
netiquette

_____

_____

_____

Read-Write Connection

If you were interviewing Dave Schaller and Susan Nagel, what questions would you ask them?

_____

_____

_____

_____

_____

_____

_____

_____

_____

_____

_____

_____

_____

_____

_____

_____

Beyond the Reading

EVALUATING WEBSITES. Visit one of the websites listed at the end of the interview. Evaluate the site on the following criteria: ease of use, interest or entertainment value, and educational value. Then write a review of the website.

GO ONLINE. To find links and additional activities for this selection, visit the EMC Internet Resource Center at **emcp.com/languagearts** and click on Write-In Reader.

Unit 8 READING Review

Choose and Use Reading Strategies

Before reading the chart and excerpt below, review with a partner how to use each of these reading strategies with informational and visual media.

1. Read with a Purpose
2. Connect to Prior Knowledge
3. Write Things Down
4. Make Predictions
5. Visualize
6. Use Text Organization
7. Tackle Difficult Vocabulary
8. Monitor Your Reading Progress

Now apply at least two of these reading strategies as you read the Geologic Time Chart and an excerpt from "The Passage of Time." The article talks about the La Brea Tar Pits in southern California. Use the margins and mark up the text to show how you are using the reading strategies to read actively. Then answer the critical thinking questions that follow the excerpt.

GEOLOGIC TIME CHART

ERA	PERIOD	EPOCH	MILLIONS OF YEARS AGO
CENOZOIC	QUATERNARY	HOLOCENE PLEISTOCENE	0.01 1.8
CENOZOIC	TERTIARY	PLIOCENE MIOCENE OLIGOCENE EOCENE PALEOCENE	5 24 38 54 65
MESOZOIC	CRETACEOUS JURASSIC TRIASSIC		145 210 250
PALEOZOIC	PERMIAN		290
PALEOZOIC	CARBONIFEROUS PENNSYLVANIAN MISSISSIPPIAN		365
PALEOZOIC	DEVONIAN		415
PALEOZOIC	SILURIAN		465
PALEOZOIC	ORDOVICIAN		510
PALEOZOIC	CAMBRIAN		575
	PRECAMBRIAN		

For thousands of years, the La Brea Tar Pits were important to the early humans who lived in what is now southern California. Indian peoples used the sticky asphalt to bind and mend things together and to glue decorative shells to stone, bone, and wood. . . .

Spanish explorers discovered the bubbling swamp in 1769. . . . When they built a settlement nearby, they used the tar as a material for waterproofing and for roofing. A century later, workers began mining the asphalt. When they found bones, the miners assumed these remains must be from the cattle and horses people had seen wandering into the pits. In 1875, however, Professor William Denton identified a tooth from the extinct saber-toothed cat. Still, excavation of the tar pits did not begin for another 25 years. Since then, more than one million bones have been removed. Evidence of past life, these fossils began forming when the bones soaked in the asphalt. . . . Over the years, layer upon layer of asphalt and sediment marked the passage of time. Today, the La Brea Tar Pits bustle with activity, as archaeologists continue to remove evidence of past life from the pits.

Many of the larger animals entombed in the pits are now extinct. They needed a cooler, wetter climate to survive. From this finding, scientists have learned that the climate in southern California is warmer and drier than it used to be.

1. By what era in geologic history did walking animals appear? By what era did dinosaurs appear? Why do you think the chart has divided the tertiary period and the quaternary period into epochs?

   _____

   _____

2. When did William Denton identify remains of a saber-toothed cat in the La Brea Tar Pits? What time period do you think the cat is from? What assumption did Denton's discovery contradict?

   _____

   _____

3. Why did larger animals trapped in the tar pits die off? Explain how their extinction led scientists to infer that the southern California climate has become warmer and drier.

   _____

   _____

WordWorkshop

UNIT 8 WORDS FOR EVERYDAY USE
glance, 306
intact, 307
perpendicular, 307

SYNONYMS AND ANTONYMS. **Synonyms** are words that mean the same or nearly the same. **Antonyms** are words that are opposite in meaning. Choose the synonym and antonym from the words listed below for each of the Words for Everyday Use. Then try to identify another synonym and antonym for each word.

at right angle to
broken
deflect
parallel
strike
whole

Word for Everyday Use	Synonym	Antonym
glance		
intact		
perpendicular		

Literary Tools

Select the best literary element on the right to complete each sentence on the left. Write the correct letter in the blank.

_____1. Directions often use _____ to help readers understand the steps of the process.

_____2. A writer's reason or purpose for writing is his or her _____.

_____3. In a(n) _____, a person asks an expert questions about a specific subject.

_____4. A(n) ____ is a kind of chart.

_____5. "What Is Your Personality Type?" is an example of a(n) _____.

a. aim, 299, 303

b. chronological order, 309

c. interview, 282, 311, 315

d. quiz, 292

e. table, 297

On Your Own

FLUENTLY SPEAKING. Conduct an interview of a classmate or other person at your school. Choose a job, hobby, or other interest of the person you are interviewing as the subject of your interview. Develop several questions; then conduct the interview.

PICTURE THIS. A picture or a diagram can help make directions more clear. Think about a simple process that you know how to do well. Prepare a series of diagrams to explain the process. Use labels and wording with the diagrams as necessary.

PUT IT IN WRITING. Write a critique of another piece of information or visual media that interests you. For example, you might choose a photodocumentary, the box score of a game, an Internet site, or an opinion piece. Examine the piece you choose. Decide what the aim of the piece is and how well it meets its aim.

Unit NINE

Developing Vocabulary Skills

TACKLING DIFFICULT VOCABULARY AS YOU READ

To understand what you read, you need a set of tools for dealing with words you don't know. Glossaries and footnotes, context clues, prior knowledge of word parts and word families, and dictionaries are tools that can help you unlock the meaning of unfamiliar words.

Using Definitions, Footnotes, Endnotes, and Glossaries

Some textbooks, like this one, provide **definitions** of selected words on the page on which the word is used. **Footnotes**, like definitions, also appear on the same page as the words to which they refer. Specifically, footnotes appear at the foot, or bottom, of a page and are numbered to correspond to the words or phrases they explain. Sometimes footnotes cite a source of information. Other times they define uncommon words and phrases. If you see a superscripted number next to a word in the text you are reading (delta[2]), but can't find the footnote at the foot of the page, check the end of the article, chapter, or book. A footnote that comes at the end of a document is called an **endnote**. A **glossary** is an alphabetized list of important words and their definitions. Glossaries usually appear at the end of an article, a chapter, or a book.

To use definitions, footnotes, endnotes, and glossaries, follow these steps:

❶ Read the paragraph or short section containing the unfamiliar word to get a sense of the meaning.

❷ Check the definition, footnote, endnote, or glossary entry for the word.

❸ Reread the paragraph or section, this time keeping in mind the definition of the new word.

NOTE THE FACTS

What should you do after checking the meaning of a word in the definition, footnote, endnote, glossary, or dictionary?

_____

_____

_____

_____

Using Context Clues

You can often figure out the meaning of an unfamiliar word by using context clues. **Context clues**, or hints you gather from the words and sentences around the unfamiliar word, prevent you from having to look up every unknown word in the dictionary. The chart below defines the types of context clues and gives you an example of each. It also lists words that signal each type of clue.

THINK AND REFLECT

If someone says, "Gregory's side of the room is always clean and neat, while Kieran's side of the room is horribly <u>unkempt</u>," what do you think *unkempt* means? **(Apply)**

_____

_____

_____

Context Clues

comparison clue	shows a comparison, or how the unfamiliar word is like something that might be familiar to you
signal words	*and, like, as, just as, as if, as though*

EXAMPLE

Brent looked as <u>dapper</u> as James Bond in his tuxedo. (If Brent looks like James Bond in his tuxedo, he must look handsome and stylish, so *dapper* must mean "stylish.")

contrast clue	shows that something contrasts, or differs in meaning, from something else
signal words	*but, nevertheless, on the other hand, however, although, though, in spite of*

EXAMPLE

Rainy days usually make me <u>melancholy</u>; however, after months of no precipitation, I was joyful to see it finally rain. (The word *however* signals a contrast between the speaker's feelings: somber and joyful. If the speaker is unusually happy that it rained, then *melancholy* must mean "depressed or gloomy.")

restatement clue	uses different words to express the same idea
signal words	*that is, in other words, or*

EXAMPLE

That thunderstorm was <u>pernicious</u>; it caused major flooding, which destroyed hundreds of houses. (As the second sentence suggests, *pernicious* means "destructive.")

examples clue	gives examples of other items to illustrate the meaning of something
signal words	*including, such as, for example, for instance, especially, particularly*

EXAMPLE

Despite its tiny size, the Chihuahua can look <u>ferocious</u>, particularly when its teeth are bared and when it growls. (The images of bared teeth and growls suggest that *ferocious* means "fierce.")

CONTINUED

cause-and-effect clue	tells you that something happened as a result of something else
signal words	*if/then, when/then, thus, therefore, because, so, as a result of, consequently*

EXAMPLE

While attempting to do a cartwheel on the beam, Victoria fell and sprained her ankle; as a result, she felt <u>apprehensive</u> about getting back on the beam. (If falling off the beam and hurting her ankle caused Victoria to feel apprehensive, *apprehensive* must mean "fearful, nervous.")

Using Your Prior Knowledge

You can often use your knowledge of word parts and other words to help you figure out the meaning of a new word.

BREAKING WORDS INTO BASE WORDS, WORD ROOTS, PREFIXES, AND SUFFIXES

Many words are formed by adding prefixes and suffixes to main word parts called **base words** (if they can stand alone) or **word roots** (if they can't). A **prefix** is a letter or group of letters added to the beginning of a word to change its meaning. A **suffix** is a letter or group of letters added to the end of a word to change its meaning.

Word Part	Definition	Example
base word	main word part that can stand alone	flex
word root	main word part that can't stand alone	phot
prefix	letter or group of letters added to the beginning of the word	con–
suffix	letter or group of letters added to the end of the word	–er

When you encounter an unfamiliar word, check to see if you recognize the meaning of the prefix, suffix, base word, or word root. In combination with context clues, these meanings can help you unlock the meaning of the entire word. On the following pages are charts listing the meanings of the most common prefixes, suffixes, and word roots.

Reading STRATEGY
REVIEW

READ WITH A PURPOSE. Rather than read the charts on the following pages all the way through from beginning to end, set a purpose for reading, and then let that purpose guide how you read the charts. For example, if you just want to become familiar with what prefixes, suffixes, and word roots are, read only a few lines from each chart, but read them carefully, studying how each word part contributes to the meaning of the words in the Examples column. Your teacher might set a purpose for you, too. If so, approach the charts as your teacher directs.

Common Prefixes		
Prefix	**Meaning**	**Examples**
ambi–/amphi–	both	ambidextrous, amphibian
anti–/ant–	against; opposite	antibody, antacid
bi–	two	bicycle, biped
circum–	around; about	circumnavigate, circumstance
co–/col–/com–/con–/cor–	together	cooperate, collaborate, commingle, concentrate, correlate
counter–	contrary; complementary	counteract, counterpart
de–	opposite; remove; reduce	decipher, defrost, devalue
dia–	through; apart	dialogue, diaphanous
dis–	not; opposite of	dislike, disguise
dys–	abnormal; difficult; bad	dysfunctional, dystopia
em–/en–	into or onto; cover with; cause to be; provide with	embark, empower, enslave, enfeeble
ex–	out of; from	explode, export, extend
extra–/extro–	outward; outside; beyond	extraordinary, extrovert
hyper–	too much, too many, or extreme	hyperbole, hyperactive
hypo–	under	hypodermic
il–, im–, in–, ir–	not	illogical, impossible, inoperable, irrational
	in; within; toward; on	illuminate, imperil, infiltrate, irrigate
inter–	among or between	international, intersect
intra–/intro–	into; within; inward	introvert, intramural
meta–	after; changed	metamorphosis, metaphor
mis–	wrongly	mistake, misfire
non–	not	nonsense, nonsmoker
out–	in a manner that goes beyond	outrun, outmuscle
over–	excessive	overdone, overkill
per–	through, throughout	permeate, permanent
peri–	all around	perimeter, periscope
post–	after; later	postgame, postpone
pre–	before	prefix, premature *CONTINUED*

Common Prefixes (continued)

Prefix	Meaning	Examples
pro–	before; forward	proceed, prologue
re–	again; back	redo, recall
retro–	back	retrospect, retroactive
semi–	half; partly	semicircle, semidry
sub–/sup–	under	substandard, subfloor, support
super–	above; over; exceeding	superstar, superfluous
sym–/syn–	with; together	sympathy, synonym, synergy
trans–	across; beyond	transatlantic, transfer, transcend
ultra–	too much, too many, extreme	ultraviolet, ultrasound
un–	not	unethical, unhappy
under–	below or short of a quantity or limit	underestimate, understaffed
uni–	one	unicorn, universe

Common Suffixes

Noun Suffixes	Meaning	Examples
–ance/–ancy/–ence/–ency	quality or state	defiance, independence, emergency
–age	action or process	marriage, voyage
–ant/–ent	one who	defendant, assistant, resident
–ar/–er/–or	one who	lawyer, survivor, liar
–dom	state or quality of	freedom, boredom
–es/–s	plural form of noun	siblings, trees
–ion/–tion	action or process	revolution, occasion
–ism	act; state; or system of belief	plagiarism, barbarism, Buddhism
–ist	one who does or believes something	ventriloquist, idealist
–itude, –tude	quality of, state of	multitude, magnitude
–ity/–ty	state of	longevity, infinity
–ment	action or process; state or quality; product or thing	development, government, amusement, amazement, ointment, fragment
–ness	state of	kindness, happiness

CONTINUED

Common Suffixes (continued)		
Adjective Suffixes	**Meaning**	**Examples**
–able/–ible	capable of	attainable, possible
–al	having characteristics of	personal, governmental
–er	more	higher, calmer, shorter
–est	most	lowest, craziest, tallest
–ful	full of	helpful, gleeful, woeful
–ic	having characteristics of	scientific, chronic
–ish	like	childish, reddish
–ive	performs or tends toward	creative, pensive
–less	without	hapless, careless
–ous	possessing the qualities of	generous, joyous
–y	indicates description	happy, dirty, flowery
Adverb Suffixes	**Meaning**	**Examples**
–ly	in such a way	quickly, studiously, invisibly
–ward, –ways, –wise	in such a direction	toward, sideways, crosswise
Verb Suffixes	**Meaning**	**Examples**
–ate	make or cause to be	fixate, activate
–ed	past tense of verb	walked, acted, fixed
–ify/–fy	make or cause to be	vilify, magnify, glorify
–ing	indicates action in progress (present participle); can also be a noun (gerund)	running, thinking, being
–ize	bring about; cause to be	colonize, legalize

Common Word Roots		
Word Root	**Meaning**	**Examples**
acr	highest point	acrobat
act	do	actor, reaction
ann/annu/enni	year	annual, bicentennial
aqu	water	aquarium, aquatic
aster, astr	star	asteroid, disastrous
aud	hear	audition, auditorium

CONTINUED

Common Word Roots (continued)		
Word Root	**Meaning**	**Examples**
bene	good	beneficial, benefactor
bibl, bibli	book	Bible
chron	time	chronic
cosm	universe; order	cosmic, cosmos
cred	believe; trust	credit, credible
cycl	circle	bicycle, cyclone
dem/demo	people	democracy
derm	skin	dermatologist
dic/dict	say	dictate, dictionary
duc/duct	lead; pull	conduct, reproduction
dyn	force, power	dynamic, dynamite
equ/equi/iqui	equal	equidistant, equitable, iniquity
fer	carry	transfer, refer
fin	end	finish, infinite
firm	firm, strong	confirm, reaffirm
flect/flex	bend	deflect, reflex, flexible
fort	strong	fortify, comfort
ge	earth	geode, geography
gress	go	progress, regress
hydr	water	hydrate
ign	fire	ignite, ignition, igneous
ject	throw	projector, eject
judic	judgment	prejudice, judicial
lect/leg	read; choose	lecture, election, collect
liber	free	liberate, liberal
loc	place	location, relocate
locut/loqu	speak	elocution, loquacious, colloquial
log/logue	word, speech, discourse	logic, dialogue
luc/lumin	shine; light	translucent, illuminate
mal	bad	malevolent
man/manu	hand	manufacture, manual *CONTINUED*

Common Word Roots (continued)		
Word Root	**Meaning**	**Examples**
metr	measure	metric
morph	form	morpheme, metamorphosis
mot	move	motor, emotion
mut	change	mutation, transmutable
nov	new	novelty, renovate
onym	name	synonym, antonym
path	feel; suffer; disease	sympathy, pathology
ped	foot, child	pedal, pediatrics
phon/phony	sound; voice; speech	symphony
phot	light	photography
physi	nature	physical, physics
pop	people	popular, populate
port	carry	transport, portable
psych	mind; soul	psychology, psychic
reg	rule	register, regulate
rupt	break	disrupt, interruption, rupture
scrib/script	write	describe, prescription
son	sound	sonic
spec/spect/spic	look	speculate, inspect, despicable
spir	breathe	spirit, inspiration
ter/terr	earth	inter, extraterrestrial, terrain
therm	heat	thermal
top	place	topography, topical
tract	draw; drag	retract, tractor, contract
typ	stamp; model	typical, type
ver	truth	veracity, verifiable
vert	turn	divert, introvert, extrovert
vid/vis	see	video, visual
viv	alive	vivacious, vivid
vol/volv	turn	evolution, revolve

The more meanings of prefixes, suffixes, and word roots you know, the better equipped you are to tackle difficult vocabulary words.

Even if you don't know the meaning of a word part, however, you can often figure out the meaning of a word using word parts. To do this, think of as many familiar words as you can that contain each part of the word.

For example, if you were tackling the word *microcosm*, you might first think of words beginning with the prefix *micro–*: *microscope*, *microorganism*, and *microsecond*. You know that a microscope, through magnification, allows you to see things that are too small for the human eye to see. You're pretty sure that the other two words also have something to do with being extremely small. (You could check out this hunch by looking in a dictionary.) Then you might think of words that contain *cosm*: *cosmos*, *cosmic*, and *cosmopolitan*. *Cosmos* and *cosmic* both have something to do with the universe. Someone who is cosmopolitan is worldly. From this information, you might guess (correctly) that *cosm* means universe or world. A microcosm is a tiny world or universe!

This process is even easier when you work with a partner. Think aloud with your partner about how to break apart a word. Then discuss the meanings of each part and a possible meaning for the entire word.

RECOGNIZING COMBINING FORMS

Some word roots have become very common in English and are used all the time in combination with each other and with base words to create new scientific, medical, and technical terms. These combining forms can look like prefixes and suffixes, but contain more core meaning. The chart on the next page defines and gives examples of some common combining forms that will help you tackle new words.

NOTE THE FACTS

Why is it helpful to know the meanings of many different word parts?

_____

_____

_____

_____

THINK AND REFLECT

Think aloud about how you would use word parts to figure out the meaning of the word *supersonic*. Record notes from your think aloud here. **(Apply)**

_____

_____

_____

_____

Combining Forms

Word Part	Meaning	Examples
acro–	heights	acrophobia
anthropo–	human being	anthropologist
archaeo–/arche–	old	archeology
astr–/astro–	star	astronaut, astrology
audio–	hear	audiovisual
auto–	self	autobiography, automatic
bi–/bio–	life	biography, biosphere
bibli–/biblio–	book	bibliography
–centric	having such a center	egocentric
chron–/chrono–	time	chronology
–cracy	form of government; social or political class	aristocracy, democracy
ethno–	race; people; cultural group	ethnography
ge–/geo–	earth; soil	geography, geology
–graph/–graphy	something written, drawn, or represented by graphics	telegraph, photography
hydr–/hydro–	water	hydroelectric, hydrometer
–logy/–ology	study of	geology, biology
mal–	bad	malfunction, malnutrition
–mania	madness	kleptomania, megalomania
–metry	having to do with measure	geometry, symmetry
micro–	small; minute	microscope, microcosm
omni–	all	omnipresent, omnibus
–onym	name	synonym, antonym
–phile	one who loves	bibliophile
–phobe	one who has an irrational fear	arachnophobe, acrophobe
–phobia	exaggerated fear of	claustrophobia, photophobia
phon–/–phone/phono–	sound; voice; speech	telephone, phonograph
phot–/–photo–	light	photograph, telephoto
physi–/physio–	nature; physical	physiological
pseud–/pseudo–	false	pseudonym, pseudointellectual
psych–/psycho–	mind	psychiatrist, psychology
–scope/–scopy	view	telescope, microscopy
–ster	one who does or is	mobster, spinster
therm–/thermo–	heat	thermometer, thermodynamics
tel–/tele–	distant	telegram, telephone

EXPLORING WORD ORIGINS AND WORD FAMILIES

The English language expands constantly and gathers new words from many different sources. Understanding the source of a word can help you unlock its meaning.

One source of new words is the names of people and places associated with the thing being named. Words named for people and places are called **eponyms**.

> **EXAMPLES**
> **frankfurter** This food is named after Frankfurt, Germany. In Frankfurt, the same food is called a *wiener*, after *Wien*, the German name of the Austrian city Vienna.
>
> **sousaphone** This instrument is named after the American bandmaster John Philip Sousa.

Another source for new words is **acronyms**. Acronyms are words formed from the first letter or letters of the major parts of terms.

> **EXAMPLES**
> **AIDS,** from *acquired immune deficiency syndrome*
> **FAQ,** from *frequently asked questions*

Some words in the English language are borrowed from other languages.

> **EXAMPLES**
> **tortilla** (Spanish), **faux pas** (French), **tapioca** (Tupi)

Many words are formed by shortening longer words.

> **EXAMPLES**
> **lunch,** from *luncheon*
> **ad,** from *advertisement*
> **lab,** from *laboratory*

Brand names are often taken into the English language. People begin to use these words as common nouns, even though most of them are still brand names.

> **EXAMPLES**
> popsicle   styrofoam   post-it note

THINK AND REFLECT

How might understanding word origins help you unlock word meanings? **(Extend)**

_____

_____

_____

_____

_____

_____

Using a Dictionary

When you can't figure out a word using the strategies already described, or when the word is important to the meaning of the text and you want to make sure you have it right, use a dictionary.

There are many parts to a dictionary entry. Study the following sample. Then read the explanations of each part of an entry below.

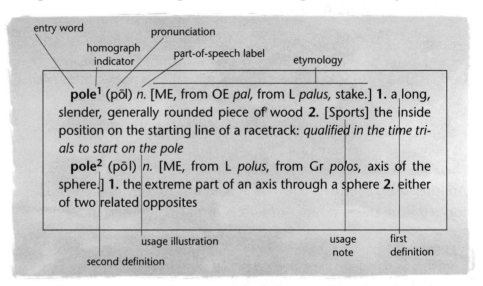

entry word

homograph indicator

pronunciation

part-of-speech label

etymology

pole¹ (pōl) *n.* [ME, from OE *pal,* from L *palus,* stake.] **1.** a long, slender, generally rounded piece of wood **2.** [Sports] the inside position on the starting line of a racetrack: *qualified in the time trials to start on the pole*

pole² (pōl) *n.* [ME, from L *polus,* from Gr *polos,* axis of the sphere.] **1.** the extreme part of an axis through a sphere **2.** either of two related opposites

usage illustration

usage note

first definition

second definition

The **pronunciation** is given immediately after the entry word. The dictionary's table of contents will tell you where you can find a complete key to pronunciation symbols. In some dictionaries, a simplified pronunciation key is provided at the bottom of each page.

An abbreviation of the **part of speech** usually follows the pronunciation. This label tells how the word can be used. If a word can be used as more than one part of speech, a separate entry is provided for each part of speech.

An **etymology** is the history of the word. In the first entry, the word *pole* can be traced back through Middle English (ME) and Old English (OE) to the Latin (L) word *palus,* which means "stake." In the second entry, the word *pole* can be traced back through Middle English to the Latin word *polus,* which comes from the Greek (Gr) word *polos,* meaning "axis of the sphere."

Sometimes the entry will include a list of **synonyms,** or words that have the same or very similar meanings. The entry may also include a **usage illustration,** which is an example of how the word is used in context.

NOTE THE FACTS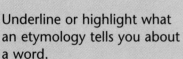

Where will you find the pronunciation in a dictionary entry? How is it set apart from the rest of the text in this sample entry?

_____

_____

_____

MARK THE TEXT

Underline or highlight what an etymology tells you about a word.

Understanding Multiple Meanings

Each definition in the entry gives a different meaning of the word. When a word has more than one meaning, the different definitions are numbered. The first definition in an entry is the most common meaning of the word, but you will have to choose the meaning that fits the context in which you have found the word. Try substituting each definition for the word until you find the one that makes the most sense.

If you come across a word that doesn't seem to make sense in context, consider whether that word might have another, lesser known meaning. Can the word be used as more than one part of speech, for example, as either a noun or a verb? Does it have a broader meaning than the one that comes to your mind? For example, the narrator in "The Tell-Tale Heart" (Unit 3, page 54) talks about listening to the deathwatches in the wall. You might know that a deathwatch involves the time spent waiting for someone or something to die, but that doesn't make sense here. The footnote at the bottom of the page tells you that *deathwatch* is a name of a wood-boring beetle.

Keep in mind that some words not only have multiple meanings but also different pronunciations. Words that are spelled the same but are pronounced differently are called **homographs**.

Understanding Denotation and Connotation

The **denotation** of a word is its dictionary definition. Sometimes, in order to understand a passage fully, it is helpful to know the connotations of the words as well. A **connotation** of a word is an emotional association the word has in addition to its literal meaning. For example, the words *juvenile* and *youthful* both denote "young," but *juvenile* has a negative connotation similar to "childish," whereas *youthful* has a positive connotation of "energetic" or "vibrant." The best way to learn the connotation of a word is to pay attention to the context in which the word appears or to ask someone more familiar with the word.

NOTE THE FACTS

What is the difference between a *denotation* and a *connotation*?

_____

_____

THINK AND REFLECT

Imagine that you are reading about two sisters, and one *demands* to use the other's tennis racquet rather than *requesting* to use it. What would that tell you about the relationship between the sisters? **(Apply)**

_____

_____

_____

_____

_____

IMPROVING YOUR ACTIVE VOCABULARY

Keeping a Word Study Notebook

Keeping a **word study notebook** is a convenient way to log new words, their meanings, and their spellings, as well as prefixes, suffixes, word roots, and other concepts. In addition, you can use your word study notebook to write down words that you have trouble remembering how to spell. You may even want to set aside a section of your notebook for word play. You can use this area to create jokes, silly rhymes, jingles, skits, acrostics, and games using the words you have logged.

When you record a new word in your notebook, include its definition, pronunciation, and origins, along with an example sentence or drawing to help you remember it.

Here is a sample page from a word study notebook.

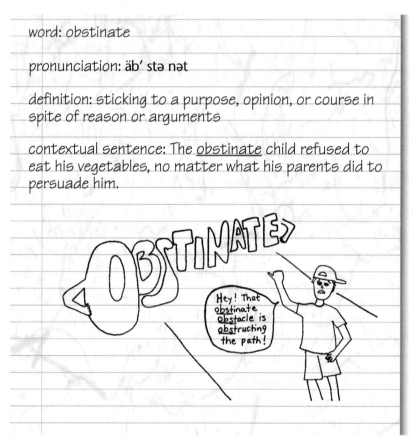

Review the words in your word study notebook and practice using the words in your speech and writing. Also, look for the words from your notebook as you read and listen. The more associations you develop and the more encounters you have with a word, the more likely you are to remember it.

Using Mnemonic Devices

A **mnemonic** (ni mä′ nik) **device** is a catchy phrase or striking image that helps you remember information. For example, you might have heard the phrase "the princiPAL is your PAL" as a trick for remembering the difference between *principal*, the person, and *principle*, the idea. The rhyme "*I* before *E* except after *C*" is a mnemonic for a spelling pattern.

Mnemonic devices are effective in learning new vocabulary words because you learn new information by linking it to words, images, and concepts that are already familiar to you. Vocabulary mnemonics can be sayings, drawings, jingles, or whatever works for you. To remember the definition of *neophyte*, you could say, "A neophyte fighter is new to fighting." To remember how to spell *museum*, you could associate the word with others like it: we are a<u>muse</u>d at the <u>muse</u>um. A mental picture can also help you remember meaning and spelling.

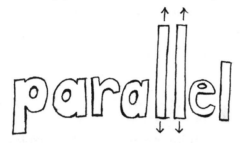

Categorizing and Classifying Words

Another technique for learning vocabulary words is categorizing and classifying the words. To categorize or classify a list of vocabulary words, sort them into groups that share a theme, topic, or characteristic. Then label each group. Like mnemonic devices, this technique works because it helps you create associations with and among new words.

For example, imagine that you need to learn the meanings of the following vocabulary words from the play *Persephone* (Unit 6, page 201).

airy	grimace	relent
desolate	haughty	smug
disclose	modesty	vigorous
distraught	plaintive	waver
fickle	quandary	

Here is how one student classified these words.

Persephone Vocabulary	
Words meaning different degrees of "upset"	desolate, distraught, plaintive
Words about making decisions	quandary, relent, waver
Words showing pride or its opposite	smug, airy, haughty, modesty
Words involving movement or change	disclose, fickle, grimace, vigorous

THINK AND REFLECT

In what other ways can these words be classified? (Apply)

_____

_____

_____

_____

_____

_____

_____

_____

Learning Synonyms, Antonyms, and Homonyms

A good way to expand your vocabulary is to learn synonyms, antonyms, and homonyms. As with using mnemonic devices and classifying or categorizing words, working with synonyms, antonyms, and homonyms will help you build associations for new words.

synonym	same (or nearly the same) meaning	danger, peril
antonym	opposite meaning	harmless, threatening
homonym	same pronunciation but different meaning	pear, pair, pare

One way of using synonyms and antonyms to make many connections to a new word is to create a **concept map**. In a concept map, you list synonyms, antonyms, examples, nonexamples, and a contextual sentence for the word you are studying. The best way to use a concept map is to fill it out with a small group or as a whole class. That way, you get to hear everyone else's associations with the word, too. Look at the concept map for *wretched* below.

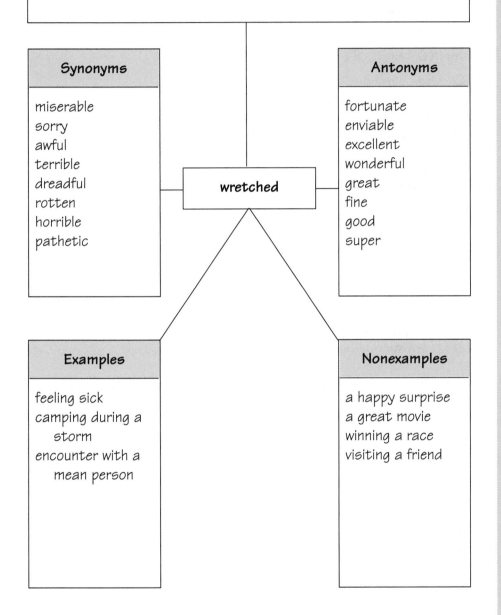

Real-Life Contexts

On the day of the big test, I felt <u>wretched</u>; my stomach was queasy, I had a headache, and I was nervous and sweaty.

The weather Tuesday made for a <u>wretched</u> picnic; it was hot, humid, and overcast, and the rain started to fall about midafternoon.

Synonyms

miserable
sorry
awful
terrible
dreadful
rotten
horrible
pathetic

Antonyms

fortunate
enviable
excellent
wonderful
great
fine
good
super

wretched

Examples

feeling sick
camping during a
    storm
encounter with a
    mean person

Nonexamples

a happy surprise
a great movie
winning a race
visiting a friend

THINK AND REFLECT

Add one more synonym, antonym, example, and nonexample to the boxes in the chart. **(Apply)**

_____

_____

_____

_____

Unit 9 VOCABULARY Review

Choose and Use Vocabulary Strategies

Before completing the vocabulary activities below, review with a partner how to use each of these vocabulary strategies.

TACKLING DIFFICULT VOCABULARY

- ❑ Use definitions, footnotes, endnotes, and glossaries
- ❑ Use context clues
- ❑ Use prior knowledge of word parts, word origins, and word families
- ❑ Use a dictionary
- ❑ Understand multiple meanings
- ❑ Understand connotation and denotation

IMPROVING YOUR ACTIVE VOCABULARY

- ❑ Keep a word study notebook
- ❑ Use mnemonic devices
- ❑ Categorize and classify words
- ❑ Learn synonyms, antonyms, and homonyms

Now use the strategies from this unit to tackle difficult vocabulary in this excerpt from "The Size of Things" by Robert Jastrow. After you finish the passage, answer the vocabulary questions that follow.

I once had the occasion to testify before the United States Senate Space and Aeronautics Committee on the scientific background of the space program; my talk dealt with the manner in which all substances in the universe are assembled out of neutrons, protons, and electrons as the basic building blocks. After I left the chamber a senior NASA[1] official continued with a summary of the major space science achievements of the last year. Apparently my scholarly presentation had perplexed the senators, although they were anxious to understand the concepts I had presented. However, the NASA official's relaxed manner reassured them, and someone asked him: "How big is the electron? How much smaller is it than a speck of dust?" The NASA official correctly replied that the size of an electron is to a dust speck as the dust speck is to the entire earth.

___

1. **NASA.** National Aeronautics and Space Administration

1. From this excerpt, the reader can guess that protons, neutrons, and electrons are ___.
   a. space programs
   b. building blocks of matter
   c. astrological terms
   d. chemicals

2. If a scholar is one who studies, *scholarly* probably means ___.
   a. universal
   b. needlessly complex
   c. knowledgeable
   d. simplistic

3. A synonym for *testify* as it is used in this passage would be ___.
   a. give evidence
   b. try
   c. assess
   d. judge

4. An antonym for *perplex* is ___.
   a. annoy
   b. confuse
   c. soothe
   d. clarify

5. Imagine that your teacher has given you the following list of vocabulary words.

conclusive	illuminate	resistance
conviction	inconceivable	scholarly
deduce	luminous	spherical
dense	minuteness	testify
diffuse	perplex	
equivalent	projectile	

Use a dictionary and your knowledge of word parts to determine the meaning of each of these words. Then, on your own paper, do the following activities:

a. Create a word study notebook entry for one of the words.
b. Create a mnemonic device for one of the words.
c. Categorize the words.

On Your Own

FLUENTLY SPEAKING. Learn the pronunciations of each of the vocabulary words from the previous activity. Then practice reading the words aloud until you can read the entire list without stumbling. Use the Word Recognition Skills: Word Race form in Appendix A, page A-4. Record your personal best time.

PICTURE THIS. Choose a story, article, or poem that contains at least three words that are new to you. For each word, create a drawing that will help you remember its meaning. Then create a drawing that illustrates some aspect of the story, poem, or article and shows that you understand it.

PUT IT IN WRITING. Find and read a book, story, article, or poem that interests you. Create a list of vocabulary words from the text you have chosen. If the text doesn't have many difficult words in it, pick easy words and use a thesaurus to learn more difficult synonyms for those words. Then use these words to create a crossword puzzle, an acrostic, or some other word game. Look at the WordWorkshop activities in the unit reading reviews in this book for ideas. Write instructions for your puzzle or game. Then have a partner study the list of vocabulary words and complete your activity.

Unit TEN

ⓣEST-TAKING Strategies

PREPARING FOR TESTS IN YOUR CLASSES

Tests are a common part of school life. You take tests in your classes to show what you have learned in each class. In addition, you might have to take one or more standardized tests each year. Standardized tests measure your skills against local, state, or national standards and may determine whether you graduate, what kind of job you can get, or which college you can attend. Learning test-taking strategies will help you succeed on the tests you are required to take.

These guidelines will help you to prepare for and take tests on the material you have covered in class.

Preparing for a Test

❑ **Know what will be covered on the test.** If you have questions about what will be covered, ask your teacher.

❑ **Make a study plan** to allow yourself time to go over the material. Avoid last-minute cramming.

❑ **Review the subject matter.** Use the graphic organizers and notes you made as you read as well as notes you took in class. Review any study questions given by your teacher.

❑ **Make lists** of important names, dates, definitions, or events. Ask a friend or family member to quiz you on them.

❑ **Try to predict questions** that may be on the test. Make sure you can answer them.

❑ **Get plenty of sleep** the night before the test. Eat a nutritious breakfast on the morning of the test.

Reading STRATEGY
REVIEW

CONNECT TO PRIOR KNOWLEDGE. Which of these test strategies do you already use? Which might help you on your next test?

_____

_____

_____

_____

_____

_____

_____

_____

_____

Answering Objective Questions

An **objective question** has a single correct answer. This chart describes the kinds of questions you may see on objective tests. It also gives you strategies for tackling each kind of question.

MARK THE TEXT

Underline or highlight the guidelines in the chart that you want to try next time you take a test.

Questions Found on Objective Tests

Description	Guidelines
True/False. You are given a statement and asked to tell whether the statement is true or false.	■ If any part of a statement is false, then the statement is false. ■ Words like *all, always, never,* and *every* often appear in false statements. ■ Words like *some, usually, often,* and *most* often appear in true statements. ■ If you do not know the answer, guess. You have a 50/50 chance of being right.
Matching. You are asked to match items in one column with items in another column.	■ Check the directions. See if each item is used only once. Also check to see if some are not used at all. ■ Read all items before starting. ■ Match those items you know first. ■ Cross out items as you match them.
Multiple Choice. You are asked to choose the best answer from a group of answers given.	■ Read *all* choices first. ■ Rule out incorrect answers. ■ Choose the answer that is most complete or accurate. ■ Pay particular attention to choices such as *none of the above* or *all of the above*.

Short Answer. You are asked to answer the question with a word, phrase, or sentence.	■ Read the directions to find out if you are required to answer in complete sentences. ■ Use correct spelling, grammar, punctuation, and capitalization. ■ If you cannot think of the answer, move on. Something in another question might remind you of the answer.

Answering Essay Questions

An essay question asks you to write an answer that shows what you know about a particular subject. Read the following essay question prompt on "The Tell-Tale Heart" (Unit 3, page 54).

> Evaluate the mental state of the narrator. Analyze the characteristics that make him seem sane and those that make him seem insane.

A simplified writing process will help you tackle questions like this. Follow these steps:

1 ANALYZE THE QUESTION. Essay questions contain clues about what is expected of you. Sometimes you will find key words that will help you determine exactly what is being asked. See the list below for some typical key words and their meanings.

Key Words for Essay Questions

analyze; identify	break into parts, and describe the parts and how they are related
compare	tell how two or more subjects are similar; in some cases, also mention how they are different
contrast	tell how two or more subjects are different from each other
describe	give enough facts about or qualities of a subject to make it clear to someone who is unfamiliar with it
discuss	provide an overview and analysis; use details for support
evaluate; argue	judge an idea or concept, telling whether you think it is good or bad, or whether you agree or disagree with it
explain	make a subject clearer, providing supporting details and examples
interpret	tell the meaning and importance of an event or concept
justify	explain or give reasons for decisions; be persuasive
prove	provide factual evidence or reasons for a statement
summarize	state only the main points of an event, concept, or debate

THINK AND REFLECT

Using the information in the chart, explain in your own words what the prompt above about "The Tell-Tale Heart" is asking you to do. **(Apply)**

_____

_____

_____

Steps for answering essay
questions:
❶ Analyze the question
❷ Plan your answer
❸ Draft your answer
❹ Revise your answer

❷ **PLAN YOUR ANSWER.** As soon as the essay prompt is clear to you, collect and organize your thoughts about it. First, gather ideas using whatever method is most comfortable for you. If you don't immediately have ideas, try freewriting for five minutes. When you **freewrite**, you write whatever comes into your head without letting your hand stop moving. You might also gather ideas in a **cluster chart**. (See Appendix B, page B-7, for an example of this kind of chart.) Then, organize the ideas you came up with. A simple outline or chart can help. For example, the following graphic organizer might help you organize an essay for the prompt on "The Tell-Tale Heart" on the previous page.

Sane Traits	Insane Traits
clear telling of story	obsession with old man's eye

Get to know other graphic organizers that might help you by reviewing those on the before-reading pages and in Appendix B of this book.

❸ **WRITE YOUR ANSWER.** Start with a clear thesis statement in your opening paragraph. Your **thesis statement** is a single sentence that sums up your answer to the essay question. Then follow your organizational plan to provide support for your thesis. Devote one paragraph to each major point of support for your thesis. Use plenty of details as evidence for each point. Write quickly and keep moving. Don't spend too much time on any single paragraph, but try to make your answer as complete as possible. End your essay with a concluding sentence that sums up your major points.

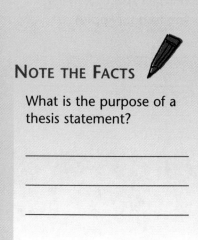

NOTE THE FACTS

What is the purpose of a thesis statement?

_____

_____

_____

❹ **REVISE YOUR ANSWER.** Make sure you have answered all parts of the question and included everything you were asked to include. Check to see that you have supplied enough details to support your thesis. Check for errors in grammar, spelling, punctuation, and paragraph breaks. Make corrections to your answer.

TAKING STANDARDIZED TESTS

Standardized tests are given to large groups of students in a school district, a state, or a country. Statewide tests measure how well students are meeting the learning standards the state has set. Other tests, such as the Scholastic Aptitude Test, or SAT, are used to help determine admission to colleges and universities. Others must be taken to enter certain careers. These tests are designed to measure overall ability or skills acquired so far. Learning how to take standardized tests will help you to achieve your goals.

You can get better at answering standardized test questions by practicing the types of questions that will be on the test. Use the Reading Skills and Test Practice questions in this book and other sample questions your teacher gives you to practice. Think aloud with a partner or small group about how you would answer each question. Notice how other students tackle the questions and learn from what they do.

In addition, remember these points:

- ❑ **Rule out some choices** when you are not sure of the answer. Then guess from the remaining possibilities.
- ❑ **Skip questions that seem too difficult** and go back to them later. Be aware, however, that most tests allow you to go back only within a section.
- ❑ **Follow instructions exactly.** The test monitor will read instructions to you, and instructions may also be printed in your test booklet. Make sure you know what to do.

Answering Multiple-Choice Questions

On many standardized tests, questions are multiple choice and have a single correct answer. The guidelines below will help you answer these kinds of questions effectively.

- ❑ **Read each question carefully.** Pay special attention to any words that are bolded, italicized, written in all capital letters, or otherwise emphasized.
- ❑ **Read all choices** before selecting an answer.
- ❑ **Eliminate** any answers that do not make sense, that disagree with what you remember from reading a passage, or that seem too extreme. Also, if two answers have exactly the same meaning, you can eliminate both.

❑ **Beware of distractors.** These are incorrect answers that look attractive because they are partially correct. They might contain a common misunderstanding, or they might apply the right information in the wrong way. Distractors are based on common mistakes students make.

❑ **Fill in circles completely** on your answer sheet when you have selected your answer.

Answering Reading Comprehension Questions

Reading comprehension questions ask you to read a passage and answer questions about it. These questions measure how well you perform the essential reading skills covered in Unit 2 of this book.

The Reading Skills and Test Practice questions that follow each literature selection in this book are reading comprehension questions. Use them to help you learn how to answer these types of questions correctly. Work through each question with a partner using a **think aloud**. Say out loud how you are figuring out the answer. Talk about how you can eliminate incorrect answers and determine the correct choice. You may want to make notes as you eliminate answers. By practicing this thinking process with a partner, you will be more prepared to use it silently when you have to take a standardized test.

The following steps will help you answer the reading comprehension questions on standardized tests.

❑ **Preview the passage and questions** and predict what the text will be about.

❑ **Use the reading strategies** you have learned to read the passage. Mark the text and make notes in the margins.

❑ **Reread the first question carefully.** Make sure you know exactly what it is asking.

❑ **Read the answers.** If you are sure of the answer, select it and move on. If not, go on to the next step.

❑ **Scan the passage** to look for key words related to the question. When you find a key word, slow down and read carefully.

❑ **Answer the question** and go on to the next one. Answer each question in this way.

Answering Analogy Questions

Analogy questions ask you to find the relationship between two words and then to recognize a similar relationship in another pair of words. In an analogy question, the symbol : means "is to" and the symbol :: means "as." For instance, the following analogy:

RUDDER : BOAT :: STEERING WHEEL : CAR

is read as

RUDDER IS TO BOAT AS STEERING WHEEL IS TO CAR.

Look at the example below.

> TAILOR : SUIT ::
> a. actor : act
> b. carpenter : nails
> c. teacher : blackboard
> d. composer : music

The example above would be read aloud as "*Tailor* is to *suit* as. . . ." Follow these guidelines for answering analogy questions:

> ❑ Think of a sentence that relates the two words. For the example above, you might think "A tailor makes a suit."
> ❑ Try substituting the words from each answer pair in the sentence.
>> "An actor makes an act."
>> "A carpenter makes nails."
>> "A teacher makes a blackboard."
>> "A composer makes music."
> ❑ Decide which sentence makes the most sense.
> ❑ If none of the options makes sense, try to think of a different sentence that relates the words, and work through the same process with the new sentence.

The chart on the following page lists some common relationships used in analogy questions.

THINK AND REFLECT

Using the process described here, how would you answer the analogy question above? **(Apply)**

_____

_____

_____

Common Analogy Relationships

Relationship	Example
synonyms	swerve : veer
antonyms	peril : safety
cause and effect	death : grief
effect and cause	odor : garbage
general and specific	reptile : snake
less intense and more intense	old : decrepit
part to whole	lens : camera
whole to part	camera : lens
age	dog : puppy
gender	chairwoman : chairman
worker and tool	painter : paintbrush
worker and product created	architect : blueprint
tool and associated action	keyboard : word-process
scientist and object of study	economist : markets
raw material and end product	paper : book
person and associated quality	psychologist : compassionate
symbol and what it stands for	cross : Christianity

Answering Synonym and Antonym Questions

Synonym or antonym questions give you a word and ask you to select the word that has the same meaning (for a **synonym**) or the opposite meaning (for an **antonym**). You must select the best answer even if none is exactly correct. For this type of question, you should consider all the choices to see which is best. Always notice whether you are looking for a synonym or an antonym. You will usually find both among the answers. Think aloud with a partner about how to answer the following question:

Mark the letter of the word that is most nearly the OPPOSITE in meaning to the word in capital letters.

1. POIGNANT
   a. touching
   b. somber
   c. dispassionate
   d. important

THINK AND REFLECT

How would you select the correct answer to this antonym question? **(Apply)**

_____

_____

_____

_____

_____

_____

_____

Answering Sentence Completion Questions

Sentence completion questions present you with a sentence that has two words missing. You must select the pair of words that best completes the sentence. The key to this kind of question is to make sure that both parts of the answer you have selected work well in the sentence. Think aloud with a partner about how to complete the following sentence.

> 2. When my father saw that my room was not ____, he became ____ because our family guests would be sleeping there.
>
>   a. clean . . . satisfied
>
>   b. painted . . . sorrowful
>
>   c. immaculate . . . furious
>
>   d. chaotic . . . stern

THINK AND REFLECT

How would you select the correct answer to the sentence completion question? **(Apply)**

_____

_____

_____

_____

_____

Answering Constructed-Response Questions

In addition to multiple-choice questions, many standardized tests include **constructed-response questions** that require you to write essay answers in the test booklet. Constructed-response questions might ask you to identify key ideas or examples from the text by writing a sentence about each. In other cases, you will be asked to write a paragraph in response to a question about the selection and to use specific details from the passage to support your answer. For example, the following prompt might occur after *Historical Photographs* by Arthur Rothstein, Unit 8, page 300.

> **Essay prompt:** What message do the photographs convey about life in the 1930s? How do they communicate that message?
>
> **Short response:** The photographs all seem to convey a message of despair and the loss of hope. In each picture, the landscape is bleak and dry, and the empty sky dominates the image. The building in the first photograph is very run-down, and the man and boy running toward it seem to be seeking shelter from blowing sand. The sand is piled everywhere, even partially blocking the entrance to the building so that it is unlikely they will be able to enter. In the second photo, the man getting water appears thoughtful and sad. In the third, a man and boy attempt to keep the sand from burying the fence, but the job seems pointless. The sand is too deep.

NOTE THE FACTS

What must you include in your answers to constructed-response questions?

_____

_____

_____

_____

Other constructed-response questions ask you to apply information or ideas from a text in a new way. For example, imagine that you have just read "The Price of Freedom" (Unit 7, page 228) on a standardized test. This article describes the author's visit to the National Prisoner of War Museum, where she encounters Lloyd, who tells her about his experience as a prisoner of war. The question might ask you to imagine that you are Lloyd and write a journal entry about your liberation. Another question might ask you to write the text for a brochure about the museum. As you answer these questions, remember that you are being evaluated based on your understanding of the text. Although these questions offer opportunities to be creative, you should still include ideas, details, and examples from the passage you have just read.

The following tips will help you answer constructed-response questions effectively.

Reading STRATEGY
REVIEW

USE TEXT ORGANIZATION.
Underline or highlight the key words in the Tips for Answering Constructed-Response Questions box. How can you tell these are the key words?

_____

_____

Tips for Answering Constructed-Response Questions

❑ **Skim the questions first.** Predict what the passage will be about.

❑ **Use reading strategies** as you read. Underline information that relates to the questions and make notes. After you have finished reading, you can decide which of the details you have gathered to use in your answers.

❑ **List the most important points** to include in each answer. Use the margins of your test booklet or a piece of scrap paper.

❑ **Number the points** you have listed to show the order in which they should be included.

❑ **Draft your answer to fit** in the space provided. Include as much detail as possible in the space you have.

❑ **Revise and proofread** your answers as you have time.

Unit 10 TEST-TAKING Review

Choose and Use Test-Taking Strategies

Before answering the sample test questions below, review with a partner how to use each of these test-taking strategies.

GENERAL STRATEGIES

- ❑ Know what will be on the test
- ❑ Make a study plan
- ❑ Review the subject matter
- ❑ Make lists
- ❑ Try to predict questions
- ❑ Preview the passage and questions
- ❑ Plan your time
- ❑ Use reading strategies to read the passage
- ❑ Come back later to questions that seem too difficult
- ❑ Save time for reviewing answers

STRATEGIES FOR OBJECTIVE TESTS

- ❑ Read each question carefully
- ❑ Read all answer choices before selecting one
- ❑ Scan the passage again if you are uncertain of the answer
- ❑ Rule out some choices
- ❑ Beware of distractors
- ❑ Understand how to answer analogy questions
- ❑ Understand how to answer synonym and antonym questions
- ❑ Understand how to answer sentence completion questions
- ❑ Fill in circles completely

STRATEGIES FOR ESSAY TESTS

- ❑ Understand how to answer constructed-response questions
- ❑ Analyze the question
- ❑ Plan your answer
- ❑ Write your answer
- ❑ Revise your answer

Now read "The Brotherhood of Sleeping Car Porters" below and answer the questions that follow. Use the strategies from this unit to complete this practice test.

People traveled by train long before planes and automobiles were invented. In the mid-1800s, however, train travel was uncomfortable. The benches were hard, the cars were full of dust and smoke, and the rough mattresses made it hard to sleep on overnight trips.

After one particularly uncomfortable ride, George Pullman decided to design a railroad car that would make the train ride more comfortable and enjoyable, especially for overnight trips. In 1864, he created a luxury sleeping car. The Pullman car had thick carpeting, beautiful woodwork, curtains, mirrors, chandeliers, and most importantly, porters to meet the needs of the passengers.

Pullman porters delivered first-class service on the Pullman sleeping cars. It was their job to get the sleeping berths ready for the passengers each night. They also cleaned ashtrays and spittoons, shined shoes, ironed clothes, polished wood, served food, hauled luggage, and did whatever other jobs the passengers desired. They were expected to be diligent and gracious and had to follow a rigid code of behavior.

Many freed slaves who were out of work in the 1860s jumped at the chance to be porters, and they were loyal and hardworking. They were used to long, difficult work and saw the trains as symbols of freedom. The Pullman Company employed African Americans almost exclusively as Pullman porters from 1868 to 1968. Although porters were respected in their communities, the pay was low and the working conditions were difficult. Porters were paid very little and were asked to work 400 hours or 11,000 miles a month, whichever came first. Porters relied on passengers' tips to supplement their meager salaries. If a passenger complained about the service, porters could be fired. Many porters endured racial insults and slurs with a smile to get tips.

After many years of being overworked and underpaid, porters decided to form a union to secure better working conditions. Porters turned to A. Philip Randolph, a well-respected African-American leader and speaker, to guide them, and in August 1925 they formed the Brotherhood of Sleeping Car Porters (BSCP).

Because Pullman was an anti-union company at the time, the BSCP and its members received threats and attacks from the company. After a twelve-year struggle, the Pullman Company finally agreed to a union contract, which was signed on August 25, 1937. This was the first contract ever won by an African-American union. The contract not only made history, but also significantly improved working conditions for Pullman porters. Salaries increased, working hours per month decreased, and porters could not be fired without a hearing. Randolph and the BSCP believed their victory made gains for all African-American workers who were seeking equality and fair working conditions. As Randolph stated, "With a union, black people can approach their employers as proud and upright equals, not as trembling and bowing slaves. Indeed, a solid union contract is, in a very real sense, another Emancipation Proclamation."

1. What is the author's main purpose in writing this article?
   a. to inform readers about the lives of Pullman porters
   b. to persuade readers that Pullman porters led lives of toil and hardship
   c. to humor readers with a silly story about a Pullman porter
   d. to criticize how Pullman porters carried out their responsibilities

2. Which of the following sets of words best describes Pullman porters?
   a. honorable and religious
   b. humorous and silly
   c. happy and friendly
   d. reliable and courteous

3. Which of the following statements best expresses the porters' reason for unionizing?
   a. Pullman porters received no health benefits or paid time off.
   b. Salaries for Pullman porters were small, but job security was guaranteed.
   c. Pullman porters were expected to work long hours and put up with poor treatment.
   d. Pay for Pullman porters was meager, and working conditions were difficult.

4. Read the following sentence from the passage:

   "Indeed, a solid union contract is, in a very real sense, another Emancipation Proclamation."

   What does this statement mean? Use details from the selection to explain the quote.

   _____

   _____

   _____

   _____

   _____

   _____

5. PULLMAN CAR : FREIGHT CAR :: HOTEL SUITE :
   a. HOTEL RESTAURANT
   b. TENT
   c. LUXURY APARTMENT
   d. TRAVEL

On Your Own

FLUENTLY SPEAKING. Use "The Brotherhood of Sleeping Car Porters" on pages 351–353 to perform a repeated reading exercise. Read the passage aloud to a partner. Have your partner record the time it takes you to read the passage and the number of errors you make. Then have your partner read the passage to you with your record time and number of errors. On your second reading, see if you both can improve your initial time and error rate and include more vocal expression. Reread the passage a third time, once again improving your time and error rate and increasing your vocal expression.

PICTURE THIS. Find an informational article on a topic that interests you. After reading the article, come up with two essay questions. Practice planning answers for essay questions by constructing a graphic organizer that will help you organize your answer for each question. For more practice on planning responses to essay questions, exchange essay questions with a partner, and plan your answer for your partner's questions.

PUT IT IN WRITING. Find and read an informational article on any topic that interests you. After you have read the article, write three multiple-choice and two constructed-response questions that test reading comprehension. As models, use the sample questions in this unit as well as those in the Reading Skills and Test Practice section that follows every literature selection in this book. Finally, exchange your passage and questions with a partner, and take one another's tests.

Appendix A:
Building Reading Fluency

WORD RECOGNITION SKILLS
INCREASE YOUR AUTOMATICITY, A-2
Crossword Puzzle, A-3
Word Race, A-4
Word Matrix, A-5

SILENT READING SKILLS
INCREASE THE AMOUNT YOU READ, A-6
How Much Can You Learn in 10 Minutes?, A-6
Free Reading Log, A-7
Pages-per-Minute Graph, A-8
Minutes-per-Section Graph, A-8

ORAL READING SKILLS
PERFORM REREADING ACTIVITIES, A-9
Repeated Reading Exercise, A-11
Repeated Reading Record, A-12
Passages for Fluency Practice, A-13

Word Recognition Skills: Increase Your Automaticity

What Are Word Recognition Skills? **Word recognition skills** are skills that help you recognize and decipher words. Learning how to read increasingly more words with faster recognition leads to **automaticity,** the ability to recognize words quickly and automatically. The activities below develop word recognition skills.

1 **Create a Crossword Puzzle.** Put together a crossword puzzle that includes clues for words you are studying and clues for facts everyone should know. Look at puzzles in the newspaper or a puzzle book to learn how to number your clues and add blank spaces. Here is how you might set up a puzzle.

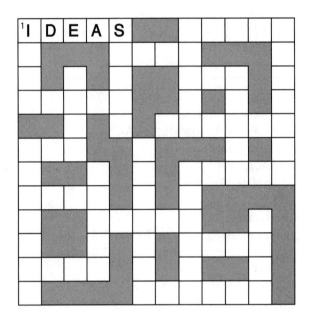

2 **Create a Word Race.** Make a list of 20 words you have studied. Practice reading the words aloud. Have a classmate keep track of how many seconds it takes you to read the entire list. Have another person keep track of the words you mispronounce. Have teams compete to see which team pronounces the same list of words the fastest with the fewest errors.

3 **Create a Word Matrix.** Choose vocabulary words that you find difficult to pronounce and place them in a chart. Add the same words to each row of your chart, but add the words to each row in a different order. Practice reading the words until you are comfortable pronouncing them. Have a partner time how many words in your chart you can read in 1 minute.

WORD RECOGNITION SKILLS: CROSSWORD PUZZLE

In a small group, list words to include in a crossword puzzle. Your list should contain 10 vocabulary words and 10 words that refer to facts that everyone knows. For instance, if the word *Washington* is on your "facts" list, add a CLUE ACROSS that says, *Our nation's first president.* Your first word down can come from one of the letters in *Washington.* For instance, the vocabulary word *wallow* can use the *w* in *Washington* with a CLUE DOWN that says, *Indulge oneself immoderately.* Use as many of the words on your list as you can (you may not be able to use all of them). Use your own paper for the CLUES ACROSS and CLUES DOWN. After you fill in your puzzle and finish your clues, make another blank, numbered puzzle. Exchange blank puzzles and clues with another group. See which group can solve their puzzle the fastest.

1.w	a	s	h	i	n	g	t	o	n			.							
a																			
l																			
l																			
o																			
w																			

WORD RECOGNITION SKILLS: WORD RACE

Create a list of 20 vocabulary words you have studied. Practice reading the list aloud. Have someone keep track of how many seconds it takes you to read the entire list. Have another person keep track of the words you mispronounce. After you have practiced the list, create teams. Have the team compete to see which team can pronounce the list the fastest with the fewest errors.

1.	11.
2.	12.
3.	13.
4.	14.
5.	15.
6.	16.
7.	17.
8.	18.
9.	19.
10.	20.

Keep track of the following data for each team member.

Number of seconds it took to read the list:
Number of words mispronounced:

WORD RECOGNITION SKILLS: WORD MATRIX

Choose 5 words that you find difficult to pronounce, and place them in the matrix below. Add the same words to each row, but use the words in a different order in each row. After a brief practice run-through, have a classmate use a clock or timer to see how many times you can make it through the chart in 1 minute. Have another classmate circle or check words you pronounce correctly. Use the second matrix below to run through your words a second time. Try to increase the number of words spoken correctly on your second reading.

Number of words correct in 1 minute: _____

Number of words correct in 1 minute: _____

SILENT READING SKILLS: INCREASE THE AMOUNT YOU READ

WHAT ARE SILENT READING SKILLS? Silent reading skills are skills you use as you read a text to yourself. Fluent silent readers can read a text quickly, easily, and smoothly. To build **silent reading fluency**, set aside time each day to read parts of a long selection or book. Most often, choose selections you consider easy and interesting. Vary the subject matter of selections you choose and, over time, include selections from several different genres—fiction, nonfiction, drama, short stories, poems, and informational and visual media. Use the charts below to keep track of your silent reading activity.

1 FILL IN A FREE READING LOG. Read silently for a sustained period several times a week. Write down what you read, the number of minutes you read, the number of pages you read, and your thoughts and reactions. Selections you read may be easy, moderate, or challenging.

2 USE A PAGES-PER-MINUTE GRAPH. Chart the number of pages you read in a 30-minute reading session. Try to increase the number of pages you read in each session. Be sure the selections you use for this activity are easy to read.

3 USE A MINUTES-PER-SECTION GRAPH. Each reading session, chart the time it takes you to read 5 pages of a selection. Try to decrease the number of minutes it takes to read 5 pages. Be sure the selections you use for this activity are easy to read.

SILENT READING SKILLS: HOW MUCH CAN YOU LEARN IN 10 MINUTES?

READING RATE. Pay attention to your silent reading rate. Do you vary your rate as you read? Do you slow down for difficult vocabulary and long sentences? Do you speed up when the ideas are easy to understand? Learn to use different reading rates with different tasks. Here are three methods to try.

Scan	Skim	Read closely
To locate particular information (to find a quotation, verify a statement, locate a word, or answer a question)	To get the overall picture (to preview or to review)	To absorb the meaning of a book you're reading for fun or a textbook on which you'll be tested (to read with understanding the first time)

Practice using different reading rates as you read silently for 10 minutes. How much can you learn in 10 minutes? Write what you learn below.

SILENT READING SKILLS: FREE READING LOG

Develop your silent reading fluency by reading silently for a sustained period several times a week. Keep track of what you read each day. List your reactions and thoughts about what you read.

Week of _____

Date/ Minutes Read	Title/Author	Pages Read From/To	Reactions/Thoughts

Total number of pages read this week:

Total number of minutes read this week:

Genres read this week: (circle)
Fiction   Nonfiction   Poetry   Drama   Informational or Visual Media   Other _____

SILENT READING SKILLS: PAGES-PER-MINUTE GRAPH

Choose an easy and interesting book. Read for 30 minutes, and count the number of pages you read. Record the number in the chart below. Try to read more pages in each practice session.

Over 10 pages										
9 pages										
8 pages										
7 pages										
6 pages										
5 pages										
4 pages										
3 pages										
2 pages										
1 page										
Practice Number	1	2	3	4	5	6	7	8	9	10
Number of Pages Read										

SILENT READING SKILLS: MINUTES-PER-SECTION GRAPH

Choose an easy and interesting book. Record in the chart below the time it takes you to read 5 pages of the book. Try to decrease the time it takes you to read 5 pages each time you read. You can time several 5-page sections in one reading by placing paper clips at 5-page intervals. Each time you reach a paper-clipped page, stop to record the time it took you to reach that page.

10 minutes										
9 minutes										
8 minutes										
7 minutes										
6 minutes										
5 minutes										
4 minutes										
3 minutes										
2 minutes										
1 minute										
Practice Number	1	2	3	4	5	6	7	8	9	10
Number of Minutes Read										

Oral Reading Skills: Perform Rereading Activities

WHAT ARE ORAL READING SKILLS? **Oral reading skills** are skills you use when you read aloud. Have you ever noticed how radio and television reporters read a news report? They do not read every word at the same speed and volume. They emphasize important points by putting more stress on some words. They use facial expressions and the tone of their voice to convey what words mean. They add pauses to give listeners time to think about what is being said. These news reporters exhibit **oral reading fluency**, the ability to read aloud smoothly and easily.

HOW CAN YOU BUILD ORAL READING SKILLS? To demonstrate that you are a fluent oral reader, you do not have to read fast without mistakes. Even the best news reporters mispronounce words or stumble over unfamiliar phrases. Good news reporters, however, use strategies that make the oral reading task easier. They read and reread material before they go on the air, and they vary their speed and vocal expression. The rereading activities below build oral reading skills.

1. **PREPARE A REPEATED READING EXERCISE.** Choose a 100–150-word passage that you consider difficult to read. With a partner, use the passage to prepare a repeated reading exercise. Read the passage aloud to your partner. Have your partner record the time it takes you to read the passage and the number of errors you make. Then have your partner read the passage to you while you record the time and number of errors. On your second reading see if you both can improve your initial time and error rate, and include more vocal expression. Reread the passage a third time, working to decrease your time and error rate and trying to increase your vocal expression.

2. **PERFORM A CHORAL READING.** Find a poem, song, or part of a story that would be fun for a group to read aloud. Practice reading the piece aloud. Everyone in the group should use the same phrasing and speed. Have group members add notes to the text that help them pronounce the words and pause at appropriate times. Poems such as "Name Giveaway" on page 109, "First Love" on page 114, and "Point Guard" on page 115 work well as choral readings.

3. **THINK ALOUD.** Read a selection aloud with a partner. As you read, discuss thoughts you have about what you are reading. Ask questions, make connections and predictions, and respond to the ideas in the selection. When you are finished with your oral reading, reread the selection again, either orally or silently.

4. **PERFORM A PLAY.** Read aloud a play you have previously read silently. Assign parts. In small groups, have each speaker rehearse his/her part several times. Present the play to an audience. Use props and costumes, if possible.

5. **WRITE YOUR OWN PLAY.** Rewrite a prose selection, or a part of a prose selection, as a play. Assign parts. In small groups, have each speaker rehearse his/her part several times. Present the play to an audience. Use props and costumes, if possible.

6. **MAKE A RECORDING.** Read a 100–150-word passage into a tape recorder or DVD player. Listen to your recording. Keep track of errors you make: mispronouncing a word, leaving a word out, or adding a word that is not there. Rerecord the passage. Try to decrease the number of errors you make, and increase the smoothness with which you read the passage. Rerecord the passage until you can read it smoothly without error.

7 **MEMORIZE A PASSAGE.** Memorize a 100–150-word passage from a selection you have read. Have a partner help you memorize the passage by chunking it. Memorize short sections at a time, and work up to repeating the entire passage from memory. Possible passages to memorize include lines from a speech or poem, such as Alfred, Lord Tennyson's poem "The Charge of the Light Brigate" on page 138 or scenes from a short story or play such as "The Tell-Tale Heart on page 55.

8 **MAKE A VIDEO.** Reread a selection with a partner. Prepare a video script that retells the selection. Record the retelling. Show the video retelling to an audience.

9 **EXPERIMENT WITH SPEED AND EXPRESSION.** Read a section of a selection silently. Reread the section aloud to a partner. Experiment with your speed and expression by rereading the section aloud in several different ways. Discuss which speed and means of expression work best.

10 **READ WITH A MASK.** Read silently, pretending that you are a character or the speaker in a selection. Reread aloud using a character or speaker mask that you hold in front of your face or wearing a costume that the character or speaker might wear.

11 **VIEW AND REENACT.** Watch a dramatic version of a selection on video. Read the print version, and reenact part of the selection.

Oral Reading Skills: Repeated Reading Exercise

❏ Choose a 100–150-word passage that you consider difficult to read. With a partner, use the passage to prepare a repeated reading exercise.

❏ Use a computer or a copier to make 6 copies of the passage: 3 for yourself and 3 for your partner.

❏ Read the passage aloud to your partner. Have your partner record the time you start reading, errors you make while reading, and the time you stop reading. Add this information to your Repeated Reading Record on page A-12.

❏ Have your partner read the passage to you. As your partner reads, record the time he/she starts reading, errors he/she makes, and the time he/she stops reading. See if your partner can improve your time and error rate. Record this information in your partner's Repeated Reading Record.

❏ Read the passage again. This time, work on varying your speed and vocal expression. Record the start/stop times and the number of errors you make, but this time your partner should listen for the meaning your words communicate. Have your partner comment on your speed and expression. For instance, your partner might note that "you read the first line too slow," "you had excellent pauses in the 2nd paragraph," or that you should "show more anger in the last line."

❏ Have your partner read the passage again. Record your partner's start/stop times and errors. Write down ways that your partner can vary his/her speed and vocal expression.

❏ You and your partner should reread the passage one more time. Continue to work on varying your speed and expression, and try to decrease your time and your number of errors. Record the information in your Repeated Reading Record.

ORAL READING SKILLS: REPEATED READING RECORD

Name: _____

Text Read: _____

Date	Evaluator	Errors	Time	Speed/Expression

ORAL READING SKILLS: REPEATED READING RECORD

Name: _____

Text Read: _____

Date	Evaluator	Errors	Time	Speed/Expression

ORAL READING SKILLS: PASSAGE FOR FLUENCY PRACTICE

from "The Epic of Gilgamesh," retold by Christina Kolb, page 158.

Gilgamesh, king of Uruk in southern Babylonia, was two-thirds divine and one-third human. He himself built the great city of Uruk. He was like a wild bull—powerful, bold, and able to best any man in combat. Perhaps because he was so very powerful, Gilgamesh was also arrogant. He drove the people of Uruk too hard, oppressing even the weak. Eventually the people of Uruk, weighed down by their heavy burdens, prayed to the gods for relief. The gods granted the people's prayers and created Enkidu.

Enkidu was a wild man, all covered with hair, and he dwelled with the animals. Enkidu was tamed by a priestess who then urged him to strive against Gilgamesh. Enkidu challenged Gilgamesh and the two wrestled like bulls. Their fight was long and terrible, but in the end Gilgamesh conquered Enkidu the wild man. From this contest and struggle of bodies emerged the bond of friendship. Together the two brave companions set out seeking adventure. In the cedar forest to the west, they killed Huwawa, a terrible monster who guarded the forest for Enlil, Lord of the Storm.

Time started:_____   Number of errors:_____   Time stopped:_____
Comments about speed and expression:

Gilgamesh, king of Uruk in southern Babylonia, was two-thirds divine and one-third human. He himself built the great city of Uruk. He was like a wild bull—powerful, bold, and able to best any man in combat. Perhaps because he was so very powerful, Gilgamesh was also arrogant. He drove the people of Uruk too hard, oppressing even the weak. Eventually the people of Uruk, weighed down by their heavy burdens, prayed to the gods for relief. The gods granted the people's prayers and created Enkidu.

Enkidu was a wild man, all covered with hair, and he dwelled with the animals. Enkidu was tamed by a priestess who then urged him to strive against Gilgamesh. Enkidu challenged Gilgamesh and the two wrestled like bulls. Their fight was long and terrible, but in the end Gilgamesh conquered Enkidu the wild man. From this contest and struggle of bodies emerged the bond of friendship. Together the two brave companions set out seeking adventure. In the cedar forest to the west, they killed Huwawa, a terrible monster who guarded the forest for Enlil, Lord of the Storm.

Time started:_____   Number of errors:_____   Time stopped:_____
Comments about speed and expression:

ORAL READING SKILLS: PASSAGE FOR FLUENCY PRACTICE

from "The *Challenger* Disaster" by Peggy Noonan, page 258

And I want to say something to the schoolchildren of America who were watching the live coverage of the shuttle's takeoff. I know it is hard to understand, but sometimes painful things like this happen. It's all part of the process of exploration and discovery. It's all part of taking a chance and expanding man's horizons. The future doesn't belong to the fainthearted; it belongs to the brave. The *Challenger* crew was pulling us into the future, and we'll continue to follow them. . . .

There's a coincidence today. On this day 390 years ago, the great explorer Sir Francis Drake died aboard ship off the coast of Panama. In his lifetime the great frontiers were the oceans, and a historian later said, "He lived by the sea, died on it, and was buried in it." Well, today we can say of the *Challenger* crew: Their dedication was, like Drake's, complete.

The crew of the space shuttle *Challenger* honored us by the manner in which they lived their lives. We will never forget them, nor the last time we saw them, this morning, as they prepared for the journey and waved goodbye and "slipped the surly bonds of earth" to "touch the face of God." ■

Time started:_____   Number of errors:_____   Time stopped:_____
Comments about speed and expression:

And I want to say something to the schoolchildren of America who were watching the live coverage of the shuttle's takeoff. I know it is hard to understand, but sometimes painful things like this happen. It's all part of the process of exploration and discovery. It's all part of taking a chance and expanding man's horizons. The future doesn't belong to the fainthearted; it belongs to the brave. The *Challenger* crew was pulling us into the future, and we'll continue to follow them. . . .

There's a coincidence today. On this day 390 years ago, the great explorer Sir Francis Drake died aboard ship off the coast of Panama. In his lifetime the great frontiers were the oceans, and a historian later said, "He lived by the sea, died on it, and was buried in it." Well, today we can say of the *Challenger* crew: Their dedication was, like Drake's, complete.

The crew of the space shuttle *Challenger* honored us by the manner in which they lived their lives. We will never forget them, nor the last time we saw them, this morning, as they prepared for the journey and waved goodbye and "slipped the surly bonds of earth" to "touch the face of God." ■

Time started:_____   Number of errors:_____   Time stopped:_____
Comments about speed and expression:

Appendix B:
Graphic Organizers for Reading Strategies

READING STRATEGIES CHECKLIST, B-2

READ WITH A PURPOSE
Author's Purpose Chart, B-3
Reader's Purpose Chart, B-4

CONNECT TO PRIOR KNOWLEDGE
K-W-L Chart, B-5
Reactions Chart, B-5

WRITE THINGS DOWN
Note Taking Chart, B-6
Pro and Con Chart, B-6
Venn Diagram, B-7
Cluster Chart, B-7
Writing Ideas Log, B-8

MAKE PREDICTIONS
Prediction Chart, B-9
Character Chart, B-9

VISUALIZE
Sensory Details Chart, B-10
Figurative Language Chart, B-10

USE TEXT ORGANIZATION
Story Strip, B-11
Time Line, B-11
Plot Diagram, B-12
Cause-and-Effect Chart, B-13
Summary Chart, B-13
Drawing Conclusions Log, B-14
Main Idea Map, B-14

TACKLE DIFFICULT VOCABULARY
Word Sort, B-15
Word Study Notebook, B-15
Word Study Log, B-16
Word Map, B-17

MONITOR YOUR READING PROGRESS
Fix-Up Ideas Log, B-18
Your Own Graphic Organizer, B-18
Reading Strategies Evaluation Chart, B-19
Books I Want to Read, B-20

READING STRATEGIES CHECKLIST

Use at least one before-, during-, or after-reading strategy listed below.

Reading Strategy	Before Reading	During Reading	After Reading
READ WITH A PURPOSE	___ I write down my reason for reading. ___ I write down the author's purpose for writing.	___ I read with a purpose in mind.	___ I reflect upon my purpose for reading.
CONNECT TO PRIOR KNOWLEDGE	___ I write down what I know about a topic.	___ I use what I know. ___ I add to what I know.	___ I think about what I learned.
WRITE THINGS DOWN	___ I have the materials I need for writing things down.	___ I mark key points. ___ I use sticky notes. ___ I take notes. ___ I highlight. ___ I react to text.	___ I summarize.
MAKE PREDICTIONS	___ I preview. ___ I guess.	___ I gather more information. ___ I guess again.	___ I analyze my predictions.
VISUALIZE	___ I picture the topic.	___ I make a mind movie. ___ I continue my mind movie.	___ I sketch or summarize my mind movie.
USE TEXT ORGANIZATION	___ I skim the text.	___ I read sections or stanzas. ___ I pay attention to introductions and conclusions. ___ I use headings and signal words. ___ I read charts and graphic aids. ___ I study the pictures. ___ I follow familiar plot, themes, and hidden outlines.	___ I use the organization to review the text.
TACKLE DIFFICULT WORDS	___ I study words beforehand.	___ I use context clues. ___ I look at prefixes and suffixes. ___ I consult a dictionary. ___ I ask a teacher or friend for help.	___ I use the words and add them to my working vocabulary.
MONITOR YOUR READING PROGRESS		**Fix-Up Ideas** ___ I reread. ___ I ask questions. ___ I read in shorter chunks. ___ I read aloud. ___ I take time to refocus. ___ I unlock difficult words. ___ I change my reading rate. ___ I create a mnemonic device.	

READ WITH A PURPOSE: AUTHOR'S PURPOSE CHART

An author may write with the following purposes in mind:

- ❑ to inform (expository/informative writing)
- ❑ to entertain, enrich, enlighten, and/or use an artistic medium such as fiction or poetry to share a perspective (imaginative/descriptive writing)
- ❑ to make a point by sharing a story about an event (narrative writing)
- ❑ to reflect (personal/expressive writing)
- ❑ to persuade readers or listeners to respond in some way, such as to agree with a position, change a view on an issue, reach an agreement, or perform an action (persuasive/argumentative writing)

The following types of writing reflect these purposes:

- ❑ Expository/informative: news article, research report
- ❑ Imaginative/descriptive: poem, short story
- ❑ Narrative: biography, family history
- ❑ Personal/expressive: diary entry, personal letter
- ❑ Persuasive/argumentative: editorial, petition

Before Reading
Identify the author's purpose, the type of writing he or she uses, and the ideas he or she wants to communicate.

During Reading
Gather ideas that the author communicates to readers.

After Reading
Summarize the ideas the author communicates. Explain how these ideas help fulfill the author's purpose.

READ WITH A PURPOSE: READER'S PURPOSE CHART

Fill in the Reader's Purpose Chart at each stage of reading to set a purpose for reading and to help you attain it.

Before Reading
Set a purpose for reading. *(Example: I am going to determine the overall mood of this poem.)*

During Reading
Take notes on what you learn. *(Example: mournful owl—sounds sad)*

After Reading
Reflect on your purpose and what you learned. *(Example: I wanted to find the overall mood of this poem. From the notes that I took, I believe the mood is melancholy and sad.)*

CONNECT TO PRIOR KNOWLEDGE: K-W-L CHART

Connect to what you know and what you want to know by filling in the first two columns before you read. Fill in the last column after you read.

What I *Know*	What I *Want* to Learn	What I Have *Learned*

CONNECT TO PRIOR KNOWLEDGE: REACTIONS CHART

Since you cannot write in, mark up, or highlight text in a textbook or library book, use this chart to record your thoughts and reactions. As you read, ask yourself questions, make predictions, react to ideas, identify key points, and/or write down unfamiliar words.

Page #	Questions, Predictions, Reactions, Key Points, and Unfamiliar Words

WRITE THINGS DOWN: NOTE TAKING CHART

Take notes in the chart below as you read nonfiction or informational selections.

Section or Page	Main Ideas	My Reactions

Summary of My Notes

WRITE THINGS DOWN: PRO AND CON CHART

As you read a persuasive or argumentative selection, take notes on both sides of each argument.

Arguments in Favor (Pro)	Arguments Against (Con)
Argument 1: Support:	Argument 1: Support:
Argument 2: Support:	Argument 2: Support:

WRITE THINGS DOWN: VENN DIAGRAM

Use a Venn diagram to compare and contrast ideas in one selection or to compare two selections.

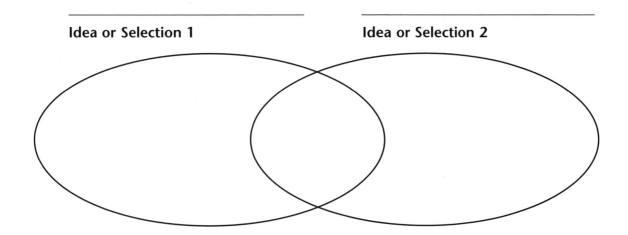

Idea or Selection 1

Idea or Selection 2

WRITE THINGS DOWN: CLUSTER CHART

Fill in the cluster chart below to keep track of character traits or main ideas. In the center circle, write the name of the character or topic. In the circles branching out from the center, write details about the character or topic.

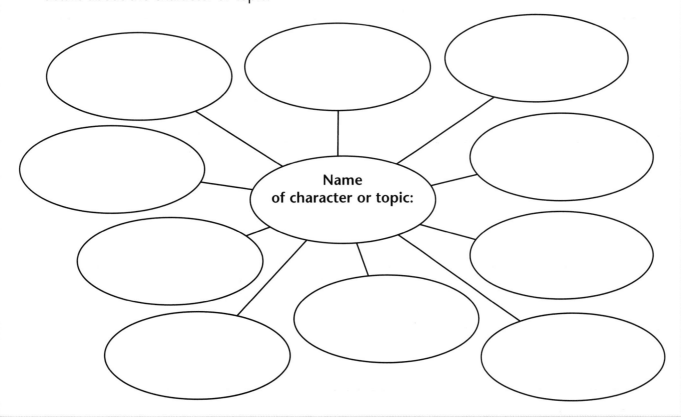

Name
of character or topic:

WRITE THINGS DOWN: WRITING IDEAS LOG

Keep track of writing ideas inspired by what you read. Draw pictures or write brief notes that you can use later in a writing assignment.

Date	Idea	Inspired By

MAKE PREDICTIONS: PREDICTION CHART

Gather information before and during reading that helps you make predictions about a literature selection. Write your predictions in the "Guesses" column. Write reasons for your guesses in the "Reasons" column. As you read, gather evidence that either supports or disproves your predictions. Change your predictions and add new ones as you learn more about the selection.

Guesses	Reasons	Evidence

MAKE PREDICTIONS: CHARACTER CHART

A **character** is a person (or sometimes an animal) who figures in the action of a literary work. Choose one character from the selection and fill in the chart below based on what you learn about the character as you read.

Character's Name:	Physical Appearance	Habits/ Mannerisms/ Behaviors	Relationships with Other People	Other Characteristics
Your description of the character at the beginning of the story				
Your predictions for this character				
Your analysis of the character at the end of the story				

VISUALIZE: SENSORY DETAILS CHART

As you read, identify images or words and phrases that contain sensory details. Write each sensory detail beneath the sense to which it appeals.

Sight	Sound	Touch	Taste	Smell

VISUALIZE: FIGURATIVE LANGUAGE CHART

As you read, identify examples of figurative language. Write down examples of figurative language in the first column below. In the second column, write down the comparison being made by the figurative language, and in the third column, describe what the figurative language makes you envision.

Example of Figurative Language	What Is Compared	What You Envision

USE TEXT ORGANIZATION: STORY STRIP

Draw pictures that represent key events in a selection. Then write a caption under each box that explains each event. Draw the events in the order in which they occurred.

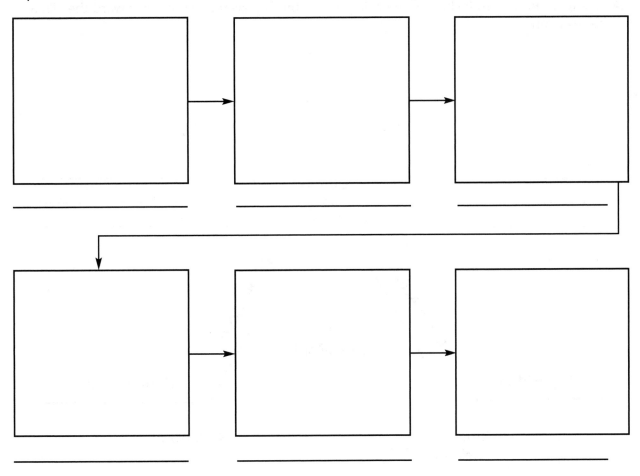

USE TEXT ORGANIZATION: TIME LINE

Use a time line to keep track of important events in a literature selection.

Dates:

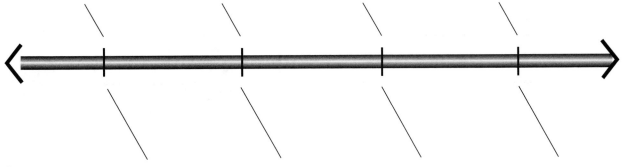

Events:

USE TEXT ORGANIZATION: PLOT DIAGRAM

Use the plot diagram below to chart the plot of a literature selection. In the spaces provided, describe the exposition, inciting incident, rising and falling action, climax, resolution, and dénouement. Be sure to include in the rising action the key events that build toward the climax of the selection.

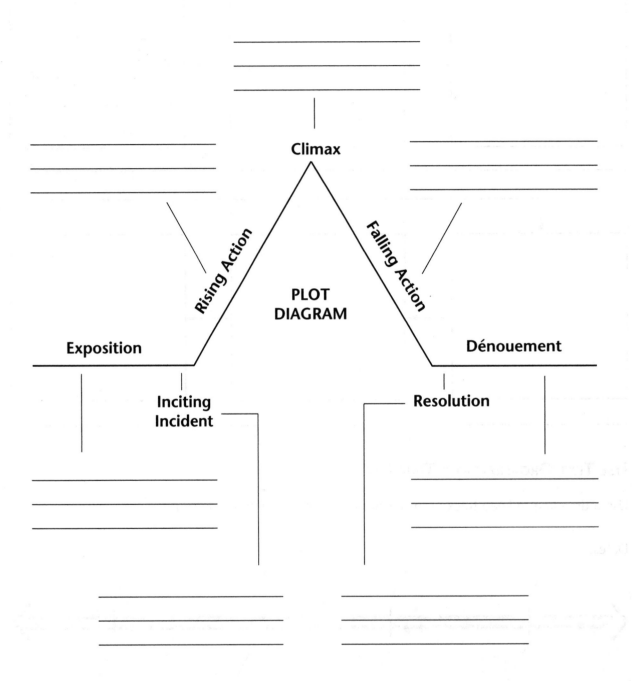

USE TEXT ORGANIZATION: CAUSE-AND-EFFECT CHART

Keep track of what happens in a story and why in the chart below. Use cause-and-effect signal words to help you identify causes and their effects. (Examples of cause-and-effect words: *as a result, because, if/then, since, therefore, this led to.*)

Cause → → → → → → → → → → → Effect

_____   _____

_____   _____

↓
↓

**Summary statement of what happened
in the selection and why:**

_____

_____

USE TEXT ORGANIZATION: SUMMARY CHART

Read and summarize short sections of a selection at a time. Then write a summary of the entire work.

Summary of Section 1:
Summary of Section 2:
Summary of Section 3:
Summary of the Selection:

USE TEXT ORGANIZATION: DRAWING CONCLUSIONS LOG

Draw conclusions about a selection by gathering supporting points for key ideas. Reread the supporting points and key ideas and draw a conclusion about the main or overall message of the selection.

Key Idea:	Key Idea:	Key Idea:
Supporting Points:	Supporting Points:	Supporting Points:
Conclusion about Overall Message:		

USE TEXT ORGANIZATION: MAIN IDEA MAP

To find the main or overall message of a whole selection or a part of the selection, gather important details into a Main Idea Map. Use the details to determine the main or overall message. Note: In fiction, the main idea is also known as the theme.

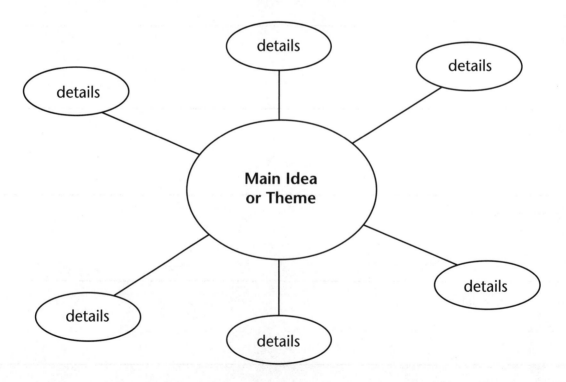

TACKLE DIFFICULT VOCABULARY: WORD SORT

Write one challenging word or phrase in each of the boxes below, along with its definition and part of speech. Cut the boxes apart. Then sort the words using one of the following methods.

- Same parts of speech
- Words with similar or opposite meanings
- Words with prefixes and suffixes
- Words that relate to each other or that can be used together
- My own sorting method: _____

Word: **Definition:** **Part of Speech:**	**Word:** **Definition:** **Part of Speech:**	**Word:** **Definition:** **Part of Speech:**
Word: **Definition:** **Part of Speech:**	**Word:** **Definition:** **Part of Speech:**	**Word:** **Definition:** **Part of Speech:**

TACKLE DIFFICULT VOCABULARY: WORD STUDY NOTEBOOK

Keeping a word study notebook is a convenient way to log new words, their meanings and their spelling, as well as prefixes, suffixes, word roots, and other concepts. When you record a new word, include its definition, pronunciation, and origins, along with an example sentence and a drawing to help you remember it.

Word: _____

Pronunciation: _____

Origins: _____

_____

Definition: _____

Sentence: _____

Drawing:

TACKLE DIFFICULT VOCABULARY: WORD STUDY LOG

Keep track of the words you gather in your word study notebook in the log below.

100								
95								
90								
85								
80								
75								
70								
65								
60								
55								
50								
45								
40								
35								
30								
25								
20								
15								
10								
5								
Total Number of Words in My Word Study Notebook	Week of	Week of	Week of	Week of	Week of	Week of	Week of	Week of

TACKLE DIFFICULT VOCABULARY: WORD MAP

Write a challenging word or phrase in the first box below. Beneath the word or phrase, include its definition, word parts you recognize, and several synonyms. In the two boxes at the bottom, write a sentence that uses the word or phrase and create a drawing that helps you remember it.

A Challenging Word or Phrase

Definition

Word Parts I Recognize

Synonyms

A Sentence That Contains the Word or Phrase

A Picture That Ilustrates the Word or Phrase

MONITOR YOUR READING PROCESS: FIX-UP IDEAS LOG

Recognizing that you don't understand something is as important as knowing that you do understand it. Sometimes you may find yourself just reading the words but not actually comprehending or getting the meaning of what you are reading. If you are having trouble comprehending something you are reading, try using some of the fix-up ideas listed below to get back on track.

- Reread
- Ask a question
- Read in shorter chunks
- Read aloud
- Retell

- Work with a partner
- Unlock difficult words
- Change your reading rate
- Choose a new strategy
- Create a mnemonic device

Problems I Encountered While Reading	Fix-Up-Ideas I Used

MONITOR YOUR READING PROGRESS: YOUR OWN GRAPHIC ORGANIZER

Graphic organizers help you understand and remember information. Use your imagination to modify a graphic organizer in this appendix, or invent a new one. Use your graphic organizer to arrange ideas as you read and to guide your discussion and writing actions after you read. Graphic organizer possibilities are endless!

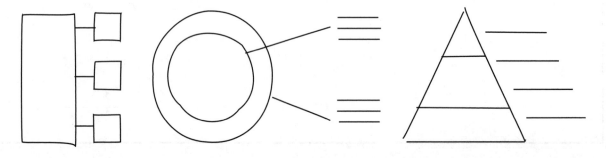

Monitor Your Reading Progress: Strategies Evaluation Chart

My Evaluation of My Progress	My Teacher's Evaluation of My Progress
Things I Do Before Reading	My Actions Taken Before Reading
Things I Do During Reading	My Actions Taken During Reading
Things I Do After Reading	My Actions Taken After Reading

MONITOR YOUR READING PROGRESS: BOOKS I WANT TO READ

Keep track of books you want to read in the chart below. Whenever you read a book on your list, add a checkmark to the first column to indicate that you have read the book.

✔	Title	Author	Genre	Notes

Literary Acknowledgments

Don Congdon Associates, Inc. "The Foghorn" by Ray Bradbury from *The Saturday Evening Post*. Reprinted by permission of Don Congdon Associates, Inc. Copyright © 1951 by the Curtis Publishing Company, renewed 1979 by Ray Bradbury.

Farrar, Straus & Giroux Inc. "The Green Mamba" from *Going Solo* by Roald Dahl. Copyright © 1986 by Roald Dahl. Reprinted in U.S. by permission of Farrar, Straus and Giroux, LLC.

Ken Haedrich. "How to Chop an Onion in Four Easy Steps" by Ken Haedrich from *Good Cook's Companion*, page 113. Reprinted by permission of the author.

Harcourt, Inc. "The Hummingbird That Lived Through Winter" from *My Kind of Crazy, Wonderful People: Seventeen Stories and a Play*, copyright 1944 and renewed 1972 by William Saroyan, reprinted by permission of Harcourt, Inc.

HarperCollins Publishers, Inc. "Point Guard" from *Sports Pages* by Arnold Adoff. Text copyright 1986 by Arnold Adoff. Used by permission of HarperCollins Publishers.

David Higham Associates Ltd. "The Green Mamba" from *Going Solo* by Roald Dahl. Copyright © 1986 by Roald Dahl. Reprinted in Canada by permission of David Higham Associates Ltd.

Houghton Mifflin Company. "Blackberry Eating" from *Mortal Acts, Mortal Words* by Galway Kinnell. Copyright © 1980 by Galway Kinnell. Reprinted by permission of Houghton Mifflin Company. All rights reserved.

Jerry Izenberg. "Roberto Clemente: A Bittersweet Memoir" from *Great Latin Sports Figures* by Jerry Izenberg. Copyright © 1976 by Jerry Izenberg. Reprinted by permission of the author.

Carl Lindner. "First Love" by Carl Lindner, originally published in *Cottonwood Review 33* (Spring, 1984), copyright by the author. Recorded by permission of the author.

Peter Lowe/Eurobook. "The Secret Name of Ra" from *Gods and Pharaohs from Egyptian Mythology* by Geraldine Harris. Copyright © 1982 by Eurobook Limited and 2004 by Peter Lowe/Eurobook.

Rona Maynard. "The Fan Club" by Rona Maynard. Copyright by Rona Maynard. Reprinted/recorded by permission of the author.

Naomi Shihab Nye. "The Lost Parrot" from *Hugging the Jukebox* by Naomi Shihab Nye. Reprinted by permission of the author.

Fifi Oscard Agency, Inc. "Appearances Are Destructive" by Mark Mathabane. Copyright Mark Mathabane. Reprinted by permission of Fifi Oscard Agency, Inc.

Poolbeg Press, Ltd. "Amaterasu" from "The Sun, the Looking-Glass, and the Eight-Headed Dragon" retold by Carolyn Swift from *World Myths and Tales*. Copyright © 1993 by Carolyn Swift. Originally published by Poolbeg Press, Ltd. Reprinted by permission of Poolbeg Press, Ltd.

Marian Reiner. "The Women's 400 Meters" from *The Sidewalk Racer and Other Poems of Sports and Motion* by Lillian Morrison. Copyright © 1965, 1967, 1969, 1977 by Lillian Morrison. Used by permission of Marian Reiner for the author.

Kenneth Rosen. "Name Giveaway" by Phil George from *Voices of the Rainbow*, edited by Kenneth Rosen. Copyright © 1993 by Kenneth Rosen. Published by Arcade Publishing, New York, New York. Reprinted/recorded by permission of Kenneth Rosen.

Sterling Partners, Inc. "Persephone," by Claire Boiko, is reprinted with the permission of the publisher, Sterling Partners, Inc. Copyright 1994. This play is for reading purposes only; for permission to produce, write to Sterling Partners, Inc., P.O. Box 600160, Newton, MA 02460.

Southern Living. "The Price of Freedom" by Cassandra Vanhooser from *Southern Living*, May 1999, page 98. Copyright © 1999 *Southern Living, Inc.* Reprinted with permission.

University of Arizona Press. "The Ground is Always Damp" from *Blue Horses Rush In* by Luci Tapahonso. © 1997 Luci Tapahonso. Reprinted by permission of the University of Arizona Press.

W. W. Norton & Company, Inc. "400-Meter Freestyle" from *Selected Poems* 1960-1990 by Maxine Kumin. Copyright 1959 and renewed 1987 by Maxine Kumin, from *Selected Poems* 1960-1990 by Maxine Kumin. Used by permission of W. W. Norton & Company, Inc.

ART ACKNOWLEDGMENTS

Cover Illustration Works; **43** © Tom Rosenthal/SuperStock; **66** © Corel; **74** © Photodisc; **114** © Photodisc; **115** © AP/Chris Gardner/Wide World Photos; **120** © Photodisc; **122** © AP/Wide World Photos; **127** © CORBIS/Chinch Gryniewicz; **132** © Photodisc; **159** © ET Archive, London; **170** © CORBIS/Gianni Dagli Orti; **185**© CORBIS/Asian Art and Archeology, Inc.; **202** © CORBIS/Mimmo Jodice; **252** © CORBIS/Bettmann; **425** © NASA; **265** © Stuart Cohen/The Image Works; **272** © Southern Living, Inc., Mark Sandlin, photographer; **300** © Library of Congress; **301** © Library of Congress; **306** © Planet Art; **312** © Educational Web Adventures LLP.